MISSOURI GENEALOGICAL

RECORDS & ABSTRACTS

VOLUME 3: 1787-1839

By

Sherida K. Eddlemon

D1526966

HERITAGE BOOKS, INC.

Published 1991 By

HERITAGE BOOKS, INC.
1540-E Pointer Ridge Place
Bowie, MD 20716
(301) 390-7709

ISBN 1-55613-447-9

ACKNOWLEDGMENTS

I want to thank my parents, Nelson and Amelia Eddlemon, for their continued support and encouragement; the staff of the Missouri State Archives; the staff of Ellis Library at the University of Missouri; and Van South for his help at the various cemeteries.

DEDICATION

This book is dedicated to the memory of my elusive French ancestor, Achille Godin (Gaudin), who died between 1812 and 1818. He left his widow Marguerite James, and his children living near the mouth of the Arkansas and Mississippi Rivers several miles below Arkansas Post; but not a footstep to show from whence he came. The search continues.

DATES TO REMEMBER

1541	The Spanish explorer Hernando De Soto first saw the Mississippi River.
1586	The Lost Colony was unsuccessfully attempted on Roanoke Island.
1607	Settlement at Jamestown.
1620	The ship "Mayflower" arrived at Plymouth, Mass.
1673	Marquette and Joliet, French explorers, discovered the Missouri River.
1682	Robert Cavelier de La Salle claimed the Mississippi Valley for France. He named the region LOUISIANA.
1700	The Mission of St. Francis Xavier was established by French priests on the present site of St. Louis. The orginal Arkansas Post was abandoned.
1722	A new settlement was formed at Arkansas Post.
1732	Settlers from what is now Illinois established a settlement at Ste. Genevieve, Missouri.
1763	French and Indian War ended. The Louisiana Territory was given to Spain. France gave Canada to the British.
1764	Pierre Laclede Liguest and Auguste Chouteau settled St. Louis.
1776	Declaration of Independence was adopted.
1787	John Dodge, an American, settled in Ste. Genevieve.
1790	Israel Dodge, an American, followed John Dodge to Ste. Genevieve.
1799	Daniel Boone moved to St. Charles County.
1800	Spain gave up the Louisiana Territory to France.

1803	France sold the Louisiana Territory to the United States.
1804	Two territories were formed out of the Louisiana Purchase.
	1. Territory of Orleans, District of Louisiana
	2. Territory of Indiana
1805	Territory of Louisiana was formed.
1809	Out of the Territory of Louisiana the Territory of Illinois was formed.
1811/12	The severe earthquake tremors known as the "New Madrid Earthquakes" that formed Reelfoot Lake in Tennessee.
1812	Part of the Territory of Louisiana became the Territory of Missouri.
1813	County of Arkansas was formed out of the Territory of Missouri.
1818	Missouri asked to be admitted into the Union.
1819	The Territory of Arkansas was formed.
1821	Missouri became the 24th state.
1836	Heatherly War
1837	Missouri gained six northwestern counties with the Platte Purchase.
1911	Capitol Fire in Missouri

G L O S S A R Y

ASSIGNEE

A person to whom a claim, property, etc. is transferred.

ET AL

And others.

WRIT

A legal document ordering or stopping some action.

WRIT OF ERROR

Usually employed for the purpose of reviewing a judgement of the courts of common law. Usually issued out of Superior Court.

WRIT OF RESTITUTION

Employed to restore to the appellant the thing lost at the time of the judgement in the lower court.

APPELLANT

A person who challenges a decision of the lower court.

EXECUTION

A process of enforcing a judgement, maybe by the sheriff or some other officer.

INTESTATE

Died without a will.

TABLE OF CONTENTS

v

C A L L A W A Y C O U N T Y
Founded 1820 From Montgomery County

C A P E G I R A R D E A U C O U N T Y
Founded 1812

C H A R I T O N C O U N T Y
Founded 1820 From Howard County

C L A Y C O U N T Y
Founded 1822 From Ray County

C O L E C O U N T Y
Founded 1820 From Cooper County

L A F A Y E T T E   C O U N T Y
Founded 1820 From Cooper County

L A C L E D E   C O U N T Y
Founded 1849 From Camden, Pulaski and Wright Counties

L I N C O L N   C O U N T Y
Founded 1818 From St. Charles County

M A C O N   C O U N T Y
Founded 1837 From Chariton and Randolph Counties

M A D I S O N   C O U N T Y
Founded 1818 From Cape Girardeau and Ste. Genevieve Counties

M A R I O N   C O U N T Y
Founded 1826 From Ralls County

MONROE COUNTY
Founded 1831 From Ralls County

MONTGOMERY COUNTY
Founded 1818 From St. Charles County

MORGAN COUNTY
Founded 1833 From Cooper County

NEWTON COUNTY
Founded 1838 From Barry County

NEW MADRID COUNTY
Founded 1812

OSAGE COUNTY
Founded 1841 From Gasconade County

PERRY COUNTY
Founded 1820 From Ste. Genevieve County

ST. CHARLES COUNTY
Founded 1812

ST. FRANCOIS COUNTY
Founded 1821 From Jefferson, Washington and
Ste. Geneveive Counties

ST. LOUIS COUNTY
Founded 1812

STE. GENEVIEVE COUNTY
Founded 1812

S T O D D A R D   C O U N T Y
Founded 1835 From New Madrid County

S U L L I V A N   C O U N T Y
Founded 1845 From Linn County

V A N   B U R E N   O R   C A S S   C O U N T Y
Founded 1835 from Jackson County

R E L A T E D   M A T E R I A L

PREFACE

This is the third volume in a series containing records from the period 1787 to 1839 which is often frustrating and difficult for the Missouri/Arkansas researcher. There is not a complete Federal census extant for Missouri until 1830. The records and information in this series are intended as a general search for the period of time indicated to help researchers find their ancestors.

The white man came early to Missouri. Spanish and French explorers were pushing deep into this virgin territory long before the English settlers thought about crossing the Smoky Mountains into Tennessee and Kentucky. The Spanish explorer Hernando De Soto first laid eyes on the Mississippi River in 1534. After De Soto's death during his expedition to explore the lands west of the Mississippi River, his successor Luis de Moscoso traveled in the area now known as Arkansas. Two French explorers, Marquette and Joliet, traveled through the Arkansas River country and pushed northward to discover the Missouri River in 1673.

But the region was still Indian country until 1682 when La Salle claimed the Mississippi Valley for France. He named the region Louisiana in honor of his King, Louis XIV. The French explorer Henry de Tonty made a settlement in 1686 that was later to be known as Arkansas Post.

Pierre le Moyne, Sieur d'Iberville, established a royal Louisiana colony in 1699 known now as Ocean Springs, Miss. Farther north French priests established the Mission of St. Francis Xavier in 1700 at the mouth of the Des Peres River.

In 1732, settlers from the area now Illinois made the first permanent settlement at Ste. Genevieve, Missouri. Civilization began to develop quickly. In 1764 Auguste Chouteau and Pierre Laclede Liguest established St. Louis. John Dodge settled in Ste. Genevieve followed three years later by Israel Dodge. Missouri no longer belonged to just the Indians, French and Spanish. By 1795 American settlements flourished along the Femme Osage Creek in St. Charles County.

In 1762 France gave this land called "Louisiana" to Spain. The Spanish gave it back to France in 1800 and three years later in 1803 France sold the area to the United States in what became known as the Louisiana Purchase. In 1804 St. Louis became the capital of the District of Louisiana. Missouri was proclaimed a territory separate from Louisiana in 1812 and became the 24th state in 1821.

This switching from France to Spain then back to France and later to the United States makes researching an early ancestor in Missouri or Arkansas extremely difficult. Even after the Louisiana Purchase the area was briefly part of the territories of Orleans and Indiana. Later the region known as the Illinois Territory was formed. It was actually six years after the purchase from France that the Missouri Territory was formed.

Not only did the settlers of Missouri, Northern Arkansas, West Tennessee and Southern Illinois have to struggle with the common problems of Indians, isolation, weather and illness, but settlers of the time period of 1811 to 1812 were faced with one more terrifying experience -- that of earthquakes. The earthquakes were so severe at one time the Mississippi River flowed backwards for over an hour and formed Reelfoot Lake in Tennessee. Some stayed and toughed it out and others left to find land that did not move.

When the Louisiana Purchase was made some of the French wanted to be considered truly American. They anglicized their names. Example: Celestine Mitchel became known as Sarah Mitchel and Achille Godin became Ashel Gordon.

Also the French used the practice of "dit" names or aliases. The early French would assume the name of a place or even another family name as a form of identity. The English or Americans did not understand this practice so the early records might be under either name or even shortened in later generations. Example: Nicholas Caillot dit Lachance. The records could be under Caillot or Lachance or even Chance. Both surnames are indexed in this volume.

All names appear as they were written on the records including abbreviations of given names. No attempt has been made to make corrections in spelling. Cemetery listings and mortality schedules include only information on those people born before 1840 and who died before 1900.

In some instances it was necessary to use abbreviations which are primarily used in tax lists. They are as follows:

SN	– Survey Number		W	– Witness
JP	– Justice of the peace		S	– Security
APT	– Appointment Date		E	– Executor
ADM	– Administrator		V	– Voucher
PD	– Probate Date		UK	– Unknown
PY	– Payment Date		MG	– Minister
RD	– Recorded Date		T	– Township
D	– Letter Date		y	– Year
L	– Letter Number		m	– month
y	– Year		R	– Ranger
S	– Section		MD	– Marriage

There was a Capitol fire in 1911 which destroyed many records of the State Auditor's Office. The documents which survived the fire were microfilmed and are simply known as the "Capitol Fire Documents." The collection is available at the Missouri State Archives. In some cases the records preserved here are not available on the county level. A complete finding aid has not been developed to date for the users of this collection.

In my search for my elusive French ancestor Achille Godin/Gaudin through these records I found a clue to the existence of a court case. I wish you luck in finding your ancestor within these pages.

Perry County, Missouri, Members Of The Grand Jury,March,1825
    Joab Waters, sr., Zar. Sturduvant, David L. Caldwell,John
Brewer, Michael Hagen, Thomas Riney, Clement Hagen, Bernard
Brown, Charles C. Walle, Henry M. Hee, sr., John May, John
M'Coy, Hillard Fowler, William Flinn, Vincent Grenney, John
Keans, Joab Waters, jr., William Searcy, Richard L. Dorsey,
John Tucker, Zachariah Layton, William Tucker,Wm. McLane,jr.

Macon County, Missouri, August, 1837, Gambling Fines.
    John Cullum, Francis Taylor, Daniel O. Marley, Austin B.
Jones, James Carter.

Detroit, 1787, Supporters of Rev. George Mitchell,John Askin
Papers, Burton Historical Collection.
    William Macomb, John Askin, James Abbot, William Harffy,
John Martin, sr, George Meldrum, John Casety,John McPherson,
George Lyons, John Dodomead, Thomas Dugan, William McNeill,
Jonathan Shiefflien, James Douglass, John Urquhart, Thomas
McCrea, William Scott, Thomas Smith, James Donalson, Nathan
Williams, John Welsh, Lieth and Sheperd, William Park, John
Laughton, Danl. McMcPhillip, Martin Theophilus Myers, Joseph
Forsth, Alexander Harrow, James Fraser, David White, Thomas
Jones, David White, Alexander McKensie, Thomas Smith (sic),
Petter Cumming, Angus Mackintosh, John Kinzei,Wm. Groesbeck,
Sharp and Wallace, Robert Stevens, William Forsith, William
St. Clair, Jno. Wheaton, James Allan, John Urquhart, James
May, Alexr. Saunders, Henry Ford, Thomas Reynalds, Mr. Cook,
Matthew Dolson, Thos. Cox, Mr. Phegan, William Bruce, James
McIntosh, Robert Gouie, Robt. Dowler, Mr. McAlpin, Mr. Hand,
Mr. McCormick, Commodore Grant, Capt. McKee,Major McGreggor,
Capt. Caldwell, Captain Elliot, Mr. Sparkman, Mr. Cornwall,
Isaac Dolson, George Forsyth, Mr. Christie, Mr. Girty, Capt.
Anderson, Mr. Lyttle, Mr. Harsen, Mr. Graverod, Dr. Harfly,
Mr. Frazer.

Ripley County, Missouri, Delinquent Tax List, 1833, Capitol
Fire Documents, Box 16, Folder 1067.
    Moses Edmunds, Samuel Edmunds, James B. Hughs, Benjamin
Hardovich, Robert Henderson, John Lewis, John Sumter, Edward
Satterfield, Robert L. Sharp, William Crickman, John Alford,
Hanah Thornton, Ligar Gordon, Elias Barker,Nathaniel Barker,
Johnathan Hubble, Obadiah Lewis (sic), Obadiah Lewis (sic),
Carter Wilburn, John West, Johnathan Dobz, Granville Fisher,
Eliza Heavington, John Harrel, John Langley,Thomas Stringer,
Richard Oaks, Jacob Shoutts, James Asly, James Elias, Westy
Riley, Sury Skaggs, Stephen Riley, William Slom,John Bucker,
William Slom, sr., Mathine Slom, Henry Zumatt, Peggy Jones,
Rutha Blackburn, Truman Chilton, John Carr,John Story, Henry
Lewis.

1

Lincoln County, Missouri, Delinquent Tax List,1834,Capitol Fire Documents, Box 16, Folder 1097.

Robert Daniel, Isaac Williams, Thomas Branable, Alexander C. Grannon, Thomas Cobb, George Stour, Bennet Nathy, Forbus Gordon, George Gills, James Galls, Joseh Evanells,William C. Downing, Andrew Evanells, Polly Evanells, Francis Auren,John T. Alexander, Adam George, George Alin, Alonzo Alford, James C. Lindsey, Tutators (sic) Stricklin, Agness Smith, Benjamin Comegys, Milton Craig, Charles Cilone, James Chak, Pleasant Cunningham, Euclid Bates, James Colland, Ralph Colland, John P. Ficklin, William B. Anderson, James Brownsnet, Johnathan R. Halcome, William Boyd, Robert Chutz, Alexander Collins, Lemuel Cox, Daniel Hawkins, Charles Holcombe, James Haywood, Howel Young, Henry Adtentine, Joel Henry, Hill H. Irby, John D. James, William J. H. Jones, Letty Setson, William Y. Knot, Jeremiah Kenny, Benjamin Kinion, jr., Morgan Sallen, Thomas Manning, jr., James Manning, Squire Moore, Samuel McGinnis, Steward Morathy, Peter Morathy, Gilbert Revisheld, Benjamin Robinson, Richardson Westz, Parker Sidney, Douglas Reynolds, James Shaw, jr., Wiley Snider, Isaac Uptergrove, Honrine H. Walton, Shadrick Woodson, William Wammock, Noah Willis,David Willon, Glenn Watkins, Thomas Stubblefield, Jacob Presley, John Foetus, William Moss, Solomon Yates.

Lafayette County, Missouri,Delinquent Tax List, 1834,Capitol Fire Documents, Box 16, Folder 1101.

Benjamin Hargrove, Jesse Hitchcock, Thornton Strother, Wm. Linsey, George Lewis, Jones Chesly, Abraham Nave, Larzarus Mathus, Horace Ressen, Thomas Moon, Thomas Shanklin, John L. Mulky, Henry Hart, Lorow Page, John Parks, Joshua Adams,John Mathus, Stephen Jesse, Danl. M'Keller, Jesse G. Grice, James H. Delap, Annias B. Davis, John C. Amos, David Burnett,David Collams, William Simpson, Cobley L. Stwinson,William Taylor, George W. Layton, John Morris, Letuton West, John Hale, Levi Bracker, David Hale, Almon Bathuck, Allison Brown, Jonathan Beckelsimer, Samuel Burnett, John Cleminson, Adam Couce,John W. Coleburn, Isham Douglas, Solomon Dixon, David Dailey,John Gaun, Henry Day, Samuel Drollinger, Aven Hor, Spencer Ellis, George L. Fulterton, John Muspeth, Markham Fristoe,Elizabeth Truman, Daniel C. Foster, Tyray Mussel, Thomas Gaylord, John Acttessel, Joseph Stephens, Henry Hicks, Philip Hicks, James Lee, William Hamilton, Jeremiah Linsey, Ricahrd Hoggard,Jos. Lane, sr., Barbara Johnson.

Callaway County, Missouri, Marriage Records, 1821 - 1839.

John Abbot and Ann Plummer, (MD) April 4, 1828, (MG) Thodrick Boulware.

--- Abraham and Rachel Sheets, (MD) October 12, 1837, Groom from Boone Co., (MG) James Barnes.

(Callaway County, Missouri Continued)

Elijah Adams and Elizabeth Leeper, (MD) April 5, 1832, (MG) David Kirkpatrick.

Isaac Agee and Cordilly Thornton, (MD) November 25, 1831, (MG) William Coats.

Ransom Agee and Siann Taylor, (MD) March 23, 1834,(MG) J. B. Morrow.

Tilman Agee and Charlotte Townsend, (MD)December 17,1835, (MG) Wm. Coats.

William Agee and Hannah M. Thornton, (MD)August 15, 1837, (MG) Jas. Suggett.

Willis B. Alexander and Jane Hopper, (MD) March 8, 1826, (JP) Thos. H. Baker.

David Allen and Anne Boone, (MD)August 9, 1829,(UK) Jabez Ham, Groom from Montgomery County.

Jesse Allen and Nancy Davis, (MD)January 13, 1831,(MG)Wm. Coats.

John Allen and Martha Sheley, (MD) September 15, 1836, (MG) Theo. Boulware.

John M. Allen and Martha Ann Smart, (MD)September 5,1833, (MG) Jas. Suggett.

John M. Allen and Mary F. Woods, (MD) September 9, 1839, (JP) Wm. H. Neal.

Thomas N. Allen and Isabella Hamilton, (MG) R. L. McAfee, (MD) April 4, 1839.

Samuel Alkire and Mahala Gibson, (MD) October 31, 1831, (JP) J. W. Johnston.

Joshua Anderson and Laurie Baker, (MD) November 13, 1825, (MG) Wm. Coats.

William Armstrong and Mary Edge, (MD) --- 1839, (JP) A. Norflet.

Samuel Ashlock and Sarah D. Hunt, (MD) May 31, 1838, (UK) Thos. M. Allen, Groom from Boone County.

Absalom Austin and Lydia Sitton, (MD) January 7, 1834, (MG) Theo. Boulware.

Anderson J. Baker and Roberta G. Wayne, (MD) August 13, 1839, (MG) Milton Cleveland.

Floyd Baker and Rachel Bell, (MD) September 23, 1830, (JP) Henry Neill.

Isaac Baker and Ann Baker, (MD) January 18, 1826, (MG) Thos. J. Stephens.

John T. Baker and Nancy Devore, (MD) December 29, 1831, (MG) David M. Kirkpatrick.

Morris Baker and Hily Haines, (MD) June 27, 1822, (JP) Patrick Fwing.

Robert C. Baker and Susanah C. Devore,(MD)April 30, 1833, (Elder) Geo. Washington.

Thomas Baker and Ann Adair, (MD) January 10, 1833, (UK) Thomas P. Stephens.

(Callaway County, Missouri Continued)

William B. Baker and Pamela Lewis, (MD)December 16, 1836, (JP) Andrew Alexander.

Joshua T. Bagby and Lucy J. Allen, (MD) January 19, 1837, (MG) J. Green.

Charles Bailey and Amelia Jameson, (MD)February 12, 1838, (MG) Theo. Boulware.

Henry Bailey and Elizabeth Glover,(MD)September 29, 1834, (MG) Theo. Boulware.

William Baly and Rebecca H. Baker, (MD)September 7, 1836, (UK) Jas. M. Jameson.

Henry Barger and Phoebe Wilfley, (MD) February 26, 1826, (JP) Wm. Martin, Groom from Boone County.

Thomas J. Barnes and Sarah L. McCray, (MD)April 28, 1836, (UK) Theo. P. Stephens.

George Bartley and Elizabeth Moore, (MD) July 8, 1827, (MG) William Coats.

John C. Baskin and Rebecca J. Neale, (MD) September 25, 1839, (MG) J. L. Yantis.

Henry Battie and Dorothy Gradavene, (MD)October 29, 1835, (MG) Wm. Coats.

Grief H. Baynham and Martha Granes, (MD)December 4, 1839, (MG) Jas. Suggett.

William G. Baynham and Tabitha Irvin, (UK)William Duncan, (MD) October 10, 1832.

William G. Baynham and Ann Grant, (MG) Theo. Boulware, (MD) April 3, 1838.

Trotter Bearn and Nancy Wilfley, (MD)March 12, 1837, (MG) John T. A. Henderson.

Ladoc Bavan and Luretta Miller, (MD) October 23, 1828, (JP) William Martin.

William Beavans and Lucinda Ferguson, (MD)April 12, 1832, (JP) Arthur Neill.

James Belama and Zerelda Emerine Roberts, (MD) November 22, 1838, (MG) Theo. Boulware.

William Bellama and Ann Tharp, (MD) March 9, 1836, (MG) Theo. Boulware.

Merdeci Bell and May Ann Day, (MD)February 9, 1832, (JP) Geo. Bartley.

John Bellows and Margaret Brown, (MD) May 25, 1837, (MG) R. L. McAfee.

Anson G. Bennet and Mollie Ann Moore, (MD)April 14,1825, (MG) Wm. Coats.

Moses Bennett and Lousinda McKamey, (MD)November 22,1834, (MG) R. S. McAfee.

Joel D. Bennett and Mary M. McAfee, (MD)February 19,1839, (MG) R. L. McAfee, Bride from Kentucky.

Jefferson Benson and Sally Hays, (MD)March 15, 1838, (JP) Joseph Scholl.

(Callaway County, Missouri Continued)

John Berry and Margaret Galbreath, (MD) March 25, 1830, (MG) Wm. Coats.

Edward G. Berry and Sally Ann Galbreath, (MD)February 14, 1833, (UK) --- Hoxsen.

George T. Berry and Jane Humphries, (MD)December 12,1833, (MG) Wm. W. Redman.

Thomas H. Berry and Mahala Davidson,(MD)February 17,1836, (JP) James Stewart.

Tyre Bishop and Rebecca W. Wilburn,(MD)June 7, 1838, (MG) Jabez Ham.

John W. Blackwell and Jane Davis, (MD)April 1, 1839, (MG) Jacob Coons.

Alexander Bleven and Emeline Zumwalt,(JP)Geo. B. Hopkins, (MD) November 21, 1833.

John Blunckall and Mary Hamblin, (MD) September 8, 1835, (MG) Jacob Ham.

John W. Blunt and Sintha Hays, (MD) September 13, 1838, (MG) John T. A. Henderson.

John W. Blunt and Jane Thomas, (MD) January 2, 1831, (MG) M. P. Wills.

David T. Boaz and Polly Brown, (MD) May 22, 1839, (MG) Theo. Boulware.

Matthew D. Boggs and Martha J. Kennett,(MD)August 2,1838, (MG) J. L. Yantis.

Robert Bogges and Lucy Jane Miller, (MD)December 8, 1832, (JP) J. W. Johnson.

Edward H. Bond and Eliz. G. Hughes, (MD) July 20, 1837, (MG) Jas. Suggett.

Edward Booker and Mary Lomax, (MD) January 6, 1836, (JP) A. G. Boone.

Benton G. Boone and Eliz. Copher Boone, (MD)June 26,1828, (MG) Jabez Ham.

Albert G. Boone and Ann Read Hamilton, (MD) July 9, 1829, (MG) T. N. Durbee.

Alonzo Boon and Mary Jane Jackson, (MD) January 2, 1834, (MG) Wm. Coats.

Jas. Madison Boone and Mary McMurty, (MD) April 7, 1831, (JP) Enoch Fruit.

Alphonso Boon and Nancy Boon, (MD) February 1, 1822, (JP) Enoch Fruit.

Stephen Boulware and Mary Ratican, (MD) April 29, 1835, (MG) Jas. Suggett.

John Bourd and Jane Callison, (MD) October 1, 1839, (MG) Jabez Ham.

Robert C. Boyce and Asinah Ann Murphy, (MD)March 24,1830, (MG) D. M. Kirpatrick.

Col. James Boyd and Mary Ann Scott, (MD) April 15, 1828, (MG) D. M. Kirkpatrick.

(Callaway County, Missouri Continued)

William Boyes and Margaret A. Barry, (JP) John K. Barry, (MD) September 8, 1831.

James Boyes and Jemina Freeman, (MD) February 12, 1833, (JP) John R. Barry.

Benjamin Braham and Mary Ann Tucker, (MG) William Coats, (MD) September 28, 1832.

Isaac Branham and Amanda Bailey, (MD) February 23, 1832, (MG) Theo. Boulware.

Felix Briant and Maxey Boone, (MD) May 3, 1832, (MG) Wm. Maxey.

William A. Brite and Mary Ann Scott, (MD) May 2, 1839, (JP) Wm. J. Gilman.

William Brockman and Agnes Hill, (MD) April 23, 1839, (MG) Theo. Boulware.

Robert Brooks and Elizabeth Rhour, (MD)September 28,1839, (JP) Robt. Brandon.

James S. Brown and Sarah Jane Hornbuckle, (MD)December 1, 1839, (MG) John Thatcher, Groom from Johnson County.

James Brown and Hannah Ann Alderson, (MD) July 5, 1835, (MG) Wm. Duncan.

Charles H. Brown and Amanda McKinney, (MD) March 9, 1837, (MG) R. L. McAfee.

Joseph Brown and Julian Pearson, (MD) April 19, 1836, (JP) Jas. Harris.

Toliver Bryant and Sarah E. Hackney, (MD)January 26,1837, (JP) Jabez Ham.

William Buchannan and Martha Warren, (MG) Theo. Boulware, (MG) February 14, 1831.

John Buckley and Eva Berkett, (MD) April 26, 1837,(JP) C. Zumwalt.

Marcus Bullard and Susannah Burnet, (MD) February 1,1835, (UL) John Selby.

Thompson Bunch and Nancy Hays, (MD) August 26, 1826, (JP) Enoch Fruit.

James Burks and Martha Newman, (MD) August 31, 1831, (UK) J. C. Berryman.

William Burns and Miss C. H. Throckmorton, (UK) Robert A. Younger, (MD) December 24, 1835.

Michael A. Burns and Mary McLaughlin, (MD) March 7, 1839, (JP) H. S. Turner.

Didymus Buzz and Sarah Langley, (MD) March 10, 1839, (UK) Geo. B. Hopkins.

Robert A. Caldwell and Mary A. Holman, (MD) July 25,1838, (UK) R. L. McAfee.

Joseph P. Callaway and Miss Nancy Coats, (MD)December 12, 1822, (MG) Robert Baker.

Joseph Callaway and June E. Craghead, (MD) April 28,1839, (MG) Jno. Pace.

6

(Callaway County, Missouri Continued)

William Callaway and Tabitha Coats, (MD) April 9, 1829, (MG) Wm. Coats.

Jas. Vinson Callaway and Susan Kemp, (MD)February 9,1832, (MG) Wm. Coats.

James Callaway and Fanny Meadows, (MD) September 2, 1839, (JP) W. J. Gilman.

William Callison and Nancy Moore, (MD) April 26, 1832, (JP) John A. Burt.

John Campbell and Nancy Boyd, (MD) January 31, 1839, (MG) J. L. Yantis.

Capt. Thomas Campbell and Martha West, (MD) September 25, 1839, (UK) Tos. P. Stephens.

Albert G.L. Carruth and Parthena Jones, (MG)Absalom Rice, (MD) September 13, 1838.

John Carrington and Elizabeth T. Randolph, (MD) December 21, 1837, (UK) Jno. T. A. Henderson.

Larkin Cason and Nancy Sucet, (MD) June 14, 1832, (UK) Ninivan Ridgway.

William Cason and Sarah Overton, (MD) September 22, 1836, (MG) Theo. Boulware.

Henry Cave and Fanny Craig, (MD) Septmber 8, 1824, (UK) Richard Cave, Groom from Boone County.

Stephen Chapman and Nancy Wood, (MD)June 8, 1826,(JP) Wm. Martin.

John H. Chariton and Nancy Carter, (MD) March 27, 1833, (UK) Geo. T. Keys.

Elisha Chase and Anna Donahoe, (MD) January 3, 1837, (MG) Alia B. Lusther.

David C. Cheatham and Martha Ratekin, (MG) Absalom Rice, (MD) July 4, 1838.

Claybourne Cheatham and Nancy Smith, (MG) William Coats, (MD) September 2, 1834.

Turley Cheatham and Molly Fort, (MD) April 15, 1839, (MG) Jacob Coons.

Francis Chick and Elenor Hays, (MD) December 16, 1835, (JP) Jno. A. Burt.

James Chriswell and Jane Allen, (MD) October 15, 1835, (MG) Jno. Pace.

James Clanton and Keziah Tharp, (MD) May 30, 1830, (JP) William Crain.

William Clark and Sarah Wadley, (MD) November 2, 1826, (JP) Jas. Henderson.

John Clatterbuck and Martha ---, (MD) April 29, 1830, (UK) D. M. Kirkpatrick.

Leroy Clatterbuck and Mary Gray, (MD) April 22, 1831, (MG) Jas. Suggett.

Milton Cleveland and Susan Beaven, (MD) April 16, 1830, (MG) William Crain.

(Callaway County, Missouri Continued)

William Coats and Cena McLaughlin, (MD) January 29, 1837, (UK) Andrew Alexander.

Hiram Coats and Pamelia Walker, (MD) September 20, 1835, (JP) James Stewart.

Jno. Coats and Sally Smith, (MD) April 16, 1821, (UK) Patrick Ewing.

James Cobb and Ann Boone, (MD) December 31, 1829.

John E. Commer and Nancy McGary, (MD) October 8, 1832, (MG) Theo. Boulware.

Stephen Conger and Lucy Jane Gordon, (MD) March 8, 1835, (MG) Jas. Suggett.

Thomas D. Conger and Moniza McCampbell, (MD) October 18, 1827, (JP) John Conger.

James H. Cook and Grizella B. Caldwell, (MD)May 16, 1839, (MG) J. L. Yantis, Groom from St. Louis County.

Grave Cook and Saffrony Sublet, (MD) March 31, 1825, (MG) William Coats.

George Coons and Sallie Bell, (MD) December 29, 1833, (MG) Samuel Day.

Joseph Corley and Felicity Parue, (MD) September 10,1822, (UK) Jonathan Holliway.

Henry Covington and Nancy Arnold, (MD) November 14, 1839, (UK) Joseph Scholl.

Stephen Craghead and Nancy Blount, (MD) March 11, 1834, (MG) William W. Redman.

Solomon Craghead and Elizabeth Dunlap, (MD) November 13, 1828, (UK) David Kirpatrick.

Robert Craghead, jr. and Nancy Hughes, (MD) February 27, 1831, (UK) George Bartley.

George Craig and Hannah Atwater, (MD) March 15, 1838, (UK) John F. Young.

William Craig and Sidney Smith, (MD) December 12, 1838, (MG) Theo. Boulware.

Larkin Craig and Anne Ficklin, (MD) June 7, 1831, (MG) Theo. Boulware.

Carter T. Craig and Mary S. Garner, (MD)October 14, 1836, (MG) James Barnes.

Thomas Crasento and Marandy Ratekin, (MD) November 14, 1839, (MG) Jas. Suggett.

George W. Creed and Eliza Miller, (MD) November 6, 1834, (MG) William Duncan.

William Crowson and Rachel Miller, (MD) May 2, 1839, (NG) Theo. Boulware.

William M. Crump and Mary Jane Shull, (MD)January 9,1834, (MG) Jas. Suggett.

Samuel Crump and Elizabeth Baker, (MD) January 7, 1830, (Elder) M. P. Wills.

Rich. W. Donell and Nancy Crosswaite, (MD)October 10,1839

(Callaway County, Missouri Continued)

Thompson Crump and Louisa Hays, (MD) December 2, 1825, (MG) William Hays.

James Crump and Sally Ratekin, (MD) November 1, 1832, (UK) David Kirkpatrick.

Bollinger Crump and Susan May, (MD) February 2, 1830, (Elder) M. P. Wills.

D. W. S. Crump and Mary Love, (MD) December 5, 1831, (JP) Enoch Fruit.

Simpson Crump and Mary Jane West, (MD) August 12, 1830, (MD) M. P. Wills.

Barnabas Davis and Julia Ann Davis, (MD)February 1, 1832, (UK) Henry Neill.

Thomas J. Davis and Loutesia V. Swan, (MD) September 1, 1829, (UK) David Kirkpatrick.

Elijah Davis and Lucinda Haynes, (MD) January 15, 1828, (UK) Thomas Stephens.

Matthew Davis and Elizabeth Wilfley, (MD) July 7, 1835, (MG) Theo. Boulware.

Madison Davis and Mary Ella, (MD) December 8, 1836, (MG) Theo. Boulware.

John B. Davis and Margaret Young, (MD) April 25, 1834, (MG) Theo. Boulware.

William Davis and Eliza Baker, (MD) May 30, 1831, (MG) Allin McGuire.

William Day and Eliza Childress, (MD) November 15, 1832, (MG) Geo. T. Key.

Charles A. Day and Nancy Walker, (MD) May 27, 1835, (MG) William Coats.

Ezekiel Day and Sarah Branson, (MD) January 25, 1838, (UK) George B. Hopkins.

John Debo and Ann Snell, (MD) September 23, 1835, (MG) Theo. Boulware.

John Decker and Mary Nance, (MD) January 13, 1831, (UK) George Bartley.

John T. Deshazo and Charlotte Walker, (MD) June 22, 1837, (JP) Jas. Stewart.

Francis W. Diggs and Mary Catherine Curd, (MD)October 18, 1838, (MG) John S. Yantis.

Charles Dile and Nancy Wadley, (MD) July 3, 1825, (JP) George King.

John T. Dill and Margaret F. Steele, (MD)February 1,1838, (MG) R. L. McAfee.

David B. Dixon and Beveline R. Crawford, (MD) August 2, 1839, (MG) Theo. Boulware,

Francis Dodds and Mehaldy Coats, (MD) September 18, 1828, (MG) Jabes Ham.

William H. Dorsey and Jane Nevins, (MD) July 2, 1829, (UK) David Kirkpatrick.

(Callaway County, Missouri Continued)

Andrew B. Dorsey and Mary Wiley, (MD) June 21, 1835, (UK) John F: Young.

John Dougherty and Rebecca Hatton, (MD)December 17, 1835, (JP) B. A. Ramsey.

William Douglas and Lucy Chick, (MD) March 29, 1832, (JP) Enoch Fruit.

William Dudley and Menerva Callaway, (MD) February 15, 1838, (MG) Jabez Ham.

William Dudley and Laurian Coats, (MD) January 12, 1832, (MG) William Coats.

David H. Duncan and Eliza Ann Morrison, (MD) January 6, 1836, (MG) Theo. Doulware.

Thomas Duncan and Polly McClure, (MD) January 21, 1836, (MG) William Duncan.

Frederick Duncan and Elizabeth Gibson, (MD) January 24, 1839, (MG) James Love.

James Dunlap and Sally Crump, (MD) December 7, 1826, (MG) William Coats.

William Dunn and Sarah Patton, (MD) February 8, 1839, (UK) John T. A. Henderson.

John Dunnica and Betsey Ferguson, (MD) April 11, 1822, (UK) Samuel Baskett.

William Duvall and Eliza Tully, (MD) February 27, 1827, (MG) William Coats.

John Dyer and Evaline Warren, (MD) February 19, 1824, (MG) William Coats.

Matthew Edwards and Margaret Ferguson, (MD) May 24, 1827, (UK) Ninian Ridgway.

Jacob Ellington and Sally Matheny, (MD)December 16, 1838, (MG) Jabez Ham.

Elias J. Emmons and Mildred Newman, (MD) December 7,1830, (JP) T. G. Jones.

Thomas Estes and Jane Calvin, (MD) January 8, 1835, (MG) William Coats.

James Faris and Rebecca M. (MD) December 6, 1838, (UK) J. T. Henderson.

Jesse Farmer and Elizabeth E. King, (MD) December 4,1833, (MG) Robert McAfee.

John Farmer and Emerald J. Major, (MD) November 12, 1829, (MG) Theo. Boulware.

Thomas Favier and Jane Phillips, (MD) August 2, 1821, (JP) Solomon Thomas.

John Alfred Fentesche and S. McClelland Baker, (MD) September 12, 1839, (UK) M. P. Wills.

Levan Ferguson and Jane Holloway, (MD) February 22, 1822, (JP) George King.

Thomas J. Ferguson and Nancy Lewis Moore, (MD) February 14, 1833, (UK) William W. Redman.

(Callaway County, Missouri Continued)

Willoughby P. Ferguson and Elizabeth Gee, (MD)January 18, 1838, (JP) Arthur Neill.

James Ferguson and Catharine Price, (MD)October 20, 1834, (UK) George B. Hopkins.

Samuel Ferrier and Alice Shannon, (MD) November 22, 1827, (UK) J. Y. Verrejot.

Beverly Allen Fields and Louisa E. West, (MD) August 11, 1836, (JP) George L. Smith.

John Finley and Nancy Woodland, (MD) January 7, 1838, (UK) Andrew Alexander.

William W. Findley and Margaret J. Campbell, (MD) October 25, 1838, (MG) Robert C. Hill.

Joseph Fisher and Mary Craighead, (MD) November 6, 1827, (UK) David M. Kirkpatrick.

Joseph O. Flecher and Lucy W. Parker, (MD) May 18, 1837, (MG) Thomas B. Sitton.

John F. Fletcher and Judith Simco, (MD) August 29, 1839, (MG) Theo. Boulware.

John Foster and Sarah Longley, (MD) April 24, 1828, (UK) David Kirkpatrick.

William A. Foster and Matilda D. Harris, (MD) August 31, 1837, (JP) R. B. Jackson.

Garner Quarels Foster and Manerva Pinkston, (MD)March 17, 1836, (MG) R. L. McAfee.

James T. Foster and Isabella Ellis, (MD) September 22, 1836, (MG) R. L. McAfee,

Elijah Foster and Elizabeth Powell, (MD) July 12, 1827, (UK) James Henderson.

Lienden Fowler and Sarah Osten, (MD) January 19, 1832, (UK) David Kirkpatrick, Bride from Boone County.

Nicholas Foy and Susan Roy, (MD) June 23, 1839, (JP) A. K. Bell.

Michael Freeman and Louisa Wilson, (MD)November 17, 1836, (UK) Greenup Jackson.

John French and Isabella Dillard, (MD) May 11, 1837, (MG) William B. Douglass.

Lewis French and Louisa Simpson, (MD) August 1, 1822, (JP) Enoch Fruit.

John Frey and Sophronia Hall, (MD) November 7, 1822, (JP) Adam Hope.

John Fullbright and Elizabeth Yount, (MD)October 2, 1828, (JP) George King.

James Galbreath and Elizabeth Galbreath, (MD) October 18, 1821, (UK) Solomon Thomas, Groom from Kentucky.

James R. galbreath and Sarah Petty, (MD)November 17,1836, (MG) Theo. Boulware.

--- Garrett and Lucy Scott, (MD) August 13, 1835, (UK) Robert A. Younger.

(Callaway County, Missouri Continued)

William J. Gilman and Vicy Ann Callaway, (MD) October 18, 1838, (MG) Jabez Ham.

William Gilmon and Charlotte Williams, (MD) February 25, 1830, (MG) William Coats.

Archibald Gilmore and Majoicrey Ferguson, (MD) December 28, 1837, (JP) B. A. Ramsey.

William Gillmore and Sarah Quinn, (MD) December 22, 1831, (JP) Horace Sheley.

John Gladwell and Sarah Ann Faber, (MD) July 19, 1838, (MG) J. S. Yantis.

Thomas M. Glendi and Ellen Shields, (MD)January 15, 1833, (UK) Benj. F. Hoxey.

Charles Glover and Mahala Davis, (MD) October 3, 1839, (MG) Theo. Boulware.

William Gordan and Livisa Meur, (MD) February 8, 1838, (JP) Arthur Neill.

Joseph Gordon and Matilda Henderson, (MD)August 22, 1822, (JP) Adam Hope.

Benjamin Goodrich and Harriet H. Thomas, (MD) October 8, 1822, (UK) Robert Baker.

Israel Grant and Mary Warren, (MD) February 14, 1831, (MG) Theo. Boulware.

George Gray and Eliz. C. Holt, (MD) November 16, 1837, (UK) John T. A. Henderson.

W. H. Grear and Rebecca Thatcher, (MD) July 22, 1831,(MG) Theo. Boulware.

William Green and Larceney Smith, (MD) March 8, 1830,(JP) Robert Davis.

Lewis Griffith and Nancy Lampkins, (MD) April 15, 1827, (JP) Solomon Thomas.

John Griffith and Eliza M. Williams,(MD)November 25,1830, (UK) David Kirkpatrick.

Ambrose Griggs and Isabella Evans, (MD) March 2, 1837, (JP) H. S. Turner.

Stephen Guerrant and Lucy Ann Hardin, (MD) March 2, 1837, (MG) Theo. Boulware.

Allen W. Gutherie and Eliz. Ann Young, (MD) September 16, 1838, (UK) Jno. T. A. Henderson.

Thomas Gylmare and Charlotte Coons, (MD)October 20, 1831, (UK) Horace Sheley.

Samuel Hall and Rachel Gray, (MD) October 29, 1835, (MG) A. Norfleet.

B. B. Hall and Mary H. Reed, (MD) May 21, 1835,(MG) Theo. Boulware.

Schuyler B. Ham and Pamelia Ann Jones, (MD) February 21, 1833, (UK) William W. Redman.

Mathew Ham and Elizabeth Gray, (MD) October 18, 1836,(JP) A. Norfleet.

(Callaway County, Missouri Continued)

John Hamblin and Elizabeth Heasick, (MD) August 18, 1836, (MG) Jabez Ham.

Andrew Hamilton and Elizabeth Callison, (MD)September 17, 1835, (MG) Jabez Ham.

William Baskin Hamilton and Margaret H. Allen, (MD) September 7, 1837, (UK) R. L. McAfee.

James Hamilton and Ann Callison, (MD) October 31, 1839, (MG) Jabez Ham.

Samuel Hannah and Susan Lowden, (MD) November 18, 1839, (UK) James Barnes.

--- Hansberry and Susannah Boulware, (MD) June 9, 1835, (MG) Jas. Suggett.

Peter Harris and Betsey Acles, (MD) May 5, 1833, (MG) Wm. Coats.

Mastin Harris and Rachel Jane Akens, (MD) June 9, 1835, (MG) William Coats.

John Harris and Rhody Townson, (MD) July 23, 1823, (MG) William Duncan.

M. Harrison and A. Craig, (MD) June 28, 1831, (MG) Theo. Boulware.

Abner Harrison and Nancy Harrison, (MD)November 11, 1834, (MG) Andrew Monroe.

Hugh Harryman and Christenny Zumwalt, (MD) May 10, 1827, (UK) Christopher Zumwalt.

James Hart and Nancy Ferguson.(MD) April 20, 1837, (UK) Condley Smith.

James O. Harver and Betsey Philips,(MD)September 22,1830, (MG) William Coats.

Thomas C. Haskins and Mary G. Anderson, (MD) February 18, 1835, (MG) Theo. Boulware.

Lewis Hawkins and Claudia Thomas, (MD) January 31, 1828, (MG) William Coats.

Samuel Haydon and Mary McClure, (MD) October 16, 1834, (MG) Theo. Boulware.

Jeptha Hayton and Elizabeth Fulks, (MD) March 10, 1833, (JP) Arthur Neill.

William Haynes and Polly Louder, (MD) February 25, 1830, (MG) Thomas Stephens.

Joseph Hays and Nancy Hays, (MD) March 18, 1825, (UK) Samuel Crockett.

Harmon Hays and Minervia Scholl, (MD)March 29, 1832, (JP) Enoch Fruit, Groom from Montgomery County.

Alfred E. Heart and Nicy Pulham, (MD) January 17, 1833, (UK) Robert L. McAfee.

Jesse C. Henderson and Nancy Hughart, (MD) April 5, 1827, (UK) James Henderson.

James S. Henderson and Emily Boone, (MD) June 6, 1831, (UK) David Kirkpatrick.

(Callaway County, Missouri Continued)

David Henderson and Mary Blattenburgh, (MD) December 11, 1834, (MG) Theo. Boulware.

James A. Henderson and Francis M. Holt, (MD) November 16, 1838, (UK) John T. A. Henderson.

James Hereford and Rosey Vincent, (MD) May 24, 1832, (UK) Thos. Stephens.

Henry Herriford and Esther Vinson, (MD) September 1,1825, (UK) Thos. Stephens.

Armstead Hickerson and Rhoda Bentley, (MD)April 12, 1832, (JP) John A. Burt.

Lewis Hockins and Claudia Thomas, (MD) January 31, 1828, (MG) William Coats.

John Hodge and Louisa Meelor, (MD) October 30, 1832, (UK) Ninivan Ridgeway.

Crowder Holloway and Mary Irvine, (MD) October 10, 1833, (JP) B. A. Ramsey.

Timothy Holt and Nancy J. Gordon, (MD) January 14, 1829, (UK) James Henderson.

John Holt and Sarah Brandon, (MD) November 4, 1835, (MG) Jas. Suggett.

William P. Holt and Polly Bly, (MD) October 24, 1839,(MG) Jas. Suggett.

Richard S. Hornbuckle and Rachel Baker, (MD) February 4, 1835, (UK) George B. Hopkins.

Richard S. Hornbuckle and Elvira Smart, (MD) October 1, 1838, (UK) Milton Cleveland.

Thomas Hornbuckle and Providence Baker, (MD)May 28, 1826, (JP) Robert Davis.

Rufus Hornbuckle and Amanda Davis, (MD) April 2, 1839, (UK) George B. Hopkins.

Joseph House and Mary Malone, (MD) January 25, 1825, (UK) Samuel Crockett.

John Houston and Permelia Branum, (MD) September 3, 1829, (UK) William P. Cochran.

Abraham Howard and Sally Alexander, (MD) March 1, 1826, (MG) William Coats.

James M. G. Howe and Anne C. Baker, (MD)November 20,1834, (MG) William Duncan.

Albert G. Hubbard and Francis M. Austin, (MD) March 18, 1835, (MG) Theo. Boulware.

Joseph T. Highhart and Ann Henderson, (MD)August 30,1827, (UK) David Kirkpatrick.

John Hughes and Mary E. Peyton, (MD) December 7, 1837, (JP) John A. Burt.

Elisha Hughes and Susan McMurty, (MD) November 8, 1838, (UK) William B. Douglass.

John Hull and Sarah E. Tucker, (MD) November 3, 1836,(JP) A. G. Boone.

(Callaway County, Missouri Continued)

Duke Hults and Margaret Love, (MD) October 23, 1827, (JP) Enoch Fruit.

Lorenzo Hultz and Melissa Vanbibber, (MD)January 12,1837, (MG) Jabez Ham.

William Humphries and Frances Muir, (MD) March 3, 1835, (MG) Theo. Boulware.

Robert Humphries and Lucy Williams, (MD)February 12,1824, (MG) William Coats.

Samuel Humphries and Louisa G. Smart, (MD) March 3, 1833, (UK) William W. Redman.

John Humphreys and Susannah Crawford, (MD) June 5, 1836, (UK) Archibald Allen.

Overton Hunter and Elizabeth Huff, (MD) December 21,1837, (UK) John F. Young.

William Hunter and Sarah Talbot, (MD) January 21, 1836, (MG) William Duncan.

Andrew Hunter and Ann Rock, (MD) February 14, 1822, (UK) Solomon Thomas, Groom from Montgomery County.

Samuel Hunter and Elizabeth Dysart, (MD)January 15, 1839, (UK) J. F. Young.

John Hutcherson and Isabel Meteer, (MD)September 21,1837, (MG) Theo. Boulware.

Alexander Irvine and M. Dunnica, (MD) March 19, 1833,(UK) B. A. Ramsey.

Robert Irvine and Evalina Scott, (MD) March 10, 1836,(UK) John F. Young.

Thomas Jackman and Dicey Potter, (MD) September 6, 1832, (JP) John A. Barry.

--- Janes and Mary Boyd, (MD) January 17, 1839, (MG) Jas. Suggett.

William James and Evaline Blackburn, (MD) May 24, 1838, (JP) R. B. Jackman.

Newton Jameson and Pamela Smith, (MD) January 21, 1836, (MG) Jas. Suggett.

David Jawan and Amy Philips, (MD) May 30, 1833, (UK) Rbt. S. McAfee.

James Jesse and Margaret Price, (UK) October 5, 1833,(UK) Thomas Stephens.

D. Johnson and M. A. Petty, (MD)August 8, 1833,(MG) Theo. Boulware.

John J. Jones and Rebecca Reynolds, (MD) May 13, 1827, (JP) Edward Ellis.

William Jones and Amanda Miller, (M) February 20, 1834, (MG) Jabez Ham.

Thomas Jones and Margaret Duley, (MD) June 8, 1837, (UK) William Martin.

William Jones and Elizabeth Jones, (MD) March 1, 1838, (MG) Jabez Ham.

(Callaway County, Missouri Continued)

Thomas Jones and Sarah Young, (MD) October 20, 1836, (UK) Jno. Pace.

Robert Jones and Tellacinda Sympson, (MD) June 10, 1830, (JP) John A. Burt.

Henry Keaton and Cyan Reed, (MD) March 21, 1833,(UK) Rbt. Younger.

John Kelison and Margaret B. Lochridge, (MD)April 8,1830, (JP) John K. Barry.

William Kemp and Lizean Gardener, (MD) October 16, 1834, (MG) William Duncan.

Robert M. Kemp and Nancy P. Craghead,(MD)January 22,1839, (MD) Theo. Boulware.

Jourdan Kemp and Mary Dunlap, (MD) May 19, 1831, (MG) Wm. Coats.

John Kenny and Lamira Yount, (MD) October 9, 1828, (JP) George King.

Samuel H. Kester and Sarah Simpson, (MD)February 11,1838, (MG) Jabez Ham.

Alfred Kibbey and Cynthia Harrison, (MD) June 9, 1831, (JP) Enoch Fruit, Groom of Montgomery County.

John Kilgore and Margaret Willingham, (MD) June 28, 1831, (JP) Isaac Black.

John H. Kilgore and Pamelia D. Kilgore, (MD) February 25, 1836, (MG) George L. Smith.

John Kilgore and Patsey Williams, (MD) December 11, 1835, (JP) H. J. Dean.

John King and Narcissus Conger, (MD) October 29, 1835, (MG) Jas. Suggett.

Allen Kinkead and Mary Price, (MD) June 14, 1838, (MG) J. S. Yantis, Groom from Saline County.

Augusta Lambert and Joanna Rhodes, (MD) November 19,1837, (JP) Arthur Neill.

William Lambert and Susannah Burnett, (MD) April 13,1828, (UK) Jas. Henderson.

Archibald Langley and Lucinda Freeman, (MD)March 24,1839, (JP) H. S. Turner.

James N. Langley and Ruth A. Newton, (MD) August 9, 1838, (UK) John Henderson.

Thomas Langley and Sally Williams, (MD) May 16, 1838,(JP) Arthur Neill.

Collett Langley and Therissa Evans, (MD)December 25,1834, (UK) George B. Hopkins.

John Langley and Elizabeth Rose, (MD) May 25, 1829, (JP) Henry Neill.

James Langley and Matilda Haynes, (MD) January 22, 1824, (UK) Jonathan Holliway.

Aaron Larue and Maria Sitton, (MD) August 31, 1834, (MG) Theo. Boulware.

(Callaway County, Missouri Continued)

Samuel Lathlin and Franky Coats, (MD) October 22, 1829, (MG) Jabez Ham.

Bailey Lathlin and Salina Agee, (MD) December 3, 1835, (MG) Jabez Ham.

Edward Lawrence and Evey Murdock, (MD) June 21, 1839, (MG) Absalom Rice.

Josiah Layson and Mary Young, (MD) December 13, 1832, (MG) Theo. Boulware.

James A. Leeper and Florence McPheeters, (MD) October 28, 1825, (UK) W. W. Robertson.

David Leiper and Martha Scott, (MD) January 25, 1832, (UK) Benjamin Hoxey.

Joseph Lenard and Sara Grant,(MD) December 10, 1826, (UK) Irvine Hockaday.

Harvey Level and Milly Boone, (MD) November 14, 1833,(MG) Jabez Ham.

Elias Lewis and Darley Philips, (MD) April 6, 1834, (MG) William Coats.

Nelson Lewis and Petheny Eakins, (MD) February 21, 1833, (MG) William Coats.

Moses Lewis and Delilah Jamison, (MD) March 7, 1833,(UK) Horace Sheeley.

Oliver Little and Jane Trimble, (MD) December 7, 1833, (MG) Jabez Ham.

James Logan and Elizabeth Talbott, (MD) May 12, 1836,(UK) John F. Young.

Joseph Darris Lorton and Nancy Williams, (MD) September 10, 1835, (JP) John K. Barny.

Charles Love and Catharine Martin, (MD) May 24, 1827, (JP) Enoch Fruit.

Washington Lynes and Susan Suggett, (MD) July 28, 1836, (MG) James Barnes.

Andrew Mahoney and Sally Ann Moxley, (MD) August 21,1828, (JP) Enoch Fruit.

John Marrow and Nancy Agee, (MD) October 15, 1835, (JP) Jas. Stewart.

Samuel Martin and Judith Wright, (MD) May 21, 1829, (MG) Theo. Boulware.

Noah Marton and Virginia Closby, (MD) February 11, 1835, (MG) William Duncan.

William Harris Martin and Sophronia McLanahan, (MD)December 26, 1835, (MG) R. L. McAfee.

Robert Martin and Ann Baker, (MD) February 22, 1827, (UK) Thomas P. Stephens.

Samuel G. Mason and Ann Eliza Dyer, (MD) January 6, 1835, (UK) Isaac S. Houser.

William Mask and Mary Andres, (MD) February 22, 1839, (UK) Joseph T. Bryan.

(Callaway County, Missouri Continued)

William Matter and Sally Hunter, (MD) August 27, 1829,
(UK) Thomas Durfee.

Briton Matthews and Miss Zumwalt, (MD) April 28, 1831,
(JP) George Bartley.

Henry Mattock and Matilda Cox, (MD) July 19, 1835, (UK)
Robert A. Younger.

Richard May and R. Crump, (MD) December 17, 1829, (MG)
Theo. Boulware.

John May and Delea Boon, (MD) February 20, 1834, (MG) Wm.
Coats.

Gabriel May and Elizabeth Craghead, (MD) December 4,1823,
(JP) Thomas Fisher.

Signor Mays and Martha Ridgway, (MD) September 18, 1835,
(MG) William Duncan.

Philip T. McAfee and Mary Ann E. Shelby, (MD)May 27,1834,
(MG) R. L. McAfee.

James E. McCall and Angelina Gilbert, (MD) November 7,
1839, (MG) Jabez Ham.

Jesse E. McCampbell and Lucinda Congo, (MD) May 9, 1824,
(JP) James Nevins,

John T. McClain and Iby J. Whittey, (MD) October 9, 1836,
(JP) James Stewart.

Elisha McClelland and Betsey Ann West, (MD)March 20,1834,
(MG) William Duncan.

Thomas McClelland and Sarah Robinet, (MD) May 1, 1832,
(UK) Theo. P. Stephens, Bride is from Boone County.

Harvey McClure and Mary Jane Davis, (MD) October 8, 1835,
(MG) Tho. Boulware.

William McClure and Eliz. M. McClure, (MD) April 16,1833,
(UK) Theo. Boulware.

William McCormack and Eliz. L. Jones, (MD)January 3,1822,
(UK) Enoch Fruit.

David McCormick and Unice Jones, (MD) March 12, 1832, (JP)
J. A. Burt.

Joel McConnell and Ann Thatcher, (MD) December 17, 1829,
(MG) Theo. Boulware.

Geo. P. McCredie and Sarah Ann McKinney, (MD) October 12,
1830, (MG) Theo. Boulware.

John McDaniel and Cynthia Alexander, (MD) August 5, 1824,
(UK) David Kirkpatrick.

John K. McDonald and Jane Burnett, (MD) July 11, 1833,
(UK) Robert S. McAfee,

Cash McDonald and Drusilla Davis, (MD) June 20, 1833,(JP)
J. M. Doan.

Joseph McDonald and Jane Cragg, (MD) December 5, 1833,
(UK) Robert A. Younger.

Isham McDonald and Jane Boyd, (MD) October 7, 1835, (UK)
Robert A. Younger.

(Callaway County, Missouri Continued)

Hugh H. McGary and Susan Davis, (MD) February 9,1837,(JP) Jas. Stewart.

Charles W. McIntire and Margaret Harrison, (MD) January 10, 1828, (MG) Theodore Boulware.

James M. McKammey and Elizabeth Murray, (MD) January 8, 1829, (UK) David Kirpatrick.

William H. McKammey and Angelina Soctt, (MD)June 17,1836, (MG) R. L. McAfee.

Charles McKinney and Mary Ann Craig,(MD)February 10,1830, (MG) Theo. Boulware.

John McKinney and Anna E. Hill, (MD) September 21, 1837, (MG) Theo. Boulware.

William McLaughlin and Leny Callaway, (MD) February 19, 1829, (MG) William Coats.

Isham McMahan and Elizabeth Duncan, (MD) January 6, 1831, (MG) Jabez Ham.

Richard McMahan and Louisa J. Love, (MD) November 1,1832, (JP) James Stewart.

Aaron McMillin and Sarah Zumwalt, (MD) January 19, 1826, (UK) James Henderson.

Levi McMurty and Fanny Chick, (MD) May 5, 1831, (JP)Enoch Fruit.

James McMurty and Serelda Hays, (MD) October 10, 1832, (JP) Enoch Fruit.

Christopher Meacham and Baersheba Neille, (MD)October 22, 1835, (UK) George B. Hopkins.

Adam Mead and Sally Clay, (MD) April 25, 1832,(JP)William Martin.

Joseph Mead and Levina Thomas, (MD) September 27, 1832, (JP) Arthur Neill.

John Mead and Mintey Punnels, (MD) August 15, 1833, (JP) Arthur Neill.

John Mede and Polley Ellice, (MD) April 3, 1829, (JP) Wm. Martin.

Alfred Menifee and Mary Hunt Mason, (MD)November 25,1830, (MG) Theo. Boulware.

Benjamin Miller and Eva Blevins, (MD) April 29, 1827, (UK) James Henderson.

John Warden Miller and Louisiana Coons, (MD) November 3, 1836, (MG) Joseph Coons.

Moses L. Miller and Louisa Ferguson, (MD) June 15, 1836, (MG) B. A. Ramsey.

Wikelif Miller and Louisa Jones, (MD) February 19, 1834, (MG) Jabez Ham.

Bailey Miller and Susan Jones, (MD) October 20, 1831,(JP) John A. Burt.

Martin A. Miller and Jane Miller, (MD) February 4, 1830, (UK) M. P. Wills.

19

(Callaway County, Missouri Continued)

Allen Miller and Mariah Reed, (MD) October 22, 1828, (JP) William Martin.

Robert W. Miller and Mary J. Paten, (MD) March 3, 1837, (UK) Elijah E. Chrisman.

George Mires and Malinda MacDaniel, (MD) August 20, 1835, (MG) Jabez Ham.

William B. Monroe and Martha Ann Tuttle, (MD) April 30, 1838, (MG) Andrew Monroe.

John Monteer and Susanna Bryan, (MD) December 21, 1837, (JP) J. A. Burt.

John B. Moore and Elizabeth Nash, (MD) January 20, 1831, (UK) George Bartley.

Wharton H. Moore and Mariah Ferguson, (MD) June 16, 1831, (MD) J. C. Berryman.

Isaac Moore and Rebecca Hart, (MD) December 24, 1834,(MG) B. A. Ramsey.

William G. Moore and Eliz. H. Long, (MD) May 1, 1838,(UK) Tho. M. Allen.

James Moore and Vicy Ann Smith, (MD) May 10, 1827,(MG)Wm. Coats.

Augustus Moore and Catharine Matier, (MD) September 22, 1831, (UK) David Kirkpatrick.

Isuau Moreor and Ophelia Livingston, (MD)February 4,1838, (JP) B. A. Ramsey.

George Mooris and Elizabeth McClelland,(MD)March 17,1827, (MG) Alan McGuire.

James Morrow and Seleta Agee, (MD) January 26, 1837, (JP) James Stewart.

John Mosely and Sophia M.C. Mahan, (MD)September 24,1833, (MG) James Stewart.

John Moss and Mary Hunt, (MD) September 28, 1826, (UK) Anderson Woods.

Augustus Murphy and Nancy Curry, (MD) November 28, 1833, (MG) Robert McAfee.

Andrew R. Murray and Nancy Sheley, (MD) December 28,1837, (MG) R. L. McAfee.

David Myers and Lucretia D. Jones, (MD) March 2, 1830, (UK) D. M. Kirkpatrick.

Benjamin Nale and Ann Walker, (MD) November 14, 1830,(MG) William Coats.

Ira P. Nash and Ann Smith, (MD) December 18, 1827, (JP) Enoch Fruit.

Alfred Nash and Miss Conger, (MD) January 11, 11831, (UK) Beverly A. Ramsey.

Hardin Nash and Sarah Adair, (MD) February 26, 1836, (MG) Wm. Duncan.

Samuel Nesbit and Polly Ann Meredith, (MD) June 14, 1838, (MG) Jacob Coons.

(Callaway County, Missouri Continued)

Thomas Nevins and Kitty Randolph, (MD) September 26,1835, (MG) Jno. Pace.

George Nicholson and Anna Zumwalt, (MD) December 11,1824, (JP) John Ferguson.

Felix G. Nichols and Eliz. Ann Renoe, (MD) February 12, 1833, (MG) Theo. Boulware.

John Nichols and Julia Lewis, (MD) October 10, 1839, (JP) A. Noflet.

Frederick Nichols and Angeline Crump,(MD)January --,1832, (MG) Theo. Boulware.

William Nichols and Hannah Jane Muir,(MD)October 22,1829, (MG) Theo. Boulware.

John F. Nichols and Sarah Blythe, (MD) June 30, 1836,(UK) David Doyle.

Thomas Nichols and Amanda Lewis, (MD) February 20, 1838, (JP) A. Northphen.

George Nichols and Hannah Brite, (MD) June 29, 1826, (MG) William Coats.

Martin Noland and Sarah Lampkins, (MD) March 2, 1826,(UK) Anderson Woods.

Abraham Norflett and Margaret Campbell, (MD) August 16, 1832, (UK) George W. Teason.

Berry Ola and Mary Meng, (MD) February 4, 1838, (JP) A. Northphen.

James Oliver and Nancy Bretton, (MD) December 13, 1832, (JP) Enoch Fruit.

Robert Ormer and Matilda May, (MD) April 5, 1838, (UK) Andrew Alexander.

Eli Overfelt and Sarah Parker, (MD) November 18, 1833, (UK) Irvine O. Hockaday.

Benjamin Overton and Ann Holt, (MD) July 15, 1830, (MG) J. A. Suggett.

James Overton and Harriet A. Baynham, (MD) October 11, 1832, (UK) William Duncan.

William Pace and Hester Kidwell, (MD) June 24, 1836, (JP) Jno. Pace.

James Pace and Zerilda Wayne, (MD) March 24, 1836, (MG) Jas. Suggett.

Washington Padget and Rebecca Jones, (MD) April 7, 1833, (JP) Geo. Bartley.

Washington Padgett and Martha Carter, (MD) June 24, 1838, (MG) George W. Morris.

Minor Pate and Sally Mays, (MD) December 12, 1833, (UK) Theo. Stephens, Groom from Boone County.

Hans Patton and Sally Hatton, (MD) March 23, 1826, (JP) William Patton.

Jacob Paulgel and Mrs. Sarah Smith, (MD) August 27, 1835, (UK) R. L. McAfee.

21

(Callaway County, Missouri Continued)

Moses Payne and Mary White, (MD) June 25, 1829, (UK) Nathaniel M. Talbot, Groom is from Boone County.

Richmond Pearson and Eliz. Allen Brown, (MD) March 15, 1832, (UK) James Barnes.

John U. Pemberton and Katharine Hunter, (MD) October 6, 1836, (Elder) M. P. Wills.

Alfred Petty and Synthia Howard, (MD) May 15, 1831, (JP) John K. Barry.

Zachariah Petty and Mary Jane Bryant, (MD) August 7,1833, (MG) Theo. Boulware.

John Petty and Patsy Bunch, (MD) April 16, 1833, (JP) John K. Barry.

James H. Peyton and Sarah Mateer, (MD) September 14,1837, (UK) R. L. McAfee.

Bethel Philips and Darly Estes, (MD) January 2, 1828,(MG) William Coats.

Moses Philips and Aney Agey, (MD) February 26, 1829, (MG) Jabez Ham.

Hiram R. Philips and Emily T. Wilkerson, (MD)November 10, 1836, (JP) James Stewart.

Nicholas Phye and Margaret Roy, (MD) October 7, 1827,(JP) John Conger.

John A. Pledge and Miriam Warren, (MD) February 14, 1831, (MG) Theo. Boulware.

Thomas Pledge and Florence C. Luper,(MD)February 22,1838, (MG) Theo. Boulware.

Elijah Potter and Rhoda Ham, (MD) June 24, 1837, (JP)John A. Burt.

Alexander Power and Patsey Ferrier, (MD)December 27,1827, (MG) William Coats.

John Pratt and Amy Baker, (MD) January 11, 1821, (MG) Robert Baker.

William Pratt and Polly Eaken, (MD) April 18, 1822, (MG) Robert Baker.

Thomas Pratt and Lucinda Patty, (MD) September 19, 1839, (MG) Jabez Ham.

Cyrus Price and Adeline Dickerson, (MD) November 2, 1837, (MG) Theo. Boulware.

Silas B. Pugh and Emeline Davis, (MD) June 16, 1825, (MG) William Coats.

Asa Pulliam and Angeline Miller, (MD) January 7, 1837, (MG) R. H. Jordon.

John W. Pullman and Elizabeth Heart, (MD) April 18, 1833, (UK) Robert McAfee.

Elisha Radican and Cena King, (MD) March 2, 1837,(MG)Jas. Suggett.

Jewel Ramsey and Caroline Conger, (MD) January 31, 1828, (JP) George King.

(Callaway County, Missouri Continued)

Robert Randolf and Amanda J. Humphries, (MD) January 14, 1836, (MG) Jas. Suggett.

Edmund Randolph and Patsy McClelland, (MD) December 4, 1832, (UK) William Duncan.

Edmond W. Ratekin and Susan Cheatham, (MD) May 8, 1838, (MG) Absalom Rice.

John Reed and Sally Moxley, (MD) October 31, 1835, (MG) William Coats.

Joseph D. Reagan and Eliz. E. Adams, (MD) July 27, 1835, (UK) D. Coultier.

Henry Rector and Eliz. L. Allen, (MD) October 26, 1833, (UK) Theo. Boulware.

Granville Reid and Nancy Black, (MD) February 21, 1837, (JP) James Barnes, Groom is from Boone County.

Mark Renfro and Nancy Ridgeway, (MD) September 18, 1825, (UK) Thos. Stephens, Groom is from Boone County.

R. D. Renoe and Jane Davis, (MD) August 9, 1838, (UK) Geo. Hopkins.

Richard Rennois and Nancy Chapel, (MD) September 28, 1836, (UK) John F. Young.

George Reanolds and Sarah Ann Harper, (MD) February 17, 1833, (UK) Thos. Hornbuckle.

Shedrick Reynolds and Nancy Wood, (MD) April 15, 1835, (MG) H. J. M. Doan.

William Reynolds and Polly Ann Day, (MD) January 1, 1835, (MG) James Baines.

Allen Reynolds and Polly B. Martin, (MD) June 2, 1833, (UK) Robert A. Younger.

Joseph W. Reynolds and Elizabeth McIntire, (MD) October 25, 1838, (MG) J. F. Young.

Samuel Rhoads and Sarah Pace, (MD) June 27, 1824, (JP) Jas. Nevins.

William Rhoades and Rosannah Dougherty, (MD) December 3, 1821, (JP) James Nevins.

Alexander Richardson and Lucy J. Shaw, (MD) September 27, 1837, (MG) Theo. Boulware.

Reason Ridgeway and Harriett Reede, (MD) September 17, 1835, (MG) William Duncan.

John D. Ridgeway and Saphira Wigginson, (MD) June 9, 1831, (UK) Theo. P. Stephens.

James Riggins and Elizabeth Haynes, (MD) September 2, 1830, (UK) Theo. Stephens.

Lenpoir Riggs and Elizabeth Lampton, (MD) December 24, 1826, (JP) George King.

C. A. Robbins and Kiturah V. Overfeit, (MD) April 28, 1835, (UK) John Rennie.

Daniel Robertson and Patsey VanCleane, (MD) September 3, 1828, (MG) Jabez Ham.

(Callaway County, Missouri Continued)

Pleasant Robinet and Catharine Hunt, (MD) February 10, 1829, (UK) Anderson Woods, Groom is from Boone County.

Arthur C. Robinson and Kansas Bradford, (MD) December 19, 1839, (UK) Joseph T. Bryan.

James Rose and Deleria Zumwalt, (MD) October 30, 1824, (JP) George King.

Bozele Rose and Sarah Bryan, (MD) March 30, 1822, (JP) James Nevins.

John Rosson and Margaret Daniel, (MD) June 25, 1839, (MG) Joseph Coons.

Andrew Roy and Temperance Shivers, (MD)September 15,1831, (UK) George Barltcy.

Richard Runols and Rachel Zummalt, (MD) April 24, 1823, (JP) George King.

Thomas Rupert and Rebecca Newsom, (MD) April 17, 1838, (UK) John T. A. Henderson.

Henley C. Rusell and Arrena Overfelt, (MD) December 6, 1837, (UK) Theo. Boulware.

William Rutherford and Jane Jahs, (MD) May 4, 1822, (JP) George King.

John Salor and Virginia Perkins, (MD) October 17, 1833, (MG) Jabez Ham, Groom is from Montgomery County.

Thomas Sallee and Margaret Games, (MD) July 9, 1834, (MG) Theo. Boulware.

Robert Samuel and Martha Overton, (MD) November 5, 1829, (MG) Theo. Boulware, Groom is from Palmyra.

Thomas Sanders and Letitia Breckridge, (MD) May 25, 1837, (UK) Thomas M. Allen, Groom is from Tennessee.

Arbuckle S. Sangstu and Eliza Jane Hamilton, (MD) June 6, 1839, (MG) J. S. Yantis.

Samuel Saulsbury and Christianna Wilson,(MD)July 19,1836, (JP) A. Northphen.

John Scoby and Polly Haynes, (MD) December 25, 1832, (UK) Thomas P. Stephens.

Matthew Scott and Eliz. J. Burns, (MD) February 11, 1836, (UK) Theo. Boulware.

Joseph Scholl and Eliza Broughton, (MD) February 24,1831, (JP) J. W. Johnston.

Thomas Scroghum and Susan Harryford, (MD) March 28, 1839, (UK) Joseph Coons.

Jesse Sleby and Elizabeth Hereford, (MD) November 5,1828, (JP) William Martin.

William Selby and Julian Turley, (MD) September 19, 1832, (UK) William Duncan.

William P. Selby and Amanda P. Anderson, (MD) March 12, 1836, (UK) Irvine O. Hickaday.

Singleton Sheley and Jane Christwell, (MD) February 18, 1834, (MG) Jas. Suggett.

(Callaway County, Missouri Continued)

James Sheley and Mary Ann Smart, (MD) November 8, 1837, (MG) Theo. Boulware.

Willis Shelton and Nancy Elston, (MD) August 30, 1821, (UK) Solomon Thomas.

James Sims and Margaret Isham, (MD) May 22, 1834, (MG)Wm. Duncan.

James Sims and Patsy Beden, (MD) February 24, 1833, (MG) Wm. Duncan.

Benjamin F. Sitton and Rebecca Austin,(MD)January 7,1823, (JP) Thomas Fisher.

Martin Sitton and Harriet Allen, (MD) August 24, 1826, (MG) William Coats.

John Sitton and Sally Jamison, (MD)November 11, 1825,(MG) William Coats.

Joseph T. Sitton and Preciller May, (MD) May 17, 1821, (UK) Whaton T. Moore.

Joseph Sloan and Irena Wilcockson, (MD) April 11, 1833, (JP) Horace Sheley.

Thomas Sloan and Sally Sherman, (MD) October 13, 1825, (UK) Christopher Zumwalt.

Ellis R. Sloan and Nancy Armstrong, (MD) August 7, 1834, (MG) Horace Sheley.

John T. Smart and Virginia L. Smart, (MD) March 5, 1837, (JP) James Stewart.

Glover Smart and Elvira Day, (MD) February 5, 1834, (UK) Geo. B. Hopkins.

James Smart and Rachel C. Ewing, (MD) February 15, 1838, (UK) Absalom Rice.

Thomas Smith and Catherine Craig, (MD) January 29, 1828, (MG) Theo. Boulware.

Thomas Smith and Mary Huddleston, (MD) August 16, 1829, (UK) David Kirkpatrick.

B. Smith and Sarah Ferguson, (MD) September 19, 1833,(MG) Theo. Boulware.

Macky Smith and Mary Cheatham, (MD) October 10, 1833,(MG) Theo. Boulware.

Owen Smith and Eliza P. Pace, (MD) June 16, 1836, (UK) John F. Young.

Richard Smith and Eliza Waggener, (MD) March 15, 1833, (JP) Beverly Ramsey.

E. Smith and Sarah Green, (MD) January 1, 1829, (MG)Theo. Boulware.

Greenup Snell and Sarah Ann Mackentire, (MD) December 14, 1837, (MG) James Barnes.

William Stanley and Nancy Jane Holt, (MD) April 28, 1836, (MG) Jas. Suggett.

Lock Stephen and Nancy Renfro, (MD) April 5, 1834, (UK) Thomas Stephens.

(Callaway County, Missouri Continued)

Hamilton Steward and Sarah Patty, (MD) August 2, 1832, (JP) Robert Davis.

Rueben Stewart and Nancy Stewart, (MD) May 29, 1831, (JP) John A. Burt.

Robert N. Stewart and Caroline M. Smith, (MD)February 28, 1839, (UK) Joseph T. Bryan.

Isaac Stites and Susan Williams, (MD) June 25, 1825, (JP) Thomas Fisher.

Henry W. Stokes and Elisha Bailey, (MD) November 28,1839, (MG) Jas. Suggett.

John H. Stone and Catharine R. Grant, (MD) February 22, 1838, (MG) Theo. Boulware.

William B. Stone and Eliz. Va. Gray, (MD) August 10,1837, (UK) Thomas M. Allen.

Jacob Strode and Frances May, (MD) July 20, 1826, (MG)Wm. Coats.

Volney Suggett and Mary H. Shortridge, (MD)March 23,1836, (MG) James Suggett.

Mentor Suggett and Louisa Petty, (MD) December 21, 1837, (MG) Theo. Boulware.

John L. Thaler and Martha Wilkerson, (MD) August 31,1835, (MG) William Coats.

Richard C. Tate amd Elizabeth Hamblin, (MD) October 17, 1839, (UK) Joeseph Scholl.

Caleb Warren Tate and Emily Hamblin, (MD) October 8,1839, (UK) Joseph Scholl.

Thomas Taylor and Lydia Dearing, (MD) March 5, 1837, (JP) James Stewart.

William Taylor and Lucy Ham, (MD) September 29, 1831,(MG) William Coats.

John Tennison and Ann McCormick, (MD) December 22, 1830, (JP) Enoch Fruit.

James A. Terrell and Hester A.R. Kelso, (MD)June 24,1833, (UK) W. W. Redman.

Jeremiah Tharp and Mary W. Kelsoe, (MD) October 5, 1837, (UK) Jno. Pace.

Joel Tharp and Susannah Hough, (MD) October 17, 1833,(MG) Theo. Boulware.

John Thatcher and Ann Hase, (MD) December 18, 1828, (MG) Theo. Boulware.

Mason Thatcher and Catherine McConnell, (MD) December 20, 1829, (UK) D. M. Kirkpatrick.

William S. Thatcher and Charlotte Westbrook, (MD) May 9, 1839, (MG) J. L. Yantis.

James Thaxton and Polly Stoker, (MD) September 12, 1839, (MG) Jacob Coons.

Solomon Thomas, jr. and Martha Gilbert, (MD) January 14, 1836, (JP) A. G. Boone.

(Callaway County, Missouri Continued)

Hiram H. Thomas and Elizabeth Meredith, (MD) February 1, 1835, (MG) Robert McAfee.

Larkin Thomas and Louisa Addar, (MD) February 12, 1833, (UK) William Duncan.

Ira Thomas and Malisa Fox, (MD) May 18, 1824, (JP) Enoch Fruit.

George C. Thompson and Eleanor Leeper, (MD) July 29,1830, (UK) David Kirkpatrick.

Joseph Thompson and Patsy Baker, (MD) January 13, 1831, (UK) Theo. P. Stephens.

David Thompson and Ann Darting, (MD) July 12, 1827, (JP) William Martin.

Robert W. Thurman and Susan E. Leeper,(MD)August 21,1838, (UK) Theo. Boulware.

Zepheniah Tod and Sally Stephens, (MD) September 5, 1839, (UK) Thomas P. Stephens, Groom is from Clay County.

Thomas Tucker and Betsy Harper, (MD) May 2, 1823, (JP) Thomas Fisher.

James Turley and Harriett Miller, (MD) December 24, 1834, (MG) William Duncan.

Graham Turner and Scithe Ann Meyers, (MD) May 14, 1836, (MG) Theo. Boulware.

Henry Turner and Mary Hook, (MD) August 12, 1830, (UK) David Kirkpatrick.

Martin Turner and Debby Hornbuckle, (MD)February 24,1825, (JP) George King.

Louis Uno and Elizabeth Surrat, (MD) October 22, 1830, (JP) Henry Neill.

William K. VanArsdall and Rosanna M. Curry, (MD) November 19, 1829, (UK) D. M. Kirkpatrick.

Mastin Vaughn and Caroline Wilburn, (MD)November 26,1834, (MG) J. Ham.

James Vest and Mary Jane Oslin, (MD) March 3, 1836, (JP) J. M. Doan.

Elisha Vincent and Nancy Heddleston, (MD) April 9, 1829, (MG) N. Ridgway.

Jesse Vincent and Jane Baker, (MD) August 11, 1825, (UK) Thos Stephens.

John Wadley and Sophiah Doyel, (MD) December 7, 1828,(JP) Robert Davis.

John Wadley and Catharine Doyle, (MD) September 30, 1838, (UK) Geo. B. Hopkins.

John Wadley and Susannah Howard, (MD) December 29, 1825, (JP) George King.

David Waggoner and Fanny Ronalls, (MD) September 18,, (JP) B. A. Ramsey.

--- Waldring and Rebecca Ransom, (MD) June 25, 1837, (JP) A. Norflet.

(Callaway County, Missouri Continued)

Jesse B. Wainscott and Eliza Langley, (MD)August 16,1838, (UK) John T. A. Henderson.

Samuel Walker and Kitty Townsend, (MD) December 31, 1835, (MG) William Duncan.

Griffin Walker and Sally Roberson, (MD) February 3, 1831, (MG) William Coats.

Julias Walls and Aley Langly, (MD) November 14, 1834,(JP) B. Ramsey.

John M. Ward and Margaret Hunt, (MD) December 27, 1839, (JP) George Morris.

James Ward and Mary Long, (MD) July 29, 1835, (MG) Theo. Boulware, Groom is from Boone County.

Charles Ward and Jane McCormick, (MD) December 21, 1826, (MG) Jabez Ham.

Joseph Watkins and Martha W. Dyer, (MD)November 22,1837, (MG) R. L. McAfee.

Temple Wayne and Elizabeth Gregg, (MD) March 12, 1835, (MG) Theo. Boulware.

William Weatherford and Evaline Harper, (MD)December 23, 1829, (JP) Robert Davis.

Thomas Webeert and Lucretia Potter, (MD)November 16,1837, (JP) John Burt.

William Wells and Elizabeth Smart, (MD) November 25,1836, (MG) James Suggett.

Curtis Wilburn and Ede Nettle, (MD) December 5, 1833,(UK) Thomas Stephens.

Harry S. Wilcockson and Rosa M. Crowson, (MD)December 18, 1838, (MG) Theo. Boulware.

Joseph Wilfley and Sally Newland, (MD) September 27,1838, (MG) Theo. Boulware.

Samuel Wilfley and Nancy Ellis, (MD) July 15, 1824, (JP) Jas. Nevins.

James Wilfley and Elizabeth Kelso, (MD) August 19, 1830, (JP) William Crain.

Moses Wilkerson and Amada Duncan, (MD)August 9,1838, (UK) Joseph Coons.

Dien Wilkerson and Harriet Dunham, (MD) August 2, 1831, (JP) J. W. Johnson.

Samuel Wilkes and Malinda Tate, (MD) June 1, 1839, (JP) Joseph Scholl.

William Willing and Eliza C. Parker, (MD) March 8, 1838, (UK) Jno. Pace.

Delona Willingham and Malinda WInscott, (MD)June 23,1831, (UK) James Barnes.

Joseph Williams and Elizabeth Langley, (MD) February 6, 1825, (UK) Felix Brown.

Caleb Williams and Sarah Updike, (MD) October 6, 1836, (JP) Jas. Harrison.

(Callaway County, Missouri Continued)

Reuben Williams and Evaline Moore, (MD) May 17, 1836,(UK) Jno. Pace.

Thomas Williams and Elizabeth Todd, (MD) January 20,1834, (MG) Jabez Ham.

John Williams and Eliza Graves, (MD) September 27, 1827, (JP) William Martin.

Robert Williams and Francis May, (MD) November 30, 1824, (UK) Felix Brown.

Galbreath Wilson and Clarissa Ann Foxworthy, (MD) October 31, 1839, (MG) J. L. Yantis.

Edward Wilson and Leeny Burket, (MD) October 13, 1825, (UK) Chris. Zumwalt.

William H. Wilson and Isabella J. Foxworthy, (MD) January 22, 1839, (MG) John Yantis.

Thomas Wilson and Deborah A. Long, (MD) November 22,1837, (UK) Thomas W. Allen.

John Wills and Mary Hughes, (MD) December 1, 1837, (MG) Jabez Ham.

Thomas Winn and Roxalina Day, (MD) August 25, 1839, (UK) Joseph T. Bryan.

John Wintertower and Elizabeth Zumwalt,(MD)April 11,1839, (JP) Abrams Nortfleet.

Francis Withurington and Polly Parker, (MD) October 31, 1827, (UK) Edward L. Ellis.

David Woods and Sarah Reynolds, (MD) October 9, 1831,(UK) Thos. P. Stephens, Groom is from Monroe County. Bride is from Boone County.

Henry Fletcher and Jane Estes, (MD) April 18, 1822.

Wm. I. Worsham and Samenta Ann Stokes, (MD)March 27,1838, (MG) R. L. McAfee, Groom is from Cole County.

Blanton Wray and Margaret Ann Hultz, (MD) July 5, 1837, (MG) James Love, Groom is from Warren County.

Oliver Wright and Veany Pratt, (MD) November 28, 1839, (UK) John Fletcher.

Wesley Wright and Polly Potts, (MD) October 12, 1826,(UK) John B. Morrow.

William Yancey and Martha Ferguson, (MD) March 14, 1839, (UK) J. F. Young.

Vincent Yates and Nancy Estes, (MD) September 9,1827,(UK) Cap. Vanquickenborne.

Jeptha Yates and Jane Harrison, (MD) April 2, 1838, (MG) Theo. Boulware.

John Yates and Ann Nichols, (MD) May 15, 1828, (MG) Theo. Boulware.

Charles H. Yeater and Judith Jameson, (MD) September 2, 1830, (MG) Theo. Boulware.

William Young and Sally Linville, (MD) April 18, 1831, (MG) William Coats.

(Callaway County, Missouri Continued)
    David Yount and Caty Waggoner, (MD) December 12, 1833,
(UK) Beverly A. Ramsey.
    Jacob Zumwalt and Sarah Zumwalt, (MD) August 18, 1836,
(JP) A. Norflet.
    Abraham Zumwalt and Juliet Hope, (MD) September 30, 1825,
(UK) Christopher Zumwalt.
    Isaac Zumwalt and Matilda Blythe, (MD) June 10, 1826,
(UK) Christopher Zumwalt.
    Elijah Harrison and Millender Rowland, (MD) July 28,1831.
    Thomas Jacobs and Lydia Dawson, (MD) November 9, 1834.
    Thomas McCullouch and Rebecca M. Craft, (MD) December 11,
1836.
    Samuel Newland and Mary W. Martin, (MD) December 12,1839.
    Perry Pollard and Bettie Henderson, (MD) October 17,1834.
    Rheuben Standley and Luthy Pulliam, (MD) March 18, 1835.
    Isaac Tate and Jane Henderson, (MD) July 14, 1830.
    Lewis B. Thomas and Polly Robertson, (MD) April 26, 1823.
    John West and Elizabeth Glaves, (MD) February 13, 1834.
    William West and Margery Miller, (MD) December 21, 1834.
    John Yates and Elizabeth Dawson, (MD) April 26, 1833.

Arkansas County, Missouri Territory, November,1810,Tax List,
Capitol Fire Documents, Folder 141.
    Widow Batte Ambroin, George Armstead, Charles Adams, John
Allison, Martin Allen, Christpher Anthony, James Alexander,
Louis Bogy, Joseph Bogy,John Baker,Elijah Bunch,Royal Bills,
Henry Baker, Christian Bringh, Widow Raphael Brimbal,Charles
Bogy, Thomas Baily, John Billingsley, James Billingsley,John
Berry, William Blakely, Jacob Bankman, Edward Bradly, Lewis
Blaylock, James Brown, Nathan P. Baforta, Jacob Barkman, Wm.
Bassite, James Currin, Lemuel Currin, Patrick Cassidy, John
Canahan, Jesse Collin, --- Cooper, James Cummins, Jean Bte.
Deruisseaux, Martin Collier, Morgan Cryer, John Dehart, John
Dudley, Winthrop, Francois Desusseaux, Louis Dumon, Wiliam
Durm, Madam Dianne, Edward Davis, Wright Daniel, Zachariah
Davis, Thomas Dooley, Jesse Dean, Hezekiah Dickson, Absalom
Edens, Reuben Easton, Joseph Egg, Thomas Frazure, Benjamin
Fooy, Hugh Flanagan, Daniel Futral, Elizzear Fulsom, William
Flanegan, Daniel Frazier, Joseph Gravier, Augustin Grander,
Anna Greenwalt, John Gossett, William H. Glass, Aaron Goza,
Thomas Green, Thomas Gray, Bartley Hamington, Anthony Haden,
Joseph Hudsell, James Hanks, John Hampton, James Henny, Jas.
Howell, Madam Hacket, James P. Howard, William Hughs, Abner
Hignight, Ezekiel Henry, John Hemphill, Edmund Hagen, Joseph
Imbau, Alexis Janels, John Jardeus,John Jones,James Johnson,
Charles Ingraham, Madam Kessler, Jos. Kuykendall, John King,
Lydia Kendrick, Jesse Killiam, Andrew Lutting, John Lavin--,
Francis Larue, Pierre Lifern, jr., Pierre Lifern, sr., John

(Arkansas County, Missouri Territory Continued)
   Benjamin Leets, Chevalier Laganern, Bryan Lynch, Robert
Leone, William Morrison, John Masten, Frenacis Mitchel,Danl.
Mooney, John B. Menard, James Murphy, Danl. Mitchell, Lydia
Missahas (sic), John Maden, John Milmurry, Silas McDaniel,
Frc--- M'Clendon, John M'Clendon,Jas. M'Clendon,Mathew Moss,
Ruth Montgomery, (Indian - No Tribe), James C. Nowell, James
Y. O'Carrol, Michel Paterson, Louis Places,William Peterson,
John Parker, Edward Proctor, Jos. G. Parry, Zackeus Philips,
Slyvanus Philips, James Pratt, John Pratt, John Pettitt,John
Shater, Charles Refelo, Tana. B. Racine, Jacko Racine,Derick
Rogers, I--- Ruchester, Andrew Robinson, James Reynolds, Wm.
Strong, Joseph Stillwell, Harold Stillwell,James Scull,Hewes
Scull, John Strong, William Smith, Jacob Stroops,John Wells,
Joab Sallion, Heirs of Jos. Trudeaus, Wylie Thompson,Absalom
Trince, Charles Vilemont, Victor Vassuer, John Weare,Francis
Vaugin, Jesse Vincent, Peter Whetstone, Joseph While, Thomas
Woolsey, Margaret Welch, Jacob Wells, Curtis Wellborne, Joel
Walker, John D. Yews, Elisha Wellborne, --- Yarberry.

Clay County, Missouri, Plat Book, 1819 - 1839.

Name	Date	Location
Thomas Allen	Oct. 7, 1836	T51-R30-S13
John Allen	Oct. 14, 1839	T51-R30-S12
John Allen	Mar. 17, 1827	T53-R30-S26
Pleasant Adams	Mar. 16, 1827	T53-R30-S35
Elizabeth Arnold	Jan. 23, 1829	T53-R30-S22
Elizabeth Arnold	Jan. 2, 1832	---
James Ater	Nov. 3, 1837	T53-R30-S11
*James Allen	Jun. 21, 1832	T50-R31-S18
*(With Nathaniel Olmstead)		
Robert Aull	Dec. 17, 1832	T50-R31-S3
*Robert Aull	Mar. 5, 1838	T50-R31-S3
*(With Samuel C. Owen)		
Novell L. Allcock	Feb. 18, 1833	T52-R31-S5
Lewis Arnold	Nov. 6, 1828	T52-R31-S1
Zachariah Avrett	Mar. 15, 1827	T52-R31-S27
Zachariah Avrett	Oct. 17, 1827	T52-R31-S34
Zachariah Avrett	Feb. 4, 1825	T52-R31-S34
William H. Arnold	Oct. 15, 1830	T54-R31-S34
William H. Arnold	Nov. 7, 1831	T54-R31-S34
William H. Arnold	Oct. 15, 1830	T54-R31-S35
Lewis B. Arnold	Dec. 7, 1835	T54-R31-S34
Joel Albright	Oct. 21, 1839	T54-R31-S33
Fauntleroy Arnold	Feb. 26, 1836	T54-R31-S33
James Arnold	Dec. 3, 1835	T54-R31-S34
James Arnold	Nov. 4, 1836	T54-R31-S34
John James Arnold	Dec. 12, 1832	T54-R31-S35
John James Arnold	Dec. 7, 1836	T54-R31-S35

(Clay County, Missouri Continued)

Name	Date	Location
John James Arnold	Jan. 19, 1837	T54-R31-S35
John James Arnold	Dec. 12, 1832	T54-R31-S34
John James Arnold	Jan. 20, 1836	T54-R31-S34
Pleasant Adams	Jul. 27, 1838	T51-R31-S35
Subael Allen	Feb. 6, 1833	T51-R31-S30
*Subael Allen	Mar. 19, 1821	T51-R31-S30
*(With John Thornton)		
*Subael Allen	Mar. 8, 1821	T51-R31-S31
*(With John Thornton)		
William Atchison	May 16, 1835	T53-R31-S7
William Atchison	Aug. 11, 1838	T53-R31-S7
Benj. A. Atchison	No Date	T53-R31-S7
Alexander H. Atchison	Aug. 29, 1829	T53-R31-S7
Samuel Arbuckle	Mar. 4, 1828	T53-R31-S1
William H. Arnold	Aug. 21, 1835	T53-R31-S2
William H. Arnold	Oct. 18, 1830	T53-R31-S3
William R. Allnut	Apr. 27, 1835	T53-R31-S2
William R. Allnut	Apr. 27, 1835	T53-R31-S11
William R. Allnut	Jul. 28, 1831	T53-R31-S12
Thomas Arnold	Dec. 6, 1828	T53-R31-S24
Thomas Arnold	Dec. 6, 1828	T53-R31-S4
Thomas Arnold	Oct. 31, 1828	T53-R31-S1
Lewis S. Arnold	Dec. 3, 1835	T53-R31-S15
Elias Anderson	Nov. 19, 1839	T53-R31-S20
Elias Anderson	Nov. 28, 1836	T53-R31-S20
Lewis S. Arnold	Nov. 4, 1832	T53-R31-S15
Lewis S. Arnold	Nov. 4, 1828	T53-R31-S10
Elizabeth Arnold	Dec. 12, 1828	T53-R31-S11
Horace P. Anderson	Nov. 19, 1837	T53-R31-S19
Horace P. Anderson	Dec. 26, 1835	T53-R31-S19
Horace P. Anderson	Oct. 26, 1825	T53-R31-S30
Horace P. Anderson	Dec. 26, 1835	T53-R31-S31
Lewis B. Arnold	Nov. 6, 1830	T53-R31-S10
Joseph Anderson	Nov. 19, 1839	T53-R31-S19
Joseph Anderson	Nov. 21, 1836	T53-R31-S19
Fauntleroy Arnold	Feb. 18, 1837	T53-R31-S4
Fauntleroy Arnold	Jun. 27, 1831	T53-R31-S4
Fauntleroy Arnold	Nov. 4, 1828	T53-R31-S25
William Alley	Feb. 29, 1836	T53-R33-S36
David Ashby	Mar. 27, 1829	T51-R33-S14
Thomas Arnold	Sep. 1, 1828	T51-R33-S26
Wyat Atkinson	Mar. 12, 1821	T50-R32-S9
Elizabeth Arnold	Nov. 14, 1825	T50-R32-S6
Elizabeth Arnold	Sep. 26, 1825	T50-R32-S6
William Adkins	Oct. 4, 1824	T50-R32-S13
Wyat Adkins	May 26, 1823	T50-R32-S15
Rufus Abbott	Oct. 22, 1835	T51-R32-S9

(Clay County, Missouri Continued)

Name	Date	Location
John Ashby	Oct. 16, 1834	T51-R32-S9
Jonathan Adkins	Nov. 20, 1833	T51-R32-S32
Jonathan Adkins	Oct. 31, 1833	T51-R32-S32
Jonathan Adkins	Feb. 6, 1836	T51-R32-S20'
Garrard Allen	Nov. 16, 1827	T51-R3?-S28
Garrard Allen	Mar. 31, 1829	T51-R32-S28
Shubael Allen	Mar. 17, 1827	T51-R32-S14
*Shubael Allen	Mar. 12, 1821	T51-R32-S26
*(With John Thronton)		
*Shubael Allen	Mar. 17, 1827	T51-R32-S11
*(With John Thornton)		
John Ashby	Oct. 16, 1834	T51-R32-S9
Henton Ashby	Jun. 2, 1835	T51-R32-S19
David Ashby	Jan. 19, 1836	T51-R32-S17
William Allen	Mar. 12, 1821	T51-R32-S19
William Allen	Dec. 27, 1828	T51-R32-S20
Arnold Garrard	Nov. 20, 1835	T51-R32-S33
Thomas Arnold	Nov. 12, 1827	T51-R32-S33
Thomas Arnold	Nov. 14, 1825	T51-R32-S34
Michael Arthur	Nov. 3, 1825	T51-R32-S14
Michael Arthur	Mar. 17, 1827	T51-R32-S14
Michael Arthur	Nov. 3, 1825	T51-R32-S23
Michael Arthur	Nov. 18, 1835	T51-R32-S23
Robert Adkins	Jan. 18, 1837	T52-R32-S29
Robert Adkins	Sep. 13, 1839	T52-R32-S29
Robert Adkins	Jan. 18, 1837	T52-R32-S29
Mary Aker	Apr. 6, 1839	T53-R32-S18
Horace L. Anderson	Apr. 23, 1839	T53-R32-S24
William Atchison	May 16, 1835	T53-R32-S12
John Aker	Apr. 18, 1831	T53-R32-S7
John Aker	Oct. 24, 1828	T53-R32-S18
John Aker	Oct. 28, 1828	T53-R32-S18
Jacob Aker	Apr. 6, 1839	T53-R32-S7
John Bradley	Nov. 9, 1835	T52-R32-S29
Van W. Brooks	Jul. 20, 1835	T52-R32-S4
Van W. Brooks	Apr. 16, 1839	T52-R32-S4
Balus Bright	Feb. 18, 1834	T52-R32-S28
Eddie Linn Breckenridge	Jul. 2, 1832	T52-R32-S4
Eddie Linn Breckenridge	Jun. 28, 1836	T52-R32-S4
Eddie Linn Breckenridge	Jun. 18, 1828	T52-R32-S5
Eddie Lin Breckenridge	Jan. 18, 1828	T52-R32-S8
Eddie Linn Breckenridge	Oct. 21, 1831	T52-R32-S8
John Boggess	Jan. 15, 1833	T52-R32-S11
John Boggess	Apr. 6, 1839	T52-R32-S11
Walker B. Bevins	Oct. 13, 1827	T52-R32-S8
Charles N. Berryman	Jan. 22, 1827	T52-R32-S6
Strother Ball	Nov. 7, 1831	T52-R32-S8

(Clay County, Missouri Continued)

Name	Date	Location
Charles L. Berryman	Jan. 22, 1831	T52-R32-S6
Robert Adkins	Jan. 18, 1837	T52-R32-S29
Robert Adkins	Sep. 13, 1839	T52-R32-S29
Robert Adkins	Jan. 18, 1837	T52-R32-S29
Robert H. Brooks	Nov. 5, 1832	T53-R32-S33
Robert H. Brooks	May 2, 1837	T53-R32-S28
Abijah Brooks, jr.	Sep. 7, 1839	T53-R32-S32
Abijah Brooks	Oct. 17, 1837	T53-R32-S33
Abijah Brooks	Sep. 7, 1839	T53-R32-S32
Abijah Brooks	Dec. 30, 1828	T53-R32-S31
Abijah Brooks	Scp. 14, 1837	T53-R32-S31
William Bennett	Dec. 11, 1834	T53-R32-S7
Jeremiah Bailey	Dec. 30, 1837	T53-R32-S14
James Butler	Nov. 30, 1832	T53-R32-S6
James Butler	Jan. 7, 1833	T53-R32-S6
Van W. Brooks	Oct. 23, 1837	T53-R32-S33
Van W. Brooks	Oct. 17, 1837	T53-R32-S28
Samuel J. Brooks	Oct. 17, 1837	T53-R32-S33
Robert H. Brooks	Oct. 24, 1837	T53-R32-S29
Robert H. Brooks	May 2, 1837	T53-R32-S33
Robert H. Brooks	Jul. 1, 1839	T53-R32-S33
Robert H. Brooks	Dec. 19, 1838	T53-R32-S33
Samuel A. Brown	Mar. 30, 1833	T51-R33-S2
Thomas Beazley	Jan. 20, 1836	T51-R33-S34
Jeremiah Burns	Jan. 6, 1834	T51-R33-S25
William Brown	Jan. 26, 1829	T51-R33-S24
William Brown	Sep. 19, 1829	T51-R33-S24
William Brown	Dec. 15, 1823	T51-R33-S23
Townsan F. Brown	Dec. 29, 1823	T51-R33-S10
John Broadhurst	Nov. 7, 1825	T51-R33-S13
John Broadhurst	Dec. 25, 1824	T51-R33-S13
Truman Bevins	Nov. 20, 1821	T51-R33-S25
Truman Bevins	Nov. 18, 1822	T51-R33-S25
Truman Bevins	Nov. 29, 1827	T51-R33-S24
Truman Bevins	Nov. 18, 1822	T51-R33-S24
David M. Bevins	Sep. 9, 1823	T51-R33-S36
Timothy Bancroft	Sep. 1, 1824	T51-R33-S36
Timothy Bancroft	Sep. 22, 1822	T51-R33-S36
Randol G. Baber	Nov. 16, 1835	T52-R33-S27
Robert Barber	Aug. 31, 1837	T52-R33-S35
Robert Barber	Nov. 9, 1839	T52-R33-S35
Jas. H. Berry and Jonathan English	May 20, 1831	T52-R33-S22
Denis H. Boggess	May 18, 1833	T52-R33-S2
Dennis H. Boggess	Sep. 7, 1839	T52-R33-S2
William Butler	Jul. 27, 1835	T54-R33-S36
Joel Branam	Oct. 5, 1832	T53-R33-S14

(Clay County, Missouri Continued)

Name	Date	Location
Abijah Brooks	Feb. 6, 1832	T53-R33-S23
Abijah Brooks	Jun. 5, 1833	T53-R33-S23
Abijah Brooks	Mar. 15, 1827	T53-R33-S26
Abijah Brooks	Feb. 15, 1827	T53-R33-S26
Abijah Brooks	Nov. 1, 1828	T53-R33-S26
Abijah Brooks	Oct. 18, 1828	T53-R33-S26
Abijah Brooks, jr.	Sep. 7, 1839	T53-R33-S27
Andrew Baldwin	Mar. 7, 1830	T52-R30-S19
Andrew Baldwin	Apr. 7, 1827	T52-R30-S20
John A. Beauchamp	Apr. 3, 1839	T52-R30-S36
Henry Bell	Nov. 17, 1832	T52-R30-S14
Henry Bell	Oct. 31, 1835	T52-R30-S14
Henry Bell	Dec. 8, 1837	T52-R30-S14
Henry Bell	Nov. 17, 1832	T52-R30-S23
Benjamin Benson	Jun. 8, 1836	T52-R30-S21
Samuel R. Blain	Oct. 8, 1830	T52-R30-S34
Samuel R. Blain	Oct. 11, 1839	T52-R30-S34
Isaac Blanton	Nov. 26, 1828	T52-R30-S20
Levi Bracken	Jun. 16, 1836	T52-R30-S27
John Braley	Aug. 8, 1838	T52-R30-S23
Catherine Brock	Oct. 6, 1827	T52-R30-S3
Edward Brock	Dec. 29, 1835	T52-R30-S23
James M. Brock	Nov. 20, 1839	T52-R30-S4
Joseph Brock	Nov. 17, 1836	T52-R30-S3
Andrew B. Brown	Nov. 11, 1822	T52-R30-S19
Griffin Bryant	Jul. 31, 1837	T52-R30-S12
Griffin Bryant	Nov. 17, 1835	T52-R30-S13
Griffin Bryant	Jan. 7, 1836	T52-R30-S22
James Baxter	Nov. 18, 1835	T54-R30-S32
Moses Belcher	Jan. 9, 1834	T54-R30-S31
Moses Belcher	Jan. 18, 1836	T54-R30-S31
Benjamin B. Blakey	May 14, 1839	T54-R30-S33
Stephen Baxter	Mar. 19, 1827	T54-R30-S5
Stephen Baxter	Apr. 10, 1827	T54-R30-S5
Stephen Baxter	Jun. 21, 1837	T54-R30-S8
David O. Brawner	Nov. 18, 1839	T54-R30-S8
David O. Brawner	Nov. 3, 1835	T54-R30-S18
John Brawner	Apr. 28, 1838	T54-R30-S22
Edward Brock	Nov. 22, 1837	T54-R30-S34
John Burton	Aug. 8, 1834	T54-R30-S19
John Burton	Aug. 11, 1834	T54-R30-S19
John Burton	May 18, 1833	T54-R30-S30
Sharod Burton	Feb. 6, 1836	T54-R30-S19
Sharod Burton	Aug. 11, 1834	T54-R30-S19
Sharod Burton	May 18, 1833	T54-R30-S30
Stephen Baxter	Mar. 8, 1821	T51-R31-S9
William H. Bell	Jun. 20, 1832	T51-R31-S10

(Clay County, Missouri Continued)

Name	Date	Location
Squire Bozarth	Apr. 18, 1836	T50-R32-S1
Squire Bozarth	Feb. 6, 1837	T50-R32-S1
Squire Bozarth	Apr. 18, 1836	T50-R32-S1
Squire Boarth	Mar. 16, 1835	T50-R32-S12
Cicero Brown	Jan. 25, 1825	T50-R32-S1
Hugh Brown	Mar. 12, 1821	T50-R32-S1
Joseph Brown	May 7, 1821	T50-R32-S10
Joseph Brown	May 23, 1837	T50-R32-S14
Joseph Brown	Feb. 6, 1834	T50-R32-S22
Joseph Brown	Feb. 6, 1834	T50-R32-S23
Joshua Broyles	Mar. 20, 1821	T50-R32-S2
Joshua Broyles	Mar. 8, 1833	T50-R32-S2
Larkin Broyles	Apr. 6, 1839	T50-R32-S15
George Burnett	Aug. 21, 1821	T50-R32-S4
George Burnett	Mar. 7, 1828	T50-R32-S4
George Burnett	Nov. 12, 1827	T50-R32-S4
George Burnett	Apr. 1, 1828	T50-R32-S4
George Burnett	Apr. 28, 1823	T50-R32-S5
Robert Barber	Jan. 15, 1830	T51-R32-S9
Richard Barnes	Nov. 27, 1827	T51-R32-S30
Jno. Bartelson	May 15, 1824	T51-R32-S25
Jno. and Andrew Bartelson	Mar. 12, 1821	T51-R32-S25
Herman Bassett	Oct. 15, 1834	T51-R32-S8
Herman Bassett	Oct. 13, 1834	T51-R32-S9
Jas. Berry	Nov. 5, 1825	T51-R32-S28
Jas. Bogie	Mar. 12, 1821	T51-R32-S24
John S. Bonds	Nov. 20, 1833	T51-R32-S21
John S. Bonds	Jun. 4, 1825	T51-R32-S29
James Buster	Oct. 31, 1835	T51-R32-S33
Jeremiah Bush	May 27, 1831	T51-R32-S5
Benj. Burns	Mar. 2, 1829	T51-R32-S8
Geo. W. Burnett	Dec. 12, 1832	T51-R32-S33
Joseph Broadhurst	Oct. 16, 1825	T51-R32-S18
Joseph Broadhurst	Feb. 18, 1839	T51-R32-S18
John Broadhurst	Feb. 8, 1837	T51-R32-S18
Squire Bozarth	May 30, 1836	T51-R32-S35
Jacob Boydston	Jan. 25, 1833	T51-R32-S17
Jacob Boydston	Aug. 28, 1832	T51-R32-S18
Patsy Bowdry	Mar. 19, 1827	T51-R32-S2
Richard Chance	Sep. 6, 1834	T53-R33-S36
Richard Chance	Dec. 20, 1834	T53-R33-S36
Richard Chance	Oct. 23, 1837	T53-R33-S36
William Corum	Nov. 17, 1832	T53-R33-S36
Samuel Crowley	Sep. 20, 1836	T53-R33-S26
Samuel Crowley	Nov. 29, 1824	T53-R33-S26
Samuel Crowley	Aug. 18, 1831	T53-R33-S26
Thomas Corum	Feb. 18, 1836	T53-R33-S11

Name	Date	Location
Thomas Corum	Mar. 15, 1827	T53-R33-S11
Thomas Corum	Apr. 1, 1831	T53-R33-S11
Samuel Crowley	Sep. 20, 1825	T53-R33-S26
Samuel Crowley	Nov. 29, 1824	T53-R33-S34
Samuel Crowley	Aug. 18, 1831	T53-R33-S14
William Corum	Nov. 17, 1832	T53-R33-S36
Richard Chance	Oct. 23, 1837	T53-R33-S36
Richard Chance	Dec. 20, 1834	T53-R33-S36
Richard Chance	Sep. 6, 1834	T53-R33-S36
John Corum	Dec. 8, 1831	T52-R33-S1
John Corum	Jan. 4, 1838	T52-R33-S12
John Corum	Sep. 28, 1832	T52-R33-S13
John Corum	Mar. 17, 1827	T52-R33-S15
Benjamin Cornelius	Sep. 8, 1825	T52-R33-S10
Robert Cain	Jan. 9, 1829	T51-R33-S14
John Catts	Feb. 8, 1837	T51-R33-S26
William Chance	Nov. 13, 1832	T51-R33-S3
William Chandler	Mar. 5, 1832	T50-R33-S12
Richard Chandler	Nov. 14, 1831	T50-R33-S12
Daniel Carry	Mar. 1, 1836	T50-R33-S1
Thomas M. Chevisi	May 8, 1837	T53-R32-S24
Jas. W. Craig	Nov. 22, 1838	T53-R32-S29
Edward Clark	Mar. 16, 1827	T53-R32-S35
Edward Clark	Sep. 24, 1832	T53-R32-S36
Edward Clark	Oct. 30, 1828	T53-R32-S36
Elisha Cameron and Thomas Pebley	Mar. 5, 1821	T51-R30-S6
Elisha Cameron	Feb. 28, 1834	T51-R30-S6
James Cameron	Jan. 8, 1830	T51-R30-S5
James Casey	May 23, 1836	T51-R30-S1
James Casey	Mar. 25, 1836	T51-R30-S12
James Casey	May 23, 1836	T51-R30-S1
Thomas Cate	Aug. 30, 1832	T51-R30-S8
William Clampitt	Apr. 30, 1839	T51-R30-S3
William Clampitt	Oct. 29, 1838	T51-R30-S11
Archibald Cleavinger	Oct. 5, 1832	T51-R30-S12
James Cleavinger	Sep. 3, 1839	T51-R30-S12
Abraham Coots	Mar. 9, 1829	T51-R30-S6
Elisha Cameron	Apr. 12, 1837	T52-R30-S19
Elisha Cameron	Mar. 5, 1821	T52-R30-S31
Elisha Cameron	Mar. 5, 1821	T52-R30-S36
John Carroll	Jul. 13, 1827	T52-R30-S6
John Carroll	Jun. 20, 1832	T52-R30-S6
Robert Carroll	Dec. 4, 1837	T52-R30-S6
Benjamin Culp	Apr. 1, 1831	T52-R30-S28
Benjamin Culp	Apr. 12, 1827	T52-R30-S19
James H. Casey	Feb. 24, 1837	T52-R30-S34

(Clay County, Missouri Continued)

Name	Date	Location
James H. Casey	Jul. 5, 1837	T52-R30-S34
Eli Chase	Jun. 25, 1836	T52-R30-S17
James C. Clark	Nov. 28, 1835	T52-R30-S24
Jesse Clark	May 12, 1829	T52-R30-S5
Jesse Clark	Jun. 18, 1829	T52-R30-S5
Jesse Clark	Nov. 28, 1834	T52-R30-S7
John Clark	Jan. 7, 1836	T52-R30-S5
Willis Clark	Jan. 17, 1836	T52-R30-S6
Willis Clark	Jan. 7, 1836	T52-R30-S6
Willis Clark	Sep. 12, 1839	T52-R30-S6
Harrison Cooley	Jul. 1, 1839	T52-R30-S35
Abraham Creek	Mar. 5, 1821	T52-R30-S34
Charity Crossett	Nov. 2, 1831	T52-R30-S4
John Crowley	Jul. 12, 1828	T52-R30-S29
Samuel Crowley, jr.	Jun. 27, 1836	T52-R30-S17
Samuel Crowley, jr.	Oct. 12, 1827	T52-R30-S20
Samuel Crowley, jr.	Dec. 3, 1827	T52-R30-S20
Samuel Crowley, jr.	Mar. 17, 1827	T52-R30-S20
James C. Clark	Nov. 1, 1831	T53-R30-S10
James C. Clark	Sep. 22, 1829	T53-R30-S15
James C. Clark	Nov. 1, 1832	T53-R30-S33
James C. Clark	Jan. 27, 1832	T53-R30-S34
James C. Clark	Mar. 21, 1832	T53-R30-S34
Porteous Clark	May 14, 1835	T53-R30-S29
Richard Clark	Jun. 20, 1829	T53-R30-S7
Thomas Clark	Oct. 31, 1832	T53-R30-S29
Timothy B. Clark	Oct. 17, 1835	T53-R30-S26
Timothy B. Clark	Oct. 17, 1835	T53-R30-S35
John Cooper	Jun. 8, 1836	T53-R30-S26
John Cooper	Jun. 8, 1836	T53-R30-S35
John Cooper	Jun. 8, 1836	T53-R30-S36
Abraham Coots	Jan. 7, 1824	T53-R30-S29
Smith Crawford	Nov. 18, 1831	T53-R30-S5
Smith Crawford	Oct. 28, 1828	T53-R30-S5
John Crosset	Nov. 14, 1834	T53-R30-S33
John Crosset	Apr. 17, 1837	T53-R30-S33
Hiram Crowley	Dec. 12, 1828	T53-R30-S26
Hiram Crowley	Feb. 11, 1836	T53-R30-S26
William Crossett	Apr. 18, 1831	T53-R30-S33
Isam Crowley	Dec. 19, 1829	T53-R30-S22
Isam Crowley	Jan. 11, 1836	T53-R30-S27
Isam Crowley	Aug. 13, 1835	T53-R30-S27
Isam Crowley	Dec. 19, 1829	T53-R30-S27
John Crowley	Mar. 17, 1827	T53-R30-S26
John Crowley	Feb. 12, 1825	T53-R30-S27
John Crowley	Feb. 4, 1828	T53-R30-S27
John Crowley	Mar. 1, 1830	T53-R30-S34

(Clay County, Missouri Continued)

Name	Date	Location
Elisha Cameron	Aug. 19, 1828	T53-R30-S24
John Carroll	Mar. 26, 1836	T53-R30-S31
Robert Carroll	Oct. 29, 1835	T53-R30-S31
Henry Clark	Dec. 2, 1835	T53-R30-S23
Nathan Culp	Jan. 19, 1836	T53-R30-S24
Samuel Crowley, jr.	Jul. 13, 1835	T53-R30-S29
Samuel Crowley, jr.	Feb. 8, 1825	T53-R30-S30
Samuel Crowley, jr.	Dec. 3, 1835	T53-R30-S30
Samuel Crowley, jr.	Dec. 29, 1828	T53-R30-S20
Samuel Crowley, jr.	Aug. 26, 1830	T53-R30-S20
Samuel Crowley	Mar. 29, 1822	T51-R31-S9
John Crowley	Mar. 3, 1821	T51-R31-S19
Jeremiah Crowley	Mar. 17, 1827	T51-R31-S10
Phineas Clark	May 19, 1824	T51-R31-S10
Phineas Clark	Aug. 22, 1825	T51-R31-S3
William Campbell	Mar. 16, 1827	T51-R31-S6
Jas. Campbell	Mar. 8, 1821	T51-R31-S20
Elisha Cameron	Sep. 16, 1824	T51-R31-S1
John Cammens	Dec. 19, 1835	T52-R31-S1
Elisha Camron	Jun. 22, 1833	T52-R31-S12
John Camron	Dec. 16, 1835	T52-R31-S1
Ambrose Carpenter	Oct. 12, 1827	T52-R31-S19
Ambrose Carpenter	Nov. 5, 1827	T52-R31-S19
Jonathan Carpenter	Dec. 9, 1833	T52-R31-S19
Jonathan Carpenter	Mar. 22, 1827	T52-R31-S19
Jonathan Carpenter	Mar. 16, 1827	T52-R31-S30
John Carroll	Mar. 8, 1821	T52-R31-S24
John Church	Dec. 4, 1828	T52-R31-S23
Charles Clark	Nov. 23, 1827	T52-R31-S6
Edward Clark	Jan. 6, 1836	T52-R31-S6
Jos. Clarke	Mar. 21, 1827	T52-R31-S21
Catharine Cogdill	Mar. 19, 1836	T52-R31-S2
Catharine Cogdill	Mar. 4, 1834	T52-R31-S11
Catharine Cogdill	Mar. 7, 1824	T52-R31-S12
Jonathan Culp	Mar. 17, 1834	T52-R31-S13
Samuel Crowley	Mar. 16, 1827	T52-R31-S2
David Crockett	Mar. 15, 1827	T52-R31-S26
David Crockett	Mar. 15, 1822	T52-R31-S26
William Creson	Mar. 20, 1823	T52-R31-S35
Jacob Cogdill	Mar. 7, 1832	T52-R31-S11
Jacob Cogdill	Jun. 20, 1832	T52-R31-S2
Jacob Cogdill	Oct. 1, 1827	T52-R31-S1
Jacob Cogdill	Mar. 19, 1836	T53-R31-S35
Jacob Cogdill	Jun. 20, 1832	T53-R31-S35
Jacob Cogdill	Jul. 13, 1832	T53-R31-S35
Elisha Cameron	Jan. 3, 1828	T53-R31-S10
Adey Carter	May 14, 1828	T53-R31-S25

(Clay County, Missouri Continued)

Name	Date	Location
Charles Carthea	Dec. 6, 1839	T53-R31-S27
Charles Carthea	Apr. 4, 1839	T53-R31-S36
Nathaniel Caviell	Mar. 10, 1835	T53-R31-S36
Edward Clark	Jun. 29, 1836	T53-R31-S31
Edward Clark	May 23, 1839	T53-R31-S31
Nelly Coffman	Nov. 6, 1828	T53-R31-S1
Joseph Courtney	Nov. 20, 1839	T53-R31-S11
Joseph Crockett	Nov. 22, 1828	T53-R31-S6
Joseph Crockett	Jun. 20, 1833	T53-R31-S7
Joseph Crockett	Oct. 26, 1825	T53-R31-S29
Joseph Crockett	Mar. 26, 1827	T53-R31-S29
John Crowley, jr.	Jan. 18, 1822	T53-R32-S3
James Crowley	Nov. 19, 1825	T53-R32-S3
Richard Chandler	Nov. 14, 1831	T53-R32-S7
Jas. Campbell	May 12, 1821	T53-R32-S3
Geo. W. Campbell	Mar. 17, 1834	T51-R32-S26
Thomas Campbell	Sep. 24, 1824	T51-R32-S23
William Campbell	Mar. 16, 1827	T51-R32-S8
William Campbell	Jul. 2, 1821	T51-R32-S17
William Campbell	Mar. 6, 1828	T51-R32-S20
Thomas Crowley	Nov. 9, 1825	T51-R32-S34
Thomas Crowley	Aug. 24, 1825	T51-R32-S34
Robert Cans	Mar. 16, 1827	T51-R32-S13
David Carey	Sep. 10, 1822	T51-R32-S31
John Cary	Nov. 17, 1828	T51-R32-S27
John Cary	Feb. 15, 1836	T51-R32-S27
John Cary	Mar. 1, 1828	T51-R32-S27
John Cary	Feb. 14, 1833	T51-R32-S27
Nathaniel Chaney	May 20, 1827	T51-R32-S1
F. B. Convisa	No Date	
John Courtney	Jun. 4, 1825	T51-R32-S29
John Courtney	Dec. 7, 1824	T51-R32-S29
James Crowley	Mar. 17, 1827	T51-R32-S35
Jno. Crowley	Nov. 7, 1831	T51-R32-S34
Edward Clark	May 2, 1827	T54-R32-S32
Thos. M. Chevisi	May 2, 1837	T53-R32-S24
Edward Clark	Mar. 16, 1827	T53-R32-S35
Edward Clark	Sep. 24, 1832	T53-R32-S36
Edward Clark	Oct. 30, 1828	T53-R32-S36
Edward Clark	May 28, 1839	T52-R32-S1
Edward Clark	Feb. 8, 1838	T52-R32-S1
Greenup Collier	Apr. 1, 1839	T52-R32-S24
William C. Colley	Apr. 14, 1837	T52-R32-S31
William Cranny	Feb. 27, 1836	T52-R32-S33
Jno. B. Cox	Dec. 2, 1836	T52-R32-S29
Robert Collins	Jul. 6, 1836	T52-R32-S18
Robert Collins	Jul. 6, 1836	T52-R32-S23

(Clay County, Missouri Continued)

Name	Date	Location
William L. Colley	Dec. 3, 1836	T52-R32-S30
William L. Colley	Apr. 14, 1837	T52-R32-S32
Daniel Carry	Mar. 1, 1836	T50-R33-S1
Richard Chandler	Nov. 14, 1831	T50-R33-S12
William Chandler	Mar. 5, 1832	T50-R33-S12
William Chance	Nov. 13, 1832	T51-R33-S3
John Catts	Feb. 8, 1837	T51-R33-S26
Robert Cain	Jan. 9, 1829	T51-R33-S14
Benjamin Cornelius	Sep. 8, 1825	T52-R33-S10
John Corum	Dec. 8, 1831	T52-R33-S1
John Corum	Jan. 4, 1838	T52-R33-S12
Milton Corum	Jan. 7, 1833	T52-R33-S2
Milton Corum	Feb. 18, 1836	T52-R33-S2
John Corum	Sep. 28, 1832	T52-R33-S13
John Corum	Mar. 17, 1827	T52-R33-S15
Wilkerson Corum	Apr. 13, 1836	T52-R33-S1
Richard Chance	Sep. 6, 1834	T53-R33-S36
Richard Chance	Dec. 20, 1834	T53-R33-S36
Richard Chance	Oct. 23, 1827	T53-R33-S36
William Corum	Nov. 17, 1832	T53-R33-S36
Weekly Dale	Mar. 11, 1833	T52-R31-S7
Weekly Dale and Timothy Dale	Feb. 17, 1838	T52-R31-S7
Weekly Dale	Jul. 26, 1824	T52-R31-S20
Weekly Dale	Oct. 9, 1838	T52-R31-S18
Weekly Dale and Timothy Dale	Dec. 19, 1833	T52-R31-S18
Weekly Dale	Jun. 18, 1827	T52-R31-S18
Weekly Dale	Nov. 13, 1832	T52-R31-S19
Weekly Dale	Jul. 26, 1834	T52-R31-S29
Weekly Dale	Nov. 21, 1825	T52-R31-S30
James Donaldson	Jan. 2, 1836	T52-R31-S21
Timothy R. Dale	Mar. 17, 1836	T52-R31-S17
Timothy R. Dale	Dec. 10, 1832	T52-R31-S7
Rawleigh Dale	Jul. 29, 1830	T52-R31-S18
Rawleigh Dale	Jul. 26, 1824	T52-R31-S17
Carter Dale	Jul. 26, 1824	T52-R31-S17
Weekly Dale	Dec. 6, 1839	T51-R31-S26
Weekly Dale	Nov. 19, 1839	T51-R31-S26
Weekly Dale	Dec. 3, 1839	T51-R31-S27
John Dean	Mar. 8, 1821	T51-R31-S30
Matthew Duncan	Nov. 15, 1827	T51-R31-S9
George Denny	Jan. 29, 1836	T53-R30-S24
Walter Davis	Nov. 13, 1828	T53-R30-S20
Walter Davis	Jul. 27, 1829	T53-R30-S21
Walter Davis	Nov. 13, 1828	T53-R30-S21
Walter Davis	Feb. 26, 1830	T53-R30-S27

(Callaway County, Missouri Continued)

Name	Date	Location
William N. Denny	Jan. 6, 1836	T53-R30-S23
Levi Denny	May 7, 1834	T53-R30-S23
Levi Denny	Jan. 29, 1836	T53-R30-S22
Levi Denny	Dec. 31, 1835	T53-R30-S28
James Dickie	Jan. 17, 1837	T52-R30-S23
William T. Davis	Feb. 7, 1837	T52-R30-S23
James Dagley	Dec. 20, 1839	T52-R30-S17
James Dagley	Jan. 18, 1832	T52-R30-S29
Archibald W. Dickie	Jan. 17, 1837	T52-R30-S23
Samuel Drollings and John Patton	Jul. 14, 1834	T51-R30-S8
Wm. H. H. Davis	Jun. 21, 1839	T54-R31-S31
William Dawson	Oct. 3, 1838	T53-R31-S34
Alexander Duerson	Nov. 11, 1837	T53-R31-S11
James Duncan	Oct. 19, 1827	T53-R31-S24
William Dunlap	May 1, 1837	T53-R31-S18
Peter Drew	Nov. 7, 1836	T50-R32-S2
Harrison Davis	Nov. 28, 1831	T50-R32-S12
David Dale	Dec. 18, 1833	T51-R32-S28
David Dale	Mar. 19, 1827	T52-R32-S32
Calvin Davis	May 24, 1823	T51-R32-S4
Michael Dressler	Apr. 25, 1828	T51-R32-S17
Robert Dunlap	Mar. 24, 1829	T51-R32-S3
Robert Dunlap	Apr. 1, 1831	T52-R32-S34
James Dunlap	Sep. 6, 1838	T51-R32-S20
James Dunlap	Nov. 24, 1837	T52-R32-S20
James Dunlap	Dec. 9, 1835	T52-R32-S24
James Dunlap	Sep. 20, 1825	T52-R32-S24
James Dunlap	Sep. 2, 1823	T52-R32-S28
James Dunlap	Sep. 24, 1839	T52-R32-S33
Jas. Dickey	Jul. 23, 1838	T52-R32-S21
Preston Dunlap	Nov. 24, 1837	T52-R32-S24
Mathew Duncan	Nov. 15, 1827	T52-R32-S13
John Dougherty	Sep. 30, 1839	T52-R32-S32
John Dougherty	Sep. 24, 1839	T52-R32-S19
William Davis	May 24, 1823	T52-R32-S33
James B. Davenport	Nov. 24, 1829	T52-R32-S6
James Duncan	Oct. 30, 1828	T54-R32-S34
James Duncan	Mar. 15, 1827	T53-R32-S4
James Duncan	Oct. 30, 1828	T53-R32-S5
James Duncan	Jul. 27, 1829	T53-R32-S5
James Duncan	Mar. 15, 1827	T53-R32-S18
James Duncan	Oct. 28, 1825	T53-R32-S20
James Duncan	Nov. 21, 1825	T53-R32-S20
James Duncan	Apr. 13, 1836	T53-R32-S21
James Duncan	Feb. 14, 1833	T53-R32-S21
James Duncan	Aug. 2, 1836	T53-R32-S21

Name	Date	Location
James Duncan	Nov. 15, 1827	T53-R32-S27
Rice B. Davenport	Oct. 28, 1831	T53-R32-S17
Rice B. Davenport	Dec. 11, 1837	T53-R32-S17
Rice B. Davenport	May 26, 1832	T53-R32-S17
Rice B. Davenport and Peter Holtsclaw	Jul. 16, 1839	T53-R32-S17
Rice B. Davenport	Apr. 2, 1838	T53-R32-S18
Rice B. Davenport	Mar. 15, 1827	T53-R32-S20
Rice B. Davenport	Apr. 2, 1834	T53-R32-S19
William Davenport	Jul. 16, 1839	T53-R32-S20
Mathew Duncan	Sep. 1, 1834	T53-R32-S19
Mathew Duncan	Nov. 21, 1825	T53-R32-S19
Mathew Duncan	Oct. 28, 1825	T53-R32-S19
Mathew Duncan	Nov. 15, 1827	T53-R32-S28
Ambrose Davis	Mar. 30, 1836	T50-R33-S1
Jno. T. Dodson	Jul. 14, 1834	T50-R33-S3
Philo Dibble	Sep. 16, 1834	T51-S33-S35
William Duncan	Oct. 28, 1825	T52-R33-S3
William Duncan	Jun. 15, 1831	T52-R33-S2
William Duncan	Jul. 11, 1835	T52-R33-S14
John Dougherty	Sep. 24, 1839	T52-R33-S24
James Duncan	Jul. 11, 1835	T52-R33-S15
James Duncan	Jun. 17, 1837	T53-R33-S24
James Duncan	Oct. 25, 1834	T53-R33-S24
James Duncan	Mar. 15, 1827	T53-R33-S24
James Duncan	Feb. 14, 1828	T53-R33-S24
James Duncan	Oct. 30, 1828	T53-R33-S13
James Duncan	Mar. 15, 1827	T53-R33-S25
Alex. B. Duncan	Oct. 29, 1832	T53-R33-S13
Alex. B. Duncan	May 8, 1834	T53-R33-S11
Alex. B. Duncan	Dec. 10, 1832	T53-R33-S11
Alex. B. Duncan	Aug. 13, 1832	T53-R33-S11
Geo. W. Douglas	Sep. 17, 1838	T53-R33-S2
Daniel Denborn	Mar. 16, 1827	T53-R33-S11
William Davenport	Oct, 19, 1827	T53-R33-S12
Rice B. Davenport	Mar. 15, 1827	T53-R33-S1
Rice B. Davenport	Mar. 21, 1833	T53-R33-S1
Rice B. Davenport	Mar. 19, 1827	T53-R33-S12
Howard Everett	Jan. 2, 1836	T52-R30-S35
William Estes	Mar. 22, 1827	T52-R30-S12
John Estes	Feb. 20, 1834	T52-R30-S22
Anderson Estes	Dec. 23, 1833	T52-R30-S12
John Evans	Jul. 9, 1821	T51-R31-S8
Thomas Estes	Mar. 19, 1821	T51-R31-S5
John Evans	Sep. 3, 1821	T51-R31-S8
John Evans	Mar. 25, 1822	T51-R31-S5
John Edwards	Mar. 15, 1827	T51-R31-S3

(Clay County, Missouri Continued)

Name	Date	Location
Thos. Estes	Sep. 18, 1823	T51-R31-S5
Thos. Estes	Mar. 16, 1827	T51-R31-S5
Thos. Estes	Nov. 17, 1831	T51-R31-S4
Littleberry Estes	Mar. 8, 1821	T51-R31-S9
Peter Estes	Nov. 22, 1824	T51-R31-S9
Peter Estes	Feb. 1, 1828	T51-R31-S10
Peter Estes	Jun. 16, 1824	T51-R31-S10
Joel Estes, sr.	Jul. 14, 1821	T51-R31-S5
Henry Estes	Mar. 19, 1821	T51-R31-S5
Archibald Estes	Sep. 25, 1827	T53-R31-S29
Henry Estes	Dec. 7, 1835	T53-R31-S15
Henry Estes	Jun. 20, 1832	T53-R31-S15
Henry Estes	Mar. 20, 1829	T53-R31-S22
Henry Estes	Nov. 18, 1839	T53-R31-S22
Henry Estes	Aug. 8, 1839	T53-R31-S22
Henry Estes	Mar. 16, 1827	T53-R31-S36
Westen J. Everett	Oct. 29, 1835	T52-R31-S28
Westen J. Everett	Jan. 26, 1829	T52-R31-S28
Westen J. Everett	Oct. 17, 1827	T52-R31-S21
Westen J. Everett	Dec. 8, 1835	T52-R31-S15
Mathew Everett	Mar. 5, 1833	T52-R31-S14
Howard Everett	Apr. 7, 1827	T52-R31-S27
Howard Everett	Mar. 21, 1827	T52-R31-S27
Howard Everett	Jan. 16, 1830	T52-R31-S27
Howard Everett	Mar. 16, 1827	T52-R31-S25
Howard Everett	Sep. 17, 1823	T52-R31-S25
Howard Everett	Apr. 17, 1827	T52-R31-S22
Howard Everett	Dec. 14, 1835	T52-R31-S15
A. D. Edwards	Mar. 15, 1836	T52-R31-S8
Littleberry Estes and Henry Estes	Dec. 14, 1824	T52-R31-S11
Littleberry Estes	Dec. 24, 1827	T52-R31-S15
Elisha Estes	Oct. 29, 1832	T52-R31-S11
Elisha Estes	Jul. 13, 1832	T52-R31-S11
Joel Estes	Nov. 23, 1824	T52-R31-S33
Joel Estes	Jan. 25, 1825	T52-R31-S33
Henry Estes	Dec. 14, 1824	T52-R31-S11
Stephen Estes	Jun. 26, 1832	T52-R31-S10
Thomas Estes	May 8, 1835	T52-R31-S28
Thomas Estes	Nov. 11, 1833	T52-R31-S28
Joel Estes	Jan. 25, 1825	T52-R31-S3
Joel Estes and Samuel C. Hall	Mar. 7, 1828	T52-R31-S3
Joel Estes	Mar. 19, 1827	T52-R31-S3
Joel Estes	Jan. 25, 1825	T52-R31-S10
Joel Estes	Jan. 15, 1825	T52-R31-S13
Joel Estes	Nov. 17, 1837	T52-R31-S14

Name	Date	Location
Roswell Evans	Mar. 3, 1835	T51-R32-S22
John Evans	Mar. 19, 1827	T51-R32-S13
Jonathan English	Nov. 20, 1821	T51-R32-S30
Simpson Emerson	Nov. 9, 1824	T51-R32-S11
William Emberer	Jul. 22, 1830	T51-R32-S10
Ambrose Embrer and Jane Raulings	Dec. 10, 1829	T51-R32-S11
John Ellis	Nov. 26, 1825	T51-R32-S4
John Ellis	Oct. 27, 1821	T51-R32-S5
Robert Elliott	Oct. 24, 1828	T51-R32-S3
Peter Elliott	Oct. 24, 1828	T51-R32-S4
Weston Everett	Mar. 16, 1827	T52-R32-S31
John Evans	Mar. 12, 1821	T52-R32-S25
Robert Elliott	Nov. 4, 1836	T52-R32-S30
John Evans	Apr. 22, 1828	T54-R32-S32
John Evans	Oct. 19, 1839	T54-R32-S32
John Evans	Mar. 13, 1828	T54-R32-S32
Henry Estes	Jul. 14, 1835	T54-R32-S36
Jefferson Estes	Dec. 7, 1835	T53-R31-S15
Jefferson Estes	Aug. 22, 1839	T53-R31-S22
John Ecton	Apr. 16, 1835	T53-R32-S26
John Ellington	Apr. 24, 1839	T53-R32-S5
John Ellington	Nov. 27, 1837	T53-R32-S8
John Ellington	Jan. 5, 1830	T53-R32-S8
John Ellington	Sep. 3, 1832	T53-R32-S8
John Ellington	Apr. 3, 1829	T53-R32-S9
Richardson Ellington	Nov. 17, 1836	T53-R32-S2
David English	Oct. 20, 1828	T50-R33-S2
Charles English	Jan. 5, 1823	T50-R33-S2
Charles English	Sep. 3, 1821	T50-R33-S2
Nancy Elliott	Feb. 16, 1836	T51-R33-S27
David L. Ferrel	Dec. 8, 1827	T52-R31-S1
David Ferrel	Dec. 5, 1827	T52-R31-S1
David L. Ferrel	Mar. 15, 1834	T52-R31-S1
David Ferrel	Jan. 9, 1838	T52-R31-S12
David L. Ferrel	Jan. 31, 1835	T52-R31-S12
Samuel D. Ferrell	Dec. 15, 1835	T52-R31-S13
William F. Franklin	Mar. 20, 1837	T52-R31-S21
Solomon Fry	Feb. 11, 1837	T52-R31-S28
Solomon Fry	Mar. 31, 1836	T52-R31-S28
Solomon Fry	Mar. 8, 1821	T51-R31-S19
Solomon Fry	Dec. 5, 1833	T51-R31-S4
Solomon Fry	Mar. 9, 1821	T51-R31-S4
Travis Finley	Mar. 8, 1821	T51-R31-S20
Henry S. Fields	Dec. 24, 1832	T51-R31-S15
John Farrens	Feb. 28, 1824	T51-R31-S9
Jesse Fletcher	Aug. 25, 1829	T53-R30-S24

(Clay County, Missouri Continued)

Name	Date	Location
George B. Finley	Nov. 24, 1835	T53-R30-S21
Travis Finley	Feb. 1, 1835	T53-R30-S31
Travis Finley	Oct. 28, 1835	T53-R30-S35
Jesse Fletcher	Jul. 10, 1828	T53-R30-S24
Jermeiah Farmer	Apr. 19, 1839	T54-R33-S36
Larshel C. Fugitt	Feb. 14, 1824	T51-R33-S14
Alex Fudge	Aug. 22, 1825	T51-R33-S25
Moses Fletcher	Feb. 24, 1829	T51-R33-S35
Moses Fletcher	Sep. 1, 1824	T51-R33-S26
Moses Fletcher	Nov. 29, 1824	T51-R33-S25
Moses Faubion	Feb. 18, 1834	T51-R33-S22
Hiram Faggitt	Feb. 14, 1829	T51-R33-S13
Jos. Fowler	Mar. 31, 1837	T50-R33-S1
Jos. Fowler	Jul. 25, 1833	T50-R33-S1
Jos. Fowler	Mar. 15, 1821	T50-R33-S2
Thos. Frost	Sep. 10, 1822	T50-R33-S2
Thomas Farmer	Aug. 28, 1837	T53-R32-S15
Thomas Fry	Feb. 6, 1836	T54-R32-S33
Thomas Fry	Dec. 17, 1832	T54-R32-S33
Thomas Fry	Nov. 13, 1827	T54-R32-S33
Thomas Fry	Apr. 17, 1827	T54-R32-S33
Thomas Fry	Apr. 22, 1837	T54-R32-S33
Elijah Fry	Jul. 19, 1832	T54-R32-S31
Abraham Faubion	Oct. 14, 1835	T51-R32-S7
Hiram Fugett	Nov. 17, 1837	T51-R32-S18
Thomas Frost	Mar. 12, 1821	T50-R32-S11
Young Fowler	Mar. 12, 1821	T50-R32-S5
Young Fowler	Jan. 29, 1824	T50-R32-S6
William T. Franklin	Oct. 21, 1828	T53-R31-S1
Asa T. Force	Sep. 18, 1834	T54-R31-S32
Thornton Guinn	Jul. 5, 1829	T51-R30-S5
Benjamin Grimm	Sep. 29, 1833	T52-R30-S32
John Gregg	Jun. 15, 1836	T52-R30-S12
John Gregg	Jun. 19, 1837	T52-R30-S23
Baily O. Gregg	Aug. 6, 1832	T52-R30-S32
Isom Gentry	Sep. 9, 1837	T52-R30-S18
Nathaniel Gates	May 7, 1839	T52-R30-S1
Gibson Gates	Jun. 1, 1836	T52-R30-S1
Erastus Gates	Dec. 5, 1837	T52-R30-S1
Garret Green	Dec. 10, 1835	T53-R30-S6
Garret Green	Sep. 11, 1832	T53-R30-S6
Garret Green	Nov. 21, 1828	T53-R30-S6
Jesse Green	Dec. 5, 1829	T53-R30-S17
Jacob Gromer	Oct. 22, 1827	T53-R30-S19
William Groomer	Sep. 1, 1836	T53-R30-S1
William Groomer	Nov. 1, 1835	T53-R30-S11
William Groomer	Nov. 10, 1835	T53-R30-S11

(Clay County, Missouri Continued)

Name	Date	Location
John O. Gross	Nov. 11, 1831	T53-R30-S10
John O. Gross	Jun. 25, 1836	T53-R30-S10
John O. Gross	Apr. 19, 1835	T53-R30-S10
Henry Gish	Dec. 21, 1835	T53-R30-S29
Henry Gish	Mar. 27, 1833	T53-R30-S28
Henry Gish	Dec. 2, 1835	T53-R30-S28
Henry Gish	Oct. 22, 1831	T53-R30-S28
Henry Gish	Sep. 12, 1829	T53-R30-S28
Henry Gish	Sep. 25, 1829	T53-R30-S28
Henry Gish	Mar. 27, 1833	T53-R30-S27
Jesse Gilliam	Jun. 29, 1836	T53-R30-S29
Jesse Gilliam	Mar. 19, 1827	T53-R30-S7
Jesse Gilliam	Jan. 29, 1832	T53-R30-S7
William N. George	Dec. 29, 1835	T53-R30-S11
Baily O. George	Dec. 29, 1835	T53-R30-S23
Abraham Groom	Mar. 8, 1821	T51-R31-S18
Robert Gladden	Oct. 8, 1823	T51-R31-S11
James Gilmore	Mar. 8, 1821	T51-R31-S15
Robert Gilliam	Feb. 15, 1825	T51-R31-S3
Pleasant Gates	Nov. 9, 1832	T51-R31-S15
Thomas Gardner	Oct. 23, 1839	T51-R31-S22
Laban Garret	Mar. 6, 1827	T51-R31-S6
Thomas Gardner	Mar. 17, 1827	T52-R31-S35
Samuel Gilmore	Feb. 27, 1829	T52-R31-S30
Augustine G. Gunter	Nov. 20, 1835	T52-R31-S11
Augustine G. Gunter	Nov. 29, 1830	T52-R31-S15
Henry Green, jr.	Aug. 26, 1833	T54-R31-S36
Henry Green, jr.	Feb. 18, 1834	T54-R31-S36
Henry Green, jr.	Nov. 20, 1823	T54-R31-S36
Jacob Gromer	Nov. 6, 1827	T53-R31-S24
Isaac Gromer	Dec. 7, 1836	T53-R31-S14
Polly Gillespie	Aug. 2, 1836	T53-R31-S20
Robert Gilmore	Sep. 22, 1824	T53-R31-S29
Robert Gilmore	Nov. 4, 1828	T53-R31-S29
Robert Gilmore	Dec. 28, 1835	T53-R31-S21
David Gromer	Oct. 22, 1827	T53-R31-S13
David Gromer	Dec. 17, 1832	T53-R31-S13
David Gromer	Nov. 28, 1827	T53-R31-S13
Jas. Griffith	Dec. 30, 1835	T50-R32-S3
Samuel Gragg	Aug. 6, 1832	T50-R32-S18
Benjamin Gragg	Apr. 22, 1833	T50-R32-S18
William Gotcher	May 26, 1836	T50-R32-S11
Joshua Gotcher	May 8, 1838	T50-R32-S12
Joshua Gotcher	Jul. 6, 1835	T50-R32-S2
Hugh Gocher	Mar. 14, 1836	T50-R32-S10
Wesley Gaines	Mar. 7, 1836	T50-R32-S7
William Groom	Mar. 21, 1821	T51-R32-S2

(Clay County, Missouri Continued)

Name	Date	Location
Benjamin Gregg	Oct. 26, 1835	T51-R32-S7
Benjamin Gregg	Jul. 11, 1825	T51-R32-S7
John Gregg	Feb. 2, 1838	T51-R32-S7
Samuel Gregg	Oct. 14, 1835	T51-R32-S7
Samuel and Benjamin Gregg	May 17, 1824	T51-R32-S6
Sarah Groom	Oct. 9, 1824	T51-R32-S12
William Groom	Mar. 12, 1821	T51-R32-S2
Joseph Grooms	Oct. 31, 1836	T51-R32-S14
Thos. Gordon	Jun. 23, 1836	T52-R32-S9
Thos. Gordon	Mar. 24, 1836	T52-R32-S9
Thos. Gordon	Dec. 12, 1833	T52-R32-S9
Thos. Gordon	Jul. 2, 1838	T52-R32-S9
Thos. Gordon	Dec. 28, 1833	T52-R32-S10
Thos. Gordon	Apr. 4, 1839	T52-R32-S17
Thos. Gordon	Aug. 20, 1839	T52-R32-S17
Thos. Gordon	Aug. 27, 1838	T52-R32-S21
Thos. Gordon	Nov. 25, 1831	T52-R32-S7
Thos. Gordon	Jun. 23, 1832	T52-R32-S8
Jno. W. Gill	Dec. 18, 1837	T52-R32-S11
Jos. Gallaway	Nov. 19, 1825	T52-R32-S15
Jos. Gallaway	Jul. 11, 1827	T52-R32-S22
William F. Griggsby	Feb. 22, 1836	T52-R32-S8
William F. Griggsby	May 1, 1838	T52-R32-S21
William F. Griggsby	Jan. 23, 1837	T52-R32-S21
William F. Griggsby	Jun. 3, 1833	T52-R32-S28
Geo. Grimes	Apr. 6, 1837	T52-R32-S17
Amos Groom	Jun. 27, 1828	T52-R32-S27
Isaac Groom	Apr. 15, 1829	T52-R32-S24
Isaac Groom	Feb. 14, 1828	T52-R32-S25
Isaac Groom	Aug. 9, 1828	T52-R32-S28
Richard Groom	Mar. 16, 1827	T52-R32-S26
Pleasant Gentry	Jan. 30, 1832	T53-R32-S5
Pleasant Gentry	Jul. 9, 1832	T53-R32-S5
Pleasant Gentry	Mar. 14, 1832	T53-R32-S6
Pleasant Gentry	Nov. 27, 1837	T52-R32-S8
Pleasant Gentry	Dec. 11, 1837	T53-R32-S8
Pleasant Gentry	Jan. 30, 1839	T53-R32-S8
Pleasant Gentry	Nov. 19, 1833	T52-R32-S8
Daniel Gaines	Mar. 7, 1836	T50-R33-S23
Wesley Gaines	Nov. 14, 1831	T50-R33-S12
Wesley Gaines	Nov. 10, 1830	T50-R33-S12
John Gash, sr.	Mar. 15, 1821	T51-R33-S11
John D. Gash	Mar. 15, 1821	T51-R33-S13
Geo. S. Goode	Dec. 25, 1829	T51-R33-S23
John Gragg	Sep. 3, 1838	T51-R33-S1
John Gragg	Dec. 21, 1829	T51-R33-S34
Samuel Gragg	Aug. 18, 1838	T51-R33-S12

(Clay County, Missouri Continued)

Name	Date	Location
Samuel and Benjamin Gregg, ex. of Henry Gregg	Mar. 3, 1830	T51-R33-S12
Samuel Gregg and D. L. Magill	Oct. 13, 1828	T51-R33-S1
David Gregg	Mar. 19, 1821	T51-R33-S35
Abner Gregg	Jul. 25, 1835	T51-R33-S34
John C. Hawkins	Nov. 21, 1837	T53-R31-S35
John C. Hawkins	Mar. 5, 1838	T53-R31-S35
David Henderson	Nov. 11, 1828	T53-R31-S13
Robert Henderson	Oct. 2, 1837	T53-R31-S14
Jesse Hickman	Jan. 26, 1837	T53-R31-S2
Noah Hickman	Nov. 5, 1835	T53-R31-S36
Harlow Hinkston	Nov. 29, 1833	T53-R31-S12
Rueben Holman	Jan. 1, 1836	T53-R31-S2
Reuben Holman	Nov. 10, 1828	T53-R31-S32
Christian Huffaker	Oct. 5, 1827	T53-R31-S24
George Huffaker	Aug. 11, 1821	T53-R31-S24
George Huffaker	Apr. 2, 1824	T53-R31-S24
James Hudgens	Mar. 24, 1836	T53-R31-S8
James Hudgens	Jul. 2, 1838	T53-R31-S9
Jno. D. Hall	Mar. 10, 1834	T53-R31-S23
Samuel Hall	Jul. 11, 1837	T53-R31-S34
Samuel Hall	Jan. 11, 1837	T53-R31-S34
Henry W. Hanson	Dec. 12, 1836	T52-R31-S18
Jeremiah Holt	Jan. 15, 1838	T54-R31-S35
Wesley Henderson	Feb. 18, 1834	T54-R31-S33
Wesley Henderson	Nov. 20, 1823	T54-R31-S33
John Hughes	Jul. 2, 1821	T52-R31-S36
William Hughes	May 7, 1821	T52-R31-S13
William Hughes	Mar. 8, 1821	T52-R31-S13
Thos. Hagans	Jan. 23, 1837	T52-R31-S7
George S. Huffaker	Apr. 2, 1821	T52-R31-S13
George S. Huffaker	Oct. 16, 1824	T52-R31-S24
George S. Hufftaker	Oct. 31, 1833	T52-R31-S25
Christopher Huffaker	Sep. 4, 1822	T52-R31-S26
Christopher Huffaker	Apr. 2, 1821	T52-R31-S26
Christian Huffaker	Apr. 2, 1821	T52-R31-S2
David Holmes	Jun. 23, 1832	T52-R31-S14
John Holman	Mar. 16, 1827	T52-R31-S19
James R. Holeman	Nov. 9, 1835	T52-R31-S3
James Hiett	Sep. 12, 1821	T52-R31-S31
James Hiett	Feb. 16, 1824	T52-R31-S31
James Hiett	Mar. 17, 1827	T52-R31-S32
Andrew, Jas., Allen, Wm., and Soloman Hixon	Jan. 15, 1835	T52-R31-S8
Thos. Hickson	Jul. 16, 1824	T52-R31-S32
Thos. Hickson	Nov. 26, 1832	T52-R31-S32

(Clay County, Missouri Continued)

Name	Date	Location
Thos. Heartt	Jan. 30, 1832	T52-R31-S22
Andrew, Jas., Allen, Wm., and Solomon Hixon	Dec. 2, 1827	T52-R31-S15
Silas Henderson	Feb. 15, 1837	T52-R31-S12
Thomas Harrington	Oct. 13, 1821	T52-R31-S25
Pitman Hanks	Apr. 3, 1827	T52-R31-S19
Samuel C. Hall	Dec. 24, 1827	T52-R31-S3
Jeremiah Holt	Jan. 15, 1838	T54-R31-S35
James Hudgens	Mar. 24, 1836	T53-R31-S8
James Hudgens	Jul. 2, 1838	T53-R31-S9
George Huffaker	Aug. 11, 1821	T53-R31-S24
George Huffaker	Apr. 2, 1824	T53-R31-S24
Christian Huffaker	Oct. 5, 1827	T53-R31-S24
Reuben Holman	Jan. 1, 1836	T53-R31-S3
Reuben Holman	Nov. 10, 1828	T53-R31-S32
Harlow Hinkston	Nov. 29, 1833	T53-R31-S12
Noah Hickman	Nov. 5, 1835	T53-R31-S36
Jesse Hickman	Jan. 26, 1837	T53-R31-S2
Robert Henderson	Oct. 2, 1837	T53-R31-S14
John C. Hawkins	Nov. 21, 1837	T53-R31-S35
John C. Hawkins	Mar. 5, 1838	T53-R31-S35
Henry W. Hanson	Dec. 12, 1836	T53-R31-S18
Samuel Hall	Jul. 11, 1837	T53-R31-S34
Samuel Hall	Jan. 11, 1837	T53-R31-S34
Jno. D. Hall	Mar. 10, 1834	T53-R31-S23
Jno. Hightower	Feb. 17, 1823	T50-R32-S5
John Havins	Oct. 17, 1835	T50-R32-S2
William Harvey	Feb. 27, 1822	T50-R32-S6
Thomas Harins	Jul. 9, 1833	T50-R32-S3
Philip Hardwick	Sep. 1, 1837	T50-R32-S7
David Hagan	Oct. 17, 1835	T50-R32-S3
David Hagan	Jan. 27, 1834	T51-R32-S35
Samuel Hadley	Dec. 12, 1833	T51-R32-S1
J.P. Hume and Jno. Thorton	Jan. 9, 1836	T51-R32-S22
William Hughes, sr.	May 7, 1821	T51-R32-S13
David Hamilton	Oct. 21, 1824	T51-R32-S30
Chas. C. Harrington	Feb. 19, 1824	T51-R32-S27
Elisha Harrington	Jan. 15, 1826	T51-R32-S8
Thos. Harrington	Mar. 7, 1836	T51-R32-S26
Thos. Harrington	Jan. 16, 1832	T51-R32-S26
Thos. Harrington	May 23, 1827	T51-R32-S27
Jno. Harris	Mar. 12, 1821	T51-R32-S18
Isaac Hiner	Aug. 8, 1836	T51-R32-S7
Ezekiel Huffman	Mar. 14, 1836	T52-R32-S5
Ezekiel Huffman	Dec. 30, 1830	T52-R32-S5
Ezekiel Huffman	May 23, 1831	T52-R32-S6
Ezekiel Huffman	Jun. 14, 1826	T52-R32-S8

(Clay County, Missouri Continued)

Name	Date	Location
Ezekiel Huffman	Mar. 16, 1827	T52-R32-S8
Ezekiel Huffman	May 9, 1835	T52-R32-S9
Ezekiel Huffman	Jun. 29, 1836	T52-R32-S9
Samuel Hiett	Apr. 3, 1827	T52-R32-S15
Samuel C. Hall	Jun. 16, 1824	T52-R32-S22
Samuel C. Hall	Jul. 25, 1825	T52-R32-S27
John D. Hall	Sep. 23, 1839	T52-R32-S17
John D. Hall	Jul. 28, 1828	T52-R32-S27
John D. Hall	Jun. 16, 1824	T52-R32-S27
John D. Hall	Mar. 12, 1826	T52-R32-S22
John D. Hall	Apr. 9, 1838	T52-R32-S20
Geo. C. Hall	Jul. 9, 1838	T52-R32-S20
Elijah Hall	Feb. 11, 1822	T52-R32-S25
Elijah Hall	Dec. 22, 1831	T52-R32-S27
Elijah Hall	May 23, 1831	T52-R32-S27
Elijah Hall	Sep. 2, 1839	T52-R32-S26
Jeremiah Hall, jr.	Aug. 20, 1832	T54-R32-S33
Jas. E. Hall	Jan. 1, 1833	T54-R32-S31
Jas. E. Hall	Feb. 1, 1836	T54-R32-S31
Elijah Hall	Apr. 26, 1827	T54-R32-S33
Eleanor Hall	Apr. 23, 1839	T53-R32-S5
John Hulce	Feb. 6, 1834	T53-R32-S7
John Hulce	Aug. 31, 1837	T53-R32-S6
Elisha Hall	Mar. 19, 1827	T53-R32-S4
Elisha Hall	Feb. 14, 1828	T53-R32-S4
Elisha Hall	Jun. 23, 1827	T53-R32-S5
Geo. C. Hall	May 30, 1833	T53-R32-S4
William Hughes	Jul. 5, 1831	T53-R32-S23
William Hughes	May 13, 1836	T53-R32-S24
Jesse G. Huffman	Dec. 4, 1834	T53-R32-S7
Jesse G. Huffman	Jun. 7, 1836	T53-R32-S21
John Harsel	Jan. 28, 1830	T53-R32-S22
John Harsel	Nov. 5, 1827	T53-R32-S23
Peter Holtzclaw	Aug. 6, 1836	T53-R32-S17
Peter Holtzclaw	Sep. 7, 1832	T53-R32-S21
Peter Holtzclaw	May 24, 1831	T53-R32-S22
Peter Holtzclaw	Aug. 3, 1832	T53-R32-S22
Peter Holtzclaw	Apr. 13, 1836	T53-R32-S22
Anthony Harsel, jr.	Jun. 14, 1836	T53-R32-S26
Anthony Harsel	Oct. 15, 1832	T53-R32-S14
Anthony Harsel	Jun. 24, 1839	T53-R32-S23
Anthony Harsel	May 31, 1831	T53-R32-S23
Anthony Harsel	Nov. 19, 1828	T53-R32-S23
Anthony Harsel	Nov. 5, 1827	T53-R32-S23
Jeremiah Hall, jr.	Aug. 20, 1832	T53-R32-S3
Mary Hensley	Mar. 15, 1836	T50-R33-S11
William Harrington	Mar. 17, 1827	T50-R33-S1

(Clay County, Missouri Continued)

Name	Date	Location
Nathan E. Harrelson	Oct. 17, 1839	T50-R33-S13
Jacob Harrington	Oct. 21, 1825	T50-R33-S2
William Hensley	Oct. 6, 1832	T50-R33-S11
Henry W. Hensley	May 4, 1832	T50-R33-S15
David Hunt	Mar. 19, 1827	T51-R33-S11
David Hunt	Sep. 11, 1829	T51-R33-S12
Daniel Hughes	Dec. 3, 1830	T51-R33-S22
Daniel Hughes	Oct. 25, 1825	T51-R33-S24
Simon Hudson	Oct. 22, 1825	T51-R33-S14
Simon Hudson	Jan. 23, 1829	T51-R33-S23
Simon Hudson	Mar. 17, 1827	T51-R33-S27
Samuel Hudson	Jun. 21, 1836	T51-R33-S22
Samuel Hudson	Sep. 28, 1832	T51-R33-S27
Samuel Hudson	Jul. 25, 1834	T51-R33-S27
Henry B. Hokit	Jul. 18, 1835	T51-R33-S27
A. L. Hokit	Feb. 16, 1836	T51-R33-S27
Robert Harris	Aug. 31, 1835	T52-R33-S13
Robert Harris	Dec. 11, 1829	T52-R33-S35
Samuel Harris	Nov. 25, 1831	T52-R33-S2
Samuel Harris	Mar. 9, 1836	T52-R33-S10
Eli P. Hardin	Nov. 23, 1837	T53-R33-S36
Robert Harris	Mar. 16, 1827	T53-R33-S1
Robert Irwin	Nov. 23, 1824	T53-R31-S29
John Irwin	Sep. 28, 1832	T53-R31-S5
Hezekiah W. Inyart	Dec. 14, 1824	T52-R32-S15
Abraham Inyart	Dec. 14, 1824	T53-R32-S27
Jas. Irvin	Aug. 15, 1831	T53-R32-S15
John Justice	Feb. 16, 1836	T52-R33-S36
Richard Jesse	Oct. 12, 1832	T52-R33-S13
John Justice	Feb. 19, 1836	T52-R33-S36
Woodford F. Jesse	Dec. 8, 1831	T52-R33-S11
John Justice	Feb. 6, 1836	T52-R33-S36
Marvel and Leander Jones	Aug. 13, 1831	T52-R33-S15
Woodford F. Jesse	Oct. 26, 1832	T52-R33-S13
Woodford F. Jesse	Mar. 17, 1827	T52-R33-S13
Woodford F. Jesse	Oct. 19, 1825	T52-R33-S12
Benj. F. Jesse	Oct. 12, 1832	T52-R33-S13
Benj. F. Jesse	Oct. 13, 1838	T52-R33-S14
Benj. F. Jesse	Sep. 14, 1838	T52-R33-S24
James James	Nov. 27, 1830	T51-R33-S22
William Johnston	Jul. 27, 1827	T51-R33-S12
William Johnston	Jun. 15, 1831	T51-R33-S12
William Jasseph	Dec. 26, 1835	T51-R33-S35
John Jeffries	Mar. 18, 1834	T51-R33-S22
John Jeffers	Oct. 10, 1827	T51-R33-S13
William L. Judy	Feb. 12, 1825	T53-R32-S31
Stephen Jones	Feb. 20, 1830	T53-R32-S27

(Clay County, Missouri Continued)

Name	Date	Location
George W. Jones	Oct. 27, 1835	T52-R32-S31
Jas. A. Johnston	Jul. 28, 1838	T52-R32-S24
Benj. F. Jesse	Oct. 13, 1838	T52-R32-S7
Zachariah Jones	Mar. 18, 1825	T51-R32-S7
Fielding Jefferies	Dec. 15, 1830	T51-R32-S18
Marvel M. Jones	Nov. 5, 1835	T53-R31-S1
Marvel M. Jones	Dec. 16, 1835	T53-R31-S2
David James	Apr. 1, 1831	T53-R31-S23
David James	Jun. 6, 1833	T53-R31-S23
David James	Jan. 19, 1828	T53-R31-S25
James James	Feb. 9, 1828	T53-R31-S10
James James	Nov. 29, 1830	T53-R31-S23
James James	Feb. 17, 1827	T52-R31-S12
Robert Johnson	Nov. 1, 1825	T52-R31-S30
John Jones	Mar. 20, 1827	T53-R31-S26
John Jones	Oct. 12, 1827	T53-R31-S34
John Jones	Dec. 7, 1827	T53-R31-S34
James James	Nov. 27, 1821	T51-R31-S1
Ambrose Jones	Apr. 15, 1829	T53-R30-S9
John Jobe	Nov. 27, 1828	T52-R30-S29
John Jobe	May 23, 1831	T52-R30-S29
William D. King	Jul. 3, 1829	T53-R30-S32
Samuel B. King	Jul. 3, 1829	T53-R30-S29
Samuel B. King	Jan. 14, 1833	T53-R30-S31
Samuel B. King	May 13, 1829	T53-R30-S32
Samuel B. King	Oct. 30, 1832	T53-R30-S32
John Kates	Apr. 18, 1823	T51-R31-S7
Solomon Kinzey	Nov. 18, 1833	T51-R31-S13
John Kuykendall	Sep. 9, 1837	T52-R32-S25
Elizabeth Kuykendall	Jan. 15, 1836	T52-R32-S14
Abraham Kutz	Jan. 22, 1822	T52-R32-S25
Solomon Kinzey	Mar. 19, 1827	T52-R32-S34
John Kerns	May 1, 1835	T52-R31-S2
John Kerns	May 15, 1837	T52-R31-S2
John Kerns	Dec. 16, 1835	T52-R31-S3
Sewell Knight	Mar. 29, 1834	T50-R32-S7
Solomon Kitchum	Jan. 12, 1837	T50-R32-S15
Jane Kincaid	Nov. 29, 1832	T51-R32-S14
Will King	Nov. 3, 1830	T51-R32-S1
James Kuykendall	Dec. 12, 1833	T51-R32-S13
James Lansing	Mar. 31, 1836	T51-R30-S1
Aarno Hart	Jun. 15, 1836	T52-R30-S24
Jas. Laney	Jun. 30, 1827	T52-R30-S27
George Lingenfelter	Apr. 6, 1827	T52-R30-S30
James H. Long	Mar. 2, 1828	T52-R30-S9
James H. Long	Mar. 20, 1828	T52-R30-S10
William B. Lafoon	May 28, 1839	T53-R30-S17

Name	Date	Location
James Lyon	Jun. 26, 1839	T53-R30-S6
William Logan	May 26, 1829	T53-R30-S23
Stewart Lewis	Mar. 20, 1821	T53-R30-S23
Abijah Lewis	Jul. 27, 1827	T53-R30-S35
Abijah Lewis	Jul. 29, 1829	T53-R30-S36
Joseph Ledgewood	Sep. 5, 1833	T53-R30-S9
William Lainhart	Mar. 19, 1821	T51-R31-S14
John Leaky	Aug. 13, 1823	T51-R31-S10
John Leaky	Feb. 13, 1830	T51-R31-S10
John Lemon and John F. Owen	Jun. 29, 1836	T51-R31-S13
Joseph Lewis	May 21, 1835	T51-R31-S27
Geo. Lincoln	Mar. 8, 1821	T51-R31-S17
Geo. Lincoln	Aug. 3, 1839	T51-R31-S23
Geo. Lincoln	Apr. 6, 1835	T51-R31-S23
Geo. Lincoln	May 13, 1839	T51-R31-S26
Geo. Lincoln	Mar. 14, 1836	T51-R31-S34
John Lincoln	Mar. 8, 1821	T51-R31-S8
John Loveless	Sep. 9, 1839	T51-R31-S22
Abraham Lincoln	Jul. 3, 1823	T52-R31-S31
Abraham Lincoln	Mar. 29, 1822	T52-R31-S31
Geo. Lingenfelter	Mar. 17, 1827	T52-R31-S23
James Lyon	Mar. 28, 1821	T52-R31-S12
James Lyon	Mar. 20, 1827	T52-R31-S26
James Lyon	Nov. 1, 1825	T52-R31-S27
James Lyon	Jan. 27, 1825	T52-R31-S34
William Locker	Dec. 28, 1827	T53-R31-S11
William Locker	Oct. 2, 1837	T53-R31-S12
Jno. Livingston	Apr. 9, 1827	T53-R31-S15
James Lear	Dec. 8, 1830	T53-R31-S9
William Laidlaw	Jul. 5, 1838	T53-R31-S35
Isaac B. Lane	Oct. 10, 1829	T50-R32-S2
John Lincoln	Mar. 12, 1821	T50-R32-S5
Granville Linville	Aug. 18, 1834	T50-R32-S9
John Linville	Jun. 16, 1824	T50-R32-S3
John Linville	Apr. 21, 1821	T50-R32-S4
John Linville	Nov. 13, 1834	T50-R32-S21
Richard Linville	Feb. 3, 1836	T50-R32-S9
John Lowry	Jan. 18, 1836	T50-R32-S2
Jas. M. Letchworth	Sep. 17, 1835	T51-R32-S5
Leonard Ligon	Jul. 26, 1824	T51-R32-S5
Leonard Ligon	Oct. 21, 1824	T51-R32-S6
John Lincoln	Mar. 12, 1821	T51-R32-S31
Jno. Linville	Dec. 27, 1823	T51-R32-S34
John Long	Mar. 15, 1827	T51-R32-S4
John Long, jr.	Feb. 22, 1828	T51-R32-S5
Reuben Long	Nov. 24, 1829	T51-R32-S12

(Clay County, Missouri Continued)

Name	Date	Location
Reuben Long	Nov. 3, 1835	T52-R32-S32
John Long	Mar. 15, 1827	T52-R32-S33
John Long	Nov. 3, 1835	T52-R32-S32
John Long	Nov. 6, 1833	T52-R32-S32
James H. Long	May 17, 1827	T52-R32-S30
Richard T. Ligon	Sep. 12, 1835	T52-R32-S32
Thos. Liggett	Sep. 21, 1839	T52-R32-S10
Thos. Liggett	Oct. 19, 1835	T52-R32-S10
Thos. Liggett	Aug. 16, 1838	T52-R32-S10
Thos. Liggett	Dec. 28, 1833	T52-R32-S10
Thos. Liggett	Sep. 11, 1828	T52-R32-S10
Josiah Letchworth	Jan. 22, 1833	T52-R32-S32
Geo. B. Lingenfelter	Oct. 27, 1834	T54-R32-S31
William Livingston	Mar. 17, 1827	T53-R32-S24
John Livingston	Nov. 24, 1838	T53-R32-S13
William Lamine	Nov. 7, 1825	T53-R32-S24
Asa Lauter	Apr. 19, 1834	T51-R33-S35
Thomas Lauter	Feb. 22, 1825	T51-R33-S26
Thomas Lauter	Dec. 11, 1833	T51-R33-S26
William Munkers	Jun. 17, 1836	T51-R30-S6
William Munkers	Jul. 17, 1828	T51-R30-S7
Richard Munkers	Nov. 21, 1831	T51-R30-S5
Richard Munkers	Apr. 6, 1836	T51-R30-S6
Felix W. McKay and William Wilson	Jun. 7, 1839	T51-R30-S13
James McCoy	Jun. 23, 1836	T51-R30-S5
Chas. R. Morehead	Apr. 9, 1839	T52-R30-S18
Benjamin Munkers	Mar. 21, 1823	T52-R30-S28
John Morehead	Oct. 14, 1839	T52-R30-S17
John Morehead	Jun. 29, 1836	T52-R30-S18
William Moss	Mar. 9, 1829	T52-R30-S28
Hugh W. Martin	Nov. 22, 1828	T52-R30-S22
Joel L. Moore	Mar. 19, 1827	T52-R30-S10
Polly Morland	Jul. 15, 1836	T52-R30-S6
Clemens Means	Mar. 18, 1830	T52-R30-S7
Zadock Martin	Mar. 15, 1827	T52-R30-S10
Zadock Martin	May 9, 1836	T52-R30-S11
Zadock Martin	Jul. 5, 1828	T52-R30-S11
Zadock Martin	Jun. 5, 1837	T52-R30-S11
Joel P. Means	Mar. 12, 1838	T52-R30-S11
Joel P. Means	Mar. 10, 1827	T52-R30-S22
David McElwee	Mar. 5, 1821	T52-R30-S27
David McElwee	Jan. 1, 1828	T52-R30-S2
David McElwee	Sep. 13, 1831	T52-R30-S23
David McElwee	Jan. 31, 1828	T52-R30-S2
David McElwee	Sep. 8, 1831	T52-R30-S22
David McElwee	Feb. 8, 1833	T52-R30-S23

(Clay County, Missouri Continued)

Name	Date	Location
David McElwee	Jan. 31, 1828	T52-R30-S25
David McElwee	Mar. 5, 1821	T52-R30-S27
William McQueamey	Jul. 17, 1821	T52-R30-S24
James Mc Kay	Mar. 10, 1830	T52-R30-S32
Erastus McClain	Jul. 3, 1839	T52-R30-S21
David McKee	Jun. 13, 1836	T52-R30-S13
David McKee	Sep. 23, 1835	T52-R30-S1
James McGuire	Nov. 29, 1833	T52-R30-S23
McCasland McCullough	Apr. 2, 1839	T52-R30-S11
James McCrorey	Jun. 20, 1832	T52-R30-S4
George McCorkle	Nov. 20, 1839	T52-R30-S11
Robert McCorkle	May 31, 1836	T52-R30-S12
Robert McCorkle	Apr. 23, 1836	T52-R30-S1
John McCorkle	Feb. 23, 1833	T52-R30-S22
John McCorkle	Oct. 6, 1834	T52-R30-S1
John McCorkle	Jan. 23, 1833	T52-R30-S2
John McCorkle	Nov. 23, 1831	T52-R30-S2
Archibald McCorkle	Jan. 4, 1836	T52-R30-S21
Archibald McCorkle	Jun. 7, 1836	T52-R30-S21
William Miller	Oct. 8, 1825	T53-R30-S20
David McElwee	Jan. 1, 1828	T53-R30-S35
Hetty McIlvain	Oct. 17, 1827	T53-R30-S18
John McTaggart	Aug. 10, 1836	T53-R30-S34
John McTaggart	May 8, 1837	T53-R30-S34
Doug McGinnis	Dec. 8, 1830	T53-R30-S19
Archibald McIlvain	Feb. 18, 1830	T53-R30-S17
Archibald McIlvain	Jun. 20, 1829	T53-R30-S17
Archibald McIlvain	Jan. 20, 1829	T53-R30-S8
Archiblad McIlvain	Apr. 6, 1829	T53-R30-S17
Archibald McIlvain	Oct. 30, 1828	T53-R30-S17
Archibald McIlvain	Nov. 1, 1828	T53-R30-S17
Nancy McIlvain	Apr. 11, 1828	T53-R30-S18
Thomas Malot	Feb. 5, 1836	T53-R30-S35
Thomas Malot	Feb. 3, 1836	T53-R30-S35
Elisha Majors	Nov. 20, 1837	T53-R30-S15
Elisha Majors	Sep. 24, 1835	T53-R30-S11
Jacob McKay	Jul. 26, 1825	T51-R31-S1
David McElwee	Oct. 30, 1828	T51-R31-S9
Thos. Mayo	May 20, 1822	T51-R31-S18
Charles McGee	Mar. 27, 1821	T51-R31-S7
Abner McKeen	Jan. 12, 1825	T51-R31-S15
Nathaniel McKeen	Jan. 8, 1825	T51-R31-S15
Elijah McCrary	Apr. 14, 1828	T51-R31-S11
Elijah McCrary	Aug. 24, 1832	T51-R31-S11
Robert McCoy	Sep. 11, 1823	T51-R31-S12
Lemuel Moore	Sep. 23, 1837	T51-R31-S15
Archibald Moss	Feb. 20, 1832	T51-R31-S11

(Clay County, Missouri Continued)

Name	Date	Location
Robert Moss	Jan. 8, 1836	T51-R31-S11
Archibald Moss	Feb. 8, 1833	T51-R31-S12
Edmund Munday	May 3, 1830	T51-R31-S14
Richard Munkers	Nov. 27, 1821	T51-R31-SI
William Munkers	Jun. 25, 1832	T51-R31-S12
William Munkers	Jun. 23, 1836	T51-R31-S12
Richard Munkers	Feb. 27, 1837	T52-R31-S12
Strother N. McGinnis	Apr. 10, 1837	T52-R31-S27
Samuel McCorkle	Feb. 4, 1825	T52-R31-S24
John McCorkle, jr.	Nov. 21, 1831	T52-R31-S24
William McAfee	Mar. 19, 1827	T52-R31-S10
Redmund Munkers	Feb. 10, 1836	T52-R31-S12
Redmund Munkers	Jan. 6, 1832	T52-R31-S13
William Moss	Mar. 17, 1827	T52-R31-S35
Wade Mosby	Mar. 16, 1827	T52-R31-S23
Joseph Moroney	Jan. 2, 1832	T52-R31-S8
Silas Moreland	May 4, 1835	T52-R31-S1
John H. Morehead	Aug. 8, 1836	T52-R31-S13
William Minter	Dec. 1, 1838	T52-R31-S21
John McQuaddy	Mar. 17, 1827	T52-R31-S10
John McQuaddy	Nov. 5, 1827	T52-R31-S9
William Miller	Mar. 23, 1827	T52-R31-S23
William Miller	Jul. 19, 1832	T52-R31-S23
William Miller	Nov. 4, 1825	T52-R31-S23
Samuel Marksbury	Dec. 5, 1836	T53-R31-S14
Samuel Marksbury	Nov. 26, 1835	T53-R31-S14
Tobias Miller	Dec. 30, 1829	T53-R31-S4
Tobias Miller	Sep. 12, 1832	T53-R31-S25
Abijah Means	Apr. 9, 1827	T53-R31-S17
William Martin	Aug. 26, 1834	T53-R31-S35
Moses Miller	Jul. 26, 1833	T53-R31-S3
Moses Miller	Dec. 1, 1832	T53-R31-S8
Moses Miller	Dec. 5, 1829	T53-R31-S3
Moses Miller	Nov. 3, 1828	T53-R31-S3
Greenfield Mathews	Oct. 15, 1833	T53-R31-S6
Taylor McCuly	Nov. 6, 1828	T53-R31-S11
James R. McGinness	Sep. 24, 1839	T53-R31-S18
James Marsh	Feb. 6, 1832	T53-R31-S30
James Marsh	Jul. 5, 1831	T53-R31-S31
James Marsh	Jan. 1, 1836	T53-R31-S31
James Marsh	Dec. 5, 1833	T53-R31-S31
James Marsh	Jul. 1, 1836	T53-R31-S31
Wm. H. McIlvain	Mar. 5, 1828	T53-R31-S12
John S. Major	Sep. 30, 1839	T53-R31-S34
John S. Major	Oct. 7, 1839	T53-R31-S33
Jesse Mundy	Mar. 5, 1836	T50-R32-S2
John McDaniel	Apr. 20, 1838	T50-R32-S9

(Clay County, Missouri Continued)

Name	Date	Location
David P. McGuire	Nov. 28, 1835	T50-R32-S8
David Magill	Nov. 28, 1835	T50-R32-S17
Benj. Munkress	Mar. 10, 1835	T50-R32-S23
Jesse Mundy	Mar. 5, 1836	T50-R32-S2
William Maids	Jun. 17, 1836	T50-R32-S2
William Monroe	Mar. 12, 1821	T51-R32-S2
William Monroe	Sep. 18, 1822	T51-R51-R32
John Meek	Jan. 22, 1833	T51-R32-S7
John Meek	Jun. 2, 1835	T51-R32-S8
Andrew Means	Jan. 15, 1822	T51-R32-S12
Jas. Mason	Sep. 8, 1824	T51-R32-S8
Zadock Martin	Jan. 26, 1825	T51-R32-S9
Zadock Martin	Sep. 10, 1823	T51-R32-S9
Zadock Martin	Dec. 3, 1835	T51-R32-S9
Jos. Martin	Jan. 4, 1830	T51-R32-S17
Jos. Martin	Feb. 18, 1825	T51-R32-S17
David Manchester	Feb. 9, 1828	T51-R32-S4
David Manchester	Aug. 12, 1822	T51-R32-S9
David Manchester	Mar. 4, 1830	T51-R32-S9
Jos. Malott	Nov. 24, 1829	T51-R32-S33
Jos. Malott	Jul. 31, 1833	T51-R32-S35
Jno. S. Malott	Mar. 12, 1821	T51-R32-S31
Jno. S. Malott	Feb. 23, 1829	T51-R32-S32
Wm. Males	Feb. 27, 1837	T51-R32-S35
Henry Males	Oct. 23, 1830	T51-R32-S33
Jno. McWilliams	Nov. 5, 1825	T51-R32-S28
Jas. H. McWilliams	Jun. 26, 1832	T51-R32-S14
Benj. McQuaddy	Dec. 1, 1824	T51-R32-S11
Jno. McKissick	Jun. 25, 1828	T51-R32-S20
Jno. McDaniel	Jul. 14, 1823	T51-R32-S6
James McDaniel	Nov. 4, 1824	T51-R32-S6
Alex McCorkle	Feb. 7, 1829	T51-R32-S3
Wm. Monroe	Jul. 20, 1821	T51-R32-S3
Wm. Monroe	Mar. 12, 1821	T51-R32-S11
Wm. Monroe	Mar. 19, 1821	T51-R32-S13
William Mothershead	Nov. 28, 1837	T52-R32-S6
Ransom P. Mahany	Feb. 8, 1837	T52-R32-S24
John Mathews	Sep. 23, 1836	T52-R32-S3
Jos. McConnell	Mar. 11, 1828	T52-R32-S23
Jos. McConnell	Nov. 8, 1832	T52-R32-S23
James McDaniel	Sep. 19, 1833	T52-R32-S31
James McDaniel and Clayton Tillery	Apr. 25, 1828	T52-R32-S31
James McDaniel	Mar. 14, 1836	T52-R32-S31
George McElwee	Dec. 9, 1835	T52-R32-S22
John McGee	Apr. 13, 1825	T52-R32-S28
Zachariah McGill	Apr. 10. 1827	T52-R32-S14

(Clay County, Missouri Continued)

Name	Date	Location
Zachariah McGill	Nov. 25, 1833	T52-R32-S12
Caleb Magill	Oct. 19, 1827	T52-R32-S29
David Magill	Mar. 12, 1821	T52-R32-S29
Samuel Magill	Mar. 12, 1821	T52-R32-S33
Sarah Musick	Mar. 31, 1835	T53-R32-S8
Sarah Musick	Nov. 15, 1827	T53-R32-S29
Sarah Musick	Dec. 18, 1833	T53-R32-S21
Sarah Musick	Mar. 15, 1827	T53-R32-S28
James Moore	Jul. 7, 1837	T53-R32-S6
Thos. J. Marsh	Dec. 16, 1837	T53-R32-S36
James Marsh	Feb. 1, 1836	T53-R32-S36
James Marsh	Dec. 16, 1837	T53-R32-S36
James Marsh	Jun. 10, 1837	T53-R32-S25
Jas. McKown	Mar. 17, 1827	T53-R32-S23
Jas. R. McGinness	Nov. 1, 1839	T53-R32-S24
Zachariah McGee	Mar. 5, 1833	T53-R32-S3
Prosper Massee	Feb. 26, 1838	T50-R33-S23
Collin Manterdeau	Oct. 31, 1836	T50-R33-S22
William Malott	Sep. 5, 1831	T50-R33-S1
William Malott	Aug. 17, 1833	T50-R33-S1
Jos. K. McWilliams	Nov. 16, 1825	T50-R33-S2
Jos. K. McWilliams	Aug. 6, 1835	T50-R33-S3
Jos. K. McWilliams	Jan. 29, 1836	T50-R33-S11
John McKissack	Sep. 17, 1831	T50-R33-S14
Isaac McCoy	Oct. 21, 1836	T50-R33-S27
John Moseley	Nov. 7, 1825	T51-R33-S2
Hyr--- Mainwaring	Jul. 18, 1828	T51-R33-S15
Bennet Morgan	May 14, 1831	T51-R33-S15
Jas. N. McWilliams	Mar. 18, 1834	T51-R33-S35
John McKissick	Sep. 3, 1821	T51-R33-S36
John McDaniel	Nov. 1, 1829	T51-R33-S1
John McDaniel	Feb. 15, 1836	T51-R33-S1
Jas. McDaniel	Jan. 15, 1830	T51-R33-S1
Jas. McDaniel	Mar. 17, 1827	T52-R33-S36
David McDaniel	Jul. 1, 1823	T52-R33-S36
Nathaniel Mothershead	Aug. 27, 1832	T52-R33-S1
David L. Magill	Jun. 18, 1835	T52-R33-S35
John Morrison	Sep. 24, 1832	T52-R33-S1
Samuel McGee	Nov. 24, 1828	T52-R33-S14
Chas. McGee	Mar. 29, 1827	T53-R33-S12
Chas. McGee	Dec, 23, 1833	T53-R33-S13
David McElwee	Aug. 13, 1828	T53-R33-S11
Peyton Nowlen	Mar. 19, 1827	T51-R31-S4
Richard Neill	Feb. 1, 1822	T51-R31-S9
Henry Neill	May 14, 1828	T51-R31-S6
Richard A. Neely	Mar. 15, 1836	T51-R31-S12
James Newberry	Dec. 13, 1834	T50-R32-S2

(Clay County, Missouri Continued)

Name	Date	Location
Wm. Nash	Dec. 23, 1835	T51-R32-S32
Jas. Nickel	Jul. 31, 1824	T51-R32-S13
Saunders Norman	Mar. 29, 1827	T51-R32-S22
Aaron Overton	Aug. 28, 1828	T51-R30-S18
David Osborn	Jul. 1, 1829	T51-R30-S14
David Osborn	Oct. 29, 1838	T51-R30-S2
Adam Overton	Mar. 29, 1828	T52-R30-S32
Job Odell	Oct. 18, 1833	T52-R30-S26
Thomas Officer	Mar. 5, 1821	T52-R30-S35
Nehemiah Odell	Feb. 5, 1836	T52-R30-S25
Nehemiah Odell	Sep. 29, 1836	T52-R30-S24
Robert Officer	Mar. 5, 1821	T52-R30-S35
James Officer	May 30, 1825	T52-R30-S10
Aaron Overton	Aug. 31, 1839	T51-R31-S26
John Owens	Mar. 8, 1821	T51-R31-S7
John S. Owens	Jun. 29, 1836	T51-R31-S24
Robert Officer	Nov. 24, 1834	T54-R31-S33
Robert Officer	Dec. 18, 1835	T54-R31-S32
Robert Officer	Aug. 1, 1834	T54-R31-S33
Robert Officer	Aug. 12, 1839	T54-R32-S32
William Oldacre	Mar. 7, 1838	T53-R31-S23
John Oldacre	Nov. 18, 1839	T53-R31-S14
Wm. Osburn	Oct. 24, 1825	T51-R32-S14
Wm. Osburn	Oct. 27, 1829	T51-R32-S15
Nicholas Owens	Apr. 1, 1831	T54-R33-S34
Robert C. Owens	Jun. 4, 1836	T53-R33-S22
Robert C. Owens	Apr. 6, 1839	T53-R33-S23
Nicholas C. Owens	May 1, 1838	T53-R33-S36
John M. Owens	Mar. 15, 1827	T53-R33-S10
John M. Owens	May 3, 1831	T53-R33-S10
John M. Owens	Mar. 15, 1827	T53-R33-S10
John M. Owens	Oct. 26, 1829	T53-R33-S10
John M. Owens	Mar. 14, 1831	T53-R33-S10
John M. Owens	Apr. 9, 1832	T53-R33-S15
Jeremiah Purdom	Apr. 1, 1839	T51-R30-S3
Thomas Pebley	Mar. 19, 1827	T51-R30-S6
Thomas Pebley	Mar. 5, 1821	T51-R30-S6
Wm. W. Price	Dec. 20, 1835	T52-R30-S25
Wm. W. Price	Nov. 21, 1834	T52-R30-S26
Winfrey E. Price	Mar. 27, 1837	T52-R30-S14
Winfrey E. Price	Jul. 18, 1839	T52-R30-S17
Napoleon S. and Wm. E. Price	Nov. 17, 1825	T52-R30-S15
Adam Pence	Jul. 12, 1830	T52-R30-S13
James F. Posey	Oct. 16, 1832	T52-R30-S11
John Potter	Nov. 13, 1837	T54-R30-S32
Allen Parks	May 15, 1837	T54-R30-S31

(Clay County, Missouri Continued)

Name	Date	Location
Samuel Parrott	Feb. 24, 1836	T54-R30-S34
Samuel Parrott	Nov. 14, 1835	T54-R30-S34
Dennis J. Parsons	Dec. 23, 1835	T53-R30-S34
Dennis. J. Parsons	Nov. 30, 1835	T53-R30-S34
Milton Payne	Apr. 30, 1839	T53-R30-S4
Adam Pence	Apr. 9, 1828	T53-R30-S30
Adam Pence, jr.	Feb. 2, 1835	T53-R30-S31
Jeremiah Pryor	Mar. 26, 1828	T53-R30-S21
Jeremiah Pryor	Jan. 10, 1828	T53-R30-S21
Jeremiah Pryor	Sep. 27, 1827	T53-R30-S21
John R. Peters	Feb. 15, 1830	T51-R31-S30
Andrew K. Poage	Feb. 15, 1833	T51-R31-S21
Wm. Perry	Mar. 17, 1827	T51-R31-S11
Geo. M. Pryor	May 26, 1836	T51-R31-S15
Geo. M. Pryor	Feb. 23, 1836	T51-R31-S21
Nelson Pullen	Apr. 3, 1829	T51-R31-S11
Milton O. Pulliam	Jun. 13, 1836	T51-R31-S22
Eldridge Potter	Nov. 19, 1831	T52-R31-S17
Eldridge Potter	Mar. 19, 1827	T52-R31-S17
Ira Peters	Jul. 26, 1837	T52-R31-S18
Ira Peters	Mar. 16, 1828	T52-R31-S7
Ira Peters	Jul. 2, 1838	T52-R31-S7
Charles J. Palmer	Jul. 31, 1835	T53-R31-S23
Charles J. Palmer	Nov. 24, 1838	T53-R31-S23
Adam Pence	Dec. 5, 1834	T53-R31-S36
Adam Pence	Nov. 2, 1835	T53-R31-S36
Andrew Pence	Apr. 9, 1828	T53-R31-S25
Jos. Pfisterer	Apr. 9, 1828	T53-R31-S33
Samuel Poteat	Jul. 25, 1833	T53-R31-S6
Peter Pelow	Jul. 6, 1833	T50-R32-S2
Nelson Potter	Feb. 19, 1825	T51-R32-S20
Robert Poage	Jan. 1, 1824	T51-R32-S12
Robert Poage	Mar. 12, 1821	T51-R32-S12
Robert Pence	Mar. 15, 1827	T51-R32-S23
Richard H. Pence	Jun. 2, 1824	T51-R32-S4
John T. Pence	Dec. 15, 1824	T51-R32-S11
John T. Pence	Mar. 19, 1836	T51-R32-S22
Eveline and Julianna Pence	Jan. 2, 1824	T51-R32-S10
Clarrisa and Emily E. Pence	Jun. 2, 1824	T51-R32-S10
Adam Pence, jr.	Mar. 16, 1827	T51-R32-S22
Adam Pence, sr.	Feb. 8, 1828	T51-R32-S15
Adam Pence, sr.	Nov. 25, 1825	T51-R32-S23
Hanah Pebley	Apr. 6, 1821	T51-R32-S15
Jas. Poteet	Jul. 3, 1834	T52-R32-S24
Jas. Poteet	Feb. 7, 1829	T52-R32-S24
A. H. F. Payne	Aug. 11, 1838	T52-R32-S2

Name	Date	Location
Jno. R. Peters	Apr. 15, 1829	T52-R32-S13
Jno. R. Peters	Feb. 20, 1828	T52-R32-S13
William Peters	Jan. 3, 1828	T52-R32-S36
Andrew M. Poague	Apr. 16, 1823	T52-R32-S35
Andrew M. Poague	Mar. 12, 1821	T52-R32-S35
Augustus H. F. Payne	Jun. 6, 1836	T53-R32-S36
Augustus H. F. Payne	Aug. 3, 1838	T53-R32-S35
Evan J. Park	Jan. 30, 1832	T53-R32-S9
Hamilton Pollard	Jun. 25, 1839	T50-R33-S12
Barruck Prather	Mar. 1, 1836	T50-R33-S12
Roswell Pindle	Oct. 21, 1835	T50-R33-S11
David Rupe, jr.	Feb. 15, 1836	T53-R33-S34
Sophia Rollins	Jun. 6, 1831	T53-R33-S12
Lee Rollins	Dec. 4, 1830	T53-R33-S12
Lee Rollins	Oct. 19, 1835	T53-R33-S13
Samuel Riggs	Sep. 20, 1825	T53-R33-S35
John Rupe	Aug. 6, 1822	T52-R33-S3
Wm. Rickman	Aug. 11, 1835	T51-R33-S15
Andrew Russel	Mar. 27, 1821	T50-R33-S1
Daniel Reed	Mar. 3, 1836	T53-R32-S6
Benj. W. Riley	Oct. 28, 1834	T53-R32-S25
H. M. Riley	Nov. 21, 1836	T53-R32-S24
H. M. Riley	Jan. 9, 1834	T53-R32-S24
H. M. Riley	Oct. 19, 1824	T53-R32-S25
Lee Rollins	May 5, 1834	T53-R32-S7
Sophia Rollins	Sep. 14, 1832	T53-R32-S6
Sophia Rollins	Feb. 17, 1838	T53-R32-S7
Louis C. Ramey	Sep. 3, 1838	T52-R32-S17
Allen G. Reed	Jan. 23, 1837	T52-R32-S28
Jno. W. Reynolds	Aug. 2, 1839	T52-R32-S12
Jno. W. Reynolds	Oct. 21, 1835	T52-R32-S12
Jno. W. Reynolds	Oct. 15, 1836	T52-R32-S12
Jno. W. Reynolds	Mar. 18, 1835	T52-r32-S12
Jno. W. Reynolds	Jan. 2, 1838	T52-R32-S12
Wilson Roberts	Dec. 16, 1833	T52-R32-S3
Obijah Roberts	Oct. 9, 1833	T52-R32-S2
Obijah Roberts	Jan. 10, 1829	T52-R32-S3·
Arnot Roberts	Jan. 10, 1829	T52-R32-S2
Arnot Roberts	Apr. 11, 1834	T52-R32-S3
James Roberts	Nov. 25, 1831	T52-R32-S2
James Roberts	Dec. 31, 1833	T52-R32-S3
Wm. Rui	Dec. 17, 1824	T51-R32-S1
Peter Rogers	Aug. 1, 1835	T51-R32-S33
William Rollins	Dec. 7, 1833	T51-R32-S4
Danl. Robinson	Dec. 8, 1824	T51-R32-S13
Aaron Roberts	Feb. 27, 1828	T51-R32-S33
Andrew Robertson, sr.	Mar. 12, 1821	T51-R32-S24

Name	Date	Location
Jonathan Reed	May 3, 1825	T51-R32-S8
Henry Renick	Jan. 24, 1828	T51-R32-S8
Joseph Roberts	Nov. 21, 1837	T50-R32-S8
Moses Roberts	May 16, 1834	T50-R32-S9˙
Moses Roberts	Sep. 24, 1832	T50-R32-S9
Saml. Roberts	Oct. 19, 1837	T50-R32-S8
Saml. Roberts	Dec. 16, 1837	T50-R32-S8
Jesse Richards	Dec. 29, 1823	T50-R32-S17
Benj. Ricketts	Nov. 14, 1831	T50-R32-S7
Aaron Roberts	Oct. 19, 1837	T50-R32-S8
Aaron Roberts	May 16, 1834	T50-R32-S8
Aaron Roberts	Mar. 31, 1835	T50-R32-S8
Aaron Roberts	May 17, 1831	T50-R32-S17
William O. Russel	Oct. 5, 1839	T53-R31-S25
William Rose	Jul. 16, 1834	T53-R31-S10
William Riley	Jun. 8, 1839	T53-R31-S20
James M. Riley	Nov. 20, 1829	T53-R31-S13
James T. Riley	Oct. 28, 1828	T53-R31-S20
James T. Riley	Apr. 15, 1829	T53-R31-S17
James T. Riley	Feb. 15, 1836	T53-R31-S20
Robert T. Ready	Jul. 16, 1834	T53-R31-S9
Benj. R. Riley	Nov. 24, 1836	T53-R31-S11
Alfred M. Riley	Nov. 17, 1828	T53-R31-S21
Benj. W. Riley	Apr. 6, 1831	T53-R31-S12
Benj. W. Riley	Nov. 10. 1834	T53-R31-S12
Benj. W. Riley	Oct. 29, 1835	T53-R31-S12
Alfred M. Riley	Nov. 19, 1839	T53-R31-S28
Alfred M. Riley	Dec. 10, 1836	T53-R31-S28
Alfred M. Riley	Apr. 24, 1839	T53-R31-S21
Alfred M. Riley	Aug. 2, 1836	T53-R31-S21
Alfred M. Riley	Jul. 31, 1839	T53-R31-S21
Samuel Riggs	Apr. 19, 1828	T54-R31-S36
Samuel Riggs	Aug. 26, 1828	T54-R31-S36
Samuel Ringo	Mar. 17, 1827	T52-R31-S9
Andrew Robertson, jr.	Jun. 20, 1832	T52-R31-S28
Samuel Ringo, jr.	Mar. 18, 1825	T52-R31-S9
Samuel Ringo, jr.	Mar. 5, 1825	T52-R31-S9
Amos Riley	Sep. 29, 1824	T52-R31-S36
Amos Riley	Jan. 17, 1825	T52-R31-S36
Andrew Robertson	Oct. 12, 1822	T52-R31-S20
Andrew Robertson	Mar. 16, 1827	T52-R31-S20
Andrew Robertson	Nov. 9, 1821	T52-R31-S20
Andrew Robertson	Sep. 23, 1825	T52-R31-S21
Andrew Robertson	May 20, 1835	T52-R31-S28
Andrew Robertson	Jun. 18, 1828	T52-R31-S29
William Rice	Apr. 4, 1839	T52-R31-S4
William Rice	Dec. 2, 1836	T52-R31-S4

(Clay County, Missouri Continued)

Name	Date	Location
William Rice	Dec. 17, 1834	T52-R31-S32
William Rice	Nov. 21, 1824	T52-R31-S29
William Rice	Nov. 11, 1834	T52-R31-S29
Samuel and Andrew H. Ringo	Dec. 20, 1834	T52-R31-S6
Jno. H. Richie	Mar. 18, 1824	T51-R31-S11
William Reed	Jan. 8, 1825	T51-R31-S15
Saml. Riggs	Jan. 26, 1825	T51-R31-S2
William W. Reynolds	Feb. 11, 1836	T51-R31-S34
John D. Richie	Jan. 18, 1836	T51-R31-S14
John D. Richie	Jan. 29, 1836	T51-R31-S14
Jeremiah Rose	Mar. 15, 1827	T51-R31-S1
Jeremiah Rose	Sep. 15, 1823	T51-R31-S2
Joseph Reed	Nov. 20, 1835	T51-R31-S13
Jesse Richards	Oct. 7, 1824	T51-R31-S29
Andrew Robertson	Mar. 8, 1821	T51-R31-S17
Joshua Reed	Jan. 7, 1836	T51=R31=S14
Jas. Reynolds	Mar. 11, 1836	T51-R31-S15
Jas. Reynolds	Nov. 13, 1832	T51-R31-S22
Levi W. Reynolds	May 30, 1836	T51-R31-S34
Lloyd Rockhold	Aug. 28, 1829	T53-R30-S24
James Reed, jr.	Dec. 14, 1836	T53-R30-S5
William Roper	Jul. 21, 1839	T53-R30-S4
William Roper	Nov. 14, 1831	T53-R30-S9
Nicholas Roberts, jr.	Jan. 5, 1836	T53-R30-S13
Nicholas Roberts, jr.	Jan. 31, 1834	T53-R30-S14
Benj. W. Riley	May 9, 1835	T53-R30-S7
Leonard N. Renict	Nov. 4, 1834	T53-R30-S9
Henry Renick, jr.	Jun. 18, 1828	T53-R30-S32
Henry Renick, jr.	Jul. 1, 1828	T53-R30-S32
James Reed, jr.	Jan. 21, 1837	T54-R30-S31
James Reed, jr.	Mar. 27, 1837	T54-R30-S33
Samuel Robertson	Jan. 1, 1836	T52-R30-S25
Lawrence Robertson	Feb. 14, 1837	T52-R30-S36
Nicholas Roberts, jr.	Mar. 25, 1830	T52-R30-S3
Ezekiel Roberts	Jun. 21, 1836	T52-R30-S3
David Rigg	Feb. 29, 1836	T52-R30-S21
David Riggs	Feb. 5, 1838	T52-R30-S21
David Riggs	Feb. 29, 1836	T52-R30-S22
Nicholas Roberts	Jan. 17, 1833	T51-R30-S5
John S. Strode	Sep. 1, 1836	T53-R33-S25
Thorton Strother	Mar. 16, 1827	T53-R33-S24
Christopher Searcy	Apr. 15, 1839	T53-R33-S3
Doctor Smith	Jul. 22, 1833	T53-R33-S13
Thorton Strother	Mar. 16, 1827	T53-R33-S10
George Smith	Aug. 3, 1832	T53-R33-S27
George Smith	Aug. 8, 1836	T53-R33-S23
Josiah Shaffer	Mar. 3, 1835	T53-R33-S14

(Clay County, Missouri Continued)

Name	Date	Location
George and Calvin Smith	Sep. 3, 1832	T53-R33-S14
George and Calvin Smith	Feb. 6, 1832	T53=R33-S15
Stephen Strode	Jun. 3, 1837	T53-R33-S24
Stephen Strode	Oct. 18, 1839	T53-R33-S25
Stephen Strode	Nov. 7, 1832	T53-R33-S25
Josiah Shaffer	Mar. 3, 1835	T53-R33-S14
Louis Shelton	Mar. 15, 1827	T53-R33-S12
George Smith	Aug. 3, 1832	T53-R33-S27
George Smith	Aug. 8, 1836	T53-R33-S23
John S. Strode	Sep. 1, 1837	T53=R33=S25
John Shaw	Aug. 9, 1828	T53-R33-S35
John Shaw	Jul. 2, 1838	T53-R33-S35
John Shaw	Aug. 27, 1828	T53-R33-S35
Humphrey Smith	Jun. 5, 1822	T53-R33-S23
Humphrey Smith	Sep. 28, 1825	T53-R33-S26
Calvin Smith	Aug. 14, 1835	T53-R33-S15
Calvin Smith	Feb. 3, 1836	T53-R33-S27
Calvin Smith	Jun. 14, 1836	T53-R33-S22
William Smith	Oct. 8, 1838	T52-R33-S1
William Smith	Aug. 19, 1831	T52-R33-S12
William Smith	Dec. 15, 1834	T52-R33-S13
Henderson Searcy	Nov. 7, 1825	T51-R33-S1
Jonas Sutton	Aug. 17, 1824	T51-R33-S35
Ambrose Scott	Sep. 16, 1834	T51-R33-S35
Strashley Searcy	Nov. 7, 1825	T51-R33-S2
Stephen Strode	Nov. 17, 1832	T53-R32-S19
Stephen Strode	Nov. 17, 1832	T53-R32-S30
John Simms	May 2, 1838	T53-R32-S35
Rowland Stark	Oct. 19, 1835	T53-R32-S32
John S. Strode	Apr. 11, 1834	T53-R32-S8
John S. Strode	Oct. 13, 1834	T53-R32-S30
Daniel Shackleford	Feb. 8, 1836	T52-R32-S18
William Smith	Jun. 20, 1832	T52-R32-S7
William Smith	Oct. 13, 1838	T52-R32-S7
Benj. A. Simms	Apr. 28, 1838	T52-R32-S1
William Stephenson	Oct. 2, 1830	T52-R32-S21
William Stephenson	Jan. 3, 1828	T52-R32-S22
George Springer	Mar. 19, 1827	T52-R32-S25
Willis Sheaver	Apr. 10, 1827	T52-R32-S26
Clark Stephens	Oct. 25, 1827	T52-R32-S33
Clark Stephens	Sep. 26, 1823	T52-R32-S33
John Simms	Dec. 18, 1837	T52-R32-S11
Harvey Springer	Jun. 3, 1833	T52-R32-S23
Jos. S. Simms	Jan. 11, 1836	T52-R32-S1
Jos. S. Simms	Jan. 30, 1838	T52-R32-S2
George Springer	Mar. 19, 1827	T52-R32-S25
Jno. H. Simms	Dec. 19, 1833	T52-R32-S2

(Clay County, Missouri Continued)

Name	Date	Location
Jno. H. Simms	Feb. 16, 1828	T52-R32-S2
Jonas Sutton	Mar. 14, 1828	T51-R32-S21
Jonas Sutton	Sep. 6, 1828	T51-R32-S21
Noah St. John	Feb. 16, 1836	T51-R32-S9
Uzziel Stevens	Feb. 28, 1834	T51-R32-S20
John Sutton	Mar. 21, 1827	T51-R32-S7
Benj. Sampson	Mar. 12, 1821	T51-R32-S30
Jacob Smith	Oct. 26, 1835	T51-R32-S7
John Smith	Oct. 1, 1832	T51-R32-S28
John Smith	Aug. 19, 1823	T51-R32-S29
Solomon Sethrow	Mar. 15, 1825	T50-R32-S8
Francis Sisson	Jun. 16, 1836	T50-R32-S10
Elisha Sollers	Jul. 22, 1833	T50-R32-S10
Joseph Sexton	Oct. 6, 1832	T50-R32-S7
Joseph Sexton	Nov. 18, 1833	T50-R32-S7
Noah Snell	May 4, 1839	T50-R32-S12
Noah Snell	Jun. 7, 1837	T50-R32-S12
Noah Snell	Jul. 2, 1838	T50-R32-S12
Jordan Stribling	Apr. 29, 1835	T53-R31-S32
William C. Shaw	Oct. 5, 1835	T53-R31-S2
Jno. D. Stothart	Mar. 29, 1837	T53-R31-S1
James Shackelford	Jun, 25, 1832	T53-R31-S3
James Shackelford	Aug. 8, 1839	T53-R31-S3
James Shackelford	Nov. 6, 1830	T53-R31-S10
Benj. Soper	Nov. 18, 1830	T53-R31-S28
Benj. Soper	May 5, 1837	T53-R31-S33
Benj. Soper	Jul. 5, 1838	T53-R31-S28
Ryland Shackelford	Sep. 21, 1835	T54-R31-S33
Ryland Shackelford	Nov. 29, 1830	T54-R34-S34
Ryland Shackelford	Dec. 18, 1835	T54-R31-S33
Henry Stone	Dec, 19, 1833	T52-R31-S4
Henry Stone	Mar. 19, 1827	T52-R31-S5
Jacob Strollings	Mar. 15, 1827	T52-R31-S22
Samuel Sweet	Dec. 3, 1834	T52-R31-S36
William Stribling	Nov. 16, 1835	T52-R31-S8
Jesse Stollings	Apr. 28, 1831	T52-R31-S28
Jesse Stollings	Mar. 26, 1827	T52-R31-S33
Jesse Stollings	Dec. 16, 1835	T52-R31-S27
Jesse Stollings	Nov. 3, 1834	T52-R31-S21
Jesse Stollings	Oct. 13, 1829	T52-R31-S27
Jesse Stollings	Jul. 22, 1835	T52-R31-S27
Lewis Scott	Nov. 5, 1830	T52-R31-S32
Richard Simms	Jun. 1, 1831	T52-R31-S6
Richard Simms	Dec. 21, 1829	T52-R31-S6
Richard Simms	Jan. 11, 1836	T52-R31-S6
William and Hugh Shaw	Jan. 27, 1832	T52-R31-S8
John Smith	Nov. 5, 1825	T52-R31-S30

Name	Date	Location
Lewis Scott	Nov. 5, 1830	T52-R31-S32
Washington Shaver	Jul. 17, 1835	T52-R31-S19
William Shaw	Dec. 20, 1828	T52-R31-S8
John W. Simms	Jan. 3, 1838	T52-R31-S18
Richard Simms	Jun. 1, 1831	T52-R31-S6
Richard Simms	Jan. 11, 1836	T52-R31-S6
Richard Simms	Dec. 21, 1829	T52-R31-S6
Roland Stark	Jul. 10, 1828	T51-R31-S12
Smith Story	Mar. 20, 1827	T51-R31-S1
William L. Smith	Apr. 16, 1822	T51-R31-S6
William L. Smith	May 3, 1822	T51-R31-S6
William L. Smith	Mar. 8, 1821	T51-R31-S20
John D. Stothart	Aug. 3, 1836	T51-R31-S13
John D. Stothart	Apr. 5, 1839	T51-R31-S22
Newman Stone	Nov. 5, 1827	T51-R30-S30
John Stephenson	Mar. 20, 1827	T53-R30-S17
John Stephenson	Jul. 9, 1827	T53-R30-S20
Vincent Smith	Jun. 29, 1829	T53-R30-S14
Rankin C. Schoolfield	Jun. 27, 1835	T53-R30-S31
William H. Shelton	May 22, 1824	T53-R30-S28
Francis T. Slaughter	Mar. 16, 1829	T53-R30-S26
Newman Stone	Nov. 5, 1827	T53-R30-S30
John Stephenson	Mar. 20, 1827	T53-R30-S17
John Stephenson	Jul. 9, 1827	T53-R30-S20
John Smith	Jun. 24, 1829	T53-R30-S14
John Smith	Jun. 30, 1835	T53-R30-S14
Alex W. Scoggins	Jun. 10, 1837	T53-R30-S3
Anderson Smith	Mar. 19, 1827	T54-R30-S31
Edward Smith	May 9, 1829	T54-R30-S32
Levi Stephenson	Apr. 11, 1839	T54-R30-S33
John Storey	May 2, 1834	T52-R30-S9
John Storey	Feb. 16, 1830	T52-R30-S9
Chas. G. Singleton	Aug. 16, 1837	T52-R30-S14
Nancy Singleton	Aug. 16, 1837	T52-R30-S12
Nancy Singleton	Jan. 9, 1836	T52-R30-S14
Nancy Singleton	Mar. 17, 1837	T52-R30-S14
John D. Stothart	Apr. 5, 1839	T52-R30-S27
John D. Stothart	Aug. 12, 1836	T52-R30-S32
Alexander Sloan	Apr. 19, 1834	T52-R30-S9
Nathan Stewart	Oct. 30, 1835	T52-R30-S29
Bluford Stanton	Jul. 10, 1828	T52-R30-S20
Robert Snodgrass	May 28, 1836	T52-R30-S13
Robert Smith	Oct. 28, 1835	T52-R30-S24
William K. Sloan	Feb. 1, 1837	T52-R30-S21
William K. Sloan	Apr. 4, 1834	T52-R30-S21
Jesse Slaughter	Mar. 22, 1827	T52-R30-S15
Thomas Slaughter	Mar. 22, 1827	T52-R30-S2

(Clay County, Missouri Continued)

Name	Date	Location
David Sloan	Nov. 15, 1828	T52-R30-S5
David Sloan	Dec. 3, 1827	T52-R30-S8
David Sloan	Feb. 21, 1833	T52-R30-S8
John Shouse	Jun. 29, 1836	T51-R30-S3
John Shouse	Feb. 22, 1836	T51-R30-S8
John Smith	Nov. 5, 1831	T51-R30-S1
John Stothart	Aug. 12, 1836	T51-R30-S5
John Stothart	Jun. 25, 1836	T51-R30-S7
John Thatcher	Jan. 1, 1828	T53-R33-S25
Eleven Thatcher	Dec. 5, 1837	T53-R33-S34
Eleven Thatcher	Mar. 7, 1828	T53-R33-S34
Eleven Thatcher	Mar. 15, 1827	T53-R33-S35
Eleven Thatcher	Dec. 5, 1837	T53-R33-S35
Eleven Thatcher	Dec. 6, 1839	T53-R33-S35
James L. V. Thompson	Jan. 4, 1820	T52-R33-S34
James L. V. Thompson	Jul. 17, 1839	T53-R32-S34
James L. V. Thompson	Aug. 30, 1836	T53-R32-S35
Rachel Thatcher	Jun. 27, 1828	T52-R33-S3
Samuel Taylor	Mar. 21, 1827	T52-R33-S2
Samuel Taylor	Nov. 22, 1825	T52-R33-S10
James Taylor	Feb. 18, 1834	T52-R33-S12
James Taylor	Jan. 5, 1830	T52-R33-S13
George Taylor	Feb. 10, 1836	T52-R33-S13
Jesse Todd	Feb. 10, 1823	T51-R33-S3
Joseph Todd	Feb. 10, 1823	T51-R33-S10
William Todd	Feb. 10, 1823	T51-R33-S14
Benj. Talbott	Nov. 23, 1827	T54-R32-S32
Reuben Tipton	Jan. 27, 1838	T52-R32-S24
William Tillery	Nov. 28, 1821	T52-R32-S36
Reuben Tillery	Jan. 1, 1824	T52-R32-S36
Danl. C. Thomas	Sep. 19, 1835	T52-R32-S29
Danl. C. Thomas	Dec. 2, 1836	T52-R32-S30
Danl. C. Thomas	Sep. 30, 1835	T52-R32-S30
Geo. Taylor	Oct. 16, 1832	T52-R32-S18
Owen Thorp	Mar. 19, 1827	T52-R32-S15
Jas. L. V. Thompson	Jul. 17, 1839	T52-R32-S4
John N. Tillery	Apr. 1, 1839	T52-R32-S23
Eppe Tillery	Mar. 12, 1821	T52-R32-S36
Jas. Tillery	Jan. 5, 1836	T52-R32-S24
Jas. Tillery	Nov. 27, 1821	T52-R32-S36
William Thorp	Nov. 17, 1823	T52-R32-S27
William Thorp	Mar. 18, 1824	T52-R32-S33
William Thorp	Sep. 18, 1822	T52-R32-S34
William Thorp	Jun. 5, 1823	T52-R32-S34
William Thorp	May 27, 1824	T52-R32-S34
Clayton Tillery	Sep. 7, 1835	T52-R32-S31
Clayton Tillery	Nov. 3, 1837	T52-R32-S36

(Clay County, Missouri Continued)

Name	Date	Location
Clayton Tillery	Nov. 27, 1821	T52-R32-S36
Clayton Tillery	Mar. 15, 1827	T52-R32-S36
John Thornton	Nov. 14, 1836	T51-R32-S36
John Thortnon	Oct. 1, 1835	T51-R32-S36
John Thornton	Feb. 11, 1836	T51-R32-S36
John Thornton	Jun. 21, 1825	T51-R32-S26
John Thornton	Feb. 17, 1833	T51-R32-S36
John Thornton	Mar. 17, 1827	T51-R32-S26
John Thornton	Jan. 31, 1828	T51-R32-S23
John Thornton	Mar. 12, 1821	T51-R32-S26
John Thornton	Feb. 6, 1832	T51-R32-S25
John Thornton	Apr. 24, 1829	T51-R32-S23
John Thornton	Jan, 9, 1836	T51-R32-S22
John Thornton	Nov. 5, 1824	T51-R32-S21
John Thornton	Aug. 24, 1821	T51-R32-S21
John Thornton	May 17, 1824	T51-R32-S10
Samuel Tillery	Feb. 17, 1829	T51-R32-S29
Samuel Tillery	Nov. 10, 1824	T51-R32-S29
William Thorp	Mar. 19, 1822	T51-R32-S5
William Thorp	Aug. 6, 1822	T51-R32-S34
William Thorp	Sep. 18, 1822	T51-R32-S3
Elisha Todd	Jan. 20, 1832	T51-R32-S18
Elisha Todd	Feb. 23, 1829	T51-R32-S19
Elisha Todd	Mar. 12, 1821	T51-R32-S19
Eppe Tillery	Jul. 5, 832	T51-R32-S1
Merrit Tillery	Nov. 13, 1824	T51-R32-S30
Greenberry Thorp	May 26, 1831	T50-R32-S15
Greenberry Thorp	Jul. 1, 1831	T50-R32-S15
John Thornton	Sep. 18, 1830	T50-R32-S3
John Thornton	Feb. 11, 1836	T50-R32-S10
John Thornton	Apr. 9, 1832	T50-R32-S10
John Thornton	Jun. 8, 1837	T50-R32-S13
William Thorp, jr.	Mar. 15, 1836	T50-R32-S24
John Toffeimier	Jan. 30, 1828	T53-R31-S36
Joel Turnham	Apr. 19, 1827	T53-R31-S23
Joel Turnham	Mar. 16, 1827	T52-R31-S10
Joel Turnham	Oct. 5, 1822	T52-R31-S3
Joel Turnham	Sep. 26, 1825	T52-R31-S20
Joel Turnham	Apr. 11, 1832	T52-R31-S29
Joel Turnham	Jun. 4, 1830	T51-R31-S29
Joel Turnham	Apr. 17, 1837	T51-R31-S33
Wm. L. Tippets	Mar. 24, 1836	T51-R31-S14
John Thompson	Jan. 5, 1825	T52-R31-S26
John Thompson	Apr. 3, 1821	T52-R31-S36
William Tapp	Oct. 21, 1839	T52-R31-S5
Joseph Thorp	Feb. 25, 1828	T52-R31-S18
Saml. R. Turner	Mar. 7, 1836	T52-R31-S13

Name	Date	Location
Jas. L. Tevis	May 23, 1836	T51-R31-S25
Walker Turner	Jun. 27, 1836	T51-R31-S12
Robert G. Thompson	Jul. 22, 1839	T51-R31-S28
William Thompson	Oct. 26, 1832	T51-R31-S2
Joel Turnham	Apr. 11, 1832	T51-R31-S29
Joel Turnham	Jun. 4, 1830	T51-R31-S29
Joel Turnham	Apr. 17, 1837	T51-R31-S33
John Thornton	Jan. 1, 1838	T50-R31-S7
John Thornton	May 17, 1824	T50-R31-S10
Ann Tarrants	Nov. 18, 1831	T53-R30-S8
Benjamin Taylor	Apr. 17, 1827	T53-R30-S19
Benjamin Taylor	Aug. 3, 1830	T53-R30-S20
William Turner	Oct. 28, 1835	T53-R30-S13
William Turner	Jul. 13, 1829	T53-R30-S23
William Turner	Dec. 7, 1839	T53-R30-S36
Richard Tate	Jan. 17, 1833	T53-R30-S15
Richard Tate	Aug. 1, 1833	T53-R30-S15
Arasmus Tarrants	Oct. 20, 1834	T53-R30-S8
Arasmus Tarrants	Dec. 16, 1835	T53-R30-S8
Littleton Turner	Jan. 28, 1836	T52-R30-S25
Jno. Taggart	Nov. 2, 1834	T52-R30-S4
David Taggart	Oct. 10, 1834	T52-R30-S4
Wm. Turnedge	Apr. 1, 1831	T52-R30-S14
Wm. Turnidge (sic)	Jan. 2, 1833	T52-R30-S25
John Taylor	Jun. 18, 1836	T51-R30-S6
Hankesson Utterback	Mar. 16, 1827	T51-R32-S22
Jos. Utterback	Mar. 16, 1827	T51-R32-S8
Daniel Varble	Mar. 14, 1833	T53-R31-S18
Singleton Vaughn	Oct. 4, 1827	T51-R32-S2
Thos. Vaughn	Mar. 20, 1827	T51-R32-S1
Thos. Vaughn	Jun. 26, 1824	T52-R32-S35
Robert Vance	Feb. 2, 1833	T52-R32-S29
Enos Vaughan	Oct. 22, 1825	T52-R32-S35
Enos Vaughan	Mar. 12, 1821	T52-R32-S35
David Vaughan	Apr. 2, 1832	T52-R32-S26
David Vaughan	Jan. 22, 1820	T52-R32-S26
Josiah J. Vaughan	Apr. 7, 1827	T52-R32-S14
Josiah J. Vaughan	Jan. 26, 1829	T52-R32-S26
Thos. Vaughan, jr.	Mar. 16, 1827	T52-R32-S13
Peter Vendemans	Apr. 4, 1839	T54-R32-S33
Daniel Varble	Jun. 8, 1835	T53-R32-S13
Solomon Vance	Mar. 16, 1827	T52-R33-S1
Solomon Vance	Oct. 31, 1828	T52-R33-S1
Solomon Vance	Aug. 2, 1836	T52-R33-S2
Solomon Vance	Dec. 5, 1832	T52-R33-S2
Handle Vance	Apr. 13, 1839	T52-R33-S11
Handle Vance	Oct. 19, 1825	T52-R33-S14

(Clay County, Missouri Continued)

Name	Date	Location
Handle Vance	Oct. 21, 1834	T52-R33-S14
Handle Vance	Sep. 24, 1832	T52-R33-S14
Handle Vance	Nov. 2, 1837	T52-R33-S14
Handle Vance	Oct. 8, 1839	T52-R33-S23
Solomon Vance	Dec. 5, 1832	T52-R33-S2
Solomon Vance	Mar. 16, 1827	T52-R33-S1
Solomon Vance	Oct. 31, 1828	T52-R33-S1
Solomon Vance	Aug. 2, 1836	T52-R33-S1
Solomon Vance	Dec. 5, 1832	T52-R33-S2
Nathaniel Vincent	Jan. 4, 1838	T53-R33-S36
Josiah Vaughn	Jan. 6, 1838	T53-R33-S25
George Withers	Apr. 13, 1831	T51-R30-S4
George Withers	Jun. 7, 1836	T51-R30-S4
George Withers	Mar. 15, 1827	T52-R30-S10
George Withers	Feb. 18, 1836	T52-R30-S21
James M. White	Mar. 5, 1821	T51-R30-S1
Shrewsbury Williams	Nov. 24, 1829	T51-R30-S7
Shrewsbury Williams	Dec. 5, 1833	T51-R30-S7
Sanford Welton	Nov. 7, 1831	T52-R30-S8
Sanford Welton	Aug. 12, 1834	T52-R30-S8
Nelson Witt	Jan. 31, 1828	T52-R30-S2
Nelson Witt	Apr. 1, 1831	T52-R30-S21
Caleb Wilson	Jan. 29, 1836	T52-R30-S4
Benedict Weldon	Jan. 7, 1833	T52-R30-S32
Benedict Weldon	Dec. 28, 1827	T52-R30-S32
Benedict Weldon	Nov. 8, 1838	T52-R30-S31
James Williams	Mar. 29, 1827	T52-R30-S29
Peter Withers	Mar. 15, 1827	T52-R30-S3
Alfred Writesman	Feb. 20, 1837	T52-R30-S33
Caleb Wilson	Jan. 29, 1836	T52-R30-S4
William Wilson	Oct. 28, 1839	T52-R30-S35
Milton H. Williams	Jun. 19, 1827	T52-R30-S9
Milton H. Williams	Sep. 17, 1827	T52-R30-S15
Michael Welton	Sep. 6, 1831	T52-R30-S15
Michael Welton	Aug. 3, 1832	T52-R30-S22
Francis Writesman	Mar. 1, 1830	T52-R30-S28
Francis Writesman	Mar. 15, 1827	T52-R30-S28
John Writesman	May 16, 1822	T52-R30-S33
John Writesman	Nov. 16, 1822	T52-R30-S33
John Writesman	Feb. 14, 1822	T52-R30-S33
Peter Writesman	Apr. 14, 1827	T52-R30-S32
Peter Writesman	May 31, 1836	T52-R30-S33
Alfred Whitsitt	Nov. 19, 1839	T54-R30-S31
Jos. Walker	Sep. 2, 1835	T54-R30-S31
Walter L. Watkins	Apr. 29, 1839	T54-R30-S33
Walter L. Watkins	Apr. 1, 1839	T53-R30-S15
James M. Watkins	May 11, 1839	T53-R30-S14

(Clay County, Missouri Continued)

Name	Date	Location
Milton N. Williams	Apr. 30, 1839	T53-R30-S15
Josiah Wilson	Nov. 20, 1834	T53-R30-S33
Anderson Wilson	Nov. 20, 1834	T53-R30-S34
Shrewsbury Williams	Dec. 24, 1824	T51-R31-S2
Shrewsbury Williams	Mar. 16, 1827	T52-R31-S35
Jas. Williams	Jul. 26, 1824	T52-R31-S17
Jas. Williams	Mar. 16, 1827	T51-R31-S35
Benedict Weldon	Sep. 3, 1821	T51-R31-S2
Wm. T. and Sarah Ward	Dec. 15, 1824	T51-R31-S3
Thos. Walker	Jul. 25, 1825	T51-R31-S4
John Wade	Dec. 19, 1827	T52-R31-S17
John Wade, jr.	Sep. 2, 1836	T52-R31-S4
John Wade, jr.	Dec. 5, 1833	T52-R31-S5
Robert Walker	Dec. 15, 1830	T52-R31-S19
James L. Walker	Dec. 25, 1829	T52-R31-S7
Samuel Wiett	Mar. 19, 1827	T52-R31-S15
James Wilhoit	Jul. 26, 1824	T52-R31-S17
James Wilhoit	Jan. 29, 1836	T53-R31-S2
Jno. S. Whorton	Nov. 22, 1839	T54-R31-S36
James Weldon	Sep. 11, 1828	T54-R31-S36
James Weldon	Aug. 13, 1828	T54-R31-S36
Jesse Wright	Sep. 20, 1839	T53-R31-S8
Peton Wade	Dec. 22, 1828	T53-R31-S9
Andrew Wilhoit	Dec. 17, 1830	T53-R31-S2
Andrew Wilhoit	Nov. 28, 1837	T53-R31-S2
Joseph Wilhoit	Jul. 25, 1837	T53-R31-S2
Thomas Wilhoit	Nov. 23, 1828	T53-R31-S11
George Williams	Jul. 26, 1833	T50-R32-S10
Thos. Woods	Apr. 1, 1831	T50-R32-S5
Thos. Woods	Apr. 24, 1834	T50-R32-S9
Littleberry Winningham	Sep. 30, 1824	T50-R32-S22
Joshua Warren	Nov. 28, 1831	T51-R32-S20
Joshua Warren	Oct. 14, 1831	T51-R32-S20
Jno. Wirt	Oct. 11, 1829	T51-R32-S10
Henry and Caleb Weeden	Mar. 12, 1821	T51-R32-S32
Jas. D. Watkins	Oct. 17, 1825	T51-R32-S15
John Warren	Jul. 21, 1832	T51-R32-S20
Humphrey Warren	Jun. 11, 1821	T51-R32-S27
Simeon Wilhite	Oct. 11, 1829	T51-R32-S18
Walter L. Watkins	Jul. 2, 1838	T52-R32-S2
Walter L. Watkins	Apr. 1, 1839	T52-R32-S3
David Wills	May 21, 1833	T52-R32-S21
David Wills	Mar. 1, 1827	T52-R32-S21
David Wills	Jan. 7, 1836	T52-R32-S22
John Walker	May 11, 1838	T52-R32-S12
William Whitlock	Feb. 18, 1834	T52-R32-S12
George Wills	Oct. 29, 1827	T52-R32-S5

(Clay County, Missouri Continued)

Name	Date	Location
George Wills	Jun. 6, 1827	T52-R32-S5
George Wills	Jun. 20, 1829	T52-R32-S5
George Wills	Jan. 22, 1830	T52-R32-S7
George Wills	Sep. 21, 1839	T52-R32-S17
George Wills	Apr. 6, 1839	T52-R32-S18
George Wills	Nov. 4, 1828	T52-R32-S18
George Wills	Jul. 18, 1828	T52-R32-S18
Jas. B. Wills	Jun. 20, 1829	T52-R32-S17
Jas. B. Wills	Feb. 27, 1837	T52-R32-S21
Jas. B. Wills	May 31, 1824	T52-R32-S21
Jas. B. Wills	Jun. 7, 1837	T52-R32-S17
William Wade	Aug. 4, 1831	T54-R32-S34
David S. Wade	Aug. 21, 1835	T54-R32-S35
John Wade, jr.	Jun. 20, 1833	T53-R32-S1
Peyton Wade	Nov. 30, 1833	T53-R32-S4
Peyton Wade	Aug. 4, 1831	T53-R32-S9
Peyton Wade	Jun. 9, 1836	T53-R32-S9
Henry Walker	Aug. 11, 1837	T53-R32-S24
Jacob Walker	Jan. 24, 1832	T53-R32-S21
James M. Watkins	May 11, 1839	T53-R32-S34
James M. Watkins	Jul. 2, 1838	T53-R32-S35
Walter L. Watkins	Aug. 3, 1838	T53-R32-S34
Walter L. Watkins	Jul. 2, 1838	T53-R32-S35
Nancy Wilhoit	Mar. 24, 1828	T53-R32-S15
Benjamin F. Wilkerson	Mar. 24, 1828	T53-R32-S30
James Winn	Feb. 8, 1830	T53-R32-S30
James Winn	Dec. 3, 1832	T53-R32-S30
John Welch	Jan. 25, 1825	T50-R33-S14
John Welch	Oct. 7, 1825	T50-R33-S14
James Wambley	Jan. 1, 1825	T51-R33-S12
William Woods, jr.	Mar. 19, 1827	T51-R33-S10
Lazarus Wilcox	Nov. 8, 1824	T51-R33-S23
William Woods	Nov. 3, 1835	T51-R33-S15
Jane Williams	Mar. 19, 1827	T51-R33-S11
Thomas Woods	Jan. 15, 1829	T51-R33-S22
John N. Williams	Jul. 18m 1828	T51-R33-S11
Peter Woods	Mar. 17, 1827	T51-R33-S23
Johnson Williams	Nov. 7, 1825	T51-R33-S12
John and Johnson Williams	May 23, 1831	T51-R33-S12
Archibald Woods	Aug. 15, 1829	T51-R33-S15
John Wilson	Nov. 15, 1823	T51-R33-S10
Archibald and Thomas Woods	Jan. 1, 1825	T51-R33-S2
Archibald Woods	Sep. 9, 1833	T52-R33-S35
Elisha Williams	Nov. 19, 1839	T52-R33-S35
Johnson Williams	Nov. 19, 1839	T52-R33-S35
Archibald B. Wills	Oct. 21, 1831	T52-R33-S11
Chas. Warren	Jan. 26, 1829	T53-R33-S25

(Clay County, Missouri Continued)

Name	Date	Location
Talton Whitlock	Feb. 8, 1836	T53-R33-S27
Talton Whitlock	Aug. 20, 1838	T53-R33-S34
Jno. M. Wilkerson	Oct. 21, 1834	T53-R33-S25
Jno. M. Wilkerson	Aug. 29, 1837	T53-R33-S25
Joseph W. Younger	Jun. 25, 1836	T52-R30-S2
John L. Yantis	Mar. 17, 1837	T53-R30-S27
Linet Young	May 19, 1836	T51-R31-S35
Henry Yates	Nov. 4, 1831	T53-R31-S10
Pleasant Yates	Nov. 15, 1827	T53-R31-S11
William Young	Jun. 24, 1839	T53-R31-S20
William Young	Mar. 9, 1836	T53-R31-S20
William Young	Jul. 2, 1838	T53-R31-S29
Charles Younger	Mar. 19, 1827	T50-R32-S5
Charles Younger	Jan. 28, 1834	T50-R32-S6
Charles Younger	Jul. 8, 1837	T50-R32-S7
Charles Younger	Nov. 26, 1832	T50-R32-S8
Charles Younger	Dec. 11, 1837	T50-R32-S8
Charles Younger	May 21, 1836	T50-R32-S13
Charles Younger	Aug. 2, 1828	T51-R32-S13
Charles Younger	Feb. 7, 1824	T51-R32-S31
Charles Younger	Dec. 4, 1830	T51-R32-S32
Charles Younger	Dec. 16, 1824	T51-R32-S34
Newman York	Apr. 5, 1827	T52-R32-S35
Jas. Yokum	Feb. 31, 1834	T53-R32-S18
Jesse Yokum	Aug. 19, 1837	T53-R32-S9
Jesse Yokum	Nov. 27, 1837	T53-R32-S7
John W. Young	Aug. 16, 1838	T53-R32-S33
John W. Young	Jan. 13, 1834	T53-R32-S30
Jos. T. Young	Feb. 6, 1832	T53-R32-S31
Coleman Younger	May 16, 1838	T50-R33-S13
Wm. Yocum	Apr. 14, 1834	T52-R33-S10
Wm. Yocum	Apr. 9, 1829	T52-R33-S11
Jesse Yocum	May 9, 1829	T53-R33-S36
Milton Younger	Mar. 11, 1836	T50-R32-S8
James Zavely	Mar. 5, 1833	T51-R31-S23
Henry Zabrisky	Jun. 21, 1836	T51-R30-S4

New Madrid County, Missouri, June Term, 1825, Members Of The Grand Jury.

Isaac Ogden, John Shanks, Martin Shaver, John Netherton, Conrad Wheat, Allen E. Alford, Isaac Phelpst, Samuel Filcher, Antoine Saffint, Alexander Newman, David Hunter, Samuel Allen, Peter A. Laforge, Robert M'Coy, Richard Phillips, Nicholas Turmot, William Sazele, Thomas Williams, Alford L. Diliard.

Scott County, Missouri, February Term, 1822, Grand Jury.

Ludwick P. Davis, James Cardin, John Ashley. John Wathan,

(Scott County, Missouri Continued)
Bartlett Conyers, Samuel Fowler, Willis Benefield, James W.
Dudley, Samuel Fowler, Robert Wood, John V. Lucas, William
Alexander, Edward Fowler, James W. Dudley, Thomas Moore,John
Friend, James Purtle, Ceburn Wiley, Silas Carpenter, George
Anderson, Solomon Hays, Barthlomew J. Evans.

Van Buren or Cass County, Missouri,Delinquent Tax List,1837,
Capitol Fire Documents, Box CFD 30, Folder 1279.
     Charles Hopper, Joseph Bevin, Joseph Swiss, Rufus Young,
William Butler, Bartlett Bingham, Elias Barnett, Johnathan
Summer, Samuel English, Robert English, Thos. Graham, John
Meard, sr., John M'Carty, Simon Malone, Warner Porter, Louis
Roy, Warner Porter, Edward Reynolds, Hugh Silvero, John M.
Savage, Nimrod Stokes, Richard Smith, Nathan Turner, James
Tunley, Pearson Teaque, Hiram Helms, Joshua Harst, Sampson
Bledsoe, William S. Caton, William Caton.

Abstract of Wm. Clark's Expeditures as Superintendent of
Indian Affairs Of The Missouri Territory, American States
Papers, January 1, 1820 to December 31, 1820.
  (1)   William Clark: a) Compensation from April 1, 1819
        to March 31, 1820, (PY) March 31, 1820, (V) 1;
        b) Compensation from April 1, 1820 to June 30,1830,
        (PY) Jul 1, 1820, (V) 2; c) Compensation from July
        1, 1820 to September 30, 1820, (PY) September 30,
        1820, (V) 3; d) Compensation from October 1, 1820
        to December 31, 1820, (PY) December 31,1820, (V) 4.
  (2)   B. O'Fallon: a)Salary as Indian Agent from October
        1, 1819 to December 31, 1819, (PY) January 1, 1820,
        (V) 9; b)Salary as Indian Agent from January 1,1820
        to June 30,1820, (PY) July 1,1820, (V) 10; c)Salary
        as Indian Agent from July 1, 1820 to September 30,
        1820, (PY) October 1, 1820, (V) 11.
  (4)   Thos. Forsyth: a)Salary as Indian Agent from April
        1, 1819 to March 31, 1820, (PY) March 31, 1820, (V)
        14; b) Salary as Indian Agent from April 1, 1820 to
        June 30,1820, (PY) June 30,1820, (V) 15; c) Salary
        as Indian Agent from July 1, 1820 to September 30,
        1820, (PY) September 30, 1820, (V) 16; d) Salary
        as Indian Agent from October 1, 1820 to December
        31, 1820, (PY) December 31, 1820, (V) 17.
  (5)   Nicholas Boilvin: a) Salary as Indian Agent from
        January 1, 1820 to March 31, 1820, (PY) March 31,
        1820, (V) 19; b) Salary as Indian Agent from April
        1, 1820 to September 30, 1820, (PY)October 26,1820,
        (V) 20; c) Salary as Indian Agent from October 1,
        1820 to December 31, 1820, (PY) December 31, 1820,
        (V) 21.

(Indian Affairs, Missouri Territory Continued)

(6)   John Ruland: a) Salary as Indian Sub-Agent from April 1, 1819 to March 31, 1820, (PY)March 31,1820, (V) 22; b) Salary as Indian Sub-Agent from April 1, 1820 to June 30, 1820, (PY) July 1,1820, (V) 23; c) Salary as Indian Sub-Agent from July 1, 1820 to September 30, 1820, (PY) October 1, 1820, (V) 24; d) Salary as Indian Sub-Agent from October 1, 1820 to December 31,1820, (PY) December 31,1820, (V) 25.

(7)   P. L. Chouteau: a) Salary as Indian Sub-Agent from July 1, 1819 to March 31, 1820, (PY) April 1, 1820, (V) 28; b)Salary as Indian Sub-Agent from April 1, 1820 to June 30, 1820, (PY) June 5, 1820, (V) 29; c) Salary as Indian Sub-Agent from July 1, 1820 to December 30, 1820, (PY) October 2, 1820, (V) 20.

(8)   Pierre Menard: a) Salary as Indian Sub-Agent from April 1, 1819 to March 31, 1820, (PY) April 1,1820, (V) 31; b) Salary as Indian Sub-Agent from April 1, 1820 to June 30, 1820, (PY) July 1,1820, (V) 32; c) Salary as Indian Sub-Agent from July 1, 1820 to September 30, 1820, (PY) October 1, 1820, (V) 33.

(9)   George C. Sibley: a) Salary as Indian Sub-Agent from October 1, 1819 to March 31, 1820, (PY) March 31, 1820, (V) 36; b) Salary as Indian Sub-Agent from April 1, 1820 to December 31,1820, (PY) December 31, 1820, (V) 37.

(10)   L. Taliaferro: a) Salary as Indian Sub-Agent, balance of second quarter ending June 30, 1820, (PY) June 30, 1820, (V) 41; b) Salary as Indian Sub-Agent from July 1, 1820 to September 30, 1820, (PY) September 30, 1820, (V) 42; c) Salary as Indian Sub-Agent from October 1, 1820 to December 31,1820, (PY) December 7, 1820, (V) 43.

(11)   John Dougherty: a) Salary as interpreter from June 1, 1819 to December 23, 1819, (PY) January 1, 1820, (V) 44; b) Salary as Indian Sub-Agent and as interpreter from December 23, 1819 to June 30,1820, (PY) July 1, 1820, (V) 45; c) Salary as Indian Sub-Agent and interpreter from July 1, 1820 to September 30, 1820, (PY) October 1, 1820, (V) 46.

(12)   John Ruland: a) Salary as translator from April 1, 1819 to March 31, 1820, (PY) March 31, 1820, (V) 49; b) Salary as tranlator from April 1, 1820 to June 30, 1820, (PY) July 1, 1820, (V) 50; c) Salary as translator from July 1, 1820 to September 30, 1820, (PY) October 1, 1820, (V) 51.

(13)   L. T. Honore: a) Salary as interpreter from January 1, 1820 to March 31, 1820, (PY) March 31,1820, (V) 56; b) Salary as interpreter from April 1,1820

(Indian Affairs, Missouri Territory Continued)
    to June 30, 1820, (PY) June 30, 1820, (V) 57; c)r
    Salary as interpreter from July 1, 1820 to Septem-
    ber 30,1820, (PY) October 1,1820, (V) 58; d)Salary
    as interpreter from October 1, 1820 to December 31,
    1820, (PY) December 31, 1820, (V) 59.

(14) Paul Loise: a) Salary as interpreter from January
      1, 1820 to March 31, 1820, (PY) March 31, 1820, (V)
      64;   b)   Salary as interpreter from April 1, 1820
      to June 30, 1820, (PY) June 6, 1820, (V) 65;   C)
      Salary as interpreter from July 1, 1820 to December
      31, 1820, (PY) December 31, 1820, (V) 66.

(15) T. Charboneau: a) Salary as interpreter from July
      1, 1820 to December 31, 1819, (PY) January 1, 1820,
      (V) 69.

(16) Narsis Franier: a) Salary as interpreter from May
      1, 1820 to September 30, 1820, (PY) September 30,
      1820, (V); b) Salary as interpreter from October
      1, 1820 to December 31,1820, (PY) December 31,1820,
      (V) 70.

(17) C. Campbell: a) Salary as interpreter from July 1,
      to September 30, 1820, (PY) September 30, 1820, (V)
      72;   b)   Salary as interpreter from October 1, 1820
      to December 31, 1820, (PY) November 15, 1820, (V)
      73.

(18) D. Campbell: a) Salary from May 14, 1820 to June
      30, 1820, (V) 74.

(19) P. Fournier: a) Salary as interpreter from October
      1, 1819 to March 31, 1820, (PY) April 1, 1820, (V)
      76;   b)   Salary as interpreter from April 1, 1820
      to June 30, 1820, (PY) June 30, 1820, (V) 77;   c)
      Salary as interpreter from July 1, 1820 to Septem-
      ber 30, 1820, (PY) October 1, 1820, (V) 78.

(20) Louis Pettle: a) Salary as interpreter from Sep-
      tember 1, 1820 to December 31, 1820, (PY) December
      31, 1820, (V) 80.

(21) J. B. Canon: a) Salary From April 1, 1820 to June
      30, 1820, (PY) June 30, 1821, (V) 81.

(22) Amasa Crane: a) Salary as gunsmith from October
      1, 1819 to March 31, 1820, (PY) March 31, 1820, (V)
      84;   b)   Salary as gunsmith from April 1, 1820 to
      September 30, 1820, (PY) September 20,1820, (V) 85.

(23) Joseph Montreny: a) Salary as interpreter ·from
      June 1, 1820 to September 30, 1820, (PY) March 31,
      1820, (V) 269.

(24) Pierre Perior: a) Salary as gunsmith from June 1,
      1820 to September 30, 1820, (PY) September 30,1820,
      (V) 275.

(25) J. B. Valle: a) By order of P. Menard, delivery

of various goods from October, 1818 to March, 1820,
(PY) March 29, 1820, (V) 122;   b) Storage and car-
tage of goods to the Kaskaskia, Piankeshaw and
Peoria tribes, (PY) March 29, 1820, (V) 123.   c)
Payment for various goods, (PY) June 27, 1820, (V)
123,   d)   Payment for various goods, (PY) June 30,
1820, (V) 171.

(26)   Francis Day: a) Payment for a horse used by the
Osage interpreter to carry a message to the Kickapoos, (PY) March 29, 1820, (V) 124.

(27)   Joseph Bogy: a) Payment for furnishing bread to
the Shawnee and Piankeshaw Indians, (PY) March 21,
1820, (V) 125.

(28)   G. Beauvais: a) Payment for goods, (PY) June 27,
1820, (V) 164.   b) Payment for various iron goods,
(PY) September 7, 1820, (V) 187.

(29)   P. Provot: a) Services as boatman in conveying
corn fron the plantation of W. Bilderback, in Illinois, to Cape Girardeau, (PY) July 30,1820, (V)181.

(30)   C. Derousse: See no. 29.

(31)   L. Allair: See no. 29.

(32)   N. Provot: See no. 29.

(33)   P. Lafleur: See no. 29.

(34)   J. and G. H. Kennerly: a) Payment for goods, (PY)
October, 1825, 1820, (V) 212;   b) Payment for furnishing clothing and sundry goods to John Tanner and
his family after their release from captivity, (PY)
October 25, 1820, (V) 212.

(35)   William G. Heiser: a) Payment for delivering beef
to the Indians, (PY) November 29, 1820, (V) 218.

(36)   Baptiste Moran: a) Payment for ferriage of seventy
Indian families across the Mississippi River, (PY)
November 29, 1820, (V) 219.

(37)   John Carpenter: a) Payment for ferriage of forty-
one Indian families across the Mississippi, (PY)
November 30, 1820, (V) 220.

(38)   Francis Montreal: a) Payment for ferriage of one
hundred eleven Indian families across the Kaskaskia
River, (PY) December 6, 1820, (V) 225.

(39)   --- Lewis: a) Payment for furnishing bread to the
Shawanee, (PY) December 13, 1820, (V) 226.

(40)   --- Walker: See no. 39.

(41)   Paschall Cerre: a) Payment for services and provisions redered to the Kickapoo Indians, (PY) March
28, 1820, (V) 340.

(42)   Nathan Mills: a) Payment for delivering beef to
the Kicakappo Indians, (PY) July 25, 1820, (V) 341.

(43)   Antoine Chenie: a) Payment for delivering bread to

(Indian Affairs, Missouri Territory Continued)
the Indians, (PY) August 1, 1820, (V) 349.

(44) Nathan Mills: a) Payment for delivering beef to
the Kickapoos in July and August, (PY) August 30,
1820, (V) 344.

(45) Lakeman: a) Payment for repairing rifles and other
goods, (PY) August 30, 1820, (V) 345.

(46) B. P. Cain: a) Payment for supplying bread to the
Kicakappos in July and August, (PY) September 1,
1820, (V) 346.

(47) Joseph Archambeau: a) Payment for ferriage of
thirty-nine Shawnees over the Mississippi River,
(PY) September 25, 1820, (V) 347.

(48) F. Montreuil: a) Payment for ferriage of ninety-
five Shawnees across the KasKaskia, (PY) September
27, 1820, (V) 348.

(49) Jacob Meyers: a) Payment for supplying bread to the
Shawanees in July, August, and September, 1820,
(PY) September 29, 1820, (V) 349.

(50) John Carpenter: a) Payment for ferriage of forty-
two shawanees across the Mississippi River, (PY)
September 29, 1820, (V) 350.

(51) William G. Heizer: a) Payment for the delivery of
beef to the Shawanees in July, August, and September, 1820, (PY) September 20, 1820, (V) 351.

(52) Joseph Bogy: a) Payment for supplying bread to the
Shawanees in July, August, and September, 1820,
(PY) September 20, 1820, (V) 352.

(53) J. B. Valle: a) Payment for delivery of beef to
the Shawanees in July, August, and September, 1820,
(PY) September 20, 1820, (V) 353.

(54) --- Pitzer: a) Payment for keeping indian horses
in St, Louis, (PY) January 12, 1820, (V) 117.

(55) --- Price: see no. 54.

(56) J. E. Welch: a) Payment of two quarters' tuition
for J. B. Charboneau, a half Indian boy, (PY) January 22, 1820, (V) 118.

(57) M. Maloney: a) Payment for supplying wood to the
Indians, (PY) January 22, 1820, (V) 120.

(58) Warner Lewis: a) Payment for supplying fodder for
public horses, (PY) February 6, 1820, (V) 121.

(59) L. T. Honore: a) Payment for the lodging of J. B.
Charboneau, a half Indian, (PY) March 31, 1820, (V)
126.

(60) J. and G. H. Kennerly: a) Payment for supplying
goods to Indians. Also, supplying sundries for J.
B. Charboneau, a half Indian, (PY) April 1, 1820,
(V) 128.

(61) M. L. Malette: a) Payment for making coats, (PY)

(Indian Affairs, Missouri Territory Continued)
          April 25, 1820, (V) 136.
  (62)   John Campbell: a) Payment for supplying goods,
         tobacco and whickey. Also, reimburse for cash paid
         to C. Towen, interpreter. He quieted a party of
         Sac Indians who were upset over the death of one of
         their party by a white man, (PY) April 2, 1820, (V)
         131.
  (63)   J. E. Welch: a) Payment for one quarter's tuition
         for J. B. Charboneau, a half Indian, (PY) April 11,
         1820, (V) 132.
  (64)   P. Chouteau: a) Payment for supplying beef, bread,
         and corn to the Sac Indians, (PY) April 11, 1820,
         (V) 133. b) Payment for supplying beef, bread, and
         corn to the Osage Indians, (PY) April 11, 1820, (V)
         134.
  (65)   Solomon Migneron: a) Payment for the repair of
         tools, (PY) April 15, 1820, (V) 135; b) Payment
         for the repair of tools, (PY) May 12, 1820, (V)
         137.
  (66)   M. Lambert: a) Payment for work done for the
         Indian Department, (PY) April 15, 1820, (V) 138.
  (67)   F. Neil: a) Payment for one quarter's tuition for
         Toussaint Charboneau, a half Indian boy, (PY) May
         17, 1820, (V) 139.
  (68)   P. G. Voorhees: a) Payment for hauling freight
         from St. Louis to Arkansas, (PY) May 24, 1820, (V)
         140.
  (69)   Louis Marly: a) Payment for supplying beef to the
         Sac and Osage Indians at St. Louis, (PY) May 25,
         1820, (V) 141.
  (70)   J. B. Simoneau: a) Payment for making coats, (PY)
         May 26, 1820, (V) 142.
  (71)   A. Honore: a) Payment for for making clothing for
         Indians at Washington, (PY) May 30, 1820, (V) 143.
  (72)   James Burrows: a) Payment for corn, (PY) June 3,
         1820, (V) 145.
  (73)   --- Bertholett: a) Payment for repairing tools,
         (PY) June 5, 1820, (V) 147.
  (74)   --- Rolette: See no. 73.
  (75)   J. Chandler: a) Payment for washing Indian clothes,
         (PY) August 29, 1820, (V) 311.
  (76)   C. Beauman: a) Payment for lodging Indians, (PY)
         August 29, 1820, (V) 312.
  (77)   Auguste Dubois: a) Payment for deer skins, (PY)
         August 30, 1820, (V) 313.
  (78)   Robert Keller: a) Payment for furnishing dinners
         for Indians and supplying horse feed, (PY) August
         30, 1820, (V) 315.

(Indian Affairs, Missouri Territory Continued)

(80) Samuel Ramsey: a) Payment for lodging Indians,
     (PY) August 30, 1820, (V) 315.

(81) Samuel Inclabb: a) Payment for lodging Indians,
     (PY) August 30, 1820, (V) 316.

(82) John C. Holland: a) Payment for riding goods, (PY)
     August 30, 1820, (V) 317.

(83) L. Cramer: a) Payment for lodging Indians, (PY)
     August 31, 1820, (V) 318.

(84) George Roberts: a) Payment for lodging Indians,
     (PY) August 31, 1820, (V) 319.

(85) John J. Feclet: a) Payment for lodging Indians,
     (PY) August 31, 1820, (V) 320.

(86) Daniel Grower: a) Payment for lodging Indians,
     (PY) September 1, 1820, (V) 321.

(87) John Lawrence: a) Payment for lodging Indians,
     (PY) September 1, 1820, (V) 322.

(88) P. Gilmoor: a) Payment for lodging Indians, (PY)
     September 1, 1820, (V) 323.

(89) Joel Medley: a) Payment for liquors, cigars, and
     horse feed, (PY) September 2, 1820, (V) 324.

(90) John Ball: a) Payment for various expenses, (PY)
     September 3, 1820, (V) 325.

(91) Robert Bowman: a) Payment for the transportation
     of Indian baggage from Louisville to St. Louis,
     (PY) September 4, 1820, (V) 326.

(92) John Bains: a) Payment for a horse for J. B.
     Chouteau, (PY) September 5, 1820, (V) 327.

(93) I. Tomilson: a) Payment for food, horse feed and
     and lodging of Indians, (PY) August 26, 1820, (V)
     328.

(94) Pierre Chouteau: a) Payment for the lodging of
     Osage Indians, (PY) August 30, 1820, (V) 330.

(95) Joseph Cotte: a) Payment for transporting black-
     smith's tools, three men, and Indian baggage in the
     Osage Nation, (PY) September 30, 1820, (V) 331.

(96) Antoine Janis: a) Payment for corn meal, (PY) Sep-
     tember 30, 1820, (V) 332.

(99) R. Paul: a) Payment for pilot bread, (PY) September
     30, 1820, (V) 333.

(100) J. St. Germanin: a) Payment for a large pirouge,
     (PY) September 30, 1820, (V) 334.

(101) R. S. Wiggins: a) Payment for ferriage of Indians
     across the Mississippi River, (PY) September 30,
     1820, (V) 335.

(102) P. L. Chouteau: a) Payment for expenses on his tour
     with the Osages, (PY) October 3, 1820, (V) 336.

(103) Christian Welt: a) Payment for various goods, (PY)
     June 5, 1820, (V) 148.

(Indian Affairs, Missouri Territory Continued)
    (104) A. P. Chouteau: a) Payment for various goods, (PY)
          June 6, 1820, (V) 149.
    (105) R. Paul: a) Payment for clothing, (PY) June 6,1820,
          (V) 150.
    (106) John W. Johnson: a) Payment for lead, (PY) June 28,
          1820, (V) 166.
    (107) Fred. Dent: a) Payment for clothing, (PY) June 30,
          1820, (V) 169.
    (108) Antoine Dangen: a) Payment for jewelry, (PY)July 1,
          1820, (V) 178.
    (109) Lilburn W. Boggs: a) Payment for various goods,(PY)
          September 24, 1820, (V) 188.
    (110) James Woods: a) Payment for a horse, (PY) September
          27, 1820, (V) 192.

Johnson County, Missouri, Carpenter Cemetery,Chilhower Township (Note:Only Those Persons Born Before 1840 and That Died
Before 1900.

Name	Born	Died
Felix Lotspeich	Nov. 23, 1813	Jan. 13, 1875
Henry Lotspeich	Feb. 10, 1810	Oct. 27, 1882
Mary Lotspeich	Apr. 20, 1812	Feb. 7, 1887
Susan Lotspeich	Mar. 20, 1812	Mar. 13, 1896
A. M. Potts	Apr. 6, 1807	Apr. 1, 1864
Hiram Hunt	Mar. 1, 1803	Nov. 14, 188-
Adaline Vance	Sep. 8, 1812	Dec. 25, 1883
George E. Moore	May 3, 1826	Jul. 18, 1826
Lucy A. Raper	Aug. 11, 1839	Oct. 29, 1883
Susam Moore	Oct. 3, 1819	Jun. 13, 1895
Alonzo Potts	Apr. 14, 1823	Oct. 17, 1879
Elizabeth Witt	Feb. 22, 1819	Feb. 19, 1893
Sarah A. Satterwhite	1827	1899
Saphronia West	Dec. 6, 181809	Jul. 19, 1894
Pleasanr R. Witt	Jan. 21, 1818	Aug. 9, 1889
Leonard A. Wisley	May 25, 1819	Oct. 1, 1897

Ste. Genevieve County, Missouri, November, 1814, Members of
the Grand Jury.
    Henry Kiel, John Corren, Louis Gurneau, James G. Brady,
William Shannon, Charles Archambeau, Ferdinand Pisier,Pierre
Leonard, Michael Goza, Thomas Eads, Michael Doolin,Sebastian
Butcher, Jacob Miller, John Burns, John A. Sturges, William
Montier, Isaac Baird, Joab Waters, Jean M. Bouchard, George
Morrow, Perfait Dufour, George Pinkley.

Perry County, Missouri, March, 1828, Members of the Grand
Jury.
    John W. Stewart, Samuel Flynn, Jeremiah Warthon, Benedict

(Perry County, Missouri Continued)
Riley, James Hagan, Joseph Manning, sr., Peter Holster, Geo.
Fenwick, George W. Sturduine, Andrew Holster,Robert Winnsot,
Abner Kinison, Jonas Winfield, Alexander Bayley,Jos. Murray,
Jacob Shamer, Robert Greenwell, Robert Mitchell, Cornelius
Manning, Martain Layton, James D. Brewer, Lewis Coteaux.

Clay County, Missouri, New Hope Cemetery, New Hope Baptist
Church, Washington Township.

Name	Born	Died
Sarah Henderson	Aug. 22, 1812	Oct. 18, 1872
Early Armstead (age: 52 y)		May 9, 1855
Louisa G. Cole	Sep. 7, 1829	Nov. 5, 1870
William Groomer (age: 70 y, 10 m, 12 d)		Feb. 5, 1858
Daniel Askew	Feb. 28, 1828	Apr. 12, 1875
William L. Yates	Jul. 10, 1802	Dec. 25, 1869
Tyra Harris (age: 65 y, 20 d)		Feb. 16, 1861
Eliz. Brockman(age: 93 y)	Sep. 7, 1829	May 18, 1881
Garret Green	Jan. 5, 1787	May 4, 1870
Mary Green	Apr. 1, 1789	Jan. 15, 1874
David O. Brawner (age: 66 y. 10 m, 20 d)		Aug. 6, 1869
Clarra Agee	Mar. 10, 1818	Feb. 5, 1869
Robert Thomason	Feb. 17, 1791	Apr. 21, 1864
Sarah S. Thompson	Apr. 15, 1803	Oct. 12, 1851
Eliza F. Cosby	Jan. 15, 1826	Oct. 10, 1848
Yelverton Green (age: 43 y, 11 m, 6 d)		Nov. 21, 1865
Elizabeth S. Baker	Jul. 6, 1807	Jun. 22, 1859
Elizabeth Groomer (age: 66 y, 1 m, 28 d)		Feb. 16, 1858
Joseph P. Dagley	Sep. 25, 1826	May 23, 1875
James Armstead (age: 69 y)		Oct. 7, 1871
Ambrose Brockman (age: 77 y, 15 d)		Mar. 11, 1862
William Bayer (age: 57 y, 7 m, 9 d)		Oct. 29, 1864
Simeon Thomason	Sep. 25, 1825	Dec. 15, 1847
Robert Harris (age: 57 y)		Jun. 20, 1857
Nancy C. Hawkins (age: 49 y, 7 m, 1 d)		Mar. 5, 1868
Emily Dagley	Oct. 1, 1819	Sep. 4, 1848
Matilda Fitzgerald (Born: Georgetown, Ky, Oct. 21, 1805; died Liberty, Mo Apr. 27, 1877, age: 71, 6 m, 6 d)		
James Wilhoit (age: 60 y, 7 m, 11 d)		Mar. 11, 1874
John Hawkins (age: 65 y, 20 d)		May 4, 1868

Scott County, Missouri, October, 1822, Members of the Grand
Jury.
James Ramsey, William Allen, David Griffith,Abner Fowler,
John Hall, John Davis, Andrew Brown, Benj. G. Gray, Robert
M'Culloch, William Gray, Johnson Woosley, Martin Fowler,Hugh
B. Virgin, Bennet Towlson, Andrew Lafont, Andrew Lafont,Jas.
Hunter, Israel Friend.

(1)   The letter concerns the resurvey of a tract in New
        Madrid Co., which is confirmed to Joseph Laplante.
        Godfrey Lesieur asks for a new survey due to fraud
        by James Tanner and --- Summers. (LD) February 4,
        1829, (LN) 1, (PG) 13.

(2)   S. G. Hopkins' correspondence regarding both New
        Madrid and private land claims. (LD) February 14,
        1829, (LN) 2, (PG) 25.

(3)   Letter regarding the platt of James Scull as stated
        in the Quapaw Treaty.(LD) February 26,1829, (LN) 3,
        (PG) 33.

(4)   Col. Bamford appoints Lt. Thomas to select a site
        for a powder magazine. Lt. Thomas contacts Col.
        George Bamford regarding a tract which adjoins
        Dusanna Dubriel under Sylvester Sarpy.(LD) June 11,
        1829, (LN) 6, (PG) 97, (SN) 374.

(5)   Letter from William Russell regarding the claim of
        John B. Dardenne in the Arkansas Territory. Also,
        concerns a survey abstract for a bill before Con-
        gress for the relief of James Russell.

(6)   The claim of Joseph Marie is confirmed. (LD) June
        18, 1829, (LN) 9, (PG) 105, (SN) 1759.

(7)   Letter from Francis Menard regarding the survey of
        Nathaniel Shaver. (LN) 11, (PG) 121, (LD) July 8,
        1821, (SN) 588.

(8)   A letter correcting the New Madrid certificate no.
        153 of Edw. Mathews, that is north of the Missouri
        River. (LN) 13, (PG) 141, (LD) July 23, 1829.

(9)   Plat of the tract of Gregory Strahern. (LN) 13,
        (PG) 153, (LD) July 25, 1829.

(10)   A letter from the Land Office in Palestine, Ill.
        regarding an error in the claim of the heirs of
        Toussant Dubois. (LN) 16, (PG) 161, (LD) August 4,
        1829, (SN) 262.

(11)   A letter acknowledging the receipt of the plats on
        on the Arkansas River for --- Scull as stated in
        the Quapaw Treaty of 1824. (LN) 17, (PG) 171, (LD)
        August 28, 1829.

(12)   A letter concerning the tract of Jacob Myers. (LN)
        19, (PG) 179, (LD) September 10, 1829.

(13)   A letter citing the holdings of Robert D. Dawson,
        assignee of R. J. Waters. (LN) 20, (PG) 187, (LD)
        September 28, 1829.

(14)   A letter regarding the survey of Thomas Riney. (LN)
        21, (PG) 203, (LD) November 7, 1829, (SN) 1844.

(15)   A letter regarding the information of the tracts of
        Wm. James, (SN) 2908; John Campbell under Elisha

(Letters from the General Land Office)
Harrington, (SN) 478; and D. Delaney, (SN) 1702.
(LN) 25, (PG) 231, (LD) March 24, 1830.
(16)   A letter from the Land Office at Edwardsville, Ill.
         regarding the survey of John Kain, June, 1818. (LN)
         26, (PG) 240, (LD) May 14, 1830.
(17)   A letter confirming the claim of Isidore Moore,
         assignee of Thomas Fenwick under the concession of
         Zenon Trudeau in Perry County. (LN) 25, (PG) 255,
         (LD) May 29, 1830.
(18)   A letter regarding the application of Mr. Hunter,
         Scott County, for the patent on survey no. 49 for
         Stephen Dunney. (LN) 28, (PG) 263, (LD) June 8,
         1830.
(19)   A letter correcting survey no. 18 for David Darst,
         sr., survey no. 1643 for David Darst, jr., survey
         no. 970 and 1307 for Js. Davis, survey no. 20 for
         D. M. Boone, and survey no. 1646 for Daniel Boone.
         (LN) 29, (PG) 267, (LD) June 11, 1830.
(20)   A letter regarding Eustache Peltier, A. Chouteau,
         and Wm. C. Carr. (LN) 31, (PG) 311, (LD) November
         8, 1830.
(21)   Plat of James Mackey, south of the Missouri River.
         (LN) 32, (PG) 319, (LD) November 12, 1830.
(22)   A letter regarding the resurvey of James Piper
         under Francis Gignares. (LN) 33, (PG) 327, (LD)
         December 4, 1830, (SN) 1775.
(23)   A letter regarding the survey of Arend Rutgers.
         (LN) 35, (PG) 339, (LD) December 16, 1830.

Obituary From The Lawrence, Kansas Republican,June 28, 1860.
     J. D. Davidson, about age 55 and formerly of Cass County,
Missouri, died on June 23, 1860.

Ste. Genevieve County, Missouri, August, 1815,Members of the
Grand Jury.
     Peter Daquiet, John Barns, Michael Goza,Abraham Newfield,
Obediah Scott, Richard Maddin, John R. Cissel, Henry Diel,
Aubene Cerre, St. Germain Bouvais, Henry Chambers, Rene Le
Meilleus, John McArthur, Richard Burnass, Jean Bta. Valle,
sr., Edmond Roberts, Jean Bta. Valle,jr., Jean Bte. Bassier,
Patrick McManes.

St. Charles County, Missouri, October, 1808, Members of the
Grand Jury.
     Ebenezer Ayers, Andrew Zumwalt, Frances Howell, Hezekiel
O'Neal, George Hoopman, Abraham Darst, William Craig, James
Baldridge, Joseph Duplcit, James Morrison, Antoine Reynolds,
William F. Lamme, William Lynn.

Monroe County, Missouri, Middle Grove Cemetery, Middle Grove.

Name	Born	Died
W. H. Dulany	Apr. 3, 1814	Mar. 4, 1819
Eliza Settle	Mar. 3, 1821	Nov. 2, 1892
Palina Davis	Nov. 25, 1822	Jul. 30, 1864
Louisa M. Noel	Mar. 2, 1827	Nov. 11, 1886
Olive Brooks (age: 36 y, 8 m, 18 d)		Aug. 28, 1855
Lydia V. Fearis	Sep. 29, 1829	Feb. 26, 1898
Briant Riley (age: 58 y, 9 m, 26 d)		Nov. 29, 1863
Portteus G. Fearis	Oct. 17, 1833	Oct. 10, 1883
George H. Bassett	Oct. 18, 1806	Oct. 9, 1895
Powel S. Ownby	Dec. 21, 1812	May 9, 1871
Philip Swartz (age: 63 y, 2 m)		Mar. 6, 1883
Ruth Harris	Feb. 15, 1828	Jul. 15, 1880
Dorothy Baker	May 26, 1786	May 20, 1853
Malka J. Hulen	Nov. 8, 1831	Sep. 27, 1884
Catharine Brooks (age: 76 y, 9 m, 4 d)		Aug. 20, 1854
T. N. Galbreath (age: 77 y, 11 m, 20 d)		May 8, 1893
Sarah J. Ownby	Jun. 4, 1817	Sep. 11, 1882
Thomas G. Bacland (age: 69 y, 9 m, 15 d)		Apr. 2, 1874
Elijah G. Broaddus	1822	1895
Riley Brown	Jun. 5, 1835	Dec. 6, 1889
Susan Bacland (age: 39 y, 6 m, 13 d)		Aug. 31, 1863
Adeline Reid (age: 76 y, 10 m, 28 d)		Aug. 6, 1887
Susan Goodnight	1829	1896
Absalom W. Stephens	Aug. 5, 1815	Dec. 25, 1889
Cath. McDowell Anderson	Jan. 30, 1817	Apr. 24, 1891
John M. Brooks (age: 59 y, 6 m, 26 d)		Dec. 5, 1878
Thomas Turk Harris	Sep. 2, 1827	Mar. 13, 1896
S. O. Hunter (age: 85 y, 10 m, 2 d)		Oct. 18, 1876
Nancy A. Evans	Nov. 17, 1829	Jul. 6, 1898
A. A. Anderson (age: 78 y)		Sep. 7, 1883
Rebecca Riley	Nov. 2, 1810	Dec. 6, 1893
Abraham Hardy	Dec. 30, 1839	Feb. 28, 1852
Joseph Stevens (age: 85 y)		Sep. 22, 1861
Morris James (age: 75 y, 5 m, 11 d)		Feb. 22, 1876
Joseph Harris	Aug. 1, 1808	Sep. 1, 1880
Catherine A. Osbourn (age:62 y,11 m,3 d)		Feb. 10, 1877
Abraham Hardy, sr. (no date)		
Bettie A. Eustace	Sep. 13, 1833	Apr. 5, 1890
Mary Neal (age: 71 y, 6 m, 7 d)		Feb. 28, 1871

Chariton County, Missouri, Deed Tax From November 4, 1824 to November 6, 1826, Capitol Fire Documents, Folder 733.

Saml. Loney, J. Whitside and Levi Davis, Thos. B. Scott, Moses Halbitt, B. Briley, E. B. Cabell, Hiram Craig, Edwd. B. Cabell, William Fleetwood, D. Ashby, S. Donohoe, Thos. Gorham, M. Finnell, Jas. Ross, I. R. White, Duff Green, Geo. Burckhartt, Thos. Watson, J. M. Baker, J. Wells, Bland Smith,

(Chariton County, Missouri Continued)
Joseph Vance, Joseph Gill, Jas. Ryan, Thos. Watson, Thos. G.
Bradford, John Bule, Saml. Davis, Jesse Hendeteter, N. Wash,
J. Parker, E. T. Hickman, J. M. Baker (sic), M. Morgan, Wm.
Ralph, J. L. Anderson, Isaac Garrett, Wm. H. Monroe, E. B.
Cabell, Thos. Watson (sic), D. E. Clayton, John Burk, Isaac
Williams, J. Dysart, Robt. Hancock, J. B. Winn, S. Smith, D.
E. Cuyler, John Presson, Wm. Lockridge, Peter B. Harris, J.
S. Watson, Geo. Vaughan, Jas. Friar, B. B. Williams, William
Rector, J. Harrison, E. Dale, Thomas Griffin, Wm. Lawrence,
E. Arterberry, S. Campbell, A. F. Walden, James Ravenscraft,
John Williams, Jas. Collins, John M'Cully, Thos. Lock, T. G.
Bradford, M. Jacobs, Patrick O. Fling, F. Redding, William
Cabeen, H. T. Williams, F. Loring, Jas. Smith, S. M. Cully,
Stephen Glascock, Jas. Sipple, J. Highnoght, Levi Fauk, Wm.
N. Fulkerson, Jas. P. Fulkerson.

Perry County, Missouri, Poll Book, 1836, Capitol Fire Docu-
ments, No. 182..
   Cinghomme Township: Alarkin Abernathy, Alonzo Abernathy,
Harley D. Abernathy, James D. Abernathy, John Adams, George
Ashly, David Bails, Frederick Ballinger, Ferdinand Belsha,
Mathias Barringer, John Bess, H. Black, Joshua Bess, Lewis
Blaze, Charles Brewer, John Brewer, Mark Brewer, John Brite,
Robert T. Brown, Thomas Brown, Vimzod (sic) Brown, William
Burrs, Adam J. Bullinger, Joab Burgee, James Burns, James
Camern, Robert Cashion, Benjamin Chambers, Wm. Cissell, John
R. Cissell, Fracis Clark, Franklin Clifton, Jacob Clifton,
Samuel Clifton, Samuel M. Cobbs, Jacob Conrad, John Conrad,
Peter Conrad, Michael Daley, Henry Deen, Peter Deen, William
Deen, Lewis Dickson, Nathaniel J. Divine, Steven Dolson, R.
S. Dorsey, Henry Drury, John M. Duvall, Joseph Eddlemon, Guy
Elder, John Farrar, Ansil Farrel, John P. Finch, Washington
Gather, Peter Flaharty, Joseph French, Silas French, Robert
L. Glascock, Henry Grounds, Peter Grounds, Mitchael Hagan,
Isadore Hagan, Edward Hagan, Seth Hall, Abram Ham, Charles
A. Harris, Frderick C. Hase, Charles Hayden, Clement Haydon,
Philemon Higgins, Casper Hunker, Austin Hogard, Wm. Hogard,
Christen Horns,Bernard Horrell, John Huffman,Nathan Jackson,
Nelson Jones, George Killion, Ansil Layton, Austin Layton,
Ignatius Layton, James Layton, John Layton, John B. Layton,
Joseph Layton, Lewis Layton, Walter Layton, Wilford Layton,
Henry Leonard, Henry Little,Ransom A. Little,Henry McAustin,
Benj. McAuley, James McAuley, Wm. McAuley, Patrick McBride,
Edward McGinnis, Michael McLaughlin, John McLean, Richard
Maddock, James Manning, Gilleson Martin, James B. Mattingly,
Joseph A. Massey, Joseph Mattingly, Wm. Mattingly, Joseph B.
Miller, James Michael, Francis Miles, Joseph Miles, Ignatus
Moore,James C. Moore, James N. Moore,Levi Moore,Lewis Moore,

(Perry County, Missouri Continued)

Martin L. Moore, Sylvester Moore, Thomas Newberry, Benjamin P. Overton, Daniel O'Meara, Alfred L. Parks,Caleb H. Perrin, Cornelius Pertle, James Philips, David Pinkleton, John Rice, Clement Powers, Jeffery Powers, P. R. Pratte,George Preston, John Pullim, Wm. Rariddon, Thomas Riney, John Ross, Charles Roy, George Ruledge, Wm. Rutledge, Alfred Saddler, Fedeston Saddler, Joseph Saddler, James Saddler, Stephen Sanders, Wm. Searcy, Francis Scools, George Scott, Reuben Shelby, Joseph Shults, Joseph D. Simpson, Felix Sims,James Skidmore, Robert Steward, Charles Stuart, Wm. Steward, John C. Sutton,William Taylor, Lewis Tharp, Archibald Thurman, Wm. R. Tompson, John P. Tucker, Robert Trotter, Francis Tucker, James F. Tucker, John T. Tucker, Joseph Tucker,Nicholas Tucker,Thomas Tucker, Wm. T. Tucker, Geo. W. Vessels, Jesse R. Walker, William A. Walker, John Waters, David Watkins, Richard Welch,Wm. White, Isaac Westover, Trenius Whelenburger, John Whitledge, Joseph Wilkinson, Wm. Winfield.

Brazean Township: Lott Abernathy, Alexander Baily, Elias Barber, Samuel Barber, Robert Black, William A. Black,Wm. A. Bull, Daniel Cline, Jessey Dickson, Leo. Fenwick, Richard N. Graham, Miles Hughes, Joseph James, Singleton H. Kimmel, Asa Trickey, Ezekiel Knox, David Luckey, David McHenry,Archibald Mickel, Joseph Murray, Lorenzo D. Myres, Columbus Price, Wm. Price, John Ross, George Seiburt,Henry Seiburt,Richard Swan, Thomson Trickey, Thomas Twyman,Thomas Wilkerson,Rbt. Wilson.

Bois Brule Township: David M. Anderson, James Beasley, John E. Burgett, Michael Burns, Logan M. C. Carver, William Cox, Thomas Ewell, James Fairhertt, Isaac Flynn, Wm. Flynn, Vincent Grenn, George Hayden, Alexander Hogard,David Waters, William P. Kenadey, Joel Kinneson, Stephen Kinneson, William Marshal, James Nickel, John Patterson, Fk. Pratt, Benjamin Williams, William Redford, Abraham Roberts,Joseph Rodes,John Sadler, Thomas Sanders, Charles W. Stewart, George Vessels.

St. Charles County, Missouri,June, 1810,Members of the Grand Jury.

John Davis, Anthony Hellar, Charles Tayon, Richard Jones, Nathan Boon, Ephraim Anderson, Alex. Allison, jr., Alexander Murdock, Paul LaCroise, Joshua Dodson, Will. T. Lema, Aruno Rutgers, Will. T. Cole, Jonathan Bryan, Will. Stewart, Janis Journey, John Lindsey, David Bryan, Henry Stephenson,Stephen Cole.

Van Buren County, Missouri,Delinquent Tax List,1838,Capitol Fire Documents, Folder 1351.

Isaac Bledsoe, Alexander Belcher, Sampson Bledsoe, David Chandler, Wm. F. Ellis, Joshua Evans, George W. Gentry, John Baskin, Jesse Houshaw, Wm. Hornsby, Irwin W. Hill, James R.

(Van Buren County, Missouri Continued)
May, David McGee, Edmund Gapper, Peter Thomas, John Porter,
Wm. Rhea, John Rollins, Thomas Smith, John Tucker, Joel P.
Walker, Gabriel Stratton.

Audrain County, Missouri, Emmanuel Evangelical German Church Cemetery, Rt. J, North of Mexico, Missoouri.

Name	Born	Died
John Hammond	Dec. 7, 1799	Oct. 1, 1871
John P. Umstattd	Nov. 18, 1815	Jul. 10, 1880
John H. Wilson (age: 86 y, 5 m, 10 d)		Mar. 24, 1870
Jane Bledsoe	Jun. 1, 1802	Nov. 17, 1869
Susanna Wilson (age: 77 y, 3 m, 14 d)		Oct. 23, 1878
W. W. Wilson	Oct. 21, 1823	Mar. 9, 1876
P. W. Gahan (age: 42 y, 1 m, 11 d)		May 25, 1877
Hester S. Price	Aug. 21, 1821	Mar. 2, 1897
John M. Price	Dec. 23, 1814	Feb. 18, 1886
Rebecca Story	Feb. 4, 1804	Mar. 12, 1879
Rachel Bozarth	Jul. 25, 1836	Aug. 25, 1878
John J. Weaver	Feb. 16, 1811	Dec. 10, 1881
Eve F. Simms	Feb. 18, 1808	Jul. 7, 1882
John Ellis	Sep. 5, 1820	Apr. 14, 1886
Rebecca Ellis (age: 43 y, 2 m, 13 d)		Nov. 3, 1868
Jane Finks	Dec. 6, 1826	May 24, 1886
Eleanor D. Weaver	1829	1893
Clarissa M. Creed	1825	Jul. 6, 1896
Rebecca Goodrich	1816	1891
*Peyton Botts	Dec. 8, 1805	Aug. 15, 1875

   *(Born in Rappahamnock County,Va.,Moved to Missouri in
      1836. Married Elizabeth Lewis,born Culpepper Co.,
      Va., April 4, 1803. Had four daughters and two sons.)

Name	Born	Died
Edmund Goodrich	1816	1890
Martin Goodrich	1798	1886
Thomas H. Fisher	1827	1885
Mrs. Sarah V. Dudley	Oct. 9, 1813	Feb. 20, 1877
J. W. Dudley	Jun. 12, 1807	Jul. 17, 1880
*William Emmons	Mar. 22, 1821	Oct. 22, 1821

   *(Born Flemming County, Ky.)

Name	Died
Nannie P. Bedford (age: 1 y, 1 m, 29 d)	Mar. 5, 1821

Ste. Genevieve County, Missouri, Delinquent Tax List, 1838, Capitol Fire Documents, Folder 1349.

Alexander Buges, William Bell, Franklin Boles, M. Cofer,
Frances Delba, John Hendrickson, James Ham, Frances Vincent,
Pierre Lajor, John Missplay, Walter M'Lain, Willis McNally,
Jos. M. Migren, Garrett McAllister, William Neal, H. Reeder,
John Patterson,James Patrick, Zeno Placet, James Strickland,
Corns. Rhodes, Charles Sibert, William Steward,Lewis Jacabo,
Gregoire V. Jones, Joseph Patterson.

Lafayette County, Missouri, Deed Book A, February 16, 1825, Persons Purchasing Town Lots In Lexington.

Henry Renick, jr., Henry Renick, sr., Spencer Estis, John Young, Jesse Hickcock, Michael Farris, Chatham Ewing, William Horn, Michael Farris, Braxton Small, Thomas Blakley, James Gray, Young Ewing, John Ingram, Alfred K. Stephens, Wm. Ellison and Abner Norris, James Whitsett, James Bounds, James Nelson, Thomas Hollingsworth, Ira Bedwell, David Ward, G. P. Buche, William Robinson, Benj. Gooch, William Wallace.

Ste. Genevieve County, Missouri, Inquests, 1788 to 1801.

Name	Date	Comments
Bethold Bonneau	1801	
Jean Gachard	1801	Autopsy
Mathew Faussee	1794	Killed by Denis and Fcois. Auge
Francois Grenon	1788	Testified on the death of sister-in-law, Mrs. Jos. Grenon (Margaret Thiery)
Joseph Grenon	1788	Death
Joseph Lalumadiere	1795	Concerning 6the death of an Englishman at Mine-a-Breton
James Ross	1795	Sudden Death
--- Paquin	1792	Sudden Death
Jean Bpt. Dorlac	1775	Sudden Death
Jn. Bapt. Lafont	1789	Body in River

Cape Girardeau County, Missouri, Merchant Licenses, September, 1825, Capitol Fire Documents, Folder 1055.

Name	Date
Dilbourn & Curopin	July 20, 1825
Cyrus Henderson	August 25, 1825
Adam Clingsmith	August 28, 1825
Robert P. Slaughter	September 1, 1825
James P. Fulkerson	September 12, 1825
M. and Z. Block	September 12, 1825
Morton & Smoot	September 13m 1825
Thomas Neal	August 19, 1825
James N. Burnett	August 19, 1825
Kimmel & Payton	August 21, 1825
N. Danhorn	September 6, 1825
D. V. Shell	September 7, 1825
I. Ralathein	September 13, 1825

St. Charles County, Missouri, February, 1811, Members Of The Grand Jury.

Jesse Morrison, Richard Law, Joseph Keithly, James Lewis,

(St. Charles County, Missouri Continued)
Zadock Woods, Martin Woods, Jacob Trask, James Baldridge, Jeremiah Geoshang, Lawrence Killekrew, Stephen Hempstead, John B. Stone, Joshua Dodson, Anthony C. Palmer, Wm. Zozanson.

Saline County, Missouri, November, 1825, Tax On Executions and Writs, Capitol Fire Documents, Folder 680.

Name	Name	Document
Philip Frammell	G. C. Hart	Execution
William Pate	Geo. Tennille	Execution
A. and A. Goodin	John Smith	Writ
James Warren	John Smith	Writ
A. Steel	A. H. Galbreath	Writ
Cornelius Davis	Francis Cooper	Execution
Rice & Eldridge	A. Galbreath	Execution
J. McMahan	John Smith	Execution
B. Romine	Hugh Tennille	Execution
Barton Lawless		Ferry Lisc.
Jesse G---	--- Lindell	Deed
Chspher. Catron's heirs	Jacob Ish	Deed
Anthony Thomas	Anthony C. Thomas	Deed

Jackson County, Missouri, November, 1827, Licenses, Capitol Fire Documents, Folder 782.

Name	Date	Type
Wilham Prime	May 21, 1827	Ferry
Anton Uneau	September 3, 1827	Ferry

Perry County, Missouri, March, 1838, Naturalization Intents.

Name	Nativity
Nicholas and Peter Gieber	France
Philip Schmaltz	Baden
Francis Dosenbach	Baden
Martin Endres	Ireland
Michael Muhlfeld	Ireland

Randolph County, Illinois, Probate Records, 1790 to 1808, Box OSC 41.

Name	Died Before
Henry O'Hara	July 5, 1808
Bridget O'Hara	July 5, 1808
Moses Oliver	February 17, 1807
Slyvester Patterson	November 15, 1806
Margaret Preston	January 13, 1803
Paul Reaum	January 23, 1795
John Richards	September 3, 1803
Josiah Ryan	December 15, 1800
Lazarus Ryan	September 11, 1805
Elisha Smith	August 8, 1808

(Randolph County, Illinois Continued)

Name	Died Before
Jacques Smith	1790
Baptiste St. Ouse	January 30, 1798
John Sharp	April 3, 1797
Mary Magdaline Tardue	September 5, 1801
Joseph Turcott	October 8, 1802
Geo. White	July 25, 1797
William Whitesides	February 7, 1801
John Williams	May --, 1805
Samuel Worley	Febraury 8, 1800

Audrain County, Missouri, October, 1838,Delinquent Tax List, Capitol Fire Documents, CFD 30, Folder 1263.

Abraham Alexander, John A. Adams, Francois Armstead, John Allen, Miller M. Barnes, Ira S. Brooks, Neal Blue, Edward H. Douglass, Duncan Blue, Richard Byran, Isaac Black, Joseph S. Delaney, John W. Barnett, Thos. M. Barnett, William Bryns, George Bomer, Joseph Brown,Elija M. Byran,Edward Beatty,John Crosswhite, Jacob Bruce, James F. Botts, William Creacy,John Creacy,John Crud,Benjamin Canterbury,Franklin P. Canterbury, Ruebin M. Canterbury, Thos. Crouch, Wyatt Cardwell, Samuel Cammel,Hugh Crockett,Madison Disard,James Davis(Beaver Dam), Mathew Davis,Joseph S. Delaney,Ephraim Davis,Wm. T. Dallins, James Davis (Littleby), Simon Davis, James Davis (Shulluck), H. J. M. Doan, Lewis Day, Wm. B. Evans, Elijah Eubanks, Wm. Eubanks, David Eubanks, John Fannery, John Faucett, Edward Faucett, Pinkney Frenth, Josiah Fugate, David I. Fort, Jas. E. Fenton, Alfred Gabreth, Daniel Galbreth, Archibald Grigg, Josiah Grant, John Goally, Hugh Gregg, John I. Greason, John Hungate, William Hunquel, Flemming B. Hubbard, David Hatten, Jonah B. Hatten, Milton Hatten, William Howard, Hiram Harry, Andrew B. B. Hayes, Elihu Hall, Joel Haynes,Wm. Hall, Jacob Haupt, Thos. Hundle, Thos. Hook,Slocum Jackson,Jas. Jackson, Greenbury Johnson, Miles Johnson, Phillip Johnson, Isam T.W. Kilgore, Greenes (sic) Jackman,Bacanah Jackson,Wm. M. Jesse, Thos. M. Joplin, Isaac Johnson, Johnson Kilgore, B. S. Mays, John H. Kilgore, Balez Kilgore,Hugh Kilgore,John B. Kilgore, G.W. Kilgore, Thos. Kilgore,Thos. I. Kecton,Henry R. Kecton, George Literal, John Lorton, jr., John Lorton, sr., William Lochridge, Thos. Lorton, John Lochridge, Jas. Lochridge, R. C. Mansfield, David Leach, Elvington Mallory,Benjamin McGee, Peyton Mahan, Drusa D. Mayse, Wm. W. Mayse, I. H. Williams, Benjamin McCarty, Daniel McSwain,David Mastin,Vincent Moore, William B. Middleton, David Mahaney, Wm. F. Metcalf, William M'Cormack, Barly Miller, David Myass, Prelby Myass, Stephen Masthena, David McCormack, Thos. McDaniel, Joseph McDaniel, jr., Joseph McDaniel, sr., Cashus McDonald, Roland McIntyre, Charles McIntyre, J. B. Mosses, I. C. Martin, J. A. Martin,

(Audrain County, Missouri Continued)
Thomason Norvell, James Oslin, Martin Oslin,Michael Perkins,
Jesse Perkins, John Perkins, Minor Pate, Nathaniel Pearson,
P.W. Pearson, Joseph A. Posey,Alfred Petty,Richmond Pearson,
William Pearson, Ruebin Pulis, P. H. Powell, John Pottz, J.
A. Pearson, Joseph Pearson, John A. Read, Wm. Reynolds, L.L.
Ramsey, Granville Read, John Smith,Abraham Smith,John Still,
John G. Swindle, Thos. Stricklin, James Spera, Andrew Still,
Meredith Still, Wm. Still, Eli Smith, George S. Smith, H. P.
L. Shock, William Shepard, Flinny Shock, Jas. H. Smith,Thos.
T. Stone, Edward Turner, Daniel W. Tally, George Tally, Wm.
Tally, John R. Tennison, Abraham   B. Tinsly, G. W. Tusley,
John Turner, Robt. Tailor, Wm. L. Wayne, A. H. Wayne, Colet
V. Williams, David Wilson, Wm. W. Welch, C. R. Ward, Roling
Watts, Caleb Williams, William Woods, Isam Willingham, B. B.
Wilkinson, P. H. Woods, Wm. C. West, William White, Lewis R.
Venibb, Wm. Willingham White,Littlebury Watts,G.P. Williams,
W. L. Williams, Joseph Watts, Temple Wayne, W.H. Wright,John
Young, John Willingham, Lewis R. Vennibb, James H. West.
    Nonresidents: John Davis, Angel Gillasby, James M'Pike,
R. H. C. Fulkerson.

Ste. Genevieve County, Missouri, November, 1815, Members Of
The Grand Jury.
    William Dillon, Patrick McMans, Julian Dessha, Beckwith
Baker, George Callaway, Louis Beuat, John Morgan, Christian
Fenton, Archibald Morgan,John Tennison,John Bte. Flubardeau,
Johnson Campbell, John A. Bossier, Henry Leek, Joab Waters,
Hezekiah P. Harris, Ferdinan Rogeer, Mathew Pusey, John Bte.
Beavuis, John Dart, Charles Ellis, William Flynn.

New Madrid County, Missouri, November, 1822, Circuit Court
Record Book.
    (PG 1)   Joseph Hunter vs. Hiram Cannon: Action for Slan-
             der.
             John Wathen, adm. for Aquilla Wathen, dec., vs.
             Charles F. Ramsey, exr. of James Brady, dec.:
             Action of Covenant.
             Joseph Hunter vs. Hiram Cannon: Action for Slan-
             der (sic).
             State vs. Hartwell Baldwin: Indicted for Assault
             and Battery.
             David Hunter vs. Stephen Ross:Action of Covenant.
             State vs. Spencer P. Biddle:Indicted for Assault
             and Battery.
    (PG 2)   Members of the Grand Jury: John Wathen, Joseph
             Marshal, William Sullen, William Winchester, John
             Lucas, Isreal Friend, Elijelot (sic) Folsom, John
             Ramsey, Thos. M'Mullin, William Actherton, Joseph

93

(New Madrid County, Missouri Continued)

Essory, Enoch Evans.

James Hutton failed to attend as a juror in the case of State vs. Spencer P. Biddle.

State vs. Chas. R. Saunders: Indicted for Assault and Battery; Jury for the trial: James Hutson, Joseph A. Hopkins, George Autherton, Theodore Kingsberry, John Winchester, Robert Ravenscraft, Eliphalet Folsom, John Wathen, Isreal Friend.

State vs. Wm. Winchester: Indicted for Larceny.

Joseph Lambert vs. Joseph Notterly: On Appeal.

James Dudley vs. Isreal Friend: On Appeal, Jury for the trial: William Netherton, Samuel Trotter, Charles R. Saunders, James Hutson, John Shank, George Huffman, James Ruth, William Winchester, Joseph Michel, Isaac Ogden, Joseph A. Hopkins, James Reagan.

(PG 3)   Robert G. Watson, assignee of Samuel Dorsey vs. Andrew P. Gillespie and James Tanner: Action of Debt.

Van H. D'Lashmut vs. Andrew P. Gillespie and James Tanner: Action of Debt.

Archibald Taylor, for the use of R. M'Farland vs. John Walters: Action of Debt.

Houts & Stallcup vs. Enoch Leggett: On Appeal.

(PG 4)   State vs. Wm. Winchester: Indicted for Assault and Battery.

Eliphalet Fulson vs. Jacob Myers: Action on a case for Slander.

Joseph Hunter vs. Hiram Cannon: Action for Slander.

James Dudley vs. Isreal Friend: On Appeal.

Thomas C. Powell vs. James Turner, Isaac Ogden, and Andrew P. Gillespie: Injunction.

(PG 5)   Isreal Friend, for the use of John Scott vs. James Tanner and Thomas H. Tindall: Action for a Covenant.

Phinehas Coburn vs. Elizabeth Phillips and Rich. Phillips: Action on the case.

Grand Jury: Charles T. Ramsey, Joseph Michel, Andrew M. Ramsey, Robert Ravenscraft, John P. Lucas, John Mathew, James Nichol, Constantine Keesler, James Simpson, William Sutton, James Dudley, James Purtle.

Eliphalet Fulsom vs. Jacob Myers: Action for a case of Slander.

Stillwell Heddy, George Shrader, joined with Enoch Legget and Lucinda Biddle vs. Wm. Maulsby: Action of Detinue (sic).

94

(New Madrid County, Missouri Continued)
          Hartwell Baldwin vs. William Bacon: Action of
          Resselevin (sic).
(PG 6)   James Evans vs. Eliza Chamberlain, adm. of Jason
          Chamberlin, dec.: Action of Trespass.
          Rachael Laugherty, adm. of Benijah Laugherty vs.
          Andrew M. Ramsey: Action of Debt.
          Alexander Miligan vs. Charles T. Ramsey, exr.:
          Action of Covenant.
          Hiram Cannon vs. Shapley Phillips: Action of
          Trespass.
          Rutter,Houts & Stallcup vs. Phillip Ross: Action
          of Debt Attachment.
          Nathaniel Shaver vs. Hartwell Baldwin: Action of
          Debt Attachment.
(PG 7)   Barny Burns, adm. of Michael Burns, dec. vs.
          James Hunter: Action of Debt.
          Anthony B. Neely, assignee vs. Jos. A. Hopkins:
          Action of Debt.
          Eastwith Prag vs. Joseph Lasermuet: On Appeal.
          William Hunter vs. Johnson Hunter: Motion to
          quash an execution.
          John Waters and the heirs of Thomas W. Waters,
          dec. vs. Henry Wait and others.
          Thomas Houts was appointed commissioner.
          Thomas Fletcher was absent.
          Hartwell Baldwin vs. William Bacon: Action of
          Resselevin (sic).
(PG 8)   David Armour vs. Christ. G. Houts and Richard
          Phillips: Action of Covenant.
          Hartwell Baldwin vs. William Bacon: Action of
          Resselevin (sic).
          John Wathen vs. Ludwell R. Davis: Action of ---.
          William Taylor vs. Ludwell R. Davis: Petition to
          Foreclose.

Ste. Genevieve County, Missouri, March, 1814, Members of the
Grand Jury, Court of Common Pleas.
    Joseph   Bequet, jr., Humphrey Gibson, Richard Moore, John
May, Samuel McCall,Edward Johnson,Michael Goza,James Rigdon,
Thomas Patterson, James McLean, Barney Burns, Andrew Fisher.

Indian Affairs,September 1, 1823 to September 1, 1824,Report
of the Second Auditor's Office by Wm. Lee to E. P. Swift,
American States Papers, Vol. 2., Pages 561-562.
    Duff   Green, Wm. P. Duval, John Brereton, Lewis Cass, Wm.
Clark, John Crowell, George Gray, Peter Pelham,Harvey Brown,
Gad Humphries, Benard Rui, G. D. Worthington, James Gadsden,
Joseph McMinn, William Ward, George Walton, Richard Graham,

(Indian Affairs Continued)

William Ward, George Walton, C.W. Fanning, Robert Crittenden, James Miller, Matthew Irwin, Benjamin F. Smith, S. Carruthers, Jasper Parish, John Johnston, John Ross, Wm. Prince, Charles B. King, Nathaniel Jewett, Isaac Cooper, Robert Malbone, Z. Lewis, Thomas Forsyth, John Hays, John Tipton, Peter Wilson, B. F. Stickney, Lawrence Taiaferro, Nathaniel Philbrook, J. B. Finley, Nicholas Noilvin, Henry Conway, Eliza Dodds, Wm. Noyes, Samuel Houston, Moses Allen, T. C. Henry, Wm. Mackey, Samuel Thompson, Albion K. Parris, O. B. Brown, Henry Hill, Jeremiah Evarts, Charles A. Burnett, Ninian Beall, Duncan G. Campbell, Hugh Gelston, H. Simpson, Henry Deringer, Richard Burgess, John B. Blake, Luther Rice.

Howard County, Missouri, 1850 Mortality Schedule, (Only Those Persons Born Before 1840).

Name	Age	Died	Martial Status	Birthplace
Harriet White	40	March	Married	Pennsylvania
Rachael Knight	44	May	Married	Kentucky
Lucy Knight	14	June		Missouri
Adam C. Woods	54	August	Married	Kentucky
Jane Perry	25	September		Kentucky
Lucy Williams	30	February	Married	Kentucky
Mary Simons	50	September	Widow	Kentucky
Lewis Wisdom	49	October	Married	Kentucky
Sarah Hayne	30	January	Married	Virginia
Elizabeth Bradley	15	September		Missouri
Robert Percival	64	June	Married	England
Ann Woods	20	December		Missouri
James Robinson	11	January		Missouri
Mary Tolson	80	March	Widow	Virginia
Mildred Tolson	50	October		Virginia
Jackson Thorp	50	November	Married	Kentucky
Joseph Fields	76	February	Widower	Maryland
Millisa Naylor	41	March	Married	Kentucky
Betsy Street	29	February		Kentucky
Abernathy D. Payne	29	August	Married	Kentucky
Louisa Lamme	21	July		Missouri

St. Charles County, Missouri, June, 1811, Members Of The Grand Jury.

Daniel M. Boone, Francis Howell, Zachariah Moore, Eleazer Clay, James Clay, John Howell, Hugh McPeters, George Zumwalt, Stephen Hancock, Joseph Taylor, George Huffman, Michael Crow, Peter Huffman, James Journey, James McMillen.

Indiana Territory, Petitioners Regarding The Sale Of Public Lands, Carter's Territorial Papers, Vol. VII.

J. Edgar, Jas. Johnson, Will. Mackintosh, Abel Westfall,

(Indiana Territory Continued)
Henry Vanderburgh, Jno. Johnson, R. Morrison, John Griffin, Wm. Morrison, Js. Edgar, James Morrison, --- Jarrot, Daniel Sullivan, Jonathan Pettit, Robt. Reynolds,Thos. Newberry,Wm. Price, Benjn. D. Price.

Chariton County, Missouri, Licenses, November, 1827, Capitol Fire Documents, Folder 782.

Name	Type	Date
John Graves	Merchant	May 28, 1827
Jas. Ross	Merchant	Jun. 22, 1827
John Graves	Mines	Aug. 25, 1827
R. B. Thornton and A. Thrask	Ferrykeeper	Oct. 11, 1827
John Boyles	Ferrykeeper	Aug. 25, 1827
Jas. Ross and Wm. Glasgow	Merchant	Nov. 7, 1827

Lafayette County, Missouri, March, 1835,Change of Venue from Ray County, Fee Bill for the State vs. James Snowden.
Johnathan T. Bunch, Thomas Edwards, Young Ewing, Markham Fristoe, Isaac Martin, Abner G. Sneed, William Brewer, Adam Black, William Black, William L. Black, John Dodson, William Fields, James Allen, Thomas Riggs, Zadoc Marken,Henry Gregg.

Greene County, Missouri, October, 1839,Election at the House of Nathaniel Boon, that was created by the death of Albert G. Herrison, Capitol Fire Documents, Folder 16217.
Joseph Morris, Archibald Morris, John Walker, B.A. James, Isaac Looney, Isaac Burgan, William Johnson, A. B. Chastain, James M. Brane, Hugh Leeper.

Lawrence, Kansas, Kansas Republican,October 17,1855,Obituary of Willis Sutton.
Willis Sutton, of northeast Missouri, died of cholera on September 9, 1855 near Osawkee on the Grasshopper River. He was traveling on Samuel Ferandis' wagon train which was en route to Ft. Riley.

St. Charles County, Missouri, November, 1811, Members of the Grand Jury.
Benjamin Emmons, David Hays, John Stewart, David Bailey, Samuel Lewis, Henry Crow, Daniel Baldridge,Isaac Hotstotter, Robert Green, Andrew Cottle, James Cottle,Christopher Clark, James Boucher, James M'Millin, Andrew Zumwalt,Peter Huffman, Louis Crow, James Beaty.

New Madrid County, Missouri, Dunklin Cemetery, (Between New Madrid and Pt. Pleasant.

Name	Born	Died
Jane E. Maulsby	Aug. 14, 1835	Jun. 15, 1868

Name	Born	Died
Susanna Dunklin	Dec. 5, 1800	Jun. 25, 1869
Eliza Toney	1797	Jan. 13, 1864
Cynthia Montgomery	1777	Jul. 2, 1830
Mary D. Hunter	Aug. 14, 1827	Jan. 22, 1847
Jefferson D. Thomas	Jul. 2, 1832	Nov. 22, 1858
Madison Imboden	Nov. 2, 1832	Sep. 28, 1867
William Dunklin	1797	Feb. 13, 1840

Cooper County, Missouri, Licenses, May, 1837, Capitol Fire Documents, CFD. 30, Folder 1216.

Name	Type
Rogers & Blythe	Merchant
Wyan & Trigg	Merchant
R. D. Bousfield	Merchant
F. B. M'Curdy	Merchant
James H. Malone	Merchant
J. Quarles	Merchant
W. W. Fields	Merchant
J. M. Cox	Merchant
F. A. Pollock	Grocer
F. A. Williams	Grocer
N. Rector	Grocer
Dobbins & McCune	Grocer
Coleman Bullard	Grocer
Joseph Akerman	Grocer
--- Benedict	Grocer
Ira E. Burdine	Grocer
--- Peebles	Grocer
John W. Sampson	Grocer

Letters to the General Land Office, 1831 to 1832, Capitol Fire Documents, CFD 203.

(1) Letter regarding survey no. 2016 of Antoine Soulard. (LD) March 21, 1831, (PG) 5.

(2) Letter regarding certificate no. 1318, which was transferred to Aug. Chouteau under Regis Loisel and Aug. Chouteau under Baptiste Boyet. (LD) June 11, 1831, (PG) 37.

(3) Letter regarding Palmyra, Missouri tracts, that were sold to Thomas Hunter. Land was permitted to enter by Dr. Green. (LD) October 29, 1831, (PG) 95.

(4) Letter regarding the correction of the survey, that belongs to Touissant Dubois in the Palestine Dist. (LD) February 6, 1832, (PG) 115.

(5) Letter regarding survey no. 2881 of Tho. W. Waters and survey no. 2560 of Etienne Dumay. (LD) February 15, 1832, (PG) 123.

(Letters to the General Land Office Continued)
  (6) Letter from John Lindsey regarding claim under the
       King of Spain. (LD) February 6, 1832, (PG) 127.
  (7) Letter regarding survey no.2918 of Philip Shackler
       and survey no. 1685 Sylvester Labbadie.
  (8) Letter regarding the correction of the claim of
       Francis Lasseur. (LD) October 27, 1832, (PG) 241.

Kansas State Journal, August 28, 1862, Obituary of Mr. Bliss.

Mr. Bliss of Weston, Missouri died of rabies Monday evening.

Buchanon County, Missouri, Patrons Atlas, 1877.

Name	Nativity	Arrival
Peter Bledsoe	Illinois	1836
C. G. H. Brand	Bourbon County, Ky.	1839
William Brittarie	Vigo County, In.	1839
Joseph Brown	Buchanon County, Mo.	1839
Mrs. K. M. Chaney	Bedford County, Tn.	1838
Richard Chaney	Clark County, Ky.	1838
Abner Copeland	Chatham County, Nc.	1839
B. F. Cornelius	Clay County, Mo.	1837
Newton Cowan	Campbell County, Tn.	1839
S. F. Cowan	Knox County, Tn.	1839
Eli G. Cummins	Franklin County, Ky.	1830
Mrs. Sarah Cummins	Franklin County, Ky.	1830
R. T. Davis	Buchanon County, Mo	1837
John G. Elliott	Anderson County, Ky.	1833
F. P. Essman	Alabama	1833
Mrs. Hannah Everett	Tennessee	1837
Weston J. Everett	Halifax County, Va.	1837
M. W. Farris	Lincoln County, In.	1837
Samuel Judah	Springfield, Ill.	1837
S. J. Jeffers	Clay County, Mo.	1839
J. M. Jeffers	Clay County, Mo.	1839
Mrs. Sytha Fidler	Boone County, Mo.	1839
Stafford Feland	Lincoln County, Ky.	1839
M. M. Witt	Buchanon County, Mo.	1836
H. R. Witt	Buchanon County, Mo.	1836
Jenkin Williams	Clay County, Mo.	1839
Van B. Wilkerson	Jackson County, Mo.	1838
James E. Wallace	Rock Castle, Ky.	1838
Mrs. Vestal	Jackson County, Mo.	1838
Elizabeth Van Bibber	Richmond, Va.	1837
John Underwood	Grant County, In.	1837
Fay Spencer	Lawrence County, Ky.	1837
John N. Smith	Lee County, Va.	1838
Benjamin Sampson	Knox County, Il.	1837
Mrs. Ruthie R. Riley	Harrisburg, Va.	1838

(Buchanon County, Missouri Continued)

Name	Nativity	Arrival
George Rapp	Germany	1837
John Patton	Tennessee	1837
Mrs. S. E. Norris	Clay County, Missouri	1838
William Nash	Clinton County, Mo.	1836
John W. Montray	Jackson County, Mo.	1839
Mrs. Jane May	Decatur county, In.	1839
W. C. Maddox	Virginia	1839
Mrs. Martha Maddox	Shelby County, Ky.	1839
Thomas T. McGauher	Davies County, In.	1839
Jolmsen McGauhey	Rowan County, Nc.	1839
Isaac Lower	Roane County, Tn.	1837
E. Y. Kirkman	Platte County, Mo.	1839
Levi J. Judah	Lawrence County, In.	1839

Benton County, Missouri, September,1835,Members Of The Grand Jury.

Hugh M. Lonaghe, Stephen A. Howser,Patterson Russell,John Roberts, Simpkin Hollyman, Daniel Nave, Moshae (sic) Willis, John Graham,sr., David Benjamin L. Fey,Maye (sic) R. Foster, Samuel Foster, sr., George Trotter, John Roberts, Ephraim Rippete, David Lynn.

Chariton County, Missouri,Fairview Cemetery,Near Bynumville, Missouri.

Name	Born	Died
Mary S. Brewer (age: 52 y)		1887
Daniel Brewer ((age: 70 y)		Jun. 29, 1898
E. J. Foster	Apr. 12, 1834	May 19, 1884
Joseph Smith	Jan. 12, 1807	Sep. 5, 1893
Rachel Smith	Mar. 14, 1810	May 20, 1894
F. B. Kyes	Sep. 10, 1834	Apr. 9, 1893
Anthony Pleyer	Apr. 6, 1829	Apr. 13, 1894
Joseph Gotterman	1824	1896
Daniel D. Davis (age: 74 y)		Jun. 11, 1896
Antonette Smith (age: 49 y)		Sep. 10, 1884
Wm. A. Gunn	Sep. 2, 1832	Jan. 26, 1898
Wm. Nelson	Dec. 13, 1826	Dec. 28, 1896
Emma Elizabeth McCarty	1839	1874
John McSparhen (age: 45 y, 2 m, 5 d)		Dec. 10, 1878
Milly A. Wood (age: 51 y, 5 m, 12 d)		Mar. 2, 1879
Frances M. Turner (age: 56 y, 4 m, 13 d)		Jan. 10, 1882
Eliza Smalley (age: 41 y)		May 6, 1880

Obituary From Texas Christian Advocate, November 10, 1859, Galveston, Texas, Vol. VI, No. 14.

Near Victoria, Tx. on Oct. 24, 1859, Miss Mary Ann Wiley died. She was born in Ste. Geneviece Co., January 14, 1836.

Abstract of Wm. Clark's Expeditures as Supertintendent of Indian Affairs of the Missouri Territory, January 1, 1821 to July 16, 1821, American States Papers.

(1) William Clark: a) Compensation from January 1, 1821 to March 31, 1821, (PY) 1821, (V) --.

(2) Benj. O'Fallon: a) Salary as Indian Agent from October 1, 1820 to December 31, 1820, (PY) January 1, 1821, (V) 12.

(3) John Ruland: a) Salary as Indian Sub-Agent from January 1, 1821 to March 31, 1821, (PY) March 31, 1821, (V) 26; b) Salary as interpreter from January 1, 1821 to March 31, 1821, (PY) March 31,1821, (V) 53; c) Salary as interpreter from October 1, 1820 to December 31, 1820, (PY) January 1, 1821, (V) 52.

(4) Pierre Menard: a) Salary as Indian Sub-Agent for the Shawnees, Piankeshaws, Delawares and others from October 1, 1820 to December 31, 1820, (PY)January 1, 1820,'(V) 3.

(5) B. O'Fallon: a) Salary for the months of January, February, March, 1821, (PY) April 1, 1820, (V) 13; b) Salary from April 1, 1821 to June 31, 1821,(PY) July 1, 1821, (V) 370.

(6) T. Forsyth: a) Salary as Indian Agent from January 1, 1821 to March 31, 1821, (PY) March 31, 1821, (V) 18; b) Salary as Indian Agent from April 1, 1821 to June 30, 1821, (PY) June 30, 1821, (V) --.

(7) Louis Pettle: a) Salary as interpreter for the Sac and Fox Nation from January 1, 1821 to March 31, 1821, (PY) March 31, 1821, (V) 79.

(8) Paul Loise: a) Salary as interpreter from January 1, 1821 to March 31, 1821, (PY) March 31, 1821, (V) 67; b) Salary as interpreter from April 1, 1821 to June 30, 1821, (PY) June 8, 1821, (V) --.

(9) John Dougherty: a) Salary as Indian Sub-Agent and interpreter from October 1, 1820 to December 31, 1820, (PY) January 1, 1821, (V) 47; b) Salary as Indian Sub-Agent and interpreter from January 1, 1821 to March 31, 1821, (PY) April 1, 1821, (V) 48;

(10) Duncan Campbell: a) Salary as Indian Sub-Agent from April 1, 1821 to June 30, 1821, (PY) June 30, 1821, (V) 1.

(11) C. Campbell: a) Salary as interpreter from April 1, 1821 to June 30, 1821, (PY) June 2, 1821, (V) 2.

(12) L. Taliaferro: a) Salary as Indian Agent from April 1, 1821 to June 30, 1821, (PY) June 18,1821, (V)--.

(13) J. Dougherty: a) Salary as Indian Sub-Agent and interpreter from April 1, 1821 to June 30, 1821, (PY) July 1, 1821, (V) 1.

(Indian Affairs Continued)

(14) T. Charbonne: a) Salary as interpreter from January to May 31, 1820, (PY) June 1, 1821, (V) 2.

(15) M. Birdeau: a) Salary as interpreter, (PY) June 1, 1821, (V) ---.

(16) D. Campbell: a) Salary as Indian Sub-Agent from July 1, 1820 to March 31, 1821, (PY) June 8, 1821, (V) 379.

(17) N. Boilvin: a)Salary as Indian Sub-Agent from April 1, 1821 to June 30, 1821, (PY) July 21, 1821, (V) 381.

(18) C. Campbell: a) Salary as interpreter from January 1, 1821 to March 31, 1821, (PY) November 21, 1821, (V) 380.

(19) P. Menard: a) Salary from April 1, 1821 to June 30, 1821, (PY) April 20, 1821, (V) 382.

(20) G. C. Sibley: a) Salary from April 1, 1821 to June 30, 1821, (PY) March 31, 1821, (V) 385; b) Salary from January 1, 1821 to March 31, 1821, (PY) June 30, 1821, (V) 388.

(21) B. Tobin: a) Compensation from attending Indian horses for two months, (PY) April 1, 1821, (V) 251.

(22) I. Lambert: a) Compensation as gunsmith and black-smith, (PY) June 30, 1821, (V) 390.

(23) John Ruland: a) Salary as Indian Sub-Agent from April 1, 1821 to June 30, 1821, (PY) June 30, 1821, (V) 392: b) Salary as French and English interpreter from April 1, 1821 to June 30, 1821, (PY) June

(24) I. L. Honore: a) Salary as Indian interpreter,(PY) 30, 1821, (V) 393.

(25) Paul Loise: a) Salary as Indian interpreter from April 1, 1821 to June 30, 1821, (PY) June 30, 1821, (V) 394.

(26) Jos. Montre: a) Salary as Indian interpreter from January 1, 1821 to March 31, 1821, (PY)May 31,1821, (V) 395; b) Salary as Indian interpreter from April 1, 1821 to June 30, 1821, (PY) July 1, 1821, (V) 396.

(27) Jacques Vanier: a) Compensation as blacksmith from January 1, 1821 to March 31, 1821, (PY) March 31, 1821, (V) 397; b) Compensation as blacksmith from April 1, 1821 to June 30, 1821, (PY) July 1, 1821, (V) 398.

(28) Louis Pettle: a) Salary as interpreter from May 10, 1817 to July 7, 1817, (PY) May 30, 1821, (V) 411.

(29) Amasa Crane: a) Compensation as blacksmith from October 1, 1820 to February 12, 1821, (PY) March 30, 1821, (V) 387.

(30) P. L. Chouteau: a) Salary as special Indian Sub-

(Indian Affairs Continued)

Agent from January 1, 1821 to June 30, 1821, (PY)
July 6, 1821, (V) 389.

(31)   H. St. Cyr: a) Compensation for 15 cords of wood.
(PY) January 15, 1821, (V) 237.

(32)   Smith & Ferguson: a) Compensation for six iron ·
squares, (PY) February 13, 1821, (V) 234.

(33)   Tracy & Wahrendorf: a) Compensation for a variety
of tools, (PY) March 1, 1821, (V) 246.

(34)   William Clark: a) Payment for hay, (PY) March 1,
1821, (V) 246.

(35)   B. Dumoulin: a) Payment for boarding two Kickapoo
Indians, (PY) March 1, 1827, (V) 247.

(36)   G. Dougherty: a) Payment for hay, (PY) March 27,
1821, (V) 248.

(37)   Jacob Fry: a) Payment for beef and bread, (PY)
March 31, 1821, (V) 250.

(38)   William Guger: a) Compensation for the transportation of sundries, (PY) June 3, 1821, (V) 418.

(39)   J. and G. H. Kennerly: a) Payment for whiskey,pork,
nails, and for the hire of a boat, sails, oars,
poles, rigging and cooking utensils from May 15,
1821 to June 16, 1821, (PY) June 16, 1821, (V) 378.

(40)   P. A. Loramier: a) Payment for the transporting of
three tierces and a barrel of goods, (PY) April 11,
1821, (V) 383.

(41)   S. Saucier: a) Payment for the transportation of
specie in 1820, (PY) April 20, 1821, (V) 384.

(42)   S. W. Boogs: a) Payment for 14 pounds of steel,
(PY) March 30, 1821, (V) 386.

(43)   Bartholomew Tobin: a) Compensation for attending
to Indian horses and other property for two months,
(PY) June 30, 1821, (V) 399.

(44)   Earl & Light: a) Payment for two ploughs for the
Kickapoo Indians, (PY) April 8, 1821, (V) 400.

(45)   A. Osborne: a) Payment for a wood axe, (PY) April
14, 1821, (V) 401.

(46)   John B. Smith: a) Payment for the boarding, care,
and clothing of an Indian girl redeemed from servi-
tude, (PY) May 2, 1821, (V) 402.

(47)   Jesse Evans: a) Payment for corn delivered to the
Kickapoo Indians, (PY) May 22, 1821, (V) 403.

(48)   Farrar & Walker: a) Payment for medical services
form June 25, 1820 to October 19, 1820, (PY) May 7,
1821, (V) 404.

(49)   Duff Green: a) Payment for tobacco, paint and provisions delivered to the Ioway tribe, (PY) May 8,
1821, (V) 405.

(50)   S. L. Migneson: a) Compensation for the repairing

of a lock, a rifle and a medal for an Ottowa chief.
(PY) May 30, 1821, (V) 406.

(51) J. L. Provanchier: a) Compensation for services in
the hunting of horses, (PY) May 30, 1821, (V) 407.

(52) Joseph Montagne: a)Payment for the repair of tools,
(PY) July 10, 1821, (V) 408.

(53) J. B. Coured: a) Payment for bread furnished to the
Indians in St. Louis in 1821, (PY) July 10, 1821,
(V) 410.

(54) L. Bompart: a) Payment for the transport of money
to St. Louis from Franklin, (PY) July 16, 1821, (V)
412.

(55) W. Hays: a) Compensation for the guarding of a
Sioux Indian confined for murder, (PY) April 30,
1821, (V) 419.

(56) P. Curry: a) See no. 55.

(57) N. Linch: a) For the transportation of Indians from
Praire Du Chien to St. Louis, (PY) May 1, 1821, (V)
420.

(58) Jane Richards: a) Payment for boarding of a sick
interpreter, (PY) May 3, 1821, (V) 422.

(59) Henry Curtis: a) Payment for the tollage of Indians
and horses, (PY) May 21, 1821, (V) 423.

(60) J. H. Dennis: a) Payment for the lodging of Indians
on their way to Vandalia to attend the trail of
three Indians charged with murder, (PY)May 21,1821,
(V) 423.

(61) Wm. Shane: a) See no. 60.

(62) G. Bullard: a) Payment for the use of a wagon and
horses transporting witnesses to the trial of the
Winnabago Indians charged with murder, (PY) May 21,
1821, (V) 422.

(63) Michael Dodd: a) See no. 62.

(64) John Sheils: a) Payment for furnishing a room for
the Indian witnesses, (PY) May 21, 1821, (V) 423.

(65) M. K. Bottsford: a) Payment for supplies and other
sundries, (PY) May 21, 1821, (V) 423.

(66) S. Blanchard: a) Payment for feeding interpreters
and Indian witnesses, (PY) May 21, 1821, (V) 423.

(67) C. F. Hammond: a) Payment for transporting interpreters and Indian witnesses to the trial of the
Winnebago Indians, (PY) May 21, 1821, (V) 423.

(68) S. Wiggins: a) Payment for the ferriage of various
persons to the trial, (PY) May 21, 1823, (V) 423.

(69) L. T. Honore: a) Payment for the board and lodging
of Indians, (PY) May 21, 1821, (V) 423.

(70) David Robeson: a) Payment for feeding the guards of
the Indian prisoners, (PY) May 21, 1821, (V) 424.

(Indian Affairs Continued)
- (71) Enoch Paine: a) Payment for feeding and lodging two interpreters, Indians, and prisoners, (PY) May 21, 1821, (V) 424.
- (72) S. Lecompte: a) For food and horse feed, (PY) May 21, 1821, (V) 424.
- (73) John Bullard: a) Payment for transporting Indian prisoners from St. Louis to Kaskaskia, (PY) May 21, 1821, (V) 424.
- (74) A. Bradshaw: a) Payment for feeding two Indians and interpreters, (PY) May 21, 1821, (V) 424.
- (75) S. Wiggins: a) Payment for ferriage of Indians,(PY) May 21, 1821, (V) 424.
- (76) A. Perault: a) Payment as interpreter at the trial of the Winnebago Indians, (PY) May 22, 1821, (V) 425.
- (77) D. Julien: a) Payment in conducting a party of Winbego Indians, (PY) June 2, 1821, (V) 426.
- (78) Colin Campbell: a) Compensation for travel expenses from St. Peter's to St. Louis, (PY) June 30, 1821, (V) 427.
- (80) --- Farebeau: a) Compensation for bringing in a witness, (PY) July 1, 1821, (V) 428.
- (81) N. Boilvin: a) Payment for provisions issued to witnesses and goods delivered to Prairie Du Chien, (PY) July 1, 1821, (V) 428.
- (82) J. B. Carou: a) Payment for provisions furnished to the Sioux and Winnebagoes attending as witnesses, (PY) July 1, 1821, (V) 428.
- (83) E. Bebe: a) Paytment for harness, (PY) February 12, 1821, (V) 245.
- (84) J. Clemons, jr.: a) Payment for ploughshares, (PY) February 8, 1821, (V) 238.
- (85) T. Goddard, jr.: a) Payment for various goods, (PY) February 13, 1821, (V) 240.
- (86) Daniel Castor: a) Payment for farm implements, (PY) February 13, 1821, (V) 242.
- (87) James Lakeman: a) Payment for repairs done for the Kickapoo Indians as the requent of Colonel Chouteau and Colonel Stevenson, (PY) February 13, 1821, (V) 355.
- (88) Jesse Evans: a) Payment for corn furnished to the Kickapoo Indians, (PY) June 21, 1821, (V) 354.
- (89) T. Sturges: a) Payment for farm implements, (PY) June 21, 1821, (V) 223.
- (90) B. P. Clain: a) Payment for bread furnished to the Shawnee and Delaware Indians between October 2, 1820 to December 31, 1820, (PY) January 1, 1821, (V) 236.

(Indian Affairs Contined)
- (91) Pierre Menard: a) Payment for goods furnished to the Delaware Indians, (PY) January 1,1821, (V) ---.
- (92) Owen Gray: a) Payment for services to the Indian Department, (PY) July 1, 1821, (V) 373.
- (93) Samuel Burns a) Payment for express services to Rogerstown, (PY) March 12, 1821, (V) 263.
- (94) H. Wigginton: a) Payment for services as an express from settlements on the upper Missouri to St. Louis, (PY) March 5, 1821, (V) 262.
- (95) Jacob Gray: a) Payment for beef furnished to the Indians at St. Louis, Sacs, Foxes, Ioway, Ottawas, Delawares and others from April 1, 1821 to July 10, 1821, (PY) July 10, 1821, (V) 409.
- (96) Reuben Lewis: a) Advance on salary, (PY) May 21, 1821, (V) ---.
- (97) Richard Graham: a) Advance on salary, (PY) May 31, 1821, (V) ---.

Cole County, Missouri, Jefferson City Cemetery.

Name	Born	Died
John H. Karges	Aug. 22, 1801	Nov. 21, 1870
Mary F. Brinker	May 21, 1829	Jan. 9, 1898
Stpehen Dorris	1792	1810
Rosina Hensel	Aug. 8, 1813	Oct. 15, 1825
Georgia V. Duoee	Mar. 10, 1822	Sep. 14, 1898
W. Andrae	May 5, 1817	May 7, 1857
William A. Miller	Apr. 19, 1832	Jun. 29, 1859
Mary A. Hunter (age: 1 y, 2 m)		Aug. 23, 1840
John F. Roesen	Oct. 9, 1828	Nov. 29, 1883
Charles L. Meredith	May 12, 1805	Oct. 29, 1862
*Mrs. Eliza Hockaday (age: 15 y)		Jun. 16, 1851
*(Died on the Steamer El Paso)		
Martha Williams (age: 27 y, died Glasgow)		Oct. 9, 1854
Alexander Davison	Sep. 23, 1813	Mar. 5, 1884
Adam Uncapner	1796	1842
Elizabeth Gundelfinger	May 19, 1832	Apr. 6, 1884
Helen B. Holt	1802	1898
Mary Creal Jones	1816	1896
George W. Haynes	Jun. 2, 1821	Mar. 10, 1846
Erich Plumb	Feb. 13, 1819	1849
William Monnaughan (age: 37 y)		May 27, 1849
Mary J. Garman	1813	1871
Mathew Wallindorf	Dec. 25, 1805	Jul. 3, 1852
Amanda Rafferty (age; 18 y, 3 m, 1 d)		Jun. 27, 1838
Frederick Berri	Sep. 12, 1809	Nov. 25, 1866
Amelia Barri	Nov. 22, 1821	Jun. 18, 1871
Edward Hofuis	Nov. 25, 1832	Jun. 11, 1872
James A. Cheffey	Dec. 25, 1810	Sep. 2, 185?

(Cole County, Missouri Continued)

Name	Born	Died
Elizabeth Phillips	Mar. 15, 1816	Sep. 14, 1897
Henrietta Lohman	Sep. 15, 1823	Jan. 26, 1892
*Chas. F. Lohman	Dec. 26, 1817	Jul. 28, 1879
*(Born: Prussia, age: 61 y)		
Sally Berr (age: 30 y)		Feb. 1, 1842
Missouri Frazier	1835	1890
Peter Miller	Sep. 14, 1810	Jul. 5, 1834
Samuel Sone	Jul. 24, 1819	Dec. 10, 1886
Elias Bancroft (age: 73 y)		Aug. 26, 1851
Maria L. Miller	Jan. 24, 1818	Jul. 30, 1851
Gilly Miller	Jan. 26, 1807	Jan. 19, 1837
Alexander Poper Dorris	Aug. 11, 1818	Jan. 31, 1873
Phillip Henry Andrae	Mar. 23, 1801	---
Henry C. Nitchy	May 23, 1824	Mar. 5, 1894
James M. Culsin (age: 45 y)		Aug. 26, 1856
Mary Dorris	Mar. 17, 1806	Aug. 15, 1899
John Endicott	Jul. 2, 1838	Feb. 16, 1880
August Hensel	Jan. 4, 1813	Feb. 16, 1880
Samllwood Noland	---	Mar. 14, 1837
Catharine Andrews	May 9, 1829	Nov. 16, 1862
Meriwether Bolton	1800	1876
Sarah Bolton	1810	1879
Rebecca M. McEldon	Aug. 9, 1836	Mar. 11, 1827
Sarah Funk (age: 72 y)		Aug. 25, 1851
Margaret Lain (age: 50 y)		Aug. 28, 1857
Sylvester Rost	May 11, 1792	Mar. 8, 1852
Joseph Brenneesen (age: 64 y)		Jun. 11, 1855
John Doehla	Aug. 10, 1824	Dec. --, 1893
John Doehlas	Aug. 10, 1824	Dec. 10, 1893
Hier Ruht	1800	1883
Josephine Dorris	1829	1838
Sarah Dorris	Apr. 4, 1796	May 22, 1838
Jane E. Dorris	Oct. 26, 1820	Nov. 17, 1835
Ann Mary Dellinger	Nov. 7, 1805	Sep. 18, 1856
Hannah Rains (age: 77 y, 7 m, 9 d)		Aug. 17, 1871
Larkin Rains (born: Va)	1789	Sep. 9, 1841
Ann Marg. Hofuis	Jun. 17, 1787	Sep. 9, 1855
John Anderson	Sep.19, 1795	Oct. 6, 1844
Helen A. Anderson	Dec. 11, 1833	Apr. 28, 1844
Margaret L. Goodwin	May 10, 1807	Jan. 25, 1861
Jonathan H. Goodwin	Jan. 13, 1804	Jan. 20, 1839
Henry P. Boggs	Feb. 27, 1830	Aug. 29, 1862
Richard Ashlon Stuart	1813	1854
Barbara Smith	May 12, 1815	Jun. 20, 1880

Buchanon County, Missouri, Members of Grand Jury,July, 1839.
Rueben R. Reynolds, John Henry, William Bledsoe, Ezekiel

(Buchanon County, Missouri Continued)
W. Smith, Elijah Martin, Abel Evans, George S. Evans, Danl.
Ferrel, Job McNense, Hugh Copeland, Hiram Rogers, Jesse R.
Barnett, Ezra Rose, Lloyd Beall, Hugh Glenn, James Carl, John
Martin.

Cooper County, Missouri, West Boonville Evangelical Cemetery, Six Miles West Of Boonville On Old Santa Fe Road.

Name	Born	Died
Christ. Wehling	Mar. 12, 1822	Mar. 11, 1888
Elizabeth S. Sommers	May 21, 1831	Jul. 9, 1893
Maria G. Neef	Dec. 15, 1803	Jan. 1, 1871
Johann G. Neef	Jun. 9, 1800	Aug. 19, 1854
Jacob Neef	Jan. 19, 1829	Oct. 10, 1864
Elizabeth J. Neef	May 13, 1823	Jan. 29, 1896
*Louis Moehle	Aug. 25, 1817	May 13, 1891
*(Born Germany)		
Elizabeth Moehle	Dec. 25, 1815	Dec. 5, 1891
Albert Heintz	May 23, 1834	Oct. 16, 1894
Charlie Fieldler	Jan. 15, 1828	Feb. 21, 1892
George Bhauer	Oct. 13, 1818	Jul, 21, 1885
Johann Bauer (age: 70 y)		Jan. 7, 1888

Boone County, Missouri, Members Of The Grand Jury, October, 1831.

Daniel Mourning, William L. Husten, Peter Austin, James
M. Alexander, George S. Grant, John Husten, James Payne, John
Osborne, Merit Vallandingham, William Russell, Daniel Grant,
Mericer Ballenger, Tyre Harris, jr., Richard Clarkson, Lewis
Anthony, Edward Perkins, James Richards, Robert F. Gibbs,
Thomas Harris.

Abstract Of Disbursements Made by Pierre Menard, Sub-Agent At Kaskaskia, Under The Direction Of William Clark, Quarter Ending, December, 1820.

(1) M. Buale: a) Conveying flour,lead, and tobacco,(PY)
October 5, 1820, (V) 5.
(2) L. Seguin: see no. 1
(3) A. Bienvenue: see no. 1
(4) James Wilson: a) Payment for lead, powder, and
tobacco, (PY) October 6, 1820, (V) 2.
(5) Raphael Widen: a) Payment for clothe, powder, and
lead, (PY) October 7, 1820, (V) 3.
(6) Edward Humphrey: a) Payment for beef furnished to
the Delaware Indians, (PY) October 14, 1820.
(7) Mrs. Lecompte: a) Payment for feeding fourteen Delaware Indians, (PY) October 19, 1820, (V) 5
(8) James Wilson: a) Payment for entertaining thirteen
Delaware Indians, (PY) October, 1820, (V) 6.

(Indian Affairs Continued)
- (9) David Anderson: a) Payment for beef furnished to the Delaware Indians, (PY) October 20, 1820, (V) 7.
- (10) V. V. Bonis: a) Payment for boarding James Wilson, the Delaware interpreter, (PY) October 25, 1820, (V) 8.
- (11) S. Wiggins: a) Payment for ferriage of Delaware Indians across the Mississippi, (PY) October 25, 1820, (V) 9.
- (12) Geo. Ramsey: a) Payment for furnishing breakfast to thirteen Indians and their horses, (PY) October 27, 1820, (V) 10.
- (13) James Butler: a) Payment for two steers, (PY) October 30, 1820, (V) 11.
- (14) Zephany Brooks: a) Payment for corn, (PY) November 4, 1820, (V) 12.
- (15) J. and M. Davis: a) Payment for chasing men that took some horses from the Delaware Indians, (PY) November 6, 1820, (V) 13.
- (16) Henry Burbeau: a) Payment for going after Delaware horses, (PY) November 7, 1820, (V) 14.
- (17) G. Beauvais: a) Payment for reparing firearms, (PY) November 14, 1820, (V) 17.
- (18) John Carpenter: a) Payment for 1,103 persons and horses crossing the Mississippi, (PY) November 15, 1820, (V) 18.
- (19) John Louvat: a) Payment for hauling provisions for Indians, (PY) November 20, 1820, (V) 19.
- (20) N. Buate: a)Payment for beef and hauling provisions to the Indians, (PY) November 24, 1820, (V) 20.
- (21) Jno. Hoggins: a) Payment for returning horses to the Delaware Indians, (PY) November 25, 1820, (V) 21.
- (22) Francis Montreuil: a) Payment for ferriage of Indians and horses across the Kaskaskia River, (PY) November 27, 1820, (V) 22.
- (23) P. Proveaux: a) Payment for beef, (PY) November 29, 1820, (V) 23.
- (24) Baptiste Moreau: a) Payment for ferriage of Indians and horses across the Mississippi River, (PY)November 29, 1820, (V) 25.
- (25) Vital St. Gumme: a) Payment for corn furnished to Indians, (PY) November 29, 1820, (V) 26.
- (26) Pierre Coline: a) Payment for corn furnished to Indians, (PY) November 29, 1820, (V) 27.
- (27) Jos. Archambia: a) Payment for beef and flour furnished to the Indians, (PY)November 30,1820, (V)28.
- (28) Francis Menard: a) Payment for beef and corn furn- to the Indians, (PY) November 30, 1820, (V) 29.

(Indian Affairs Continued)
- (29) Michael Placet: a) Payment for ferriage of Indians across the Mississippi, (PY) December 1, 1820, (V) 30.
- (30) Wm. Gillis: a) Payment for beef and making a coffin for a Delaware Indian accidently killed, (PY)December 2, 1820, (V) 31.
- (31) Wm. Bilderback: a) Payment for corn for Delaware Indians, (PY) December 4, 1820, (V) 32.
- (32) A. Montreuil: Payment for two steers, (PY) January 2, 1821, (V) 33.
- (33) J. B. Valle: a) Payment for beef, flour, salt, and tobacco, (PY) January 4, 1821, (V) 34.
- (34) P. Delchemendy: a) Payment for flour delivered at St. Genevieve for the Delaware Indians, (PY) January 6, 1820, (V) 35.
- (35) Francis Janis: a) Payment for corn delivered to the Delaware Indians, (PY) January 6, 1820, (V) 36.
- (36) Michael Danis, sr. : a) Payment for corn delivered to the Delaware Indians, (PY) January 13, 1820, (V) 37.
- (37) A. Bienvenue: a) Payment for two steers, (PY) January 20, 1820, (V) 38.
- (38) J. B. Lashpelle: a) Payment for corn delivered to the Dleaware Indians, (PY) January 20,1820, (V) 29.

Benton County, Missouri, May, 1836, Members Of The Grand Jury.

John Holloway, Jonas Dawson, Joseph Sharp, John Davidson, Nathan Berhue, Daniel Lake, Middleton Berhue, John Robert, Benjamin L. Fey, James Graham, Hezekiah Robertson, Ferdinand Herrin, James Foster, Lewis Riddle.

Boone County, Missouri, February, 1832, Members Of The Grand Jury.

William Luetz, Edrom Tipton, Peter Kemper,Elijah Johnson, Martin Baker, William Huggart, William Goslin, James Turner, George Newland, John H. Baker, Robert Johnson,Thomas Taylor, Alexander Douglass, Benjamin G. Griffin, Benjamin Scrivener, John G. Phillips, William Cave, sr., Simeon W. Robinson,Joel Penick, John Dawson, Solomon Mordica.

Cole County, Missouri, Pleasant Hill Cemetery.

Name	Born	Died
B. A. Stark (age: 60 y)		Nov. 23, 1886
Robert Scott	Jun. 17, 1806	Apr. 10, 1883
Sarah Kennon	Mar. 10, 1799	Aug. 3, 1860
Sarah Howser	Jul. 10, 1814	Mar. 17, 1892
Lilburn Howard	Aug. 5, 1815	Aug. 4, 1883

(Cole County, Missouri Continued)

Name	Born	Died
John Bates	May 21, 1837	Nov. 25, 1895
Herman Bates	Jul. 31, 1775	Jul. 7, 1776

Jackson County, Missouri, Delinquent Tax List, 1832.

Levi Arthur, Joseph Austin, Lewis Bartlett, John Bowlin, Elihu Cleaveland, John Chase, Dennis Dunham, George Frazier, Elijah Green, Softeau Frenchman, Robert Parsons, Peter Wilson, Elkard Strickland, Munsell Stephenson, Wm. Stringham, Nathan Hudspeth, George Wilson, Briant Teaque.

Cooper County, Missouri, Bethlehem Cemetery, Eighteen Miles South On Rt. 5 Near Boonville.

Name	Born	Died
Matilda Daniel	Aug. 9, 1811	Sep. 19, 1873
Geo. T. Bailey (age: 75 y)		May 2, 1895
Archilles J. Eubank	Feb. 28, 1831	Sep. 27, 1896
Richard Eubank (age: 52 y, 2 m, 7 d)		Jul. 8, 1880
Nancy Eubank	Feb. 7, 1814	Feb. 22, 1884
W. T. Reaves	Sep. 14, 1811	Nov. 22, 1877
Sarah Crist	Jul. 6, 1811	Jul. 27, 1879
J. Varner (age: 59 y, 4 m, 5 d)		Jun. 24, 1871
Mary A. Varner (age: 64 y, 9 m, 4 d)		Dec. 11, 188
David Franklin Grove	1838	1864
*Capt. Charles W. Daniel	Jul. 25, 1807	Dec. 18, 1867
*(Born Kentucky)		
Jacob Crist	Jul. 22, 1807	Apr. 24, 1873
A. J. Reaves	Nov. 11, 1838	May 12, 1890
William Sole	Apr. 22, 1825	Sep. 7, 1895
Nancy Thompson	Sep. 7, 1829	Oct. 3, 1873
Mary Ann Denny	Aug. 9, 1819	Apr. 1, 1884
Frederick Marye	May 2, 1811	Oct. 10, 1844
Job Denny	Feb. 6, 1809	Jan. 16, 1895
Ann Sole	Sep. 6, 1788	Jun. 19, 1886
W. F. Reaves	Sep. 14, 1811	Nov. 22, 1877
Sarah E. Rothgeb (age: 79 y, 7 m, 4 d)		Oct. 14, 1882
Elizabeth Smith (age: 51 y, 3 m, 29 d)		Aug. 20, 1889
Mary A. Reaves	Dec. 16, 1817	Jan. 18, 1877

Sullivan County, Missouri, Patrons Of The Atlas, 1877 (Note: Only Persons Before 1840)

Name	Post Office	Nativity	Arrived
J. G. Smith	Kiddville	Boston, Ma	1839

Buchanon County, Missouri, November, 1839, Members Of The Grand Jury.

Philip P. Midget, Joseph Wayhart, James Hudspeth, Abraham Brubaker, John McKirtle, Allen Stephens, Isaac Clanton, John

(Buchanon County, Missouri Continued)
I. Hard, Richard Bagsby, Jepthah Todd, Davis H. Cochran, Wm.
Shaw, Frances Wrightman, Zachariah Martens, John Carey, John
Bill, Avery Ballard, Robert Henton, Claiborne F. Parmer.

Jackson County, Missouri, Delinquent Tax List, 1831.
   Francis August, Lewis Batlot, Benjamin F. Burns,Aike Box,
Anthony Bledsoe, William Burgen, C. Cardinal, Oran Creason,
James Gibson, Ruben Holeman, John R. Johnson, James Palmer,
Benjamin Jennings, William Malett, John H. Moorehead, Joseph
Pelky, Lewis Pelky, James Palmer, Joseph G. O'Connor, Parson
Teaque, John Roylance, Sampson Smith, Peter P. Wells, Henry
J. Henry, John Parsons, William Barnes.

Stoddard County, Missouri, March, 1836, Members Of The Grand
Jury.
   Samuel Lesley, Andrew Neale, Benjamin Taylor, Levi Baker,
Frederick Varner, Ephraim Snider, Jacob Crites, William W.
Hicks, William V. Carlock, Geo. Slinkard, Daniel Bollinger,
Frederick Slinkard, Peter Proffer,Henry Miller,Thomas Neale,
Henry Ashbranner,Wm. W. Hicks,Samuel Moore,Horatio Lawrence.

Indiana Territory, November, 1803, Memorialists, Carter's
Territorial Papers, Vol. II.
   William Adams, Henry Carr, Caldw. Cairns, William Carns,
Leonard Carr, James Gillham, Thomas Gillham,David Whiteside,
James Thomas, Wm. Moss, Mark Thomas, William Scoby, Absalom
Bratcher, John Byrum, Joseph Hogan,William Clover,John Kidd,
Miles Hotchkiss, Oliver Reuben, Wm. Wilson, Nathan Rumsey,
James McNabb, James Morrison, John Bloom, Philip Rouke, John
Locke, Jesse Griggs, Simon Macaffery, Thos. Newberry, James
Cooper, James Dockerry, Parker Grovenor, Daniel Link, George
Atchinson, Jorge Tery, Daniel Stone, Ichabod Badgley, David
Badgley, Francis Pelham, John Mssinger (sic), George Dement,
John Whiteside, Wm. Murrey,Abraham Teter,William Goings,jr.,
John Pulham, Robt. McMahon, William Goinges, Sollomon Shook,
Henry Noble, ---- Hornback,John O'Hara, James Wilson, Davis
Waddell, Alexander Waddell, David Waddel, sr., Martin Mauch,
Thomas Porter, Danl. McCann, Pierre Beguin, John Hays, Amos
Squire, --- Martine, --- Perey, Josephe Manegre, John Lyle,
Baptist Boulin, John Hay, William Ratcliff, --- Jarrot, John
Moredock, William Atcheson, Shadrach Bond, --- Darneille.

St. Francois County, Missouri, April, 1822, Members Of The
Grand Jury.
   David F. Marks, Archibald McHenry, Ganum Estes, William
Spradling,Tho. George,Jno. Baker,Hardy McCormick,George Tay-
lor,Wm. Gillespy, Dubart Murphy, Isaac Mitchel, Jno. Burnham
Lemuel Holstead, Jesse McFarland, Leroy Matkin, Isaac Estes.

(St.Francois County, Missouri Continued)

St. Louis County, Missouri, Compton Hill Cemetery.

Name	Died	Age
Henry Regualdis	March 11, 1822	45
Adelia Adams	June 28, 1887	81
Sarah Ransons	October 6, 1885	60
Lunconia Clinefelter	July 14, 1891	69
Mrs. Purdy	February 24, 1882	81
Jonathan Bigelow	July 12, 1888	68
Robert Pierce	February 11, 1883	52
Fred Eickerman	November 15, 1885	57
Louis Oakes	February 20, 1893	62
Paulina Davis	April 12, 1889	78
Jeremiah W. Northup	July 19, 1881	54
Mrs. Harriet Dening	December 17, 1886	58
Joseph P. Murrell	November 13, 1887	72
Margaret Edward	May 30, 1895	73
Dorothy A. Dueke	November 15, 1898	60
Thomas A. Morris	December 4, 1899	68
Eliza J. Ripley	August 24, 1883	73
Charles Choate	April 15, 1892	60
Eleanor Fairbridge	September 20, 1895	85
John Moffot	December 26, 1886	58
Mrs. Good	September 5, 1881	52
Christine Eisenburg	July 12, 1896	65
Annie Oakes	March 17, 1898	64
William E. Harrison	May 14, 1891	86
George A. Coan	August 22, 1892	75
William E. Hill	October 8, 1892	63
Mrs. McMahan	January 31, 1891	78
William A. Lewis	January 8, 1893	57
Rhoda Coffin	February 16, 1895	75
Rachel Haviland	October 12, 1889	65
Mrs. McFadden	July 13, 1891	83
Matthew R. Cullen	February 17, 1893	64
Richard S. Janes	December 27, 1889	61
Jane McIntyre	April 21, 1896	70
Dora Dempewolf	September 14, 1893	65
Margaret Reed	March 6, 1891	52
Mrs. Woolwitch	May 11, 1891	73
Henry Tesle	April 28, 1887	87
George Denison	December 3, 1896	65
James S. Purdy	August 7, 1885	52
Ellen Woodruff	March 26, 1891	52
Melissa Seaman	February 8, 1882	73
William A. Dorey	March 5, 1895	63
John Murdock	October 27, 1881	47

(St. Louis County, Missouri Continued)

Name	Died	Age
William M. Frazel	July 8, 1890	56
Pauline Morgan	November 6, 1887	73
Dora Grey	December 26, 1889	62
William A. Mephans	August 10, 1894	62
Addie Hayden	December 18, 1883	80
Jarius McLead	December 3, 1896	79
Elizabeth B. Lampton	September 20, 1895	75
Duncan McIntyre	March 8, 1887	66
Elizabeth E. Hooper	June 20, 1891	83
Ive McCarthy	July 23, 1883	74
John M. Jackson	January 7, 1899	88
Mrs. Rydeberg	October 24, 1885	55
William Wilcox	October 11, 1887	49
Lynolan Smith	August 1, 1894	66
Sarah A. Youbrook	February 1, 1884	73
George M. Welsh	October 3, 1888	83
William C. Turries	March 26, 1895	80
Mahala Wakefield	March 28, 1886	90
Charlotte Stussel	April 24, 1896	62
Lucy C. Wislizenns	April 29, 1895	73
Annie E. Warren	April 16, 1893	66
Mrs. Mary White	March 1, 1886	68

Jackson County, Missouri, Delinquent Tax List,November,1827.

Willis Crump, Jos. M. Kinion,Isaac Hitchock,Andrew Godak.

Madison County, Missouri, July, 1819, Members Of The Grand Jury.

Jason Harrison, John White, Adam Ground, John Clement, Jacob Shook, Elisha Bennett,Thomas Cooper,Nicholas LaChance, Lee Pettitt, John B. Deguire, Alexander Fletcher, John Best, William Dillard, James Pettitt, Thomas Crawford,Peter Sides, John Sides, Henry Whitner, John Wright, E. Mitchell.

Morgan County, Missouri, Versailles City Cemetery.

Name	Born	Died
Mary Clifton Kavanuagh	Jan. 26, 1822	Oct. 14, 1870
Olivia Holder	Jul. --, 1818	Jul. --, 1897
Anderson W. Anthony	Jun. 18, 1829	Dec. 20, 1893
Aaron Wear	Feb. 14, 1802	Mar. 28, 1867
Sarah Kelley	Dec. 22, 1822	Sep. 12, 1893
Catherine Argenbright	Aug. 23, 1804	Oct. 5, 1872
Will Johnson	Jun. 20, 1827	---
Catherine Tutt	Jul. 10, 1797	Oct. 5, 1852
J. H. Lotchworth	Jul. 9, 1830	Jan. 13, 1866
Louis Joachimi	1816	1893
Catherine Burns	May 27, 1821	Oct 14, 1858

(Morgan County, Missouri Continued)

Name	Born	Died
Rice Hulett	Jul. 7, 1816	Apr. 30, 1886
Christina Argenbright	Aug. 23, 1776	Jun. 19, 1867
Catherine S. Holder	Feb. 7, 1838	Dec. 8, 1859
Lucy Lotchworth	Feb. 15, 1833	Aug. 4, 1894
Jacob Rains	1822	1898
Nancy R. Thruston (age: 69 y, 2 m, 22 d)		Jan. 22, 1888
Sarah Mills	Mar. 15, 1837	Jun. 17, 1890
Narcissa R. Salmon	Dec. 4, 1805	May 15, 1845
A. J. Gunn	Mar. 17, 1828	Feb. 26, 1878
Louise Jacobs	1807	1892
Wm. W. Crook	Mar. 4, 1808	Jan. 9, 1862
Agnes Lutman	Mar. 23, 1815	Sep. 18, 1833
Mark K. Sullens	Oct. 25, 1837	Oct. 15, 1880
John Argenbright	Apr. 1, 1779	May 30, 1860
Charles D. Bowen	Apr. 8, 1825	Apr. 7, 1899
Carolina Joachime	1821	1896
Maj. George A. Stover	Jan. 3, 1823	May 6, 1897
Martha A. MacLeod	Jul. 5, 1825	Jan. 27, 1852
Daniel S. Snyder	Jul. 10, 1815	Feb. 18, 1862
Telitha B. French	Aug. 6, 1831	Mar. 7, 1890
Elizabeth Hanney	Apr. 1, 1815	Jun. 8, 1889
Mary D. Gray	Mar. 15, 1796	Nov. 27, 1879
Dr. John B. Thurston	Mar. 30, 1815	Mar. 25, 1891
Capt. W. A. Mills	Jun. 22, 1829	Aug. 28, 1885
Judge James P. Ross	Dec. 14, 1809	Apr. 17, 1893
W. A. Parker	Dec. 10, 1820	Jan. 29, 1888
*Ezekiel James Salmon	Jul. 5, 1798	Sep. 15, 1851
*(Born: South Carolina)		
*Eliz Young Salmon	Dec. 22, 1759	Oct. 18, 1849
*(Born: South Carolina)		
Martha J. rains	1822	1898
*Beverly R. Richard (age: 69, born: Canada)		Mar. --, 1899
Elias John RObinson	Dec. 10, 1836	Jun. 2, 1884

St. Francois County, Missouri, July, 1825, State Of Missouri vs. Daniel Coffman, Indictment.
    Jury: Dubart Murphy, Jno. Vance, William H. Delney, John Kennedy, Isaac Burnham, sr., Watson Cole, Henry Hampton,Jno. Baker, Palaske C. Duckworth, William Alley,Samuel Brown,Jas. Wilborn.

Ray County, Missouri, October, 1822, Bills Of Indictment By The State.

Name	Charge
James Snowden	Larceny
Lovell Snowden	Stabbing with intent to kill
Snowden and Martin	Assault and battery

(Ray County, Missouri Continued)

Name	Charge
Martin and Boyd	Assault and battery
Joseph Keeny	Assault and battery
Caleb Odell	Assault and battery
Snowden and Weld	Assault and battery

Cole County, Missouri, "No Name Cemtery", Two Miles North Of
Tuscumbia On Highway 17.

Name	Born	Died
David Hawken	Jan. 22, 1812	May 1, 1891
John Ashley	Sep. 4, 1825	Apr. 30, 1866
Clara Ashley	May 4, 1823	Nov. 19, 1866
Hannah Weitz	Nov. 12, 1838	Sep. 27, 1865
Chathrene Francher	May 1, 1819	Sep. 26, 1865
Charles Smith	Dec. 1, 1761	Oct. 20, 1850
Martha W. Smith	Jun. --, 1814	Apr. 26, 1871

Newton County, Missouri, Patrons Of The Atlas, 1882.

Name	Post Office	Nativity	Arrival
Madison Spurgeon	Neosho	Missouri	1839
T. Rutledge	Neosho	So. Carolina	1833
Joel Spence	Granby	Tennessee	1835
Jacob McClendon	Neosho	Indiana	1837
Jas. T. Boyd	Neosho	Tennessee	1838
E. D. Boyd	Neosho	Tennessee	1838
J. R. Smith	Kent	Kentucky	1836
Moses Powers	Granby	Illinois	1832
M. S. Greer	Granby	Tennessee	1839
Sandford Hutchison	Ritchey	Missouri	1839
M. H. Ritchey	Ritchey	Tennessee	1832
W. D. Reynolds	Pierce City	Tennessee	1839
A. H. Brown	Newtonia	Virginia	1837
Jasper Buzzard	Racine	Missouri	1839
Jonathan Buzzard	Racine	Ohio	1838
Andrew Sparlin	Seneca	Pennsylvania	1833
Joshua Cox	Racine	Missouri	1838
Wm. Jackson	Shoalsburg	Indiana	1839
Daniel Sherer	Seneca	Missouri	1838
J. E. Lankford	Seneca	Kentucky	1839

Adair County, Missouri, Patrons Of The Atlas, 1877.

Name	Post Office	Nativity	Arrival
F. M. Weatherford	LaPlata	Missouri	1831
O. Ownbey	Kirksville	Tennessee	1837
H. M. Barnes	Kirksville	Missouri	1839

St. Francois County, Missouri,March, 1825,Grand Jury Members

Jesse McFarland, William Posten, John Cartee, John Alley,

(St. Francois County, Missouri Continued)
Benjamin Crump, Robert Gurthee, Hardy John McKee,Luke Davis,
Watson Cole, Alexander McCoy, John Murphy, Jas. Cunningham,
Seth H. Moore, Alexander Boyd, Solomon Griffin, John Horton,
Jacob McFarland, William Simpson, Joseph Hays, John Tullock.

Ray County, Missouri, February, 1821, Members Of The Grand Jury.

John Bartlettson, Samuel Tilford, Howard Averett, James
Williams, Jonas Miller, James Snowden, Thomas Bruer, William
Black, Walker McFarland, Robert Poage, Thomas Edwards, James
E. Buchanon, Jonathan Leggett, Joseph Wills,William Officer,
John Turner.

Morgan County, Missouri, Marriage Records, 1833 to 1839.

Layton Adair And Edith Summers, (JP) Phillip Barger,
(MD) March 28, 1833.

Willim Fitzhugh and Mary Upton, (JP) Homer Howser, (MD)
February 7, 1833.

Willim F. Willett and Irena Howard, (JP) Homer Howser,
(MD) May 23, 1833.

Calvin Williams and Annaretta Adair, (JP) John B. Fisher,
(MD) June 2, 1833.

James Allard and Nancy Weaver, (JP) James G. Wooten, (MD)
November 7, 1833.

William Boys and Francis W. Crain (MG) Littleton Lunceford, (MD) August 29, 1833.

George Estes and Matilda Barger, (JP) John B. Fisher,
(MD) December 20, 1833.

Amos Elliot and Ann Sulcher, (JP) William Poer, (MD) December 24, 1833.

Isham Hatfield and Martha Rine Clay, (JP)James G. Wooten,
(MD) July 23, 1833.

John Hook and Elizabeth C. Graves, (JP) J. B. Steel, (MD)
November 4, 1833.

William Lowe and and Mary Kelsay, (JP) Dunnegar, (MD) August 29, 1833.

James Stinson and Sarah Robertson, (JP) Zackus German,
(MD) July --, 1833.

Samuel Arbuckle and Francis Evans, (MG) Stemp Scott, (MD)
December 29, 1834.

Martin Bogaer and Kesire Johnson, (MG) Jacob Chisum, (MD)
December 30, 1833.

William Deckens and Jane Eavins, (MG) David Allee, (MD)
January 9, 1834.

Richland Fisher and Thursay Wootten, (JP) R. B. Harris,
(MD) June 27, 1833.

George Hatfield and Indianna Morrisson, (MG)George Mehon,
(MD) November 16, 1834.

(Morgan County, Missouri Continued)

John Mica Hughs and Caroline Seats, (MG) J. Chisum, (MD) December 14, 1834.

Thomas Letchworth and Margaret Robinson, (JP) John B. Fisher, (MD) September 25, 1833.

Thomas McGee and Susannah Donaldson, (MG) Josiah Conn, (MD) October 22, 1834

James R. Miller and Polly Rhea, (MG) Little Lunceford, (MD) December 18, 1834.

Silas May and Polly Jones, (UK) John B. Huff, (MD) March 2, 1834.

Green Moore and Elizabeth Deakins, (JP) Buford Allee, (MD) December 21, 1834.

Samuel Payton and Sarah Cabel, (JP) Seth Howard, (MD) January 20, 1834.

Alford Runnolds and Elizabeth Heather, (JP) James McCutchen, (MD) May 22, 1834.

William Callison and Polly Cooper, (MG) Benjamin Jackson, (MD) June 1, 1837.

John Cooper and Isabella Masters, (MG) Benjamin Jackson, (MD) June 28, 1837

Lone Lime and Sophia Potter, (MG) Benjamin Jackson, (MD) February 8, 1838.

John McGee and Hannah Gest, (JP) John B. Fisher, (MD) September 3, 1837.

Fleming Meader and Sally Hughes, (MG) Benjamin Jackson, (MD) November 9, 1837.

James Prather and Mary Hawkins, (JP) Buford Allee, (MD) July 7, 1839.

Martin G. Phillips and Susan Hoff, (MG) F. Dunnegar, (MD) December 18, 1835.

William Ross and Josephine Davidson, (MG) Wlliam Mobley, (MD) September 27, 1835.

Oliver H. P. Briscoe and Ursula P. Huff, (MG) Archibald McCordi, (MD) April 7, 1836.

Perry Berry and Lucynda May, (MG) George Gehon, (MD) October 15, 1835.

John Boran and Rhoda McPherson, (JP) P. Barger, (MD) September 25, 1834.

Richard Chilcote and Sarah Harmon, (JP) Wm. Anthony, *MD) August 2, 1838.

Jackson Cook and Ann Merritt, (JP) P. Barger, (MD) January 10, 1839.

Wiley B. Cooper and Nancy Ann Blakely, (MG) Jacob Chism, (MD) December 19, 1839.

Thurman Daniel and Sintha Hill, (JP) Buford Allee, (MD) March 28, 1839.

Washington Darrell and Agnes Asbourne, (MG) J. Chisum, (MD) February 4, 1836.

(Morgan County, Missouri Continued)

Aron Estes and Elizabeth Wilson, (JP) William K. Anthony, (MD) November 1, 1838.

Henry Green and Rachael Wood, (JP) R. B. Harris, (MD) April --, 1839, (RD) November 27, 1839.

Thomas Guyer and Mary Ann Dobbins, (MG) Jacob Chisum, · (MD) May 28, 1837.

Stephen Howard and Sarah Stinson, (JP) Phillip Barger, (MD) October 18, 1838.

William McBrown and Hannah Gist, (JP) Phillip Barger, (MD) August 1, 1839.

John McPherson and Sarah Newkirk, (JP) Phillip Barger, (MD) September 22, 1838.

Thomas P. Morrisson and Jane Steward, (JP)Wm. K. Anthony, (MD) September 16, 1838.

Charles Newkirk and Dysa Bowen, (JP) Phillip Barger, (MD) May 30, 1839.

Robert Richardson and Cinderilla Estes, (JP) Phillip Barger, (MD) January 4, 1835.

Robert Morris and Elizabeth McPherson, (JP) Wm. Fulks, (MD) March 16, 1837.

George Nixson and Phebe Boonard, (JP) John P. Fisher, (MD) August 4, 1836.

Charles Pierson and Sarah Calfee, (JP) William Poer, (MD) April 25, 1837.

Thomas Francis Smith and Talitha Foley, (JP)William Rhea, (MD) June 25, 1837.

William Thurman and Martha Adkinson, (UK) Thompson Scott, (MD) September 3, 1836.

Julius Woodford and Martha J. Huff, (MG)Jacob Chism, (MD) May 9, 1839.

William Baughman and Rachel Slater, (JP) Edmond Chapman, (MD) February 26, 1839.

Shannon Akin and Kulbery Durnang, (CLRK) Thomas G. Davis, (MD) June 28, 1836.

John Campbell and Elizabeth Lanier, (JP) Edmond Chapman, (MD) December 30, 1838.

Squire Boone Campbell and Emeline Taylor, (MG) Jacob Chisum, (MD) August 23, 1838.

William W. Cook and Ann M. Davis, (MG) Jacob Chism, (MD) August 13, 1839.

Hardin Cox and Martha A. Brown, (JP) Edmond Chapman, (MD) April 8, 1838.

Sylvester R. Cox and Susan Harris, (JP) E. Chapman, (MD) June 15, 1838.

John Estes and Heziah Summers, (JP) John Chism, (MD) December 7, 1835.

Isaac French and Nancy C. Monroe, (MG) J. Chisum, (MD) June 23, 1836.

(Morgan County, Missouri Continued)

William H. Fench and Comfort E. Parkes, (MG) Abraham Milce, (MD) March 29, 1836.

Valentine Harmon and Sarah Jones, (JP) R.B. Harris, (MD) March 23, 1839.

Alfred Hatfield and Gustin Catherine Nixson, (UK) Joseph M. Bomane, (MD) December 24, 1835.

Samuel Hix and Salina Gehon, (MG) J. Chism, (MD) June 13, 1836.

C. Johnson and Susan Barlett, (JP) Robert Wilson, (MD) June 16, 1836.

William H. Lebo and Caroline McFarland, (MG) Alx. McFarland, (MD) April 24, 1838.

Alexander Findley and Jane Carroll, (JP) Robert Wilson, (MD) June 19, 1836.

Hardin Hix and Altezora Spencer, (JP) Robert Wilson, (MD) May 24, 1835.

John Barnett and Jane McCombs, (JP) Zackens German, (MD) January 18, 1838.

J. M. Bills and Mary Ellis, (JP) Zacken German, (MD) September 2, 1837.

Ed Boles and Lucinda Williams, (UK) Thomas J. Donthit, (MD) April --. 1838, Groom from Cooper County.

James Boyd and Malinda Adams, (JP) John B. Fisher, (MD) December 4, 1836.

Alexander Burd and Matilda Phillips, (JP) Zackus German, (MD) December 27, 1838.

James W. Kelly and Nancy Taylor, (JP) William Fulks, (MD) June 9, 1837.

Gabriel L. Parks and Joanna Hale, (JP) Zackeus George, (MD) February 5, 1837.

Jacob Vandergraph and Margaret Gilmore, (JP) John B. Fisher, (MD) September 12, 1833.

David Vaught and Saphony Combs, (JP) John B. Fisher, (MD) April 6, 1837.

Jarrad Trent and Elizabeth Bartlett, (JP) J. W. Findley, (MD) June 27, 1839.

Moses Woodfin and Eliza Chenault, (JP) John B. Fisher, (MD) June 27, 1838.

James M. Wood and Catharine Adair, (JP) John B. Fisher, (MD) July 20, 1837.

Joseph Bollinger and Mary Spencer, (MG) Benjamin Jackson, (MD) October 18, 1836.

Charles M. Collins and Louisa Ellen Merry, (MG) Benjamin Jackson, (MD) June 4, 1837.

Hiram Medcalf and Elizabeth Upton, (JP) William Poor, (MD) December 29, 1835.

James Goodrich and Charity Phillips, (JP) G. L. Parker, (MD) October 13, 1836.

(Morgan County, Missouri Continued)

John Dobbins and Elizabeth Richardson, (JP) William Poer, (MD) October 18, 1835.

John P. W. Burns and Lucinda J. Burker, (MG) P. G. Rea, (MD) November 7, 1839.

Isaac Perkins and Nancy Bell, (JP) G. L. Parkes, (MD) December 8, 1836.

David Shuman and Martha Kelsay, (JP) G. L. Parkes, (MD) August 24, 1837.

Garret N. Steward and Sarah B. Goodrich, (JP)G.L. Parkes, (MD) June 6, 1837.

William Bowlinger and Nancy Lamb, (MG) David Lenox, (MD) June 5, 1836.

William Bass and Mary Epperson, (JP) Zealy M. Wynn, (MD) April 17, 1836.

Levi Byee and Jale Birdsong, (MG) Kemp Scott, (MD) May 15, 1839.

James Bybee and Elizabeth Kemp, (JP) Buford Allee, (MD) February 26, 1839.

Philip Stevens and Sarah M. Howard, (JP) Buford Allee, (MD) August 6, 1839.

Jonathan G. Thomas and Talitha Smith, (JP)Wm. K. Anthony, (MD) July 20, 1837.

Larken Weaver and Martha McCulah, (JP) J. B. Steel, (MD) August 27, 1835.

Walter McFarland and Parmelia Barnett, (JP) W.S. Barnett, (MD) October 6, 1835.

Richard Fisher and Betsy Summer, (JP) Phillip Barger,(MD) October 24, 1835.

Thomas Davidson and Juleann Pickens, (JP) P. Barger, (MD) October 12, 1836.

Samuel Dennis and Forlee Green, (MG) Little Lunceford, (MD) February 8, 1835.

Calvin Drummond and Elizabeth Brein, (MG) William Mobley, (MD) January 27, 1839.

Jonathan M. Houston and Tatimey Estes, (JP) J. M. Wyne, (MD) April 14, 1836.

James Jones and Mary Ann Self, (JP) Edmond Chapman, (MD) April 11, 1839.

John Jacobs and Auri Jane Hix, (JP) John Chism, (MD) --- 2, 1837.

Thomas Dobbins and Pelina Sullivan, (JP) William Hix, (MD) December 1, 1839.

William A. Thruston and Mary Ann Walton, (MG)Jacob Chism, (MD) November 7, 1839.

John B. Thurston and Nancy R. Walton, (MG) Jacob Chism, (MD) June 29, 1837.

John H. Taylor and Lemisey Seat, (MG) Jacob Chism, (MD) January 11, 1835.

(Morgan County, Missouri Continued)

William Taylor and Jane Barnett, (MG) Thomas Campbell, (MG) October 1, 1838.

John M. McClanahan and Mildred T. McCord, (MG) Jacob Chism, (MD) September 5, 1839.

Joseph Hatfield and Polly Heather, (MG) George Gehon, (MD) October 29, 1836.

John Everly and Isaphena Seat, (MG) Jacob Chism, (MD) November 6, 1839.

Abraham Kellison and Mary Palmer, (JP) G. L. Parkes, (MD) August 31, 1837.

Robert Mock and Polly Blassengame, (JP) R.B. Harris, (MD) August --, 1839, (RD) November 27, 1839.

Job Moon and Katharine Allen, (JP) J. B. Steel, (MD) March 1, 1835.

Charles Starkes and Elizabeth Maner, (JP) G. L. Parkes, (MD) June 13, 1836.

William Lowery and Mary Fitzhugh, (JP) William Poor, (MD) May 26, 1836.

Foster P. Wright and Nancy McLanahan, (MG) Benj. Jackson, (MD) August 29, 1837.

Peyton Wilcox and Sarah Mitchel, (JP) William Hix, (MD) November 13, 1839.

John Upptergrove and Nancy Bolan, (JP) Wm. Kirkpatrick, (MD) August 25, 1836.

Thomas Stewart and Janean Donaldson, (JP)Wm. Kirkpatrick, (MD) June 30, 1836.

David C. Moore and Clementine S. Ellis, (MG) Thomas B. Litton, (MD) January 4, 1838.

Jacob H. McFarland and Mary Ann Barnett, (MG) Abraham Malice, (MD) December 31, 1835.

William Richardson and Nancy Summers, (JP) P. Barger, (MD) February 7, 1839.

Daniel Shurley and Mary Gilmore, (JP) W. S. Barnett, (MD) October 30, 1835.

James Sumers and Rhoda Barger, (MG) J. Chisum, (MD) October 15, 1834.

Joseph M. Taylor and Emily Findley, (MG) Jacob Chism, (MD) August 6, 1839.

James Turner and Nancy Jones, (JP) G. Barger, (MD) July 27, 1836.

Samuel M. Wilson and Mary Oleany Jonican, (MG) A. McFarland, (MD) December 12, 1838.

Cape Girardeau County, Missouri, Public Monies Received By The County Clerk, November 1, 1827 to October 2, 1828, Capitol Fire Documents, Folder 558, CFD 25.

Name	Date
John Bland	November 1, 1827

(Cape Girardeau County, Missouri Continued)

Name	Date
Charles G. Ellis	November 1, 1827
John Hendricks	November 2, 1827
R. Guild	November 11, 1827
Thos. Byrne	November 12, 1827
A. P. Ellis and John Judin	November 12, 1827
Oliver Creath	November 13, 1827
Isaac Jutton	November 13, 1827
William Randles	November 13, 1827
R. Daugherty	November 14, 1827
Stephen Myers	November 16, 1827
Jacob Sike	November 17, 1827
John C. Miller	November 20, 1827
Geo. F. Bollinger	November 21, 1827
Jonathan Johnson	November 25, 1827
John Sheppard	November 25, 1827
M. A. Knon	November 31, 1827
Henry Hill	November 31, 1827
Jaco Runyan	January 1, 1828
Wm. M. Bonnett	January 30, 1828
Lindsey J. D'Lashmuitt	February 1, 1828
Alex. Buckner	February 1, 1828
Nathan Vanhorn	February 1, 1828
C. G. Ellis	March 17, 1828
John H. Lockhart	March 3, 1828
Welton O'Bannon	March 5, 1828
Jacob Clodfelter	March 5, 1828
Richd. Swan	March 5, 1828
John Zillifro	March 22, 1828
Wm. M'Guin	March 24, 1828
Henry Sanford	March 24, 1828
Cross & Garner	March 26, 1828
John M. Daniel	March 26, 1828
James Little	March 26, 1828
Jos. Seawill and J. Ranney	April 4, 1828
Benjamin Hempstead	April 21, 1828
Jas. C. Lewis	May 3, 1828
Menard & Valle	May 8, 1828
Terry Pac, jr.	May 10, 1828
Eli Erwin	May 10, 1828
John Harris	May 12, 1828
V. B. D'Lashmutt	May 12, 1828
B. H. Groves	May 12, 1828
John Hall	May 12, 1828
Chas. G. Ellis	May 12, 1828
Wm. Thompson	May 14, 1828
Johnson Ranney	May 16, 1828
Hardy Brooks	May 26, 1828

(Cape Girardeau County, Missouri Continued)

Name	Date
Lindsey J. D'Lashmutt	June 30, 1828
Joseph C. Lewis	June 6, 1828
John Dunn	June 7, 1828
Benj. F. Wheeler	June 9, 1828
William Garner	June 9, 1828
Robert Brevard	June 14, 1828
Thomas Byrne	June 17, 1828
A. G. Dussey	June 18, 1828
Lewis Wadkins	June 19, 1828
John Giles	July 3, 1828
John N. Adams	July 7, 1828
John McLean	July 4, 1828
H. Sanford	July 22, 1828
Evan M. Daugherty	July 30, 1828
George Cook	July 31, 1828
Ralph Guild	August 11, 1828
Daniel Crader	August 15, 1828
Miles Randol	August 15, 1828
Hardy Brooks	August 23, 1828
E. McDurmitt	August 25, 1828
Joseph Baker	August 25, 1828
William M. Bennett	September 2, 1828
Michael Eaker	September 5, 1828
Robert Brooks	September 12, 1828
Charles G. Ellis	September 12, 1828
Belemus H. Groves	September 12, 1828
R. Daugherty	September 22, 1828
G. F. Bollinger	September 22, 1828
William Boner	October 2, 1828
John D. Talbot	October 3, 1828
J. B. Thomas	October 3, 1828
John Wilson	October 3, 1828
Henry Fellows	October 13, 1828
Robert Brooks	October 22, 1828

Morgan County, Missouri, Tax List, 1837, Capitol Fire Documents, Folder 1219, CFD 30.

Name	Acres	Original Claimant
Thomas Adair	80	Y. Adair
Buford Alle	80	B. Alle
Buford Alle	80	B. Alle
James Birdsong	80	M. Martin
Willis Brockman	80	D. M'Gee
John Butler	73	T. H. Berry
John Carpenter	80	J. Carpenter
John Carpenter	80	J. Carpenter
James Dooley	80	B. Dooley

(Morgan County, Missouri Continued)

Name	Acres	Original Claimant
John C. Findley	80	J. Chitwood
John B. Fisher	80	J. B. Fisher
Catharine Fisher	80	T. Fisher
Zacheus German	80	Z. German
Zacheus German	80	Z. German
Zacheus German	44	Z. German
John Gest	138	J. Gest
Benjamin Gest	80	B. Gest
Seth Howard	62	S. Howard
Warner Howser	97	W. Howser
Warner Howser	18	W. Howser
Alexander S. Hill	80	J. Stephens
Rowling H. Hill	40	G. Hill
Green B. Hill	40	G. Hill
George Hawk	40	J. Robertson
Lott Howard	80	L. Howard
Ruben B. Harris	80	R. Hatfield
Waid Howard	80	S. Vinston
John Ingram	40	J. Robertson
John Johnston	80	J. Smith
Monroe William	80	J. C. Boggs
Monroe William	35	Z. German
Thomas J. Morris	80	T. J. Morris
Joseph M'Pheron	80	J. M'Pheron
James Morris	140	J. Morris
David M'Gee, adm.	80	P. Rogers
Joshua M'Perion	80	J. M'Pherion
Aaron M'Pherion	80	F. Thomas
John D. Miller	80	T. Fisher
William McFarland	80	D. M'Kenzie
James M'Cutchen, sr.	80	J. M'Cutchen
James M'Cutchen, sr.	80	J. M'Cutchen
Charles Newkirk	80	R. Rogers
Nicholas Ownbey	102	N. Ownbey
Powel S. Ownbey	64	N. Ownbey
Derrin Pulley	40	D. Pulley
William Poor	80	W. Poor
John Russel	80	J. Russell
John Robertson, sr.	80	R. Robertson
John Robertson, sr.	80	W. Howard
Samuel Smith	80	S. Smith
Samuel Smith	80	G. M'Farland
Joseph B. Steele	80	J. Chitwood
Joseph B. Steele	80	W. Steele
James Spencer	80	J. Walton
Josiah S. Waltop	80	J. Walton
Nancy Wilson	80	E. Anderson

(Morgan County, Missouri Continued)
Nonresidents:

Name	Acres	Original Claimants
Andrew Estes, sr.	150	A. Estes
Wm. H. Shanklin	80	W. H. Shanklin
David Taylor	80	A. W. Caslin
Edmond Wilkes	80	E. Wilkes
William D. Walden	80	J. D. M'Cutchen

Benton County, Missouri, Delinquent Tax List, Capitol Fire Documents, 1837, Folder 1207, CFD 30.

William Ater, William Combs, Richd. Fisher, James Roberts, James Hefflinger, Noah Lindsey, Dugald M'Call, Wm. Stephens, Allen Tate, Saml. Thompson, Thos. Crenshaw.

Montgomery County, Missouri, November, 1837, Capitol Fire Documents, Delinquent Tax List, Folder 1235, CFD 30.

John Becksler, jr., John Ellis, Benjamin Ellis, Shelton T. Green, Thomas Heskene, Robert Hunter, John H. Hunter, E. O. H. Logsdon, Laswell Lasefield, Thomas Musick, John Boice, John Plowman, James Pack, Jacob Quick, jr., William Quick.

Laclede County, Missouri, Lebanon City Cemetery, Lebanon, Missouri,(Note: Only Those Persons Born Before 1840 And That Died Before 1900).

Name	Born	Died
Joseph W. Windle	Aug. 15, 1832	Oct. 15, 1888
Sarah E. Watters	Mar. 6, 1829	Jan. 21, 1893
Nancy J. Mansfield	Jan. 1, 1816	Jul. 26, 1893
Elizabeth Eilenstine	Jun. 2, 1839	---
Mary Appersom	May 20, 1812	Jul. 23, 1890
*Karan Ulimoen	May 1, 1811	Apr. 7, 1890
*(Born: Norway)		
Francis Bradshaw	Oct. 24, 1833	Mar. 30, 1891
Celia R. Biggs	May 26, 1821	Sep. 27, 1898
Henry Peyton	Feb. 12, 1789	Dec. 15, 1858
Mary Ellis	1818	1898
Cynthia Breech	May 15, 1830	Jun. 15, 1862
Green Cook	Dec. 7, 1830	Jul. 14, 1877
Charles H. Corser	Jul. 8, 1823	Apr. 28, 1896
Helen B. Wilson	Jun. 7, 1825	May 11, 1884
Linton Taylor	May 25, 1828	Mar. 19, 1898
Mary Price	Nov. 9, 1824	Nov. 1, 1884
Priscilla Duval	Dec. 27, 1814	Nov. 30, 1878
Nancy D. O'Brien	Dec. 24, 1824	May 9, 1873
Vin. A. O'Donnell	Sep. 15, 1815	Dec. 14, 1870
Martha A. Williams	Jan. 15, 1833	Nov. 2, 1854
Martha Smith	Oct. 28, 1819	Dec. 9, 1891
M. M. Miller	Jun. 11, 1815	Feb. 4, 1885

(Laclede County, Missouri Continued)

Name	Born	Died
Robert Mansfield	Dec. 31, 1807	Jan. 14, 1887
Francis Apperson (age: 82 y)		Jul. 19, 1887
Marion L. Walker	1836	1892
Thomas Peyton	Feb. 2, 1836	Nov. 17, 1·858
D. B. Armstrong	Oct. 28, 1819	May 25, 1870
Wilson O. Duval	Apr. 15, 1810	May 2, 1861
John N. McAlpin	Jun. 8, 1832	Nov. 30, 1878
*Guldbrand Ulimoen	Oct. 1, 1812	Oct. 2, 1876
*(Born: Norway)		
Andrew L. Wilson	Aug. 26, 1820	Mar. 27, 1897
James W. Rider	May 18, 1817	May 12, 1855
C. N. Dodd	Jul. 11, 1837	Jul. 9, 1837
Louisa A. Burks	Aug. 11, 1822	Dec. 13, 1882
Daniel D. Bacon, sr.	Nov. 26, 1811	Nov. 9, 1889
Matt H. Hooker	Mar. 6, 1809	May 3, 1844
John Sidler	Jul. 6, 1817	Jan. 22, 1887
Susan J. Williams	Sep. 22, 1830	Aug. 1, 1886
Josiah Ivey	Aug. 31, 1824	Feb. 1, 1890
Mary Marcella Adams	Jan. 27, 1817	Dec. 20, 1882
Caroline Mendler	Mar. 28, 1826	May 16, 1877
Mary Gillespie	May 15, 1817	---
Emeline Vier Johnson	1831	1898
Louisa Atchley	May 31, 1821	Apr. 27, 1877
Mary Keen	May 9, 1835	---
Joseph McCray	Feb. 9, 1820	Sep. 21, 1896
Rolly Crunk	1831	Jul. 6, 1888
Margaret J. Newhouse	Jun. 30, 1838	Jan. 13, 1897
T. A. Booten	Sep. 9, 1828	Jul. 9, 1886
Louisa A. Corser	Oct. 15, 1829	Jan. 25, 1899
Sallie Evington	Feb. 10, 1836	Mar. 20, 1883
Martha M. Billings	Dec. 29, 1821	Aug. 26, 1891
August J. Windsor	Sep. 5, 1806	Jan. 26, 1879
Celia Wilson Windsor	Feb. 25, 1807	May 5, 1896
Joseph F. Smith	Sep. 15, 1816	Dec. 21, 1898
Hugh McCoin	1820	1873
Louis Detweiler	May 1, 1811	Dec. 7, 1893
John L. Mustard	Aug. 4, 1831	Mar. 14, 1885
Daniel L. Price	Jan. 1, 1823	Jan. 20, 1898
John Coye	Oct. 15, 1831	Mar. 26, 1885
Abraham Price	Jun. 27, 1819	Aug. 28, 1897
John Lankford Herndon	Feb. 15, 1818	Oct. 5, 1885
S. R. Allen	Mar. 30, 1815	Mar. 12, 1892
Lt. A A. West	Apr. 12, 1834	May 1, 1899
Elizabeth S. Medley	Sep. 11, 1810	Nov. 13, 1882
J. W. Scott	Feb. 27, 1827	Jan. 23, 1896
Wm. B. Taylor	Mar. 4, 1828	Mar. 23, 1898

Ripley County, Missouri, Delinquent Tax List, 1837, Capitol Fire Documents, Folder 1242, CFD 30.

Current River Township: G. W. Coppage, John Hobaugh, jr., Poncetheen Burlson, Hiram Hobaugh, Samuel Keen, Elijah Owen, Madison Laughlin, John Laughlin,Henry Laughlin,Joel Wherley, William Watkin, Wm. Mahan, sr., Robert Mills, Geo. Wherely.

Carter Township: Thomas Cook, George Lorenzo, John Fry, Neeley Thomas, Joseph Davidson, Anthony Deaning, Wm. Farmer, Newton Jackson, Lewis Levell, John Rodman, Daniel Rose, John Slusher, Samuel West.

Kelly Township: John Alfred, George Andrew,Thomas Spiver, Michael Burget, Thomas Buman, James Dickson,John Hobs,Thomas Langley.

Washington Township: James Brown, James Eidson, Westmoreland Hugh, Anis Flaney, James Hemby, Jaom (sic) Lancey,Moses Smith, James Morrow, William Matney, Harrel Street,John Lee, Henry Poplin, Silas Lemons, Daniel Emons, Griffin Emons,Jas. Dawson, Dempsy Odom.

Union Township: Willis Dodd, William Drake, Joseph Lure, James Harbeson, David Lure, Thomas Langley, William Little, Joseph Phipps, John Brice, Miles Poers, Jeremiah Odle, John Poke, James Pierce, Bright Turman, Peter Vanbbibber, Joseph Vanbbier, John Wallace.

Moore Township: Matthew Capps, William Galehar, William Keel, William Lundy, Isaac Romine, James Turman.

Logan Township: William Black, James Clark, Isaac Mein, John Chromester, Noah Dent, Joel Leach, Moses Morris, Simon Stacy, John Mills, jr., Sally Mill, Abraham Miller, Edward Watson.

Black River Township: Seton Ueher, Thomas Buford, Vance Calahan, George Hauk, Benj. Henwick, John Jamison, sr., John Jamison, jr., James Jamison, Watty Jordan, Ezkiel Kinslow, William King, John W. Lewis, Edward Leisster, William Long, George Long, John McCabe, Edward Memiston, John Maberry, Wm. Stricklin, Solomon Mayberry, James Oxford, Elizabeth Oxford, Riley Radford, Neil Stricklin, jr., George Sumpter, Jonathan Shumley.

Callaway County, Missouri, Antioch Christian Church Cemtery, South Of Willsburg, Missouri.

Name	Born	Died
Elizabeth M. Mahan	May 15, 1814	Dec. 17, 1895
Ann B. Cobbs	Feb. 11, 1811	May 10, 1899
Mary E. Gates (age: 63 y)		Sep. 17, 1889
Pearcy Arnold (age: 73 y, 5 m, 15 d)		Oct. 12, 1875
Charles Love	1805	1881
Elizabeth Boone (age: 67 y, 7 m, 18 d)		Jun. 10, 1878
Mary E. Hults (age: 69 y)		Nov. 15, 1897
Caroline Scholl Arnold	Aug. 29, 1823	Aug. 31, 1899

(Callaway County, Missouri Continued)

Name	Born	Died
Lucy J. Harrison	1838	1891
William Arnold	Mar. 2, 1817	Oct. 10, 1875
James Hults (age: 60 y, 7 m 2 d)		Aug. 2, 1889
Louis Arnold	May 25, 1821	Jan. 9, 1893
W. C. Crews (age: 80 y, Mason)		Feb. 14, 1888
Pleasant C. Arnold	Sep. 15, 1821	Aug. 1, 1864
Isaac H. Kelly	Apr. 17, 1813	Sep. 23, 1882
Mary Ann White (age: 49 y)		Nov. 30, 1856
D. P. Allen	Jun. 18, 1803	Jun. 11, 1871
James Love (age: 79 y, 2 m, 18 d)		Dec. 21, 1886
Mrs. Frances A. Darby	Nov. 28, 1827	Mar. 15, 1899
Milton Gates	Nov. 30, 1821	---
Morgan Bryan White (age: 82 y, 9 m, 28 d)		Mar. 28, 1883
Robert Arnold, sr. (age: 81 y, 1 m, 10 d)		Mar. 23, 1867
Rodalpho Boone (age: 72 y, 1 m, 14 d)		Mar. 31, 1880
---- Gill, the wife of John Gill	Apr. 9, 1835	Jul. 17, 1892

Ste. Genevieve County, Missouri, Territorial Tax List, 1814.

Antoine Aubashon, Bazeal Aubashon, David Adams, Charles Arshanberry, Michael Ammauins, Francois Aubason, Thomas Allen, Augustus Aubashon, Btst. Aubashon, Turner Abnather, Francois Aubashon, sr., Peter Aubashon, Antoine Aubashon, Wm. Baker, Joseph Amineaux, Julian Ammeaux, Francis Aubashon, Augustin Aubashon, Peter Aubashon, William B. Block, Michael Butcher, James Berry, Peter Bequit, Michael Bardo, Louis Buatt, James Bosia, John B. Bosia, Amos Bird, John Bequit, Joseph Brown, John Bailey, Widow Berk, Joseph Belott, Pamida Bovia, Louis Bolduke, Antoine B. Buatt, Antoine Buegins, Vital Bovia, John M. Bushard, Joseph Bogy, George Butott, John Burguett, Mark Brooks, William Bean, Barney Burns, Joseph Bequett, James Burns, William Burns, Widow Burns, Anter (sic) Burns, Elisa Belshy, Richard Buress, Michael Bodaux, John Bell, Barney Brown, Brown, Roland Barlow, Francois Bequet, William Cebran, Joseph Cears, Berwill Calvert, Louis Carow, Btst. Carow, Jesse Calaway, Joseph Carow, Francois A. Cisel, John Cowin, George Campster, Thomas Cothran, Louis Corteen, Clement Cissel, Wm. Counins, Gabriel Caliott, Robert Clealand, Joseph Charleveal, Bater (sic) Bequit, sr., Widow Coldwell, David Campbell, Wm. Cheek, Robert Coldwel, Robert Coldwell (sic), David Coldwell, Henry Chambers, George Crow, Daniel Counsel, John Dart, John Donohue, Michael Doland, Francois J. Dumas, Perfect Defour, Thomas Donohue, John Donohue, adm. of J. Donohue, dec., John Daily, Btste. Dequer, Louis Degeas, Julian Depeston, Peter Dogy, Widow Parent and Dubra, P. Detchemendz, William Doial, Louis Dixon, Henry Dickinson, John Deveal, Wm. Dunn, Thomas Dodge, Henry Dodge, Widow Delouisses, Isreal G. Dodge, Henry

(Ste. Genevieve County, Missouri Continued)
Elliott, Rhueben Estes, Lunchbow Ellis, Charles Ellis, Jesse
Euiess, Elizabeth Eviner, Michael Goza, Samuel Flint, Dodge
Lamar Ellis, Wid. F. Frazierur, William Flynn, Samuel Flynn,
Christian Fender, Thomas Fenwick, Ezekiel Fenwick, Patrick
Fenwick, James Fenwick, John Frauk, F. Fenwick, adm. of G.A.
Hamistian, John Btst. Forta, Louis Gornoe, Michael Govirox,
Edward Gibson, Charles Gregois, Joseph Gale, Antoine Giel,
John Guitarsh, James Grason, John Greenwalt,Isaac Greenwalt,
John Greenwalt (sic), Wm. Greene, David Goodspeed, Louis and
Joseph Gairron, John Goseshow, Peter Gornoe,Charles L. Goin,
Joseph Goiroiuex, Charles H. Henry, Richard Hawkins, Aquilah
Hagan, Hezekiah Harris, Wid. Haden, Peter Holster, John Bte.
Hubardoo, Peter Holster, jr., William How, Wid. Hinch, James
Huchau, Levi Hagan, Edward Hempstead, Francois James, Batest
Janice, Mark Johnston, Robert Jamerson, William James,George
E. Jackson, Joseph Jarett, John Iola, John Btst. Jamill,sr.,
Henry Kile, Philip Kanady, William Kanady, John Kenearsin,
Timoth (sic) Kily, John Kily,Joel Kinerson,Absalom Kinerson,
Francois Keanes, Kenes, John Lansbanca, Harvey Lane,Nicholas
Laplant, John Bta. Laganois, Louis Laclave,Francois Laelare,
Thomas Long, James Logan, John Linkhorn, Benard Layton, John
L. Lytin, Francois Laumandier, James Lundon, James Locket,
Ignatuis Layton, Abner Loos, Joseph Labuman, Louis Laport,
Adrien Langlois, Francois Laburndier, John Bte. Lalumadier,
Joseph Lalumardiet, sr., Louis Laplaint, Zachariah Layton,
John McArthur, George Morow, Thomas McKnight, Btst. Morow,
Archibald Morgan, Benaja Morgan, David Morgan, John Morgan,
Richard Moore, Alexander McCoughae, John Moen, Peter Miller,
Daniel Meudett, Joseph Mossey, Samuel G. M'Donald, Roland
Meredith, John McCall, Joseph Manning, James Matingly, John
McLehan, Isidore Moore, Nicholas Miott, John Manning, Robert
Manning, Nicholas Miles, Henry Miles, Nicholas Moore, Iaco
Meesia, John Meesia, Joseph Morow, James McLain,Henry Moris,
John May, Thomas Madin, Major James Moore, James Manning,
Absalom Newfield, Charles Nelson, Wid. Newsom, Clement Nott,
Francois Ogia, Francois Ogia, jr., Thomas Oliver, John Btst.
Pratt, Jacob Philipson, Micael Placett, Thomas Paterson,John
Paterson, Alexander Paterson, William Paterson,Wid. Preston,
Frances Philips, Joseph Pratt, George Pinkley, Widow Pratt,
Nicholas Paschall, Joseph Placee, Paul Robert, Julian Ratia,
Francois Rongilia, Lothar Rangea, Benedict Riley, Augustus
St. James, John Scott, Thomas Sims, Wm. Severy,John Stewart,
Walter Smoot, Asap Smith, John Smith, jr., Robert Smith,John
Btst. St. James, Vital St. James, Joseph St. James, Obediah
Scott, Barney Smith, Titus Strickland, Francois Simmoe, Wm.
Shannon, Bartholomew St. James, Raphial St. James, Antoine
Simione, John Smith, Widow Samuels, Antoine Tomier, Nicholas
Tucker, James Thompson, James Tucker, Henry Tucker, Francois

(Ste. Genevieve County, Missouri Continued)
Tucker, Thomas Tucker, Peter Tucker, Joseph Tucker, sr.,
Nicholas Tomier, Bazeal Tomish, Peter Turick, Louis Treado,
Gabriel Tomwier, Theodore Tinque,Wid. Tiniver,Rueben Thomas,
Nicholas Vidmore, Nathan Vanhorn, John Btst. Vabia, John Bt.
Vabia, jr., Louis Valia, Btst. Vital Wm. Varner, Christopher
Wright, Dubia Velar, Peter Winsfield, Wid. Watson, Ignathius
Zeto, Joseph Wilkerson, Joab Waters, Tunnis Quick, Coleman
Whitlow, James W. Wright.

Montgomery County, Missouri, A List Of Public Securities For
Twelve Months Ending October 30, 1830, Folder 909, Capitol
Fire Documents, CFD 28.

Name	Date
J. M. Davis	November 10, 1829
Jno. and Willis Bryan	November 10, 1829
Jeremiah Muir	November 25, 1829
Bast and Sharp	November 25, 1829
Edward Ford	January 14, 1830
John Jones	January 25, 1830
William Timberlake	January 26, 1830
Alexander Logan	February 2, 1830
Andrew Zumwalt	February 8, 1830
Thomas Beatty	February 9, 1830
George W. Yeater	February 9, 1830
John Lee	February 10, 1830
Daniel Skinner	March 1, 1830
William Skinner	March 1, 1830
William Leatt	March 1, 1830
Stephen Ellis	March 15, 1830
E. B. Crump	March 19, 1830
Henry S. Crump	March 19, 1830
William Knon	March 19, 1830
Henry Clark	March 20, 1830
Charles Hubbard	April 10, 1830
Joseph Carpenter	April 17, 1830
Joel Pearl	May 14, 1830
Saml. Pearl	May 14, 1830
Abner Bryan	June 1, 1830
A. M. McKinney	June 1, 1830
J. C. Darst	June 1, 1830
Abraham Davidson	June 5, 1830
A. J. Long	June 17, 1830
M. Haun	June 25, 1830
A. Shobe	July 7, 1830
U. Pringle	August 4, 1830
M. Brown	August 4, 1830
J. C. M. McKinney	August 5, 1830
Lavina Holdin	August 10, 1830

(Montgomery County, Missouri Continued)

Name	Date
John Robinson	August 18, 1830
Ruce (sic) Bryan	August 18, 1830
Wm. Hancock	August 30, 1830
Wm. H. Tanner	September 11, 1830
James Cain	September 11, 1830
Daniel Robinson	October 9, 1830
David Bryan	October 28, 1830

Boone County, Missouri, Rockyford Primitive Baptist Church Cemetery, Hinton, Missouri.

Name	Born	Died
John Davenport	Apr. 24, 1793	Sep. 5, 1874
Frances Pigg	Nov. 2, 1803	Jul. 22, 1881
William F. Wilhite	Dec. 25, 1830	Jun. 8, 1899
David S. Shock	Oct. 8, 1800	Mar. 8, 1880
William R. Trunde	Nov. 25, 1829	Apr. 26, 1895
Ann Fowler (age: 78 y, 5 m, 16 d)		Jul. 9, 1879
Riley Brown	Jan. 18, 1830	Jun. 18, 1882
Susana Sublette (age: 69 y, 8 m, 15 d)		Sep. 30, 1852
William B. Dennis	Apr. 25, 1826	Jul. 23, 1876
John M. Cornielson	Nov. 2, 1820	Dec. 24, 1897
Wilet Coats (age: 70 y)		Mar. 20, 1886
John Warnock	Nov. 2, 1812	Jul. 22, 1858
Catharine Noe (age: 86 y)		Oct. 13, 1871
S. B. Turner	Jul. 6, 1819	May 14, 1886
Elizabeth Coats (age: 29 y)		Jun. 14, 1858
Zerelda Bradley	1820	1896
Nancy Jones	1821	---
Thomas Wingo (age: 83 y, 8 m, 16 d)		Oct. 8, 1870
Samuel Dysart (age: 49 y, 1 m, 20 d)		Apr. 26, 1879
Nancy Ellen Holloway	Jul. 24, 1835	Apr. 14, 1871
Polly McKenzie	Mar. 4, 1814	Dec. 3, 1891
Renard A. Pigg (age: 79 y, 7 m, 18 d)		Jan. 24, 1873
Caleb Fenton (age: 70 y, 6 m, 22 d)		Apr. 3, 1867
Henry C. Brown	May 30, 1835	Dec. 28, 1880
Jane Fenton (age: 84 y, 2 m, 15 d)		Jun. 15, 1872
John S. Barkwell (age: 75 y)		Feb. 18, 1898
India Palmer	Feb. 28, 1818	Mar. 15, 1897
Joseph Toalson (age: 62 y, 4 m, 1 d)		Jan. 18, 1893
Lemuel Batterson (age: 68 y, 3 m, 21 d)		Feb. 8, 1870
John Pigg	Sep. 27, 1830	1863
Miram Barrett (age: 72 y, 10 m, 29 d)		Jul. 19, 1883
Abigail Goslin (age; 77 y, 11 m, 8 d)		Feb. 22, 1893
Joanah W. Cowle	May 19, 1820	Apr. 3, 1852
Andrew J. Fenton (age: 42 y, 8 m, 8 d)		Oct. 23, 1871
Nathaniel McKenzie (age: 71 y)		Apr. 6, 1882
Rebecca B. Atkisson	Jun. 11, 1812	Jun. 8, 1896

(Boone County, Missouri Continued)

Name	Born	Died
Sylvester Goslin	Jul. 10, 1810	Jan. 27, 1894
James J. Fenton	Jan. 5, 1820	Feb. 5, 1869
John C. Fenton	1827	1897
Feruby C. Caldwell	Sep. 20, 1824	Dec. 11, 1885
Lettice Fenton	Jun. 20, 1811	Feb. 12, 1873
Thomas Caldwell (age: 66 y, 3 m, 29 d)		Feb. 12, 1885
Nancy Davenport (age: 69 y)		Oct. 24, 1866
Sarah Wolfe (age: 70 y, 9 m, 13 d)		Dec. 20, 1867
Stephen W. Piss	Mar. 1, 1833	Aug. 31, 1895
Tobitha D. McKenzie	Jun. 30, 1817	Nov. 28, 1893
Sallie Ann McKenzie (age: 66 y, 1 m, 19 d)		Sep. 19, 1889
Susan Wheatley (age: 77 y)		Jan. 22, 1892
James Bradley	1810	1896
Rebbeca Sullins	Oct. 18, 1833	May 13, 1894
James Atkisson (age: 68 y, 6 m, 27 d)		Nov. 2, 1880
Narcissus Cornielson	May 11, 1833	Apr. 24, 1897

St. Clair County, Illinois, Kaslaskia Land Office, Vol. 49A, Militia Land Claims, August 1, 1790, Aprroved By The Gov. In 1797.

George Atchison; Thomas Todd; John Moredock; Joseph Ogle, sr.; Samuel Morris; Jesse Waddle; Joseph Ogle, jr.; Benjamin Ogle; Edward Todd; Leonard Harness; George Hendricks; James Henderson; Benjamin Rodgers; James Lemon; Peter Casterline; John Moore; George Biggs; William Piggott; Laton White; Wm. Murray; Henry O'Hara, jr., John O'Hara; George Wilkerson,Wm. Chalfin; James Scott; Samuel Worley; Wm. Arundel; Francois Villaret; Bartholomew Provost; Daniel Schultz; Daniel Raper; Antoine LePage; Joseph Manegre; John Sullivan; Thomas Mars; George Powers; Michel Beaulieu; William Robbins; Alexander Dennis; Pierre LaPerche; Isaac Bryson; Joseph Mendoza; Isaac Bryson; Francois LaPence; George Luntsford; Thomas Mars;Wm. Jones; John Porter; Hardy Ware; Robert Seybold;Jesse Ratnor; John Jack; James Head; Michael Huff; William Moore; Ebenezer Severns; Timothy Ballew; James Bryan; Levi Piggot;Wm. Grotz; Isaac West; Alexander Waddle; James Garrotson;William Jones; Christopher Smith; David Waddle; Henry McLaughlin; Ebenezer Bowen; Thedious Bradley; James McRoberts; John Worley; Isaac Chalfin; Louis Gervalis; Bazile Beaulieu; Antoine Labuxiere; Amable Macon; Pierre Chartier; Claude Chenier; Jean Munier; Joseph Marie;Bazele LaFlamme;Francois Demeter alias Francois Dinesne; Gebriel Tellier; Henri Biron; Michel Longval; Jean Baptiste Harmand; Antoine Harmand, jr.; Hubert Delorme; John Baptiste Chenie; Joseph Hymon; Framcois Longval; Jacque St. Albin; Charles Cadron, jr.; Pierre Bourassa; Etienne Cadron; Pierre Dubois, jr; Hippolite Longval; Francois Campeau; Jean Baptiste Methode; Louis Harmand; Paschal Lefevre; Claude St.

(St. Clair County, Illinois Continued)
Aubin; Joseph Demaret; Louis Begeron; Hubert Longval; Louis LaBuxiere; Joseph Parisen; Michel Pilet; Francois LeFevere alias Courie, jr.; Joseph LePage; Joseph Chenie; Louis Gaud, jr.; Charles Buteau, jr.; Edward Hebert; Joseph Leplante; Joseph Poirie; Joseph Goneville;Pierre Chretien;Louis Rehle; Jean Beaulieu; Pierre Picard;Pierre Clermont;Louis Bouliard; August Clermont; Joseph Touchet; Louis Gondron;Louis Bisson; Dennis Lavertu; Julien Mercier; Jean Batiste Rapelais alias Gonville; Francois Pancrass; Joseph Archambeau; John Brady; Simon Lepage; Louis Coste; Louis Goneville; Jean Lyle; Jean Baptiste Fleurant; Antoine Grandbois; Dennis Valentin; Jean Lerenard; Francois Labbe; Joseph Grondine; Joseph LaChance; Pierre Lize; Alexis Chartran; Jean baptise Champlain; Pierre Reihle; Jean Baptiste Champlain; Gabriel Marleaux, jr.; Jean Baptiste Marleaux; Francois Labuxiere; Samson Canadien; John Ritchie; Joseph Trotier, son of Loius; Gabriel Marleaux;Paul Poirier; Alexis Brisson; Louis Beaulieu; Auguste Biron; Jean Baptiste Girrad dit Jean Pierre; Nicholas Turgeon; Francois Grondine; Jean Baptiste Leblanc; Louis Giroux;Louis Mullote; Louis LaFlamme; Louis Larmarche; Louis Pincomeau; Jean Noel Godin; Andre Boquet; Louis Vadbononcoeur; Pierre Guittard, jr.;Laurent Lefevere; Marrian Pancrass; Louis Grosle; Ignace Grondine; Antoine Cabassier;Joseph Cabassier;Francois Lemay; Francois Cabassier; Michel Metivier; Andrew Marlow; Pierre Cabassier; Francois Ranousse; Jean Baptiste Cabassier;Thomas Winn; Armant Tellier; Thomas Chartran; Pierre Martin, jr.; Jacque Magiot; Joseph Deloge, jr.; Pierre Godin; Jean Bapt. LaLande; Raphael Daubuchon; Jacque Latrourneau; Louis Morin; Paschal Letang; Louis St. Germain; Antoine Courtois; Joseph Boland; Constant Longtemp; Charles Pilet; Etienne Nicholle; Rene Zureau; Jean Baptiste Charterau alias Lebeuasse;Laurent Jean Berger; Pierre Antoine Tabeaux; Isidore Lacroix; Joseph Vizina; Jean Marie Caomparet; Jean Marie Bissonet; Francois Young; Joseph Grenier; Hubert Mercier; Etienne Pincomeau; Joseph Vaudry, jr.; Alphonse ---; Jean Baptiste Provost;Jean Vandett; Louis Bibeaux; Toussant Chartran;Pierre Lecuyer dit St. Sauveur; Louis Bibeaux; Michel Rocher;Charles Cabassier; Julien Nicholle; Louis Allaire; James McNabb; Joseph Danis; Bartholomew Tardiveau; Francois Janis; Francois Doin; John Rice Jones; Antoine Barutel dit Noel Toulose; Jean Baptiste Germain; Manuel Portugais; Charles Robin, jr.; Alexis Doza; Antoiny LaChapelle; Bazile LaChapelle; Louis Germain; Joseph Anderson; Baptiste LaChapelle; Joseph LaChapelle; John Cook; Francois Barutel Toulouse; Philip Derousse St. Pierre; Louis LaChapelle; Francois Lemieux; Jerome Derousse St. Pierre;Wm. Young Whiteside; Michel St. Pierre; Henry Cook; Adam Cook; William Morrison; Joseph Derousse St. Pierre;Pierre Grenier; Jean Baptiste Derousse St. Pierre; Jacque Gossiaux;Alexander

134

(St. Clair County, Missouri Continued)
McNabb; Henri Bienenu;Michel Bienvenu; Bazile Alary;Nicholas Cassou; Louis Lemieux; Charles Danis, fils; Pierre Barutel Toulouse; Henri Barutel Troulouse; Samuel Judy; Jean Baptist Taumur, jr.; Anthony Buyat, jr.; David Gray; Augustin Royer; Louis Sequin dit Laderoute; Jean Baptiste Gendron, jr.; Levi Theel; Joseph Thuillier; Jerome Thibault; Pierre Basque;Jean Baptiste Morris; Pierre Menard; Vital Bauvais, jr.; Michel LaSource; Louis Buyat, jr.; Pedro Christofal; Francis Clark; Phillip Galloher; Thomas Callahan; Joseph Longal;Jacob Judy; Antoine Labriere; Hipolite LaFarme; Louis Charleville; John Huaresborough Simpson; Hugh McDonald Chissolm;Jos. Fernande; Francois Montrie; Ignace LaGauterie; Joseph Chevalier.

Militia Of The Missouri Territory, October 1, 1814.

Name	Rank	Unit
William Clark, Gov.	Commander in Chief	
Henry Dodge	Brigadier General	
Alexander McNair	Adj. General	
St. Louis County		
Tho. F. Riddick	Major	1st Reg.
Richd. Chitwood	Major	2nd Reg.
Jedathun Kendall	Major	3rd Reg.
Peter Chouteau	Major	4th Reg.
Robert A. Smith	Captain	1st Co,1st Bat
Hubert Guyon	Lieutenant	1st Co,1st Bat
Frederick Geizer	Ensign	1st Co.1st Bat
Paul L. Chouteau	Captain	2nd Co,1st Bat
Henry Battu	Lieutenant	2nd Co,1st Bat
George Tompkins	Ensign	2nd Co,1st Bat
Louis Courtoix	Captain	3rd Co,1st Bat
Louis Courtoix, jr.	Lieutenant	3rd Co,1st Bat
Francis Roi	Ensign	3rd Co,1st Bat
Zeph. Sappington	Captain	4th Co,1st Bat
Thos. Sappington	Lieutenant	4th Co,1st Bat
William L. Long	Ensign	4th Co,1st Bat
James Musick	Captain	1st Co,2nd Bat
Elisha Patterson	Lieutenant	1st Co,2nd Bat
Green Baxter	Ensign	1st Co,2nd Bat
Hyacinth Dehetre	Captain	2nd Co,2nd Bat
J. M. Courtoix	Lieutenant	2nd Co,2nd Bat
Joseph Aubuchon	Ensign	2nd Co,2nd Bat
John Miller	Captain	3rd Co,2nd Bat
John Kinkead	Lieutenant	3rd Co,2nd Bat
Gabriel Long	Ensign	3rd Co,2nd Bat
John E. Allen	Captain	4th Co,2nd Bat
Joseph Lard	Lieutenant	4th Co,2nd Bat
William McDowns	Ensign	4th Co,2nd Bat
James McCullock	Captain	1st Co,3rd Bat

(Militia Continued)

Name	Rank	Unit
Jacob Collins	Lieutenant	1st Co,3rd Bat
John Horine	Ensign	1st Co,3rd Bat
Abner Vansant	Captain	2nd Co,3rd Bat
David Brook	Lieutenant	2nd Co,3rd Bat
Benjamin Johnston	Ensign	2nd Co,3rd Bat
Thos. Williams	Captain	3rd Co,3rd Bat
William Ink	Lieutenant	3rd Co,3rd Bat
Hardy Ware	Ensign	3rd Co,3rd Bat
Benjamin Hatherly	Captain	1st Co,4th Bat
Saml. Cantley	Lieutenant	1st Co,4th Bat
Lewis Hall	Ensign	1st Co,4th Bat
John Maupin	Captain	2nd Co,4th Bat
Joshua Brock	Lieutenant	2nd Co,4th Bat
John Sappington	Ensign	2nd Co,4th Bat
Augte. Chouteau	Captain	3rd Co,4th Bat
John Washington Thompson	Adjutant	Regmtl. Staff

Ste. Genevieve County

Name	Rank	Unit
Nathl. Cook	Lt. Colonel	2nd Reg.
Jno. Donohue	Major	1st Bat.
Jno. Callaway	Major	2nd Bat.
Thomas Oliver	Captain	1st Co,1st Bat
Jno. McArthur	Lieutenant	1st Co,1st Bat
Jos. Hertick	Ensign	1st Co,1st Bat
Jno. Bossieur	Captain	2nd Co,1st Bat
James Rigdon	Lieutenant	2nd Co,1st Bat
Jos. Amoureux	Ensign	2nd Co,1st Bat
Richd. Moore	Captain	3rd Co,1st Bat
Tho. Riney	Lieutenant	3rd Co,1st Bat
Tho. Patterson	Ensign	3rd Co,1st Bat
Frs. B. Cessell	Captain	4th Co,1st Bat
Mark Brooks	Lieutenant	4th Co,1st Bat
Saml. McCall	Ensign	4th Co,1st Bat
William Dillon	Captain	1st Co,2nd Bat
William Sims	Lieutenant	1st Co,2nd Bat
Benjamin LaChance	Ensign	1st Co,2nd Bat
Andw. Miller	Captain	2nd Co,2nd Bat
Isaac Murphy	Lieutenant	2nd Co,2nd Bat
John Burnham	Ensign	2nd Co,2nd Bat
Henry Poston	Captain	3rd Co,2nd Bat
Archibald Huddleston	Lieutenant	3rd Co,2nd Bat
Alexr. Craighead	Ensign	3rd Co,2nd Bat
Joseph Hertick	Paymaster	Regtml. Staff
Wm. McFarland	Adjutant	Regtml. Staff

(Militia Continued)

St. Charles County

Name	Rank	Unit
Daniel M. Boone	Lt. Colonel	3rd Reg.
Peter Journey	Major	1st Co
Robert Spencer	Major	2nd Co
Benjamin Cooper	Major	3rd Co
John McConell	Captain	1st Co,1st Bat
Peter Teague	Lieutenant	1st Co,1st Bat
Joseph Yardley	Ensign	1st Co,1st Bat
Isaac Vanbber	Captain	2nd Co,1st Bat
William Cassio	Ensign	2nd Co,1st Bat
Anthony Head	Lieutenant	2nd Co,1st Bat
Sanml. Ginson	Captain	3rd Co,1st Bat
Isaac Hostetter	Lieutenant	3rd Co,1st Bat
Robert Gray	Ensign	3rd Co,1st Bat
Nathl. Simonds	Captain	4th Co,1st Bat
Roswell Dusky	Lieutenant	4th Co.1st Bat
Wm. Ewing	Ensign	4th Co,1st Bat
Elisha Collard	Captain	5th Co,1st Bat
James Lewis	Lieutenant	5th Co,1st bat
Jacob Groshong	Ensign	5th Co,1st Bat
William Hartt	Captain	1st Co,2nd Bat
Osborn Knott	Lieutenant	1st Co,2nd Bat
Ralph Flaugherty	Ensign	1st Co,2nd Bat
Henry Hight	Captain	2nd Co,2nd Bat
Sylvestrie Pattie	Lieutenant	2nd Co,2nd Bat
Charles Dennis	Ensign	2nd Co,2nd Bat
Saml. Griffith	Captain	3rd Co,2nd Bat
Charles Soucier	Lieutenant	3rd Co,2nd Bat
Eben Ayres	Ensign	3rd Co,2nd Bat
Sarchal Cooper	Captain	1st Co,3rd Bat
Wm. McMahan	Lieutenant	1st Co,3rd Bat
Benjamin Cooper, jr.	Ensign	1st Co,3rd Bat
Jas. Alexander	Captain	2nd Co,3rd Bat
Jno. Morrow	Lieutenant	2nd Co,3rd Bat
Amos Barnes	Ensign	2nd Co,3rd Bat
William Head	Captain	3rd Co,3rd bat
David McQuitty	Lieutenant	3rd Co,3rd Bat
John Berry	Ensign	3rd Co,3rd Bat
Frs. Coursolle	Captain	Sans Dessein
Jos. Rivard	Lieutenant	Sans Dessein
Louis Deherte	Ensign	Sans Dessein
Henry Hight	Judge Advocate	Regtml. Staff
Jas. Beatty	Adjutant	Regtml. Staff
Stephen Hempstead	Quartermaster	Regtml. Staff

Cape Girardeau County

Name	Rank	Unit
Stephen Byrd	Lt. Colonel	4th Reg.

(Militia Continued)

Name	Rank	Unit
Geo. Bollinger	Major	1st Bat.
James Brady	Major	2nd Bat.
Abrm. Byrd	Captain	1st Co,1st Bat
Austin Young	Lieutenant	1st Co,1st Bat
Andrew Byrne	Ensign	1st Co,1st Bat
Geo. C. Miller	Captain	2nd Co,1st Bat
H. Bollinger	Lieutenant	2nd Co,1st Bat
Daniel Krytz	Ensign	2nd Co,1st Bat
Wm. Johnson	Captain	3rd Co,1st Bat
John Baker	Lieutenant	3rd Co,1st Bat
Thos. Izner	Ensign	3rd Co,1st Bat
Adam Ground	Captain	4th Co,1st Bat
Adam Shell	Lieutenant	4th Co,1st Bat
John Ground	Ensign	4th Co,1st Bat
Abm. Dougherty	Captain	1st Co,2nd Bat
Jacob Sheperd	Lieutenant	1st Co,2nd Bat
Elijah Dougherty	Ensign	1st Co,2nd Bat
Jesse Jeffery	Captain	2nd Co,2nd Bat
Jacob Fryend	Lieutenant	2nd Co,2nd Bat
John Fryend	Ensign	2nd Co,2nd Bat
James Ravenscraft	Captain	3rd Co,2nd Bat
Medad Randall	Lieutenant	3rd Co,2nd Bat
Elijah Randall	Ensign	3rd Co,2nd Bat
Geo. Jameson	Captain	4th Co,2nd Bat
Charles Logan	Lieutenant	4th Co,2nd Bat
Wm. Ingram	Ensign	4th Co,2nd Bat

New Madrid County

Name	Rank	Unit
Jno. E. Hartt	Lt. Colonel	5th Reg.
Stephen Ross	Major	1st Bat.
Jos. Hunter	Major	2nd Bat.
Elisha Winsor	Captain	
Thos. Winsor	Lieutenant	
Joseph Shields	Ensign	
Edwd. Matthews	Captain	
Jos. Smith	Lieutenant	
James Lucas	Ensign	
Saml. Cooper	Captain	
Robert Boyd	Lieutenant	
Alexr. LaForge	Ensign	
Benja. Myers	Captain	
Jno. Walker	Lieutenant	
Joseph Westbrook	Ensign	
Edward Tanner	Captain	
Andw. Robertson	Lieutenant	
Danl. Stringer	Ensign	
Jno. Hines	Captain	

138

(Militia Continued)

Name	Rank	Unit
Alex. Willard	Lieutenant	
Jacob Gibson	Ensign	
Richd. H. Waters	Judge Advocate	Regmtl. Staff
Jno. Walker	Adjutant	Regmtl. Staff

Washington County

Name	Rank	Unit
William H. Ashley	Lt. Colonel	6th Reg.
Andrew Henry	Major	1st Bat
Martin Ruggles	Major	2nd Bat
Jacob Pettit	Captain	1st Co,1st Bat
William James	Lieutenant	1st Co,1st Bat
Stephen F. Austin	Ensign	1st Co,1st Bat
Jesse Blackwell	Captain	2nd Co,1st Bat
Anthony Wilkinson	Lieutenant	2nd Co,1st Bat
Beja. Horne	Ensign	2nd Co,1st Bat
Robert F. Brown	Captain	3rd Co,1st Bat
James H. Moutree	Lieutenant	3rd Co,1st Bat
Drury Gooche	Ensign	3rd Co,1st Bat
Joshua Morrison	Captain	1st Co,2nd Bat
Zach. Goforth	Lieutenant	1st Co,2nd Bat
Thomas McLaughlin	Ensign	1st Co,2nd Bat
Timothy Phelps	Captain	2nd Co,2nd Bat
William Reed	Lieutenant	2nd Co,2nd Bat
James Gray	Ensign	2nd Co,2nd Bat
Job Westover	Captain	3rd Co,2nd Bat
John Baker	Lieutenant	3rd Co,2nd Bat
Joseph Wood	Ensign	3rd Co,2nd Bat

Arkansas County

Name	Rank	Unit
Anthony Haden	Lt. Colonel	7th Reg.
Danl. Mooney	Major	1st Bat.
Alexr. Kendrick	Captain	1st Co,1st Bat
William Glassen	Lieutenant	1st Co,1st Bat
William Dunn	Ensign	1st Co,1st Bat
James Scull	Captain	2nd Co,1st Bat
Peter Lefevre	Lieutenant	2nd Co,1st Bat
Charles Bougy	Ensign	2nd Co,1st Bat
Samuel Mosely	Captain	3rd Co,1st Bat
Lemuel Currin	Lieutenant	3rd Co,1st Bat
Edward Hogan	Captain	1st Co,2nd Bat
John Payatte	Lieutenant	1st Co,2nd Bat
Joseph Duchassin	Ensign	1st Co,2nd Bat
Jno. C. Newell	Captain	2nd Co,2nd Bat
Benjamin Murphy	Lieutenant	2nd Co,2nd Bat
Geo. Rankin	Ensign	2nd Co,2nd Bat
William Berney	Captain	3rd Co,2nd Bat
Isaac Cates	Lieutenant	3rd Co,2nd Bat

(Militia Continued)

Name	Rank	Unit
Saml. Cates	Ensign	3rd Co,2nd Bat

Volunteer Companies

Name	Rank	Unit
Jno. Scott	1st Lieutenant	Cavalry
E. A. Elliott	2nd Lieutenant	Cavalry
Jas. C. Young	Cornet	Cavalry
Wm. James	Purser	Cavalry
Joshua Dodson	2nd Lieutenant	Cavalry
Jno. B. Stone	Cornet	Cavalry
Jona. Riggs	Purser	Cavalry
John W. Thompson	Captain	Cavalry
Alexander Lucas	1st Lieutenant	Cavalry
Absalom Link	2nd Lieutenant	Cavalry

Mounted Riflemen

Name	Rank	Unit
James Rankin	Captain	
Jno. Geoger	Lieutenant	
Joseph Andrews	Ensign	
Joseph Hanks	Purser	
Morris Young	Captain	
Thomas Wyley	Lieutenant	
James Patterson	Ensign	
Tho. McWilliams	Purser	
John Hughes	Captain	
William Strother	Lieutenant	
Thomas Reed	Ensign	
Tim. Phelps	Purser	

Infantry

Name	Rank	Unit
Joseph Conway	Captain	
Richard Caulk	Lieutenant	
Thomas Caulk	Ensign	
Joseph Millard	Captain	
Stephen Martin	Lieutenant	
Anthony Bridger	Ensign	
Manuel Lisa	Captain	
Barthelemy Berthold	Lieutenant	
Francis Guyol	Ensign	

Artillery

Name	Rank	Unit
Charles Lucas	Captain	
John McKnight	1st Lieutenant	
Joseph Henderson	2nd Lieutenant	

Marion County, Missouri, Circuit Court, Causes, 1827 to 1838

Name		Name	No.
Thomas Newell	vs	George McDaniel	1

Name		Name	No.
George McDaniel	vs	Martin Gash, sr.	2
Richard W. Newell	vs	Moses D. Bates	5
Josiah Culbertson	vs	John C. Walker	7
Joseph Maxwell	vs	Richard W. Newell	9
Abraham Huntsberry	vs	Vanlandingham and Duncan	10
B. and I. Forman	vs	George McDaniel	12
R. B. Bartlett	vs	Joseph H. Brather	13
R. W. Newell	vs	Robert M. Easton	14
R. W. Newell	vs	Hawkins Smith	15
R. W. Newell	vs	Charles Smith	16
R. W. Newell	vs	Amelia Parish	17
R. W. Newell	vs	Moses D. Bates & others	18
R. W. Newell	vs	John Howell	19
R. W. Newell	vs	Brun and Eastin	20
Thomas Newell	vs	George McDaniel	21
Lewis Masquerier	vs	Elijah Haydon	22
Christopher Kieser	vs	Edward White	23
Robert Irvine	vs	Willis H. Chapman	24
Robert Miller	vs	Saml. and John Maxwell	25
State	vs	James Whaley	26
John Sear	vs	Albert Callis	27
State	vs	Jacob Fry	28
Elisha Freeman & wife	vs	Richd. DeCarnap	29
Woolfolk & Wilson	vs	Jacob Fry	30
Simon and Hyman Gratz	vs	C. Kieser	31
Charles Smith	vs	Robert B. Bartlett	34
Israel B. Grant, adm.	vs	J. McWilliams & others	36
Joseph M. Phillips	vs	C. P. Bullock and Jno. Godman	37
A. F. Boyce	vs	James White	38
R. B. Bartlett	vs	Albert G. Reynolds	39
David Ruth's admr.	vs	J. Glenday and O. Dickerson	41
Robert B. Bartlett	vs	Jas. and Thos. Glenday	42
Samuel Wilson	vs	John N. Boulware	43
Robert Miller	vs	Samuel Maxwell	44
Nathaniel Dunn	vs	Samuel S. Wilson	45
Robert B. Bartlett	vs	Moses D. Bates	47
Thomas P. Ross	vs	Abraham K. Frye	48
Albert G. Reynolds	vs	Robert B. Bartlett	49
Abraham Huntsberry	vs	Alfred Frazier	50
John S. Jenifer	vs	Elizabeth Culbertson	51
Zachariah G. Draper	vs	Robert B. Artlett	52
Raichard VanCarnap	vs	Elijah Craig	53
Tho. W. Bartlett, ass.	vs	Richd. W. Newell	54
State	vs	John Ward	55

Name		Name	No.
State	vs	Washington Young	56
Elijah Haden	vs	Thomas Haden	57
Edward White	vs	Hugh W. Shannon	58
Jas. Clemens, assignee of Hall & Trotter	vs	C. Kieser	59
George Harrison	vs	Montillion H. Smith	60
James Wood	vs	Buchannon V. R. Crews	61
Rpbt. B. Bartlett	vs	G. Ruth and D. Hendericks admrs.	62
Abraham Huntsberry	vs	Thomas J. Wise	63
Samuel Morton	vs	Robert Nisbet	64
Samuel Morton	vs	Elijah Smith	65
James T. Moore	vs	Crittemden Ferquerman	66
James Clemens	vs	C. Kieser and Jno. Sites	67
Samuel Morton	vs	Robert Nisbet	68
Albert G. Reynolds	vs	Robt. B. Bartlett	69
Stephen Glascock	vs	Bartlett, Fry & Beach	70
Samuel Morton	vs	Elijah Smith	71
Stephen Glascock	vs	Rbt. B. Bartlett & others	73
Z. W. Skinner	vs	Nicholas Werneck	76
Gay & Estes	vs	Nicholas Werneck	77
Robert B. Bartlett	vs	Z. G. Draper	78
Jesse Gentry	vs	John C. Smith	79
William Philips	vs	Henry Mathews	80
Robert Irvine	vs	Wylly H. Chapman	81
Charles Smith	vs	Robert B. Bartlett	83
Samuel S. Wilson	vs	Elijah Hayden	84
Zachariah G. Draper	vs	Robert B. Bartlett	85
State	vs	Wm. Patterson	86
State	vs.	Hiram Woolworth	87
Edward White	vs	Hugh W. Shannon	89
Elijah Haydon	vs	John H. Smith & others	90
William A. Maddox	vs	Elijah Haydon & others	91
Peter Cochran	vs	Robert Cruise	92
Saml. Allen and Wm. Lamme	vs	Squire Bozorth	93
James C. Hawkins	vs	Squire Bozorth	94
James C. Hawkins	vs	Edward White	95
Samuel Morton	vs	William Miller	96
Samuel Morton	vs	Joseph Trotter	97
Squire Bozorth	vs	Edward White	98
James Clemens	vs	Z. G. Draper	99
George and Andrew Buchanan	vs	Phil R. Thompson	101
Moses Gentry	vs	Zephaniah Robnett	102
John Hicklin	vs	Robt. Lanier	103
Frances Lowen	vs	James T. Crenshaw	104

(Marion County, Missouri Continued)

Name		Name	No.
Robert B. Bartlett	vs	George McDaniel	105
James McWilliams	vs	George McDaniel	106
Andrew Hunsaker	vs	James Cockman	108
Matthew W. Steel	vs	Peter Cochran	110
Samuel Daniel	vs	Isaac Reed	111
John G. Haydon	vs	Silas Reddick	112
James C. Hawkins	vs	Nisbet and Wm. Blakey	113
C. and J. Jackson	vs	J. Fry and J.C. Ferguson	114
William Forman	vs	Inskeep Forman	115
Benjamin Means	vs	Edward White	116
Clement Cannon vs.	vs	John Bozorth	117
Albert G. Reynolds	vs	Goodrich Slaughter	118
John Lee and William Beard	vs	Jacob Fry	119
John Hollyman	vs	Charles N. Calbert	120
State	vs	Lite T. Hampton	121
State	vs	James F. Coger	122
State	vs	Thomas A. Young	123
Leavin Adams	vs	C. Kieser	124
C. and J. Jackson	vs	J. Fry and J.C. Ferguson	125
A. Carnes and J. Green	vs	Samuel Burkes	126
Robert Crews	vs	Jacob Long	127
Jacob Cragbarn	vs	William Wylie	128
Jno. T. A. Henderson	vs	Clayburne Chandler	129
James C. Hawkins	vs	Samuel C. Reed	130
Middleton S. McNanama	vs	Clark Green	131
Richard Matson	vs	Jacob Smith	132
Claybourne Chandler	vs	R. McNulty and S. --akey	133
George T. Tilford	vs	Thomas J. Wise	134
Peter Cochran	vs	Robert Crews	136
Hiram McManama	vs	Willis M. Green	137
Richd. Payne, assignee Kenley	vs	Frye and Ferguson	138
William Glass	vs	William Mallio	139
Leslie Combs	vs	John Thrasher, jr.	140
B. and J. Forman, adm.	vs	S. C. Reed and P. Pritchard	141
Marion Co, Circ. Court	vs	J. Fry, guardian	142
William G. Coger	vs	James F. Coger	143
Elizabeth Forman	vs	Benjn. Forman	144
State	vs	Jacob Weaver	145
State	vs	Randolph Marlow	146
State	vs	P. Allen and F. Hunt	147
State	vs	Daniel Fletcher	148
Charles Bullock	vs	Thomas P. Lair	151
Scott Z. Rule	vs	Benjamin Rule	152
J. Abbey,jr. & J. Ely	vs	Benjn. Forman	153

(Marion County, Missouri Continued)

Name		Name	No.
Wm. M. Clifford	vs	Albert G. Reynolds	155
Robert Samuel	vs	Albert G. Reynolds	156
James C. Hawkins	vs	Albert G. Reynolds	157
S. C. Reed and G. Slaughter	vs	Albert G. Reynolds	158
Samuel C. Reed	vs	J. Fry, guardian	160
J. C. Hawkins, assignee --- White	vs	E. Walter and A. G. Reynolds	161
Randolph Marlow	vs	Stephen Cooper	162
Jno. Pope, trustee of E. Hall	vs	C. Kieser, ass. -- Sites	163
Randolph Marlow	vs	Stephen Cooper	164
James Boyce	vs	Parthenia Boyce	165
Alexander Shannon	vs	Albert G. Reynolds	167
Joseph Brown	vs	George McDaniel	169
William Blakey	vs	Albert G. Reynolds	170
J. C. Hawkins, ass. E. White	vs	Walter and Reynolds	171
Jno. Vanner	vs	---	172
John Ewing	vs	William Bourne	173
John Warburton	vs	Nicholas Wernick	174
James C. Hawkins	vs	James Jameson	175
William Massie	vs	Wm. S. Bates	176
Samuel Morton	vs	Epaphroditus Cossitt	177
Benjamin Duncan	vs	John Vaunoy	178
State	vs	John H. Mockbee	180
State	vs	Elisha Fisher	181
State	vs	Samuel Morton	182
State	vs	Robt. R. Vanlandingham	183
State	vs	Clement White	184
State	vs	John H. Mockbee	185
State	vs	Randolph Marlow	186
State	vs	Allen McDonel	187
State	vs	William Richardson	188
State	vs	Wm. H. McIlvaine	189
State	vs	John Longmire	190
State	vs	Daniel Hendricks	191
State	vs	Samuel C. Reed	192
State	vs	George McDaniel	193
State	vs	William Briggs	194
State	vs	Eli Murrell	195
State	vs	John Harding	196
State	vs	Martin Gash, jr.	197
Zachariah G. Draper	vs	R. K. Hamilton	198
Parmenas B. Pritchett	vs	A. Huntsberry & others	199
William Blakey	vs	Abraham Blessing	200
John H. Bullock	vs	Robt. G. Dudley	201

1Marion County, Missouri Continued)

Name		Name	No.
Aaron Lewis	vs	Samuel Smith	202
Joseph Holdman	vs	R. K. Hamilton	203
George T. Tilford	vs	A. G. Reynolds and O. Dickerson	205
John Mays	vs	Saml. C. Reed and G. Slaughter	207
James Glensay	vs	W. G. Petters and R. B. Bartlett	208
Joseph Holderman	vs.	Robt. K. Hamilton	209
Daniel Bradley	vs	Joseph L. Stephens	210
Geo. T. Tilford	vs	J. Fry and D. Gentry	211
William Garner	vs	John A. Irvine	212
William Duncan	vs	James Lauter	213
Samuel Martin	vs.	John G. Ferguson	214
Lucas Brodhead	vs	John Bullock	215
Robert B. Bartlett	vs	George McDaniel	216
William Simmons	vs	James B. Marmeduke	217
State	vs	Allen B. McDonald	218
State	vs	Adam Bird	219
State	vs	G. T. Hawkins	220
State	vs	Wm. Briggs	221
William Barns	vs	Chilton B. Tate	222
State to use William P. Frazier	vs	B. Dinning	223
Edward White	vs	H.W. Shannon & J. Smith	224
Abraham Blessing	vs	Wm. Blakey & E. Merrell	225
Enoch Hooton	vs	Joseph D. Pettus	226
James M. Welch	vs	James Lanter	227
Sally Welch	vs	James Lanter	228
Lucas Brodhead	vs	John H. Bullock	229
Andrew Hamilton	vs	John H. Bullock	230
Thomas Morgan	vs	Abel Cottrell	231
William McDaniel	vs	Seth Wood & others	232
Samuel Crocker	vs	Samuel Smith	233
George Carisle	vs	Wm. Montgomery	234
Robert A. Moffett	vs	Milford Moberly	235
O. Dickerson, trustee P. Mann	vs	Aaron S. Fry	236
A. B. McDonald	vs	Joseph D. Gash	237
Charles P. Bullock	vs	Edward Fowler	238
Christopher Tompkins	vs	John Anderson	239
State	vs	Joseph H. Forbes	240
State	vs	John Anderson	241
State	vs	Samuel McFall	242
State	vs	Robert H. Courtney	243
State	vs	Wm. H. McIlvaine	244
State	vs	Wm. Richardson	245

Name		Name	No.1
Ahab Bean	vs	Marshal Mann	246
Joseph Whitton	vs	Marion Co. Court	249
Samuel Miller	vs	Abraham Huntsberry	250
Bradford Noyes	vs	John D. White	251
Bradford Noyes	vs	Joseph D. Pettus	252
E. Cossitt	vs	O. Dickerson, guardian	253
Wm. Blakey	vs	Albert G. Reynolds	254
Joseph Haydon	vs	John C. Johnson	255
Andrew Hamilton	vs	John H. Bullock	258
Moses B. Morrison	vs	James Porter	259
Thomas Morgan	vs	Abel Cottrell	260
Dulles Z. Wilcox	vs	Wm. Muldrow	261
Searcy & Claggett	vs	Leroy Kesee	262
Kesee & Sayre	vs	Wm. Claggett	263
Elijah Haydon	vs	John G. Haydon	264
James Clemens, jr.	vs	Z. G. Draper	265
John G. Ferguson	vs	John Whaley	266
Crittington Forqueran	vs	James Lowen	267
George Collier	vs	O. Dickerson and Wm. Blakely	268
Abraham Stewart	vs	James Holland	269
State	vs	John B. Lee	270
Stephen Glasscock and D. O. Glasscock	vs	Jno. Batthrop & others	271
Gabriel Rush & others	vs	Martha Rush	272
William Phillips	vs	Edward Lafon	273
Asa Glascock	vs	James R. Garnett	274
John B. Righter	vs	S. W. B. Carnegy	275
O. Dickerson		In Chancery	276
Joseph Dismukes	vs	David Nelson	277
William Robey	vs	Hezekiah Robey	278
Zachariah Draper and John B. Agnew, adm. of Jas. Agnew	vs	Arthur L. Johnson and Jacob Smith	279
J. H. Flournoy, ass. of Matthew Jefferys	vs	Hy. Sullivan	280
Phineas Block, ass. of Wm. Carlow	vs	Jacob Jones	281
Thomas Norris	vs	George D. Tobin	282
State	vs	Mark Phillips	283
Overton & Rabin	vs	Wright,Carnegy & Green	***
*** 283 1/2 (sic)			
State	vs	Chauncey Durkee	284
S. C. Sloan	vs	John G. Haydon	***
*** 284 1/2 (sic)			
S. C. Sloan	vs	Ilan Wheat	285
Jacob L. Mills	vs	John C. Fitzgerald	286

(Marion County, Missouri Continued)

Name		Name	No.1
John B. Whits	vs	County Court	287
Samuel Smith	vs	Robert McKitchen	288
Thomas C and Callender Price	vs	Jacob Smith and Arthur L. Johnston	289
Simeon Conway	vs	Marjara Conway	290
Wm. Forman's heirs		Proceeding in Partition	291
Allen Cale and Dennis Marks, ass. of Justus P. Stevens	vs	Parmelia Mann	292
Michael Singleton to the use of Hiram Gibbs, ass. Marshal Mann admr. Saml. W. Allen			293
Robert B. Bartlett	vs	Edmund Hyde	294
Henry L. Cox	vs	Caleb Ferguson and O. Dickerson	295
Andrew Muldrow	vs	Isaac R. Gibbons	296
Henry L. Coxe	vs	Jno. Anderson and Geo. M'Daniel	298
Phineas Block	vs	Thomas M. Dickson	299
Charles Hampton	vs	James C. Lamkin and Wm. Poor	300
Vairu & Reel	vs	Jacob Smith and Arthur L. Johnson	301
Bank of Kentucky	vs	David Clark and Wm. I. McElroy	302
Robt. Matterson	vs	Jno. H. Bullock and P. B. Pritchett	303
Isaac Bland	vs	John H. Bullock	304
Vairin & Reel	vs	William P. Richardson	305
John Goodman	vs	Parmena B. Pritchett	306
George McDaniel	vs	Thomas Mitchell and John E. Trabue	307
Joseph S. Stephens	vs	Wallace & McCreery	308
Marders & Abernathy	vs	Merryman C. Bradshaw	309
Allen B. M'Donald	vs	John Nichols	310
James Dalton	vs	Thomas Slatey	311
Marshall Mann, adm. of S. W. Allen	vs	Ahab Bean	312
John Wharburton and Luke Riley	vs	Nicholas Wernick	313
State	vs	--- Morehead	314
State	vs	William S. Dickerson	315
State	vs	Zachariah G. Draper	316
George Collier, ass.	vs	George Winlock	317
Thomas J. Davis	vs	Elizabeth Davis	318
Simeon Conway	vs	Joseph Conway & others	319
Jno. Taylor and wife	vs	Susannah Merrill	320
Elias Barbee	vs	William Buckner, jr. and Andre McElroy	321

(Marion County, Missouri Continued)

Name		Name	No.1
David Clark	vs	E. C. Hayden and B. C. Forman	322
Ephraim Hopkins	vs	Ahab Bean	323
Edward Fowler	vs	Samuel C. Reed & others	324
Joseph L. Stevens	vs	Isaac Lansdale	325
P. W. and R. McQueen	vs	Jacob Smith and A. L. Johnson	326
Lawrence Brown	vs	William Buckner, jr.	327
Elisha Freeman	vs	Nicholas Watkins	328
James C. Hawkins	vs	S. W. B. Carnegy and A. Huntsberry	329
William Garvin	vs	Kemp P. Anderson	330
Clifton Rodes	vs	C. M. Wallace and M. G. McCrary	331
Waddy S. Cobbs	vs	Enoch Hayden	332
Enoch Dyer	vs	Levi Dyer	333
John F. Nelson	vs	Francis Lowen	334
Francis Lowen	vs	John F. Nelson	335
Elizabeth Haff	vs	Danl. amd Matthias Brant	336
Bank of Commonwealth of Kentucky	vs	William G. Briggs	337
Christian Catron	vs	Parmena B. Pritchett	338
John Long	vs	James Porter	339
Thomas Harrison	vs	C. Chandler & others	340
Nicholas Warfield	vs	Thomas M. Dickson	341
Joseph S. Stephens	vs	Joseph Hayden	342
O. Dickerson trustee for P. Mann	vs	Samuel Bowen	343
O. Dickerson trustee for P. Mann	vs	Z. G. Draper	344
O. Dickerson trustee for P. Mann	vs	Jas. Symms	345
Samuel Crocker	vs	Marshal Mann	346
Wm. G. Overton	vs	Robt. Rabe	347
John F. Todd	vs	Samuel A. Bowen	349
Thos. J. Davis, adm.	vs	Richd. Von Carnap	350
John F. Todd	vs	Samuel A. Bowen	351
Jacob Fry	vs	Lemuel Shugart	352
Thos. Keenan	vs	O. Dickerson trustee for P. Mann	353
Hy. Brant	vs	Matthias & Daniel Brant	354
Isaac Ely	vs	Jacob Lodowsky	355
Ephraim Hopkins	vs	William Bollins	356
State	vs	Leggs Harris	357
Acquilla Hornback	vs	John Whaley	358
Caleb Forquerean	vs	John Whaley	359
Obadiah Dickerson	vs	A. S. Fray	340

148

Name		Name	No.1
State	vs	Richard Pemberton	361
Aaron B. Glascock	vs	David Sheperd	362
Jacob Brown	vs	Isaac Reed	363
Abijah C. Abernathy	vs	Heirs H. Marders, sr.	364
State for the use of D.		Fry, A. K. Fry, W. Blakey	
Gentry & wife	vs	and O. Dickerson	365
David Gentry	vs	Jacob Fry, guardian	366
Peter Knip	vs	Josiah Swearingen	367
Thomas Keenan	vs	Alexander Burton	368
Joseph Tabor	vs	Robert H. Courtney	373
Sarah W. Dudley	vs	Wm. Dudley and the heirs	
		of R. Dudley, dec.	374
Samuel Merry	vs	Stephen Glascock	376
Granville M. Godman	vs	Wm. Carson & others	377
David Gentry	vs	County Court	378
Abraham Huntsberry	vs	Isaac Reed	379
John Whaley	vs	Aquila Hornback	380
State	vs	Samuel Crocker	381
Benjamin Means	vs	Edward Sanders	382
State	vs	Griffin Tuggle	384
State	vs	Griffin Tuggle	385
State	vs	John Pool	386
James B. Logsden	vs.	John White	387
Benoist & Lane	vs	Willis M. Green	388
Herman L. Hoffman	vs	James Wallace	389
Wm. M. Clifford	vs	C. Reed & wife	390
Emery Wheeler	vs	Wm. Muldrow and David	
		Nelson	392
Benjamin Forman	vs	Isaac B. Gibbons	393
Wurts & Reinhart	vs	Buckner & McElroy	394
Shelby Simpson	vs	Perkins Benning	395
John D. Daggett	vs	Grigsby & Chandler	396
Matthew Barqfow	vs	Matthew Roy	397
Daniel Fletcher	vs	Jno. Ferqueran	398
John Norris	vs	William I. Norris	399
Jos. Hardy, adm. of			
C. Catron	vs	Wm. Kelly	401
David Gentry	vs	Willis M. Green and W.	
		P. Richardson	402
Joseph Longmire	vs	Jas. Kendrick, adm. T.	
		P. Rois	404
Elizabeth Davis	vs	Thomas J. Davis	405
Thomas J. Davis	vs	Est. of Shadrach Davis	406
Elizabeth Davis	vs	Thomas J. Davis	407
State	vs	Lorenzo D. Nelson	408
State	vs	George Glascock	409
State	vs	Spencer Glascock	410

(Marion County, Missouri Continued)

Name		Name	No.1
State	vs	Wm. Buckner, jr.	411
State	vs	Rhoda, a slave	412
State	vs	Anthony Pool	413
Joseph J. Clark	vs	Henry Vanderslic	414
Adelia Vanderslic	vs	Henry Vanderslic	415
Eli Merrel	vs	Caly Foreman	416
James H. Walter	vs	Thomas J. Wile	417
George Davidson	vs	Orion Sparks	418
John Whaley	vs	Daniel Hendricks	419
Samuel Pennington	vs	Lewis Cattleman	420
Charles Smith	vs	Elizabeth Parrish	421
James Anderson, jr.	vs	Elijah Harcall	422
Staunton Buckner	vs	Josiah Swearingam	423
Thomas S. Crutcher	vs	John Anderson	424
Andrew McElroy	vs	George Winlock	425
Edward Fowler	vs	J.W.B. Carnegy & others	426
Jas. P. Shropshire	vs	Wm. B. Broughton	427
James Kendrick	vs	Washington & Lair	428
Wm. Boswell	vs	Wm. B. Broguhton	429
Wade H. Pottan	vs	Wm. B. Broughton	430
Shamuel Shepperd	vs	Joseph Hayden	431
M. D. Bates and U. Wright	vs	Gartell & Gooch	432
Willis M. Green	vs	Wm. Massie & others	433
Joseph Hardy	vs	Jno. L. Ward and M. Shannon	434
Jos. Hardy,adm. Catron	vs	Theodrick Massie & others	435
State	vs	Wm. Massie & others	436
State	vs	R. H. Courtney and F. Lowen	437
Tarlton	vs	John Anderson	438
Stepney	vs	John Anderson	439
Lucy Jane	vs	John Anderson	440
Mary Ann, alias Marrietta Ann	vs	John Anderson	441
Cely	vs	John Anderson	442
Dennis Ouan	vs	Thomas Gatewood	443
Berkly S. Summers and Jno. Smith	vs	W. R. Simmons	444
Moses D. Bates	vs	E. Hopkins, H. Hopkins and R. Crews	445
Samuel Shepherd	vs	Jas. B. Ryland	446
Samuel Shepherd	vs	Wm. Muldrow & others	447
Samuel Shepherd	vs	William Muldrow	448
Jas. Kendrick,adm Ross	vs	Charles Smith	449
E. Hopkins	vs	James M. Clark	450
Charles C. Gilchrist	vs	Giles Thompson	451

(Marion County, Missouri Continued)

Name		Name	No.1
State	vs	John Wiley	452
State	vs	Jacob Fry	453
State	vs	Thomas Mitchell	454
George W. Lane	vs	Henry Paore	455
Hugh Anderson	vs	Benjamin Roberts	457
John Wiley, jr.	vs	Jeremiah Brower	458
James Gooch's adm.	vs	Elizabeth Glascock	459
Thompson Bird	vs	Stephen Glascock	461
John H. Gay	vs	Robt. H. Courtney and Robt. Rabe	462
Thomas J. Crutcher	vs	John Anderson	463
William Carson, adm. of Stephens	vs	Jno. Anderson	464
William Whaley	vs	William Lander	465
Thomas Lizenby	vs	Hosea and Cyrus Blizenby	466
David O. Glascock	vs	Wm. Massie & others	468
Richd. D. Carnap	vs	Thomas Stacy	469
George Winlock	vs	Wm. Buckner and Jno. LaLafford	470
Wm. J. McElroy	vs	Robt. Rabe, G. W. Lane and Jno. LaSafford	471
Ridgely & Billow	vs	Robt. H. Courtney	472
Wash & Nunn	vs	Est. of John Redding	473
J.P. & J.E. Shropshire	vs	Wm. P. Richardson	474
Obed M. White	vs	Fountain Jones	475
State	vs	A. H. Dixon	476
State	vs	R. B. Bartlett	477
State	vs	R. D. Carnap	478
State	vs	Hy. Wilcox	479
State	vs	Jno. T. Worthington	480
Jno. A. Lyell	vs	John Gay	481
Thos. Kiser, adm. V. Brewer	vs	Giles Thompson	482
Thos. Kess part. of Wm. Keenan	vs	Giles Thompson	483
Mitchell & Harris	vs	Giles Thompson	484
Mitchell & Keyte	vs	Giles Thompson	485
J. P. Shropshire, sur. part. T. P. Ross	vs	Giles Thompson	486
L. A. Bowen	vs	W. G. Whitfield	487
W. Shelby	vs	G. Donally	488
R. B. Bartlett	vs	T. Glascock	489
R. B. Bartlett	vs	T. Glascock	490
Muldrow & Durbin	vs	J. D. Gash	491
G. D. Owen	vs	Rabe & others	492
R. M. Eastin	vs	T. Massie & others	493
W. Gillaspie	vs	T. Massie & others	494

(Marion County, Missouri Continued)

Name		Name	No.1
John D. Owen	vs	John Lafford	495
T.P. & J.E. Shropshire	vs	A. B. Glascock	496
T. P. Shropshire	vs	A. B. Glascock and Wm.	
		Green	497
J. Vannoy	vs	T. W. B. Carnegy	498
J. Vannoy	vs	John Dye	499
John Kizer	vs	J.F. Safford and R. Rabe	500
Anderson	vs	Nash & McCord	501
Buckner & Winlock	vs	Buckner	502
J. Gentry, adm. of W.			
Stephenson	vs	J. Gay	503
Thos. Walthall	vs	Robt. Rabe	504
Benja. Whaley	vs	Benj. Means	505
Carthall	vs	Kendrick	506
D. Hendrick & G. Rush	vs	P. Rush	507
G. B. Nelson	vs	J. B. Marmaduke	508
State	vs	J. P. Shropshire	509
State	vs	Tina, a slave	510
Rush's heirs	vs	Rush's heirs	511
State	vs	Robt. Rabe	512
T. Glascock	vs	M. D. Bates	513
J. F. Lafford	vs	J. Mcaffee	514
R. Croughton	vs	R. B. Bartlett	515
R. Berry	vs	J. F. Lafford	516
R. Buchannon	vs	H. Rollins' heirs	517
O. Dickerson	vs	W. G. Cogan	518
J. P. Shropshire, part.			
of Ross	vs	R. Rabe	519
J.P. & J.E. Shopshire	vs	R. Rabe	520
Kelly	vs	White	521
Anderson & Evans	vs	Nash & McCall	522
D. Brown	vs	Peter Johnson's heir	523
J. J. Clark, adm. B. O.			
Clark	vs	A. Callis	524
J. Lail	vs	Righter & Callaway	525
A. J. Lewis	vs	Grisby	526
Hawkins	vs	Bradly	527
B. Pritchett	vs	Wade H. Pollard	528
T. McDonald	vs	Rabe	529
L. Payne	vs	I. Miller	530
J. Lidick	vs	Wm. P. Richardson	531
L. A. Bowen	vs	A. Curts	532
Wm. C. Duffield	vs	Blakey	533
W. R. Allen	vs	Rabe & Lafford	534
U. Wright	vs	J. C. Pickett	535
W. P. Frazier	vs	L. Bozorth	536
P. Fry	vs	D. Lewis	537

(Marion County, Missouri Continued)

Name		Name	No.1
L. Payne	vs	I. Dudley	538
Shropshire	vs	Hooten	539
Jn. H. Brasheon	vs	T. A. Bowan	540
A. C. Abernathy	vs	Wm. P. Richardson	541
Naff Wanton & Co	vs	W. P. Richards	542
J. Dye	vs	Lage	543
J. H. Curo	vs	C. Lewis	544
State	vs	Jesse Wilcoxan	545
L. A. Bowan	vs	J. H. Boagien	546
State	vs	Henry Wilcox	547
W. B. White	vs	B. Tennile	548
Mcgruder & Herndon	vs	L. Shugart	549
J. Reinhart	vs	John Dye	550
C. J. Morris	vs	M. Higgins	551
F. Patterson	vs	L. Caldwell	552
J. Neal	vs	J. Evans	553
T. Barclay	vs	Barclay & Rabe	554
State	vs	E. L. Ely	555
A. Callis	vs	Clark	556
J. B. Gibbons	vs	McDaniels	557
Stop. Bradley's heirs	vs	Danl. Towly	558
Burdett	vs	Hickman	559
Shropshire	vs	Kendrick	560
M. A. Mitchell	vs	E. Merrill	561
P. Elliott	vs	J. Uannoy	562
T. Tman	vs	Rabe & Carson	563
T. Jones	vs	Danl. Bradly's heirs	564
Bird Pritchett	vs	R. B. Bartell	565
D. Hornican	vs	C. Smith	566
J. H. Brazier	vs	L. A. Bowen	567
J. C. Goodwin	vs	Absalon Glenn (sic)	568
J. C. Goodwin	vs	J. A. Jackson	569
J. C. Goodwin	vs	M. L. Barnett	570
E. Durbin	vs	W. Blakey	571
M. Garner	vs	J. Garner	572
J.M. & V.D. Boone	vs	A. Alsonon (sic)	573
J. Bosley	vs	Robt. Hayes	574
J. Bosley	vs	Wm. Winslow (sic)	575
Ferguson Jones & Co	vs	K. M--- (sic)	576
R. McKee	vs	B. --- (sic)	577
Rapier & Anderson	vs	B. Means	578
A. & R. R. Griffin	vs	Ayres & Matthews	579
Titer Price	vs	B. Means	580
Cormier	vs	Kendrick	581
F. D. Ortley	vs	R. B. Bartlett	582
T. Francis	vs	T. J. Pollard	583
L. Lamb	vs	B. Means	584

(Marion County, Missouri Continued)

Name		Name	No.1
R. Watson	vs	K. B. Bartlett	585
A. Brown	vs	J. Darnell	586
Peabody Riggs & Co	vs	Ayres & Mathews	587
G. R. Gather	vs	Aires & Mathews (sic)	588
A. G. Anderson	vs	A. Callis	589
K. A. Buckner	vs	W. Buckner	590
E. Brookins	vs	C. Parker	591
J.P. & J.E. Shropshire	vs	Rabe & Walttas (sic)	592
J. Leak	vs	T. Massie	593
C. Taylor & King	vs	C. W. Hall	594
Lafford	vs	Rabe	595
W. B. White, adm. of --- Massie	vs	W. Gleason	596
R. Rabe	vs	J. P. Shropshire	597
J. Clemens, jr.	vs	R. Rabe	598
J. Clemen, jr.	vs	Rabe & Barclay	599
W. W. Elgin	vs	P. W. Lewis	600
T. J. Davis	vs	County Court	601
H. L. Wills	vs	R. Rabe	602
Bartlett	vs	Jewell	603
J. Clemens, jr.	vs	Geo. W. Lane	604
State	vs	E. L. Ely	605
State	vs	Wm. Muldrow	606
Saml. Jones	vs	Benj. Means	607
J. W. Eastin	vs	E. Easton	608
Chapron & Nicholas	vs	B. Means	609
J. T. Swearingen	vs	Wm. P. Richardson	610
T. W. B. Carnegy	vs	Bradly's admr.	611
J. H. Keach	vs	W. L. Keach	612
Sheriff Marion Co.	vs	Wright & Rabe	613
W. Bowlin	vs	L. V. V. Bohannan	614
W. E. Culvar	vs	Ira Stout	615
Culvir & Craig	vs	V. Pratt	616
S. C. Sloane	vs	V. & E. G. Pratt	617
Shropshire & Owsley	vs	J. T. Mahan	618
A. C. Abnernathy	vs	Mardis' heirs	619
J. M. Holt	vs	W. J. McElroy	620
R. Rabe	vs	W. & B. Pritchett	621
T. Jones	vs	J. P. Vance	622
Laflett	vs	Carson	623
H. Withers	vs	Rabe & Lafford	624
Roadham Routt	vs	John Gay, jr.	625
Franklin Whaley	vs	R. B. Bartlett	626
David Rodgers	vs	Virgil Pratt	627
John White	vs	William Wist	628
Robert Toland	vs	Benj. Means	629
A. Alsman	vs	T. Harris	630

(Marion County, Missouri Continued)

Name		Name	No.1
E. Davis	vs	T. J. Davis	631
L. H. Mays	vs	T. Hollyman	632
R. Cobbs	vs	T. Hollyman	633
Thomas Ross	vs	Wm. Wright	634
John P. Rutter	vs	Lewis H. Mays	635
David Clark	vs	William Ringer	636
William Singleton	vs	Andrew M. Francis	637
Simeon Ryder	vs	Ira Stout	638
Wm. B. White, adm.	vs	Wm. Gleason	639
Ridgley & Billow	vs	Saml. A. Bowen	640
Caldwell & Son	vs	Virgil Pratt	641
Trustees of M. College	vs	Stone	642
Wm. H. Holmes	vs	Loring & Martin	643
Thos. Williams	vs	Clark Muldrow	644
E. Searcy	vs	J. Gobbons	645
William Carson	vs	Eli Murell	646
Wm. G. Cogan	vs	James Dunn	647
Saml. Jones	vs	Benj. Means	648
Thos. C. Rockhell	vs	Benj. Means	649
S. & J. Tarns	vs	Benj. Means	650
J. T. Swearingen	vs	Benj. Means	651
Cave & Schaffer	vs	Benj. Means	652
David Willock	vs	Thos. Spence	653
Green White	vs	McElroy & Anderson	654
Stephen Glascock	vs	R. B. Bartlett	655
Conrad & Kelly	vs	Benj. Means	656
James F. Mahn	vs	Jacob Sowdosky	657
Lesly Price	vs	Ira Stout	658
Rufus Hastings	vs	C. M. Reynolds	659
Wm. B. White	vs	S. E. Richardson	660
A. C. Abernathy	vs	H. P. Richardson	661
Anderson & Evans	vs	M'Cord & Nash	662
Bartlett & Price	vs	Jno. H. Milton	663
John Withers	vs	John F. Safford	664
State	vs	J. C. & --- Beaty	665
Cochran & Daily	vs	Haines & Danah	666
Gray Derioe & Co	vs	Thomas B. Glivenz (sic)	667
Isaac B. Owsly	vs	Richd. Sharp	668
James Barnes	vs	William Ringer	669
James Barnes	vs	William Ringer	670
G. & J. Erskin	vs	Benjamin Means	671
Hildebrum & Watson	vs	Ths. B. Stevens	672
James Muldrow	vs	J. Spear & L. Dunn, adm. of L. Wilson	673
Jamerson Lamuel	vs	Virgil Pratt	674
Robt. B. Bartlett	vs	Steven Glascock	675
Henry Willis	vs	Andrew P. Ringer	676

Name		Name	No.1
Jos. H. Brashear	vs	Saml. A. Bowen	677
A. Huntsberry	vs	J. B. M'Kown	678
A. Huntsberry	vs	Joseph M'Kown	679
Huntsberry & Walker	vs	Joseph M'Kown	680
Wm. Wright, adm. of			
M. Pratt	vs	Virgil Pratt	681
Thos. J. Davis	vs	Waller & Uriel Wright	682
Elvira Gentry	vs	David Gentry	683
Frances H. Edmondson	vs	E. G. & U. Pratt	684
State, for the use of			
D. Gentry	vs	Ja. Fry	685
Moses D. Bates	vs	J. P. Shropshire	686
Moses D. Bates	vs	G. W. Lane	687
William Morton	vs	F. B. Stevens and J. W.	
		Haydon	688
J. & O. P. Markle	vs	Steamboat Qunicy	689
William G. Ward	vs	W. H. & T. J. Pollard	690
Alford C. Brown	vs	John H. Sallee	691
Jeremiah Lalor	vs	Simpson Oldham	692
Josiah Elliott	vs	J.C. Richards & Bringley	693
Thomas Ross	vs	Wm. Wright	694
Murphy Evans	vs	D. F. Greenwood	695
John B. Righter	vs	G. M. B. Carnegy	696
Jacob Moberly, adm.	vs	O. Dickerson	697
Wm. H. Pope	vs	Thomas W. Stevens	698
State	vs	Benjn. Ingram	699
State	vs	John C. Miller	700
State	vs	Jacob C. Richards	701
State	vs	Wilsom R. Simmons	702
State	vs	Hirman G. Wellz	703
State	vs	William J. Howell	704
State	vs	William J. Howell	705
State	vs	William J. Howell	706
State	vs	William J. Howell	707
Sublett & Campbell	vs	Tompkins & Willett	708
John R. Swearninger	vs	Edward Calle	709
State	vs	A. P. Ringer	710
Bancroft Hyde & Co	vs	L. B. Envoy	711
Moses D. Bates	vs	Eph. Hopkins	712
A. G. W. and John Kerr	vs	W. J. M'Cormick	713
Bancroft Hyde & Co	vs	James Ford	714
Haines & Darrah	vs	M. O. Willes	715
John B. Matthews	vs	Joseph Long	716
John B. Matthews	vs	Joseph Long	717
E. G. & U. Pratt	vs	J. C. Richards	718
W. H. Hutchison	vs	Silas M. Rossau	719
Proctor Palmer & Felt	vs	James Ford, jr.	720

Name		Name	No.1
R. & S. Smith	vs	T. Lucket & J. Robertson	721
S. Ryder & C.S. Frost	vs	T. B. Stevens	722
Wm. G. Overton	vs	Samuel Agnew	723
R. F. & P. C. Lane	vs	Humphrey Peake	724
T. L. Anderson	vs	Saml. Agnew	725
Joshua Gentry	vs	Joseph Looy	726
Wm. Henry	vs	John M'Kee	727
Thos. J. Wise	vs	John M'Kee	728
John H. Tayler	vs	John Markle & Son	729
Edmund Tyler	vs	Robert Ghsklett (sic)	730
Joseph Long	vs	John B. Matthews	731
State	vs	William Rouse	732
Goodnoe Eastman & Co	vs	J. F. Jenkins	733
William Blakey	vs	Edison G. Pratt	734
Ira Stout	vs	Jno. Patridge	735
J. W. Craig and H. M. Turner	vs	J. C. Richards	736
Wm. Rogers	vs	Trustees of M College	737
Chas. S. Baker	vs	D. O. Glascock	739
Kindrow S. Felts	vs	A. M'Elroy	740
Jno. P. Rutter	vs	Enoch Haydon	741
Louis J. Fourniquet	vs	Thos. W. Stephens	742
Saml. Ringgold	vs	Robt. B. Bartlett	743
Cochran & Daily	vs	Poor	744
John Full	vs	Hardy & Feazle	745
Von Phull & M'Gill	vs	Ira Stoutt	746
John Full	vs	Gash & Blakey	747
Jno. W. Hunt	vs	J. & S. W. B. Carnegy	748
Thos C. Rockhill	vs	Wade H. Pollard	749
Sandford & Berthold	vs	E. G. & V. Prat	750
Newton M. Turner	vs	Saml. Stone	751
Tavna Snell	vs	John & J. Longmire	752
Tavna Snell	vs	Saml. Ringgold	753
Wm. Blakey	vs	Carson & Hayden	754
Tabor, Shaw, & Tatum	vs	Markle & Son	755
State	vs	David Miller	756
P. & J. Powel	vs	Thos. G. Stephens	757
John Barr, guardian	vs	Shaw	758
John B. White	vs	Ulade H. Pollard	759
Tabor, Shaw, & Tatum	vs	Markle & Son	760
John B. White	vs	Robt. B. Bartlett	761
Nancy Davis	vs	Jos. and Jas. Bosby	762
Joseph T. Holmes	vs	D. Ralaforia	763
John B. White	vs	Wright & Bartlett	764
Saml. Ringgold	vs	Wright & Bartlett	765
Kilgore Tailor	vs	J. H. Milton	766
Stark Fielder	vs	E. G. and -- Pratt	767

Name		Name	No.1
Von Phull & M'Gill	vs	J. H. Milton	768
Caleb W. Gay	vs	T. J. and G. Wise	769
Carlin West	vs	Humphrey Peake	770
Withers & Lamme	vs	Tarner Snell	771
Chas. Gratiott	vs	Chas. Gratiott, jr.	772
Francis Lowen	vs	Wm. Blakey	773
John Johnson	vs	Joseph Poque	774
Thos. Steward	vs	F. H. Edmondson	775
T. Jones	vs	Clark, Spear & Anderson	776
Jos. M'Koun	vs	Cochran Mahain	777
William Weight	vs	Cornelius Malone	778
A. Bird & A. Fry	vs	Jessee Carter	779
William R. Simmons	vs	M'Kee, Hanna & Co	780
Robt. Shaw	vs	Trustee M. College	781
Thos. G. Settle and Dalrymple	vs	R. B. Bartlett	782
Niff Wanton & Co	vs	D. F. Greenwood	783
Cochran & Daily	vs	D. T. Anderson	784
John W. Bowen	vs	Wm. Poor	785
Jas. G. Wiley	vs	Wm. Wiley, admr.	786
J. C. Hankins	vs	Robt. Rabe	787
State	vs	Francis Hewett	788
Marshall Kelly	vs	Johnson & Pollard	789
John C. Pickett	vs	J. W. Haydon	790
William Ringer	vs	Wm. M'Cormack	791
James A. Felps	vs	Edwin G. Pratt	792
Madison Fugate	vs	Wm. B. Lear	793
State	vs	John Martin	794
State	vs	George Nelson	795
State	vs	John M. Johnson	796
State	vs	George Glascock	797
State	vs	Haydon & Sterling	798
State	vs	P. A. McAlister	799
State	vs	A. H. & L. Crenshaw	800
State	vs	A. H. & L. Crenshaw	801
State	vs	John Garner	802
State	vs	A. Ingram	803
State	vs	A. Ingram	804
State	vs	John Miller	805
State	vs	W. R. Simmons	806
State	vs	J. C. Richards	807
State	vs	J. Eastin	808
Nancy W. Leaque	vs	George Leaque	809
Richard Watson	vs	Carstarshen (sic)	810
L. P. Vanlandingham	vs	S. C. Sloan	811
Tingley & Johnson	vs	Pollard & Johnson	812
Merrie & Bullin	vs	D. F. Greenwood	813

(Marion County, Missouri Continued)

Name		Name	No.1
W. and C. Fellow	vs	D. F. Greenwood	814
W. H. Loyd & Co	vs	D. F. Greenwood	815
Jas. Low & Co	vs	D. F. Greenwood	816
Henry Wilcox	vs	M. R. Bower	817
Abraham McElroy	vs	Jemina McElroy	818
Joseph Long	vs	Pollard & Wise	819
Andrew P. Ringgo	vs	W. Muldrow	820
Andrew P. Ringgo	vs	W. Muldrow	821
Andrew P. Ringgo	vs	W. Muldrow	822
Ira Stout	vs	Saml. Sainrr	823
R. S. Lewis	vs	James Gallaher	824
Haines & Darrah	vs	Robt. Shaw	825
Tilman & Crook	vs	W. R. Simmons	826
Bird Griffith & Co	vs	A. P. Ringer	827
Mary Monniju	vs	C. Hodges	828
Wilson H. Williams	vs	G. Williams	829
Thos. Ross	vs	S. C. Reed	830
Moses Graham	vs	Jas. Connroy	831
State	vs	Anthony Pool	832
James Amet	vs	James West	833
Jos. Long	vs	James McManama	834
A. B. Glascock	vs	H. Shaelett	835
R. M. Eastin	vs	T. G. and W. H. Pollard	836
Thos. C. Rockhill	vs	W. Pollard	837
L. C. Dobyn	vs	Wesley W. Hyde	838
John A. Simpson	vs	George Edelin	839
John Homes	vs	Cunningham & Hunter	840
John Blue	vs	L. Hyde	841
Dwight Porter	vs	Jas. M. Clark	842
Kindall F. Edgile	vs	Corpin & Sharp	843
N. H., A. R., and W. Downing	vs	Matrick	844
Doremus	vs	McKee	845
Marion County	vs	Richard & Brune (sic)	846
Benj. Forman	vs	George Hubbert	847
Von Pull & M'Gill	vs	Wm. Muldrow	848
Jas. Lane	vs	Thos. Spencer	849
A. B. Glascock	vs	Jas. & Jno. Longmire	850
Haines & Darrah	vs	Bennet & Berry	851
Haines & Darrah	vs	Jos. Berry	852
M. D. Bates	vs	Wm. Muldrow	853
Robt. C. Gest	vs	Wm. Poor	854
Robt. C. Gest	vs	G. G. Muldrow	855
Robt. C. Gest	vs	Wm. West	856
John Homn	vs	Jos. Hardy	857
Von Pull & M'Gill	vs	Stone & Strode	858
Cliften R. Rajen	vs	E. S. Ely	859

(Marion County, Missouri Continued)

Name		Name	No.1
S. Shepard	vs	Anderson & Raely	860
Worburton & King	vs	D. T. Anderson	861
Haines & Darrah	vs	N. H. Downing	862
Thos. Taylor	vs	Wm. Taylor	863
Hiram Taylor	vs	John Milton	864
Edward McLane	vs	Wm. West	865
John Varney	vs	Clayton Camur (sic)	866
Jos. C. Milles	vs	Virgil Pratt	867
John Shaeleford	vs	John Milton	868
W. G. Overton	vs	Jas. Looy	869
J. B. Eversoll	vs	Clark, Fremont & Co	870
George Pasku (sic)	vs	W. R. Campbell	871
Wm. Sallee	vs	Matlock, M'Gee & Co	872
H. N. Davis	vs	Clark, Forman & Co	873
J. Francois	vs	J. A. Felps	874
G. Glascock	vs	R. B. Bartell	875
J. B. Schoot	vs	J. B. Willis	876
J. Cannoy	vs	W. R. Simmons	877
D. and J. Clark	vs	Will Muldrow	878
Beng. Forman	vs	W. Muldrow	879
A. R. Downing	vs	W. Muldrow	880
Hood & Abbott	vs	T. Snell	881
Abrm. Huntsberry	vs	J. W. Haydon	882
State	vs	L. H. Mays	883
John Chapman	vs	M. Fannin	884
H. F. Thompson	vs	Trustees Marion College	887
L. George	vs	W. H. Pollard	888
Benj. Forman	vs	McHee & Muldrow	889
W. H. & J. W. Thompson	vs	S. Avoy	890
Courtney & Agnew	vs	J. C. Bonham (sic)	900
Haines & Darrah	vs	J. I. T. McElroy	901
Haines & Darrah	vs	Wm. Guyman	902
State	vs	Francis Hart	903
Thos. Sweringen	vs	J. W. Haydon	904
Thos. P. Ross' heirs	vs	Longmire & Whaley	905
M. V. D. Gartrell	vs	Read & Pemino	906
John Bozorth	vs	S. W. B. Camegy	907
Cowling & Agnew	vs.	Pres & T. of M. College	908
McKee & Co	vs	Cowling & Agnew	910
G. Glascock	vs	J. Long	911
A. P. Ringer	vs	M. W. Singleton	912
M. R. Bennet	vs	J. Smoot	913
Bennet & Berry	vs	D. T. Anderson	914
Josiah Abbott	vs	Abrm. Leford	915
Saml. Beckett	vs	J. and A. J. Houghton	916
State	vs	J. C. Bohn	917
Hibuling Dunning	vs	Ira Stoull	918

(Marion County, Missouri Continued)

Name		Name	No.1
Jas. D. Tapley	vs	McK--- & Brisson	919
Jas. McManama	vs	C. D. & J. O. Pratt	920
Hannah Willcoxin	vs	J. C. Miller	921
Anderson Brown	vs	Danl. Cooper	922
Sml. Beckite	vs	Jas. Houghton	923
State	vs	C. Brown	924
State	vs	Josiah Warner	925
State	vs	Morton Bringley	926
State	vs	John Miller	927
State	vs	Truman Oaks	928
State	vs	A. B. Lansing	929
State	vs	McElroy & Edelin	930
Swan Burditt	vs	John Howe, adm.	931
State	vs	Bazil Maddox	932
State	vs	J. Davis and M.J. Pepper	933
State	vs	Hawkins & Bohn	934
State	vs	Perry B. Moore	935
State	vs	Saml. B. Colwell	936
State	vs	Saml. Beckett	937
State	vs	Caleb Taylor	938
State	vs	Ira Stoutt	939
State	vs	John Bush	940
State	vs	David O. Glascock	941
State	vs	E. Hopkins	942
State	vs	J. B. White	943
State	vs	Wm. Boulware	944
State	vs	George Lilford	945
Saml. Matue	vs	Saml. Ringold	946
John Lear	vs	Benj. F. Robb	947
Haines & Darrah	vs	L. S. Cropper	948
Jno. Martin	vs	Tavnu (sic) Suell	949
Wood & Abbott	vs	Cooper & Sharp	950
Pollard & Johnson	vs	Robt. Edwards	951
Jas. T. Snyder	vs	Thos. Ross	952
T. J. Pollard	vs	Jos. Long	953

****** These Cases were listed out of order.******

Name		Name	No.1
J. B. Camden	vs	Pollard & Johnson	891
David M. Dixon	vs	L. C. Dobyon	892
J. W. Bowen	vs	Searcy & Miles	893
Coulny & Agus	vs	Marion College	894
William Maseau	vs	Muldrow & Haines	898
J. W. Bowen	vs	L. Caldwell	899
Haines & Darrah	vs	A. P. Ringer	954
Tullott	vs	Tullot	955
Andrew Avirat	vs	Pollard & Johnson	956
Micajah Matin	vs	Pollard & Johnson	957
Thomas Spence	vs	Henry Millan	958

(Marion County, Missouri Continued)

Name		Name	No.1
Wm. Blakey	vs	W. R. Limmons	959
Graham Williams	vs	Wm. N. Tandy	960
Wm. R. Campbell	vs	Joseph Long	961
Haines & Darrah	vs	James F. Mahan	962
Joseph Linz	vs	Enoch Hooton	963
James & Sherman	vs	Jenkins & Ferguson	964
James F. Mahan	vs	Jacob Sodowsky	965
William Blakely	vs	John W. Bowen	966
William Blakely	vs	James D. Johnson	967
Hanson & Everett	vs	Thomas Hoke	968
John R. Copeland	vs	Jenkins & Ferguson	969
Thos. D. Allen	vs	James D. Johnson	970
Samuel Shepherd	vs	E. J. Pratt	971
Cowling & Agnes	vs	T. J. Davis	972
Miller & Janney	vs	Bancroft, Hyde & Co	973
Walten Withers	vs	Jno. H. Milton	974
Huntsberry & Walker	vs	Joseph Ling	975
Lucy Lipscomb	vs	Long & McKee	976
T. J. Wise	vs	William Haydon	977
Jas. Lagman	vs	Joseph Long	978
Hiram Hungerford	vs	D. L. Anderson	979
Sarah Gaineto	vs	David T. Anderson	980
Hawkins & Pickett	vs	William Hayden	981
Samuel Smith	vs	J. H. Sallee	982
Marshall Kelly	vs	S. W. B. Carmegy	983
F. Lowen	vs	Kelly O. Johnson	984
Rhodes Gentry	vs	Bullock & Haydon	985
John McKee & Co	vs	Nash & Briggs	986
T. J. Settle	vs	David C. Glascock	987
Edmund Roberts	vs	Joseph Long	988
Beverly Allen	vs	Haines & Darrah	989
O. Dickerson	vs	Campbell & Millon	990
James Lee	vs	Muldrow & Feagan	991
A. H. Kemper	vs	Robert Kemper	992
Jonas Houghton	vs	Haydon & Bartlett	993
J. P. Shropshire	vs	James R. Garnett	994
G. and M. L. Troutman	vs	Caper & Sharp	995
Theodre Jones	vs	James Davis	996
Henry Chouteau	vs	Lunis (sic) C. Dobyn	997
Marion College	vs	Nash & Stone	998
Z. G. Draper	vs	Jno. C. Bonham	999
James L. Peake	vs	J. W. Haydon	1000
Hogan & Thompson	vs	Saml. T. Cluff	1001
Baird & Fanell	vs	Cooper & Shacklett	1002
J. Davis use of Mudlow	vs	Jas. Davis, jr.	1003
Robert Shaw	vs	William Wirt	1004
John Bosley	vs	E. Dearing	1005

(Marion County, Missouri Continued)

Name		Name	No.1
William Sallee	vs	Mallack May	1006
Newkirk, White & Co	vs	David Glascoe	1007
Haines & Darrah	vs	James Da---	1008
Haines & Darrah	vs	J. M. M'Coin	1009
Barkley S. Summuins	vs	Haines & Darrah	1010
H. Hungerford	vs	Jenkins & Fergsin	1011
Saml. Shepherd	vs	C. Binnot	1012
Thos. W. Lane	vs	C. Brown	1013
John Longmine	vs	R. R. Vanlandingham	1014
Haines & Darrah	vs	Marion College	1015
T. E. Brittingham	vs	A. W. & E. C. McDnl.	1016
N. Tucker & Co	vs	W. J. & J. M. McCormack	1017
N. B. Buford	vs	John Gay, jr.	1018
John Gregory	vs	John McKee	1019
Francis Brown	vs	J. C. Ferguson	1020
William Wright	vs	Jas. D. Johnston	1021
William Johnsan (sic)	vs	James Porter	1022
John W. Bowen	vs	Francis Lowe-- (sic)	1023
Henry Cook	vs	Enoch Hooton	1024
Rongrow D. Watson	vs	Lewis C. Doley	1025
William Barr	vs	Robert Shaw	1026
Thomas J. Wise	vs	James T. Williams	1027
Marion County	vs	Gasg & Callaway	1028
Obadiah Dickerson	vs	Haydon & Stevens	1029
William Gooch	vs	John W. Fraizer	1030
McKee, Stewart & Co	vs	Shubael & Avery	1031
William Bowling	vs	Jacob Jefferies	1032
J. A. Dudley	vs	Jacob Jefferies	1033
John F. Hawkins	vs	Jacob Jefferies	1034
John F. Hawkins	vs	Jacob Jefferies	1035
Ira Stout	vs	Jacob Jefferies	1036
Phillip Dilloss	vs	William Biggs	1037
Willian M. Turner	vs	Enoch Haydon	1038
Geo. W. Bird	vs	J. G. Ferguson	1039
Geo. W. Bird	vs	J. G. Ferguson	1040
B. & J. Hickey	vs	Clark Forman & Co	1041
T. &. I. Homer	vs	W. W. Hyde	1042
Geo. H. McDaniel	vs	Benj. Forman	1043
Jas. Caldwell	vs	McKee & Wright	1044
Peckett & Hawkins	vs	Clark Forman & Co	1045
Peckett & Hawkins	vs	David Ford	1046
Von Phul & McGill	vs	J. W. Eastin	1047
Haines & Darrah	vs	Joseph Clark	1048
J. J. Owens	vs	Marion College	1049
Dunn	vs	Marion College	1050
Joseph Hardy	vs	R. B. Bartlett	1051
Saml. Merton	vs	A. B. Hawkins	1052

163

Marion County, Missouri Continued)

Name		Name	No.1
Winlock	vs	G. P. Haines	1053
Yeateman, Wilborn & Co	vs	Clark Forman & Co	1054
Caleb Cope	vs	Jno. E. Shropshire	1055
J. E. Shropshire	vs	A. and S. Hawkins	1056
Wm. G. Overton	vs	Jas. W. Eastin	1057
Thos. L. Anderson	vs	Will Muldrow	1058
Wm. Sallee	vs	Mallack, Magee & Co	1059
Doctor D. Carson	vs	Marion College	1060
Wm. Assaw	vs	Muldrow	1061
Z. G. Draper	vs	Saml. Shepherd	1062
Oakley	vs	Marion College	1063
Owens	vs	Marion College	1064
Greenlee	vs	Marion College	1065
J. Dunn	vs	Marion College	1066
Willis	vs	Lance	1067
Cowling & Agnew	vs	Jos. Conway	1068
John H. Curd	vs	Shacklett & Lovelace	1069
Geo. K. McGunniagle	vs	S. Avery	1070
Geo. K. McGunniagle	vs	James Davis	1071
T. L. Anderson	vs	Benj. Forman	1072
T. L. Anderson	vs	Benj. Forman	1073
Geo. K. McGinnigle	vs	Muldrow & Wright	1074
Peckett, use of McDaniel	vs	Long & McKee	1075
J. R. Gameton	vs	J. T. McCleams	1076
Wm. Blakely	vs	E. & J. M. Hyde	1077
G. K. McGannegle	vs	Clark, Spear & Co	1078
James C. Agnew	vs	Clark, Spear & Co	1079
M. D. Bates	vs	R. P. Jenkins	1080
Richard Norris	vs	Robt. Edwards	1081
Jas. Smith	vs	D. T. Anderson	1082
R. Norris	vs	J. Sodowsky	1083
W. Marshall	vs	Wm. Tullock	1084
G. E. Williams	vs	J. P. Shropshire	1085
Wurts Musgrove	vs	Nask & Mitchell	1086
Moses Burton	vs	Robt. Shaw	1087
Haines & Darrah	vs	Will Muldrow	1088
John Elliott	vs	Mill (sic) Muldrow	1089
Cunningham	vs	Marion College	1090
M. Criswell	vs	D. T. Anderson	1091
Geo. O'Connor	vs	Jos. Long	1092
Geo. Flynn	vs	Jos. Long	1093
G. Robert	vs	G. Shepherd	1094
Geo. O'Connor	vs	D. Hounican	1095
Wingate & Gaskill	vs	G. Shepherd	1096
A. B. Hawkins	vs	Thompson & Dill	1097
Josiah Spalding	vs	Geo. McKee	1098

Name		Name	No.1
Saml. H. Wilbrune	vs	J. W. Haydon	1099
Taylor & King	vs	Chas. Whall	1100
Anderson Brown	vs	Cooper & Leatt	1101
R. C. Gest	vs	Saml. Muldrow	1102
Jno. N. Bowles	vs	Shaw & King	1103
Jno. W. Bowen	vs	M. J. Norman	1104
R. Shaw, use of T. Bates	vs	Marion College	1105
J. W. Bowen	vs	T. J. Wise	1106
Gartrell	vs	Peake	1107
R. C. Gest	vs	Isaac Marshall	1108
Riney	vs	Shropshire	1109
McElroy	vs	Marion College	1110
McKown, for use of Galaher	vs	Marion College	1111
Cope	vs	Marion College	1112
Simpson	vs	Clark & Spear	1113
Rogers	vs	Marion College	1114
Walsh	vs	Milton	1115
Walsh	vs	Milton	1116
Gentry	vs	Marion College	1117
Walsh	vs	Mulock & Seal	1118
Shepherd	vs	Marion College	1119
McKown, for the use of Galaher	vs	Marion College	1120
Pye	vs	Marion College	1121
Von Phul& McGill	vs	Overton & Anderson	1122
Potter	vs	Bywater	1123
Haines & Darrah	vs	Marion College	1124
Pollard	vs	Marion College	1125
Barton	vs	Marion College	1126
Reeves & Co	vs	Wm. Kelly	1127
Milton	vs	Stanfield	1128
Cooper	vs	Nelson	1129
Morton	vs	Tate	1130
McMurry	vs	Burnett	1131
Bosley	vs	Dearing	1132
Castaphern	vs	Furman	1133
Netherland	vs	Ringer	1134
Dunnwitt	vs	Ringer & Muldrow	1135
Arthur & Co	vs	Holiday	1136
Coats	vs	Muldrow	1137
Gest	vs	Jenkins & Ferguson	1138
Campbell	vs	Shackelford	1139
E. S. Ely	vs	Marion College	1140
Pye	vs	Hassinger	1141
Settle	vs	Bartlett	1142

(Marion County, Missouri Continued)

Name		Name	No.1
Darr	vs	Peake	1143
Stephens	vs	Darrah	1144
Vannoy	vs	Carmegy	1145
Kissee & Woolfolk	vs	Millan & Overton (sic)	1147
Fraizer	vs	Snell	1148
Overton	vs	Juileius	1149
Hawkins	vs	Pollard & Berryman	1150
Vanphul & McGill	vs	Pollard & others	1151
Hallowell & others	vs	Pollard & Johnson	1152
Rodes	vs	Ingraham	1153
See	vs	Wright	1154
Freiyer & Fisher	vs	Ferguenan (sic)	1155
Campbell	vs	Elliott	1156
Kendrick, admr.	vs	Pollard	1157
Hawkins	vs	Gay	1158
Flynn	vs	Long	1159
Campbell	vs	Long	1160
Dunn	vs	Singleton	1161
Simpson	vs	Harbour	1162
Williams, admr.	vs	McKee & Walker	1163
Pye	vs	Harbour	1164
Shepherd & Ford	vs	Avery	1165
Dobyn	vs	Minnes	1166
Rush, use of Woolrick	vs	Maddock	1167
McCormack	vs	Ringer	1168
Phillips	vs	Walker	1169
Shropshire & Owslet	vs	McAfee	1170
Hawkins	vs	Stringer	1171
Hawkins	vs	Stringer	1172
William Stevens	vs	Jos. Conway	1173
Ira Stout	vs	Manfrid Mimans (sic)	1174
Cooper & Shacklett	vs	T. L. Mitchell	1175
H. and W. Collins	vs	Jas. Conway	1176
Robert Bartlett	vs	Saml. Ringold	1177
Cushing & Huntington	vs	G. W. Bancroft	1178
James C. Goodwin	vs	B. L. Hyatt	1179
Williamson & Wallace	vs	Jno. F. Austin	1180
Jno. Lowler	vs	Wm. L. Robinson	1181
State	vs	Rulles	1182
John Millin	vs	Robt. Williamson	1183
Joshua Hickey	vs	Clark Forman	1184
Muldear (sic) Davis	vs	Clark Forman	1185
Clark Forman	vs	Wm. Ringer	1186
Josiah Abbott	vs	Geo. W. Leonard	1187
Banister Hickey	vs	Clark Forman	1188
S. S. Matson, admr.	vs	John C. Pickett	1189
Henry Shaw	vs	Marion College	1190

(Marion County, Missouri Continued)

Name		Name	No.1
Othow & Ebekee (sic)	vs	Marion College	1197
Dav Hough	vs	Hawes & Davis	1198
Hempstead & Beebe	vs	Wm. R. Campbell	1199
Edwd. Hales	vs	Benj. Forman	1200
William H. Holeues	vs	Sidney P. Hae (sic)	1201
State	vs	Thos. Sear	1202
State	vs	Saml. Bledsoe	1203
State	vs	John Withers	1204
State	vs	Ira Stout	1205
Wm. J. Ringer	vs	Marion College	1206
Janney S. Canes (sic)	vs.	Bancroft & Co	1207
R. H. & P. C. Love	vs	T. & S. Rudd	1208
Jacob Righter	vs	Haines & Darrah	1209
Guenant Mosley	vs	William Poor	1210
R. Q. Nunn	vs	I. Jefferies & others	1211
O. Dickerson	vs	Campbell & Milton	1212
John Smith	vs	Wm. Guynn	1213
McKee, Stewart & Lind	vs	Josiah Ellis	1214
Will R. Pye	vs	Thos. W. Potters	1215
A. Buckley	vs	I. Righter	1216
W. Blakely	vs	I. Righter	1217
John C. Johnson	vs	Saml. Kean	1218
Tiffany Duvall	vs	Pollard & Joh. (sic)	1219
Henry Cook	vs	Josiah Abbott	1220
T. I. Pollard	vs	Saml. Tull	1221
E. Anderson	vs	E. Merrill	1222
Charles & Blew	vs	I. W. Bowers	1223
Wm. Tull	vs	Constantine Brown	1224
Haines & Darrah	vs	W. C. Eayes	1225
J. Longmire	vs	J. Elliott	1226
William R. Campbell	vs	J. Elliott	1228
O. Hite	vs	Kelly, Pollard & Johnson	1229
Jno. McKee	vs	W. Cannon	1230
Thos. Ross	vs	Dickson & McLean	1232
Thos. Ross	vs	R. B. Bartlett	1234
Thos. Ross	vs	Dennis Magan	1235
M. Higgintotters	vs	Jas. Long	1237
D. Dunn	vs	H. L. Millan	1238
Wright & Shropshire	vs	A. Cannon	1239
Geo. Hollingworth	vs	I. A. Filfert (sic)	1240
H. Wilcoxan, admr.	vs	T. M. Dixon	1241
Glassglow, Shaw & Co	vs	D. O. Glascock	1242
Tabor, Shaw & Tate	vs	W. R. Summins	1243
Benj. Coates	vs	Jno. McKee	1244
David M. Wilson	vs	I. C. Ferguson	1245
Jas. L. Polhermus	vs	McKee & Muldrow	1246
D. T. Anderson	vs	I. Clark	1247

(Marion County, Missouri Continued)

Name		Name	No.1
Andrew King	vs	A. M. Manifee	1248
Clayborne Chander	vs	Will Muldrow	1249
John Hall	vs	Shubail Avery	1250
Joseph Litling	vs	P. P. Jenkins	1251
Jas. L. Pease	vs	Searcy & Miles	1252
Will B. White	vs	Saml. Muldrow	1253
D. T. Anderson	vs	Will Muldrow	1254
Michael Turnan	vs	Jacob Sodowsky	1255
Michael Urnan	vs	L. D. & L. Wiseman	1256
Tiffany Duvall	vs	Pickett & Hawkins	1257
A. & G. W. Kerr	vs	W. I. and M. W. McDaniel	1258
John Tapley	vs	J. D. Gash & J.G.L. Sains	1259
Von Phul & McGill	vs	J. H. Milton	1260
Kilgore, Taylor & Springer	vs	J. H. Milton	1261
Siter, Price & Co	vs	Pollard & Johnson	1262
Wm. P. Stewart	vs	Pollard & Johnson	1263
John F. Darby	vs	Cowling & Agnew	1264
William Swan	vs	Jno. McKee	1265
James R. McDaniel	vs	J. E. Shropshire	1266
Wood, Slacker & Co	vs	Isaac B. Owsley	1267
Jarvis, Trabue & Curd	vs	Kelly & Johnson	1268
S. Martin	vs	R. Matson	1269
G. C. Wood	vs	D. T. Anderson	1270
Hicks, Ewing & Co	vs	Cowling & Agnew	1271
R. P. Pulliam	vs	S. C. Ely	1272
G. D. Barnes	vs	Muldrow & McKee	1273
Geo. Collier	vs	Wm. Muldrow	1274
Riley & Dillon	vs	Bartlett	1275
Tiffany Duvall & Co	vs	Haines & Co	1277
Heiskill & Hoff	vs	Cowling & Agnew	1278
John C. Wright	vs	W. & C. Pratt	1279
Enoch Hoolow (sic)	vs	Wm. J. Howell	1280
Philip D. West	vs	Orran Smith	1281
Lewis County	vs	Shropshire	1282
R. P. Pulliam	vs	S. Caswell & Ely	1283
William Cooper	vs	I. Forman	1284
William Cooper	vs	Saml. W. King	1285
David C. Tuttle	vs	Constantine Brown	1286
Thos. Frances	vs	Henry Callaway	1287
Saml. Elzie	vs	Robt. Black (sic)	1288
W. R. Brown	vs	Tavmner Snell	1289
John W. Keale	vs	T. M. & A. H. Smith	1290
Jas. R. McDaniel	vs	J. E. Shropshire	1291
Benj. Farnan	vs	Ross & Jones	1292
John B. Haeslip	vs	Jno. Shackleford	1293
Isaac B. Diamon	vs	Reddick & McKee	1294

(Marion County, Missouri Continued)

Name		Name	No.1
William Blakey	vs	John Shackelford	1295
Sublett & Campbell	vs	Cowling & Agnew	1296
T. C. Rockhill	vs	Saml. Cluff	1297
Richardson & Davis	vs	H. & W. Collins	1298
J. H. & I. W. Tompson	vs	Jones, Turpin & Tavener	1299
J. P. Shropshire	vs	J. R. Berryman	1300
Haines & Darrah	vs	J. Abbott & Co	1301
Shropshire & Owsley	vs	Josiah Abbott	1302
Charles & Blow	vs	Edgar & Fromberger	1303
Haines & Darrah	vs	Jas. Long	1304
Haines & Darrah	vs	I. Tomsan	1305
Edeline & McElroy	vs	A. McAfee	1306
Ferguson & Hall	vs	G. S. Patterson	1307
Abbott & Brothers	vs	Shropshire & Owsley	1308
Timothy Oakly, jr.	vs	Wm. P. & A. B. Owsley	1309
Cresson & Coupland	vs	Shropshire & Owsley	1310
Jno. Lee	vs	Shropshire & Ownsley	1311
Caleb Cope	vs	Wm. P. Owsley	1312
Tiffany Duvall	vs	Williams & Shropshire	1313
Caleb Cope	vs	James P. Shropshire	1314
Powell, Lamot & Co	vs	Jas. P. Shropshire	1315
Eli Upton	vs	R. Rabe	1316
State	vs	Cortney Lewis	1317
David O. Glascock	vs	B. Gilbert	1319
H. Wilcoxan	vs	Peake & Lane	1320
Thos. E. Alsop	vs	S. A. Bowen	1321
Spalding & Randolph	vs	Ira Stout	1322
Benj. Forman	vs	Theodore Jones	1323
A. H. Evans	vs	E. McDonald	1324
Ira Y. Mann	vs	Cooper & Shacklett	1325
Crow & Lewis	vs	L. C. Hawkins	1326
Gaily & Coonee	vs	Jas. Conway	1328
Saml. Shade	vs	W. & P. Bird	1329
J. P. Shropshire	vs	Jas. Mitchell	1330
Jesse Ewing	vs	A. G. Anderson	1331
Skinner & Thomas	vs	R. B. Bartlett	1332
Bank of Missouri	vs	L. C. Dobyn & P---	1333
James Kindrick	vs	Kelly ------	1334
Z. G. Draper	vs	James Brady	1335
Henry Chouteau	vs	Hyde & Butler	1336
Hood & Abbott	vs	Cowling & Agnew	1337
J. Magoffin (sic)	vs	Wm. Muldrow	1338
Thos. W. Lane	vs	Thos. G. Mitchell	1339
Chas. P. Jennings	vs	C. R. Lewis	1340
Chaliss & Blow	vs	J. H. Milton	1341
J. Charless	vs	Winlock & Scott	1342
C. T. Harrison	vs	Levering & Co	1343

Name		Name	No.1
Price, Newlin & Co	vs	Kelly & Johnson	1344
B. Allen	vs	Haines & Darrah	1345
Elmaker & Dunn	vs	Kelly, Pollard & Johnson	1346
Hicks, Ewing & Co	vs	Jenkins & Ferguson	1347
Wm. Caiman	vs	S. W. B. Comegy	1348
J. M. Clemens	vs	Marion College	1349
S. Wonderly & Son	vs	Kelly & Johnson	1350
Maberry, Gellier & Co	vs	Kelly & Johnson	1351
Reese & Glenn	vs	Wm. P. Owsley	1352
Jno. Siles	vs	J. E. Shropshire	1354
Hallowell & Ashbridge	vs	Shropshire & Owsley	1355
J. McCarmick	vs	J. P. Rutter	1356
J. P. Shropshire	vs	Henry Cook	1357
McKee, Harding & Co	vs	Haines & Darrah	1358
Hallowell, Ashbridge	vs	Conner, Peake & Co	1359
R. C. Gest	vs	S. P. Haines	1360
Jas. C. Lampkin	vs	Jno. E. Shropshire	1361
Gill, Ford & Co	vs	W. H. Huskill	1362
Jno. H. Curd	vs	Shacktill & Lovelace	1363
I. Kendrick, admr.	vs	W. H. Pollard	1364
William Carman	vs	Robt. Stewart	1365
L. Harwood	vs	Pollard & Johnson	1366
R. Shaw	vs	Marion College	1367
Thomas Green	vs	Jeter Hicks	1368
M. M. Proctor	vs	T. C. Jefferies	1369
Shropshire & Owsley	vs	E. Haydon	1370
Haines & Darrah	vs	Geo. D. Slaven	1371
Bird, Griffith & Co	vs	Jno. Randall	1372
J. S. Buckanan	vs	J. Auginul	1373
John Birch	vs	J. & G. Slaven	1374
William Kirby	vs	R. B. Bartell	1375
Joel Free	vs	Ira Stout	1376
Jones & Sherman	vs	C. Forman	1377
State	vs	Winn	1379
State	vs	D. Corlew	1380
Haines & Darrah	vs	--- Pratt	1381
J. W. Eastin	vs	Dillingham	1382
W. P. Brown	vs	Bowen & Buckner	1383
Bird, Griffith & Co	vs	Marmaduke	1384
Bird, Griffith & Co	vs	Wm. N. Tandy	1385
Bird, Griffith & Co	vs	Marmaduke & Allison	1386
Bird, Griffith & Co	vs	Wm. D. Marmaduke	1387
Haines & Darrah	vs	J. Long	1388
Jas. W. Eastin	vs	H. I. Millin	1389
Wm. R. Davis	vs	J. J. Everett	1390
R. C. Gest	vs	J. Long	1391
Micajah Waters	vs	D. Magnedes (sic)	1392

(Marion County, Missouri Continued)

Name		Name	No.1
E. J. Wilson, admr.	vs	I. Gillespie	1393
Haines & Darrah	vs	C. Brown	1394
Elgin & Lewis	vs	Wm. N. Tandy	1395
Haydon & Pulham	vs	R. B. Bartell	1396
R. C. Gest	vs	David B. Lowen	1397
Haines & Evereet	vs	J. J. Everett	1398
S. Hargis	vs	Jos. Long	1399
J. R. Montgomery	vs	I. R. Gillespie	1400
Jacob Holliday	vs	Ginella S. Gay	1401
Geo. W. Todd	vs	Wm. Taylor	1402
W. Levier	vs	William Carman	1403
H. Wilcox	vs	W. D. Marmaduke	1404
Haines & Darrah	vs	Long	1405
W. R. Simmons	vs	J. H. Milton	1406
W. R. Simmons	vs	J. H. Milton	1407
Huntsberry & Walker	vs	Poor & Allen	1408
Wm. R. Roberts	vs	Tarner Snell	1409
Danl. Parker	vs	B. & C. Forman	1410
E. Hooton	vs	Jesse Poor	1411
Alex. Anderson	vs	Wm. Bowen	1412
Wm. R. Pye	vs	Joseph C. Harbour	1413
John H. Melin	vs	Vanlandingham	1414
James G. Wright	vs	Wm. Forman	1415
E. Hooton	vs	Jacob Howell	1416
State	vs	Geo. Glascock	1417
State	vs	Thomas Ross	1418
State	vs	Thomas Ross	1419
State	vs	Thomas Ross	1420
State	vs	John H. Curd	1421
Wm. Amos	vs	Pollard & Johnson	1422
Johnson & Langley	vs	Pollard & Kelly	1423
Silas Price	vs	Kelly, Pollard & Co	1424
R. & R. McDowall	vs	Pollard & Johnson	1425
Hord & Gray	vs	J. E. Shropshire	1426
P. Littiz & Son	vs	Haines & Darrah	1427
R. H. & P. C. Lane	vs	J. P. Shropshire	1428
Smith & Brothers	vs	Shropshire & Owsley	1429
S. Wonderly	vs	Shropshire & Owlsey	1430
Cook & Marlin	vs	R. Shacklett	1431
M. D. Bates	vs	Sodowsky & Edwards	1432
Haines & Darrah	vs	Ringer	1433
Pukill (sic) & Hawkins	vs	J. P. Shropshire	1434
McKee, Harding & Co	vs	Wm. Wright	1435
Caleb Cope	vs	J. P. Shropshire	1436
Eastin	vs	A. N. Wright	1437
State	vs	J. M. Clark	1438
State	vs	J. M. Clark	1439

(Marion County, Missouri Continued)

Name		Name	No.1
State	vs	Thos. M. Dickeson	1440
State	vs	Wade Pollard	1441
State	vs	John H. Martin	1442
State	vs	Michael Butcher	1443
State	vs	Wilson R. Simmons	1444
Reed & Perin	vs	John D. Foster	1445

Chariton Loan Office, 1822 and Ending Date October 15, 1822, Capitol Fire Documents, CFD 69, Folder 6547

Debtor	Security(1&2)	Loan Date	Due Date
Chas. Harryman	T. C. Burch Job Harryman	Sep. 1,1822	Dec. 1,1822
J. T. Burch	H. Craig Jno. Moore	Jun. 1,1822	Sep. 1,1822
Jas. Medley	E. Moore R. D. Malone	Sep. 1,1822	Dec. 1,1822
Jno. King	Jas. Anderson Jas. Linnel	Sep. 1,1822	Dec. 1,1822
W. B. Marrs	L. Marrs David Manchester	Sep. 1,1822	Dec. 1,1822
Andrw. King	John King Joel King	Sep. 1,1822	Dec. 1,1822
Wm. Lewis	Wm. Lewis Francis Dunkard	Sep. 1,1822	Dec. 1,1822
J. Hutchins	M. Parmer Wm. Parmer	Aug. 1,1822	Dec. 1,1822
Wm. Pearson	P. Wright T. Crocket	Aug. 1,1822	Nov. 1,1822
D. Lears	J. Allen R. Jack	Jul. 1,1822	Oct. 1,1822
Isom Douglass	J. Moore D. Green	Sep. 1,1822	Dec. 1,1822
Hiram Craig	Jno. Moore Ephm. Moore	Aug. 1,1822	Nov. 1,1822
E. B. Cabell	P. Browder F. A. Bradford	Aug. 1,1822	Nov. 1,1822
J. Finnel	Jno. King I. Anderson	Aug. 1,1822	Nov. 1,1822
Mos. King	Andrw. King Joel King	Aug. 1, 1822	Nov. 1,1822
E. Moore	J. Moore H. Craig	Aug. 1,1822	Nov. 1,1822
J. Moore	E. Moore H. Craig	Aug. 1,1822	Nov. 1,1822
N. Pepper	T. Pepper D. H. Campbell	Jul. 1,1822	Oct. 1,1822

(Chariton Loan Office Continued)

Debtor	Security(1&2)	Loan Date	Due Date
Lewis Newton	J. Newton Wm. Newton	Aug. 1,1822	Nov. 1,1822
H. H. Bradford	E. B. Cabell F. A. Bradford	Aug. 1,1822	Nov. 1,1822
Wm. W. Monroe	E. B. Cabell H. Stephenson	Sep. 1,1822	Dec. 1,1822
Jos. Watson	Thos. Watson J. D. Fowler	Jun. 1,1822	Sep. 1,1822
Jas. Earickson	Jno. Dorsey H. T. Williams	Aug. 1,1822	Nov. 1,1822
Jas. Holloway	Jas. Tooley Jas. Morica (sic)	Aug. 1,1822	Nov. 1,1822
Jas. Richardson	Wm. Witt L. B. Witt	Aug. 1,1822	Nov. 1,1822
Po. P. Head	S. C. Davis H. T. Williams	Aug. 1,1822	Nov. 1,1822
Danl. Riggs	Jno. Graves H. T. Williams	Aug. 1,1822	Nov. 1,1822
Geo. Craig	Fos. Freeman Wm. W. Mouier	Aug. 1,1822	Nov. 1,1822
Uria Bailey	A. McKinney T. Tate	Aug. 1,1822	Nov. 1,1822
P. Browder	E. B. Cabell F. A. Bradford	Aug. 1,1822	Nov. 1,1822
E. Samuels	A. Hatfield F. Samuels	Jul. 1,1822	Oct. 1,1822
F. Kinedey	T. Morris Jas. Simpson	Aug. 1,1822	Oct. 1,1822
T. Marrs	Geo. Delaney Jas. Richardson	Aug. 1,1822	Nov. 1,1822
F. A. Bradford	E. B. Cabell P. Browder	Aug. 1,1822	Nov. 1,1822
J. Burnum	D. Dunkin Josa. Sharp	Aug. 1,1822	Nov. 1,1822
W. E. Green	Jno. King Wm. Green	Aug. 1,1822	Oct. 1,1822
R. Hancock	W. Barbee E. Moore	Aug. 1,1822	Nov. 1,1822
Nat. Ford	Pet. Lord Boaze (sic) Maxey	Sep. 1,1822	Dec. 1,1822
Wm. Parmer	Wm. Parmer J. Hardwick	Aug. 1,1822	Nov. 1,1822
Jona. Eppler	G. T. Foster Jos. Foster	Aug. 1,1822	Nov. 1,1822
Amos Barnes	Jos. Gillum J. Belcher	Sep. 1,1822	Dec. 1,1822

Debtor	Security(1&2)	Loan Date	Due Date
T. J. Eldridge	M. Rice J. T. Gillet	Sep. 1,1822	Dec. 1,1822
H. T. Williams	E. Williams T. B. Williams	Sep. 1,1822	Dec. 1,1822
J. T. Burch	H. Craig J. W. Moore	Aug. 1,1822	Dec. 1,1822
Jos. Sharp	Joel Burmum J. Dunkin	Sep. 1,1822	Dec. 1,1822
Jas. Holloway	Jas. Morin Thos. Patterson	Aug. 1,1822	Nov. 1,1822
E. B. Witt	E. B. Witt Wm. Witt	Sep. 1,1822	Dec. 1,1822
Jas. Ramsey	A. Williams C. Simmons	Jul. 1,1822	Nov. 1,1822
C. Simmons	G. T. Foster Jas. Ramsey	Aug. 1,1822	Nov. 1,1822
F. Drinkard	Wm. Drinkard Wm. Lewis	Sep. 1,1822	Dec. 1,1822
J. M. Fowler	Wm. McCullom T. Watson	Aug. 1,1822	Nov. 1,1822
Jas. Barnes	Jas. Holman E. Moore	Sep. 1,1822	Dec. 1,1822
Jas. Tooley	Jno. Tooley Jac. Bailey	Oct. 1,1822	Jan. 1,1823
Jona. Finnel	D. Dunkin Jas. Finnel	Oct. 1,1822	Jan. 1,1823
Jno. Means	D. Todd Jesse Samuels	Oct. 1,1822	Jan. 1,1823
Jona. T. Lindsey	H. Y. Bingham W. J. Reed and D. Todd	Oct. 1,1822	Jan. 1,1823
J. M. Fowler	J. D. Fowler T. Watson	Aug. 1,1822	Nov. 1,1822
Thos. Fristoe	J. Campbell T. Williams	Oct. 1,1822	Jan. 1,1823
Sol. Kinsey	--- Hugh Jno. Braly	Oct. 1,1822	Jan. 1,1823
Jac. Medley	Joel King Jos. Head	Oct. 1,1822	Jan. 1,1823
Joel King	Mos. King Andw. King	Oct. 1,1822	Jan. 1,1823
Jackn. Tharp	Thos. Morris Thos. Tharp	Oct. 1,1822	Jan. 1,1823
Jos. Watson	Jas. Fowler Thos. Watson	Sep. 1, 1822	Dec. 1,1822
Jas. Finnel	Jona. Finnel D. Dunkin	Oct. 1,1822	Jan. 1,1823

(Chariton Loan Office Continued)

Debtor	Security(1&2)	Loan Date	Due Date
Abm. Lock	Jas. Earickson Jno. Bull	Oct. 1,1822	Jan. 1,1823
Thos. T. Lock	D. Green Thos. D. Lonney	Oct. 1,1822	Jan. 1,1823

Jackson Loan Office, Fifth Loan District, January 1, 1830 to December 31, 1830, Capitol Fire Documents, CFD 69, Folder 6568.

Debtor	Note	Due Date	Security
Gustavus A. Bird	180.00	Oct. 25, 1823	Personal
Jenifer T. Spring	180.00	Oct. 25, 1823	Personal
E. B. Herrick	180.00	Oct. 25, 1823	Personal
Jesse Haile	426.00	Mar. 30, 1823	Mortgage
Jesse Haile	125.00	Apr. 27, 1823	Personal
George Fricke	125.00	Apr. 27, 1823	Persoanl
Wm. Bancroft	125.00	Apr. 27, 1823	Personal
James Neals	200.00	Mar. 30, 1823	Personal
Thos. Craddock	200.00	Mar. 30, 1823	Personal
J. G. Mccabe	200.00	Mar. 30, 1823	Personal
E. B. Herrick	171.00	Oct. 25, 1823	Personal
G. A. Bird	171.00	Oct. 25, 1823	Personal
J. T. Sprigg	171.00	Oct. 25, 1823	Personal
Jno. McArthur	200.00	Mar. 26, 1823	Personal
Jas. Holman	200.00	Mar. 26, 1823	Personal
J. W. Miller	200.00	Mar. 26, 1823	Personal
Jno. Kinnison	200.00	Nov. 27, 1823	Personal
Presly Kinnison	200.00	Nov. 27, 1823	Personal
K. B. New--	200.00	Nov. 27, 1823	Personal
John Brown	200.00	Oct. 25, 1822	Personal
George Fricke	200.00	Oct. 25, 1822	Personal
Jas. Tanner	200.00	Oct. 25, 1822	Personal
Lewis F. Linn	500.00	Apr. 1, 1823	Mortgage
Priscilla Johnson	130.00	Mar. 30, 1823	Mortgage
Charles Ellis	199.50	Oct. 20, 1822	Mortgage
Henry Dodge	199.50	Oct. 20, 1822	Mortgage
J. Caruth	199.50	Oct. 20, 1822	Mortgage
D. Hiles	100.00	Apr. 6, 1823	Mortgage
Wm. Cracraft	100.00	Apr. 6, 1823	Mortgage
A. Creath	100.00	Apr. 6, 1823	Mortgage
Enoch Evans	100.00	Oct. 27, 1823	Mortgage
Thos. S. Sublett	53.25	Apr. 27, 1823	Personal
W. P. Lacey	53.25	Apr. 27, 1823	Personal
T. W. Graves	53.25	Apr. 27, 1823	Personal
Wm. G. Byrd	46.85	Mar. 20, 1823	Personal
Stephen Byrd	46.85	Mar. 20, 1823	Personal
Wm. McGuive	46.85	Mar. 20, 1823	Personal
Wm. Cracroft	90.00	Dec. 15, 1823	Personal

(Jackson Loan Office Continued)

Debtor	Note	Due Date	Security
Morgan Ryan	90.00	Dec. 15, 1823	Personal
N. D. D'Lashomitt	200.00	Oct. 26, 1823	Personal
S. Glascock	200.00	Oct. 26, 1823	Personal
U. Seavers	200.00	Oct. 26, 1823	Personal
William Hickman	450.00	Dec. 20, 1823	Mortgage
Samuel McFarland	408.75	Dec. 11, 1822	Mortgage
Gilbert Hector	195.85	Oct. 31, 1823	Personal
Jno. Glascock	195.85	Oct. 31, 1823	Personal
M. Randol	195.85	Oct. 31, 1823	Personal
Chs. Leaven	180.00	Dec. 5, 1823	Personal
Micholas Leaven	180.00	Dec. 5, 1823	Personal
M. Grady	180.00	Dec. 5, 1823	Personal
Lewis Pra---	97.50	Dec. 15, 1822	Personal
-- Cracroft	97.50	Dec. 15, 1822	Personal
Jacob M. Miller	1200.00	Dec. 22, 1822	Personal
W. Walkison	1200.00	Dec. 22, 1822	Personal
James Simons	200.00	Dec. 22, 1822	Personal
J. O. Clark	200.00	Dec. 22, 1822	Personal
A. Brother	200.00	Dec. 22, 1822	Personal
N. W. Watkins	150.00	May 1, 1823	Mortgage
N. W. Watkins	200.00	Dec. 15, 1822	Personal
Jno. Payne	200.00	Dec. 15, 1822	Personal
G. W. Davis	200.00	Dec. 15, 1822	Personal
Henry Elliott	200.00	Dec. 11, 1822	Personal
G. A. Bird	200.00	Dec. 11, 1822	Personal
Z. Priest	200.00	Dec. 11, 1822	Personal
W. H. Brooks	199.50	Dec. 12, 1822	Personal
W. Wilkinson	199.50	Dec. 12, 1822	Personal
E. H. Bennett	199.50	Dec. 12, 1822	Personal
Jas. Ravenscroft	1000.00	Dec. 31, 1822	Mortgage
Jesse Baker	180.00	Dec. 19, 1823	Personal
Geo. Ruddle	180.00	Dec. 19, 1823	Personal
E. Tanner	180.00	Dec. 19, 1823	Personal
Edward Tanner	180.00	Dec. 21, 1823	Personal
Geo. Ruddle	180.00	Dec. 21, 1823	Personal
J. Baker	180.00	Dec. 21, 1823	Personal
Geo. Ruddle	180.00	Dec. 19, 1823	Personal
E. Tanner	180.00	Dec. 19, 1823	Personal
J. Baker	180.00	Dec. 19, 1823	Personal
James Evans	1000.00	Oct. 26, 1822	Mortgage
Sarah Campbell	400.00	Dec. 15, 1822	Mortgage
Saml. Dixon	135.00	Dec. 7, 1823	Personal
J. T. Sprigg	135.00	Dec. 7, 1823	Personal
G. A. Bird	135.00	Dec. 7, 1823	Personal
A. P. Gillaspie	200.00	Oct. 25, 1822	Personal
Jas. Tanner	200.00	Oct. 25, 1822	Personal
M. H. Stallcup	200.00	May 1, 1823	Personal

(Jackson Loan Office Continued)

Debtor	Note	Due Date	Security
A. P. Gillaspie	200.00	May 1, 1823	Personal
J. G. Vance	200.00	May 1, 1823	Personal
Saml. S. Strothers	200.00	May 1, 1823	Personal
J. Myers	200.00	May 1, 1823	Personal
Stephen Ross	200.00	Oct. 25, 1822	Personal
Walter Wilkinson	800.00	Dec. 22, 1822	Mortgage
James Tanner	200.00	Oct. 25, 1822	Personal
Jno. Brown	200.00	Oct. 25, 1822	Personal
R. Tanner	200.00	Oct. 25, 1822	Personal
James Tanner	400.00	Dec. 20, 1822	Mortgage
Richard S. Thomas	800.00	Oct. 26, 1823	Mortgage
P. Bolduc	199.75	Mar. 27, 1823	Personal
Geo. Monoey (sic)	199.75	Mar. 27, 1823	Personal
E. Bolduc	199.75	Mar. 27, 1823	Personal
John G. W. McCabe	500.00	Mar. 30, 1823	Mortgage
Henry Millard	199.76	Oct. 26, 1822	Personal
J. Millard	199.76	Oct. 26, 1822	Personal
H. Land	199.76	Oct. 26, 1822	Personal
Wm. G. Shade	170.00	May 25, 1823	Personal
Jno. Payne	170.00	May 25, 1823	Personal
S. J. Whittenburg	170.00	May 25, 1823	Personal
Wm. Clark	200.00	Aug. 2, 1823	Personal
R. Montgomery	200.00	Aug. 2, 1823	Personal
G. Simons	200.00	Aug. 2, 1823	Personal
T. Crawford	200.00	Dec. 4, 1822	Personal
J. Crawford	200.00	Dec. 4, 1822	Personal
S. Campbell	200.00	Dec. 4, 1822	Personal
W. Long	53.25	Dec. 15, 1822	Personal
G. Hector	53.25	Dec. 15, 1822	Personal
Wm. Cracroft	53.25	Dec. 15, 1822	Personal
C. G. Houts	200.00	Dec. 7, 1822	Personal
R. Tanner	200.00	Dec. 22, 1822	Personal
Jas. Tanner	200.00	Dec. 22, 1822	Personal
Jno. Brown	200.00	Dec. 22, 1822	Personal
R. Mather	200.00	Dec. 22, 1822	Personal
Jno. Mather	200.00	Dec. 22, 1822	Personal
I. Mather	200.00	Dec. 22, 1822	Personal

Chariton 1st Loan Office, July 7, 1823 to July 7, 1825, Capitol Fire Documents, CFD 69, Folder 6549.

Debtor	Due Date	How Secured
John M. Fowler	Nov. 1,1822	J. D. Fowler & T. Watson
John M. Fowler	Nov. 1,1822	W. McCollum & T. Watson
Thomas Kinsey	Dec. 1,1822	T. Morris & J. Simpson
Solomon Kinnsey	Jan. 7,1823	H. Braly & Jno. Braly
James Richardson	Nov. 1,1822	Wm. Witt & L. B. Witt
Martin Parmer	Nov. 1,1822	M. Parmer & J. Hardwick

(Chariton Loan Office Continued)

Debtor	Due Date	Security
William Parmer	Nov. 1,1822	M. Parmer & J. Hardwick
Andrew King	Dec. 1,1822	Jno. King & Joel King
Moses King	Feb. 7,1823	Joel King & Andrw. King
Joel King	Jan. 7,1823	Moses King & Adw. King
James Tooler	Jan. 7,1823	Jno. Tooley & Jac. Baily
Pleasant Browder	Nov. 1,1822	E. B. Cabell & F. A. Bradford
F. A. Bradford	Dec. 1,1822	E. B. Cabell & P. Browder
Charles Simmons	Feb. 7,1823	G.L. Foster & Jas. Ramsey
John M. Bell	Sep. 1,1822	Jno. Doxey & H. T. Williams
Wm. J. Rector	Oct. 1,1822	A. Heavans & W. J. Redd
Wm. J. Redd	Oct. 1,1822	J. Graves & F.A. Bradford
Isaac Campbell	Nov. 1,1822	T. Fristoe & E. B. Cabell
Richard Byrd	Jul. 1,1822	B. Stapp & Jno. Burch
Hiram Craig	Feb. 7,1823	Jno. Moore & E. Moore
Hiram Craig	Feb. 7,1823	Jno. Moore & E. Moore
Edward B. Cabell	Nov. 1,1822	P. Browder & F. A. Bradford
Edward B. Cabell	Nov. 1,1822	P. Browder & F. A. Bradford
Edward B. Cabell	Jan. 7,1823	Mortgage on real estate
Thos. Conway	Oct. 1,1822	H. T. Williams & Jas. Semple
Thos. Fristoe	Jan. 7,1823	J. Campbell & H. Williams
Robt. W. Morris	Jan. 7,1822	Gray Bynum & A. Frye
Jerh. Murphy	Jan. 20,1822	R. W. Morris & A. Storrs
Moses Hutchings	Oct. 1,1822	Jno. Hutchings & M. Parmer
A. Barnes	Dec. 1,1822	Jos. Gilliam & I. Belcher
U. Bailey	Nov. 1,1822	A. McKinney & T. Tate
Geo. Craig	Nov. 1,1822	Foster Frunian & Wm. W. Monroe
Saml. Marrs	Feb. 7,1823	G. Delaney & Jas. Richardson
Wm. Pearson	Nov. 1,1822	P. Wright & T. Crockett
Jacob Medley	Jan. 1,1823	E. Moon & N. D. Malone
Jacob Medley	Jan. 7,1823	Joel King & Jas. Head
Wm. Lewis	Dec. 1,1822	F. Drinkard & Wm. Lewis
Augs. Evans	Dec. 1,1822	Mortgage on real estate
John Miller	Jan. 7,1823	B. Stapp & T. B. Kinney
James Semple	Apr. 19,1822	Jno. Moore & E. Moore
James Holloway	Nov. 1,1822	Jno. Tooley & Jas. Morin
Wm. Pearce	Feb. 7,1823	Jno. Gaither & Mary Carthurs
Saml. McMeis	Sep. 1,1822	A. H. Evans & G. Gary
A. Hancock	Sep. 1,1822	G. Gary & S. McMeis

Debtor	Due Date	Security
Martin Mars	Dec. 1,1822	S. Mars & D. Manchester
Bengn. Banks	Mar. 1,1823	E. B. Cabell & Jno. Holman
G. B. Beall	Jan. 7,1823	C. W. Williams & N. M. Thompson
S. Newton	Nov. 1,1822	J. & Wm. Newton
John Hardwick	Dec. 1,1822	L. Hardwick & M. Parmer
Hugh Stephenson	Dec. 1,1822	Nancy Stephenson & Wm. W. Mound
D. Sears	Oct. 1,1822	J. Allen & R. Jack
F. Drinkard	Dec. 1,1822	W. Drinkard & Wm. Lewis
Saml. Gilmore	Jan. 7,1823	J. Gilmore & Wm. Doherty
Josia Tharp	Dec. 1,1822	J. Burnum & Ja. Dunkin
James Barns	Dec. 1,1822	Jos. Holman & E. Moore
John Means	Jan. 7,1823	David Todd & Jesse Samuel
Nat Ford	Dec. 1,1822	Peter Ford & B. Maxey
L. B. Witt	Dec. 1,1822	E. B. Witt & Wm. Witt
H. H. Bradford	Feb. 7,1823	Mortgage on real estate
James Semple	Mar. 7,1823	Mortgage on real estate
James Morin	Aug. 1,1822	J. Holloway & Tho. Miller
John Tharp	Jan. 7,1823	Jas. Richardson & Jas. Morin
J. S. Findley	Jan. 1,1823	H. F. Bingham, W. J. Redd & D. Todd
Jonn. Eppler	Nov. 1,1822	G.S. Foster & Jos. Foster
G. S. Foster	Aug. 1,1822	C. Simmons & Jas. Foster
Duff Green	Nov. 16,1822	Mortgage on real estate
Thos. P. Gage	Jan. 15,1822	Mortgage on real estate
J. Eldridge	Dec. 1,1822	M. Rice & S. Gillet
Josa. Watson	Sep. 1,1822	T. Watson & J. D. Fowler
Josa. Adams	Oct. 1,1822	J. Hutchings & M. Parmer
H. H. Bradford	Feb. 7,1822	Mortgage on real estate
Baley George	Sep. 1,1822	M. Parmer & J. Ledgewood
Ezek. Williams	Dec. 1,1822	A. Barns & D. Munro
H. Wigginton	Feb. 7,1823	Mortgage on real estate
E. Moore	Feb. 7,1823	J. Moore & H. Craig
Thos. Watson	Nov. 2,1822	Mortgage on real estate
A. Barns	Dec. 1,1822	M. Rice & J. Gillet
Wm. P. Short	Oct. 1,1822	P. B. Harris & G. Gary
Isom Duglass	Dec. 1,1822	Jn. Moore & H. Craig
Jas. Leeper	Sep. 1,1822	Jas. Leeper & William Fleetwood
Saml. Curtis	Apr. 11,1822	G.S. Foster & Jos. Foster
H. H. Bradford	Nov. 1,1822	E. B. Cabell & F. A. Bradford
E. Samuels	Oct. 1,1822	A. Hatfield & F. Samuels
Jno. Miller	Oct. 1,1822	B. Stapp & L. B. Kinny

(Chariton Loan Office Continued)

Debtor	Loan Date	Security
Wm. W. Monroe	Dec. 1,1822	H. Stephenson & E. B. Cabell
Chas. Harryman	Feb. 7,1823	D. Green & T. D. Long
E. Young and T. Gage	Jan. 7,1823	Mortgage on real estate
J. Brunum	Feb. 7,1823	D. Dunkin & Jose Tharp
Jon. Finnel	Jan. 7,1823	D. Dunkin & Jas. Finnel
Reubn. Clark	Aug. 1,1822	J. Clark & H. Clark
J. T. Burch	Dec. 1,1822	H. Craig & Jno. Moore
J. T. Burch	Sep. 1,1822	H. Craig & Jno. Moore
M. Gaither	Feb. 7,1823	Wm. Pearce & Jno. Gaither
Jas. Gilmore	Jan. 1,1823	J. Finnel & D. Dunkin
L. Hardwick	Aug. 1,1822	M. Parmer & A. Hardwick
Edwd. Williams	Oct. 1,1822	R. Wasson & Wm. Hooton
Jas. Earickson	Nov. 1,1822	Jno. Doxey & H. T. Williams
A. Lock	Jan. 7,1823	Ja. Kanckin & Jno. Bull
E. Williams	Oct. 1,1822	R. Wasson & W. Hooton
R. Hancock	Nov. 1,1822	Wm. Barbee & E. Moore
Thos. S. Lock	Nov. 1,1822	D. Green & T. D. Loney
I. Hutchings	Dec. 1,1822	Wm. Parmer & M. Parmer
J. Holman	Mar. 1,1823	B. Banks & E. B. Cabell
Eliz. Williams	Mar. 1,1823	T. B. Williams & H. J. Williams
H. H. Williams	Dec. 1,1822	E. Williams & T. B. Williams
Allen Hoskins	Apr. 25,1822	J. D. Fowler & T. Watson
R. S. Davis	Mar. 1,1823	H.T. Williams & A. Thrash
Benj. Ray	Mar. 1,1823	Wm. Gabeer & J. Holman

Cooper 2nd Loan Office, Public Accounts Reported from June 1, 1830 to January 1, 1831, Capitol Fire Documents, CFD 69, Folder 6558.

Debtor	Securities
Geo. C. Hartt	Robt. P. Clark
Jas. Bruffee	Marcus Williams
Eli Hammond	---
Isaac Clark	Peter Stephens & Jas. Bruffee
Thos. Rogers	Chl. B. Ross
Thos. Dinsman	Sam. Sapsley
John F. Ton	Robt. Pogue
Jas. Alexander	Sam. Sapsley
Ira A. Emmons	Ezekiel Emmons
Henry Hammon	Geo. Cathey
Marcus Williams	Robt. P. Clark
Marcus Williams	Benj. F. Hickcox
Justinian Williams	Eli E. Hammons

(Cooper Loan Office Continued)

Debtor	Securities
Justinian Williams	Robt. Boyd
Robt. Boyd	Benj. F. Hickox
Benj. F. Hickox	Robt. Boyd
Britton Williams	William Savage
Wm. Savage	Wm. Curtis
Ezekiel Williams	Absalom Bram
Jas. L. Collins	Libbum Wright
Wm. Ross	Chl. B. Ross
Reuben B. Harris	Jas. Edgar
Henry Ruby	Thos. Ruby and Wm. Rud
Jas. Brown	Rubin B. Harris
Geo. Edgar	Rubin B. Harris
Wm. Savage	Mortgage

Cape Girardeau County, Missouri, Treasury Department Notice, Auditor's Office, March 10, 1834, Jefferson City, A List Of Lands To Be Sold For Unpaid Taxes For 1833, CFD 69, Capitol Fire Docuemtns, Folder 6569.

Assessed To	Acres	Org. Claimant	Sold To
John Abernathy,for			
heirs of Lewis Tash	170	Lewis Tash	State
David Greer, agt. for			
David Armour	1ot	(Jackson)	M.S. Cowan
Thomas W. Graves	204	Edw. Robinson	State
Enos Hannah	250	James Hannah	John Landers
Thomas W. Graves	100	Ramsey Bennet	State
Thomas W. Graves	1ot	(Cape Griardeau)	F. M. Means
Jacob Huffman, agent for		Phillip	
J. Huffman	320	Shackler	Wm. W. Means
David Harris	250	David Harris	State
Nathl. Watkins, agent for		Wm. Harrison	
Henry Clay	640	under -- Hubble	J.S. Rollins

Young County, Texas,1860 Mortality Schedule,(Note:Only Those Persons Born In Missouri And Born Before 1840

Name	Age	Martial Status	Cause Of Death
Ed. Cornet	30	Widower	Killed by Indians

Jackson County, Missouri, Delinquent Tax List, January, 1831

Abner J. Adair, Whitfield Boeng, John Bostick,Peter Hart, Martin Cooper, Charles Cardinal,Henry Clemens,William Prine, Larkin Johnson, Will. McCarty, jr., Ashford Noland, Samuel Saunders.

Marion County, Missouri, Members Of Grand Jury,February,1828

John Thrasher, sr., Green Lee Sams, Robert Joiner, Elijah Baxter, Thomas Threlkeld, Nathaniel Shannon, John Sites,jr.,

(Marion County, Missouri Continued)
John Farmer, William Lair, Robert Irvine, Charles Smith, Wm.
Whaley, Elijah Haydon, Nathaniel Foster, Banister Gregory,
John Moss, Joseph Hawkins.

Appointments Made By Gov. Meriwether Lewis, April 1, 1807 To March 31, 1808.

(1) Thomas C. Scott: (APT) May 7, 1807; Clerk of the
Court of Common Pleas and Quarter Sessions in the
District of Cape Girardeau.

(2) James Austin: (APT) May 8, 1807; Justice of the
Peace of the District of Ste. Genevieve.

(3) William James: (APT) June 8, 1807; Justice of the
Peace of the District of Ste. Genevieve.

(4) Joshua Pennyman: (APT) June 13, 1807; Justice of
the Peace for the Distrcit of Ste. Genevieve; (APT)
June 22, 1807, Commissioner of Rates and Levies for
District of Ste. Geneveive; (APT) June 24, 1807,
Impowered to administer the oaths of office.

(5) Silas Bent: (APT) June 14, 1807; First Justice of
the Court of Common Pleas and Quarter Sessions for
the District of St. Louis.

(6) Enoch Evans: (APT) June 16, 1807; Justice of the
Court of Common Pleas and Quarter Sessions for the
District of Cape Girardeau.

(7) Thomas Oliver: (APT) June 22, 1807, Commissioner of
Rates and Levies for the Dist. of Ste. Genevieve;
(APT) June 23, 1807, Judge of the Probate Court for
District of Ste. Geneveive.

(8) Joseph Whittlesey: (APT) June 27, 1807, Captain of
a Volunteer Infantry Company in the District of
Ste. Genievevе.

(9) Thomas Scott: (APT) June 27, 1807, Ensign in Jos.
Whittlesey's Volunteer Infantry Company in the
District of Ste. Genevieve.

(10) Ebenezer Armstrong: (APT) June 27, 1807, Lieutenant
in Joseph Whittlesey's Company of Volunteer Infantry for the District of Ste. Genevieve.

(11) James Green: (APT) July 7, 1807, Coroner of the
District of St. Charles.

(12) Michael Amoreux: (APT) July 7, 1807, Notary Public
for five years in the District of New Madrid; (APT)
July 7, 1807, Recorder and Probate Judge for the
District of New Madrid.

(13) Bernard Gains Farrar: (APT) July 20, 1807, (APT)
Surgeon First Regiment.

(14) William Sullivan: (APT) July 14, 1807, Coroner of
District of St. Louis.

(15) Thomas F. Riddick: (APT) July 14, 1807, Impowered

(Appointments Continued)

to administer the oaths of office; (APT) July 10,
1807, Clerk of the Court of Common Pleas and
Quarter Sessions for the District of St. Louis;
(APT) July 9, 1807, Commissioner of Rates and
Levies for one year from next August 15th for the
District of St. Louis.

(16) Mary Phillip LeDuc: (APT) July 18, 1807, Notary
Public for five years for the Dist. of St. Louis.

(17) Otho Shrader: (APT) August 14, 1807, Captain of a
Cavalry Company in the District of Ste. Geneveive.

(18) Henry Dodge: (APT) August 14, 1807, First Lieutenant in Otho Shrader's Company.

(19) Andrew Henry: (APT) August 14, 1807, Second Lieutenant in Otho Shrader's Company.

(20) John B. LeBrun Bossieur: (APT) August 14, 1807,
Cornet in Otho Scrader's Comapny.

(21) Charles Elliott: (APT) August 14, 1807, Burser in
Otho Shrader's Company.

(22) Henry Hight: (APT) July 18, 1807, Recorder and Probate Judge for the District of St. Charles.

(23) Benard Pratte: (APT) July 18, 1807, Treasurer for
the District of St. Louis; (APT) August 20, 1807,
Judge of the Court of Common Pleas and Quarter
Session for a period of four years in the District
of St. Louis.

(24) George Henderson: (APT) July 20, 1807, Recorder,
Probate Judge and Treasurer for the District of
Cape Girardeau.

(25) Thomas Kibbey: (APT) August 20, 1807, First Judge
of the Court of Common Pleas and Quarter Sessions
for the period of four years in the Distrct of St.
Charles.

(26) Francois Saucier: (APT) August 20, 1807, Judge of
the Court of Common Pleas and Quartes Sessions for
the period of four years in the District of St.
Charles.

(27) James Flaugherty: (APT) August 20, 1807, Judge in
the Court of Common Pleas and Quarter Sessions for
the period of four years in the District of St.
Charles.

(28) Silas Brent: (APT) August 20, 1807, First Judge in
the Court of Common Pleas and Quarter Sessions for
a period of four years in the Dist. of St. Louis.

(29) Charles Gratiot: (APT) August 20, 1807, Judge of
Court of Common Pleas and Quarter Sessions. He
declined the appointment.

(30) Louis LeBeaume: (APT) August 20, 1807, Judge of the
Court of Common Pleas and Quarter Sessions for a

(Appointments Continued)
period of four years for the District of St. Louis.

(31) Benj. Johnson: (APT) August 20, 1807, Justice for
Joachim Township, St. Louis.

(32) Jno. Allen: (APT) August 20, 1807, Justice for St.
Ferdinand Township, Louis.

(33) Geo. Fallis: (APT) August 20, 1807, Justice for St.
Ferdinand Township, St. Louis.

(34) Vincent Carico: (APT) August 20, 1807, Justice for
St. Ferdinand Township, St. Louis.

(35) James Mackay: (APT) August 20, 1807, Justice for
St. Louis Township, Louis. He declined to accept
the appointment; (APT) August 20, 1807, Justice for
Bon Homme Township, St. Louis.

(36) Kincaid Caldwell: (APT) August 20, 1807, Justice
for Bon Homme Township, St. Louis.

(37) Pierre Chouteau: (APT) August 20, 1807, Justice for
St. Louis Township, St. Louis.

(38) Richard Caulk: (APT) August 20, 1807, Justice for
Bon Homme Township, St. Louis.

(39) Jeduthan Kendal: (APT) August 20, 1807, Justice for
Joachim Township, St. Louis.

(40) M. P. LeDuc: (APT) August 20, 1807, Justice for
St. Louis Township, St. Louis.

(41) Thos. F. Riddick: (APT) August 20, 1807, Justice
St. Louis Township, St. Louis.

(42) Alexander McNair: (APT) August 20, 1807, Justice
for St. Louis Township, St. Louis.

(43) Amos Byrd: (APT) August 20, 1807, First Judge for
Court of Common Pleas and Quarter Sessions for a
period of four years in the District of Ste. Genevieve.

(44) F. M. Benoist: (APT) August 20, 1807, Justice for
St. Louis Township, St. Louis.

(45) William Gaines: (APT) August 20, 1807, Judge for
the Court of Common Pleas and Quarter Sessions for
a period of four years for the District of Ste.
Genevieve.

(46) St. James Beauvais: (APT) August 20, 1807, Judge
for the Court of Common Pleas and Quarter Sessions
for a period of four years for the District of Ste.
Genevieve.

(47) Joshua Humphreys: (APT) August 20, 1807, Justice
for New Madrid Township, District of New Madrid.

(48) Edmund Hogan: (APT) August 20, 1807, Justice for
Tywappity Township, District of Cape Girardeau.

(49) John Byrd: (APT) August 20, 1807, Judge for the
Court of Common Pleas and Quarter Sessions for
District of Cape Girardeau.

(Appointments Continued)

(50) Christ. Hays: (APT) August 20, 1807, First Judge
for the Court of Common Pleas and Quarter Sessions
for the District of Cape Girardeau.

(51) John Andrews: (APT) August 26, 1807, Justice for
Big River Township, Ste. Genevieve.

(52) Robert Green: (APT) August 20, 1807, Judge for the
Court of Common Please and Quarter Sessions for the
District of Cape Girardeau.

(53) Isidore Moore: (APT) August 256, 1807, Justice for
Cling Homme Township, Ste. Genevieve.

(54) Joshua Penniman: (APT) August 26, 1807, Justice for
Ste. Genevieve Township, Ste. Geneveive.

(55) Jno. Wellborn: (APT) August 20, 1807, Justice for
Tywappity Township, Cape Girardeau.

(56) Geo. A Hamilton: (APT) August 26, 1807, Justice for
Cling Himme Township, Ste. Genevieve.

(57) Elisha Baker: (APT) August 26, 1807, Justice for
Belle View Township, Ste. Genevieve.

(58) John Callaway: (APT) August 26, 1807, Justice for
St. Michael Township, Ste. Genevieve.

(59) Michael Hart: (APT) August 26, 1807, Justice for
Breton Township, Ste. Genevieve.

(60) Nathl. Cook: (APT) August 26, 1807, Justice for
St. Michael Township, Ste. Genevieve.

(61) Jonathan Weeds: (APT) August 20, 1807, Justice for
Lower Cuivre Township, St. Charles.

(62) Christopher Clark: (APT) August 20, 1807, Justice
for Upper Cuivre, Township, St. Charles.

(63) Thomas Smith: (APT) August 20, 1807, Justice for
Femme Osage Township, St. Charles.

(64) Daniel Boone: (APT) August 20, 1807, Justice for
Femme Osage Township, St. Charles.

(65) Warren Cottle: (APT) August 20, 1807, Justice for
Dardenne Township, St. Charles.

(66) William McConnell: (APT) August 20, 1807, Justice
for Dardenne Township, St. Charles.

(67) Antonie Janis: (APT) August 20, 1807, Justice of
St. Charles Township, St. Charles.

(68) Francis Duquette: (APT) August 20, 1807, Justice of
of St. Charles Township, St. Charles.

(69) James Morrison: (APT) August 20, 1807, Justice of
St. Charles Township, St. Charles.

(70) Ebenezer Ayres: (APT) August 20, 1807, Justice of
Portage des Sioux Township, Missouri.

(71) Francois LeSieur: (APT) August 20, 1807, Justice of
Portage des Sioux Township, St. Charles.

(72) Jacob Kelly: (APT) August 20, 1807, Justice of St.
Francois Township, Cape Girardeau.

(Appointments Continued)

(73) Enoch Evans: (APT) August 20, 1807, Justice of Cape Girardeau Township, Cape Girardeau.

(74) Stephen Ross: (APT) August 20, 1807, Justice of Big Prairie Township, New Madrid.

(75) Benj. Shell: (APT) August 20, 1807, Justice of German Township, Cape Girardeau.

(76) Frederick Bollinger: (APT) August 20, 1807, Justice of German Township, Cape Girardeau.

(77) John Davis: (APT) August 20, 1807, Justice of Byrd Township, Cape Girardeau.

(78) William Mathews: (APT) August 20, 1807, Justice of Byrd Township, Cape Girardeau.

(79) Obadiah Woodson: (APT) August 20, 1807, Justice of New Madrid Township, New Madrid.

(80) Edward Matthers, jr.: (APT)August 20, 1807, Justice of Tywappity Township, New Madrid.

(81) Francois LeSieur: (APT) August 20, 1807, Justice of Little Prairie Township, New Madrid.

(82) George Ruddell: (APT) August 20, 1807, Justice of Little Prairie Township, New Madrid.

(83) Robert Blair: (APT) October 1, 1807, Justice of the Peace, Cape Girardeau Township, Cape Girardeau.

(84) Alexander McNair: (APT) December 14, 1807, Commissioner of Rates and Levies for the District of St. Louis. Appointment is until August 15, 1809.

(85) Samuel Solomon: (APT) January 29, 1808, Coroner for District of St. Louis. He declined the appointment.

(86) David Delaunay: (APT) December 14, 1807, Commissioner of Rates and Levies. Appointment is until August 15, 1808.

(87) James McCulloch: (APT) January 24, 1809, Justice of the Peace for Joachim Township, St. Louis.

(88) Eli B. Clemson: (APT) December 20, 1807, Justice of the Peace for St. Ferdinand Township, St. Louis.

(89) William Russell: (APT) October 23, 1807, Justice of the Peace for St. Louis Township, St. Louis. He declined the appointment.

(90) James Mackay: (APT) January 20, 1808, Justice of the Peace for Bon Homme Township, St. Louis.

(91) Joseph Tucker: (APT) October 14, 1807, Justice of the Peace for Ste. Genevieve Township, Ste. Genvevieve.

(92) James Rankin: (APT) October 9, 1807, Captain of a Mounted Riflemen, Third Battalion, First Regiment.

(93) Michael Armoureaux: (APT) January 10, 1808, Impowered to administer the oaths of office.

(94) Thomas Comstock: (APT) October 9, 1807, Justice of the Peace, Joachim Township, St. Louis.

(Appointments Continued)
  (95) John Perry: (APT) October 3, 1808, Justice of the
       Peace, Breton Township, Ste. Genevieve.
  (96) Thomas Oliver: (APT) September 1, 1807, Notary Pub-
       lic for a period of five years for the District of
       Ste. Geneveive.
  (97) Joseph Perkins: (APT)September 26, 1807, Lieutenant
       in Richard G. Bibb's Volunteer Company of Riflemen,
       Second Battalion, Second Regiment.
  (98) Jeduthan Kendall: (APT) September 26, 1807, Major
       Third Battalion, First Regiment.
  (99) Richard G. Bibb: (APT) September 26, 1807, Captain
       of Volunteer Company of Riflemen, Second Battalion,
       Second Regiment.
 (100) Job Westover: (APT) September 26, 1807, Ensign in
       Richard G. Bibb's Company of Volunteer Riflemen.
 (101) Elisha Goodrich: (APT) April 4, 1808, Justice of
       the Peace St. Charles Township, St. Charles.
 (102) Jno. E. Hart: (APT) April 4, 1807, Sheriff of Dis-
       trict of New Madrid.
 (103) Rysdon H. Price: December 20, 1807, Justice of the
       Peace St. Ferdinand Twonship, St. Louis.
 (104) Joseph Hunter: (APT) January 10, 1808, Judge of the
       Court of Common Please and Quarter Sessions for a
       period of four years for the Dist. of New Madrid.
 (105) William Reed, sr., : (APT) January 8, 1808, Justice
       of the Peace for Belle View Township, Ste. Gene-
       vieve.
 (106) John Coons: (APT) February 1, 1808, Coroner for the
       District of St. Louis.
 (107) Saml. Hammond, jr.: (APT)February 29, 1808, Sheriff
       of the District of New Madrid. He declined the
       appointment.
 (108) Joseph McFerron: (APT) March 15, 1808, Clerk of the
       Court of Common Pleas and Quarter Sessions, (APT)
       March 16, 1808, Impowered to administer the oaths
       of office.
 (109) Benard Pratte: (APT) March 16, 1808, Impowered to
       administer the oaths of office in the Louisiana
       Territory.
 (110) Thomas Comstock: (APT) March 11, 1808, Lieutenant
       in Captain Rankin's Company of Mounted Riflemen.
 (111) William Gibson: (APT) March 11, 1808, Ensign in
       Captain Rankin's Company of Mounted Riflemen.
 (112) John Steward: (APT) March 11, 1808, Burser in Capt.
       Rankin's Company of Mounted Riflemen.
 (113) Benjamin Baker: (APT) March 11, 1808, Adjustant and
       Paymaster for Captain Rankin's Company of Mounted
       Riflemen.

(Appointments Continued)

(114) Mackay Wherry: (APT) April 4, 1808, Captain of a Cavalry Troop in St. Louis.

(115) Joseph Beaty: (APT) April 4, 1808, Lieutenant in Mackay Wherry's Troop of Cavalry.

(116) James Callaway: (APT) April 4, 1808, Cornet in Mackay Wherry's Troop of Cavalry.

(117) Benj. Allen: (APT) April 4, 1808, Burser of Mackay Wherry's Troop of Cavalry.

(118) Robert McKay: (APT) May 16, 1808, Coroner of the District of New Madrid.

(119) John Baptiste Olive: (APT) May 16, 1808, Treasurer of New Madrid.

(120) Joseph Lafresniere: (APT) May 16, 1808, Justice of the Peace for New Madrid Township, New Madird.

(121) John E. Hart: (APT)May 16, 1808, Colonel Commandant of the Fifth Regiment.

(122) Stephen Ross: (APT)May 16, 1808, Major of the First Battalion, Fifth Regiment.

(123) James Trotter: (APT) May 16, 1808, Captain First Battalion, Fifth Regiment.

(124) Robert Trotter: (APT) May 16,1808, Lieutenant First Battalion, Fifth Regiment.

(125) Amos Rawls: (APT) May 16, 1808, Captain Second Battalion, Fifth Regiment.

(126) Franklin J. Smith: (MD) May 16, 1808, Surgeon Fifth Regiment.

(127) Joseph N. Armoureaux: (APT) May 16, 1808, Paymaster Fifth Regiment.

(128) Joseph Jacobs: (APT) May 16, 1808, Quarter Master Fifth Regiment.

(129) Thomas Ward Cauk: (APT) May 16, 1808, Lieutenant Second Battalion, Fifth Regiment.

(130) James Faris: (APT) May 16, 1808, Ensign Second Battalion, Fifth Regiment.

(131) John G. Heth: (APT)June 6, 1808, Clerk of the Court of Common Pleas and Quarter Sessions for the St. Charles District; (APT) July 7, 1808, Justice of the Peace for the District of St. Charles; (APT) July 8, 1808, Treasurer for the District of St. Charles.

(132) Manuel Andre Roche: (APT) July 25, 1808, Justice of the Peace for St. Charles Township, District of St. Charles.

(133) Stephen Byrd: (APT) August 5, 1808, Judge for the Court of Common Pleas and Quarter Sessions for the District of Cape Girardeau.

(134) Benjamin Fooy: (APT) May 18, 1808, Justice of the Peace for Arkansas Township, New Madrid District.

(Appointments Continued)
- (135) George Armistead: (APT) May 18, 1808, Justice of the Peace for Arkansas Township, New Madrid District.
- (136) Francis Vaugine: (APT) August 20, 1808, Judge of the Court of Common Pleas and Quarter Sessions for a period of four years for the Arkansas District.
- (137) Joseph Stillwell: (APT) August 22, 1808, Judge of the Court of Common Pleas and Quarter Sessions for a period of four years for the Arkansas District.
- (138) Charles Refeld: (APT) August 22, 1808, Judge of the Court of Common Pleas and Quarter Sessions for a period of four years for the Arkansas District.
- (139) Benjamin Fooy: (APT) August 22, 1808, Judge for the Court of Common Pleas and Quarter Sessions for a period of four years for the Arkansas District.
- (140) Jno. Honey: (APT) August 22, 1808, Clerk of the Court of Common Pleas and Quarter Sessions for the District of Arkansas, (APT) August 22, 1808, Probate Judge, Treasurer, and Recorder for the Arkansas District.
- (141) Andrew Fagot: (APT)August 22, 1808, Coroner, Notary Public and Justice of the Peace for the District of Arkansas.

Marion County, Missouri, Members Of The Grand Jury, October, 1828.

John Gash, John McWilliams, George W. Lane,William Ralls, John David, Thomas Cobb, John Randol, Joshua Feazel, William McRae, Thomas Lewis, John F. Thrasher, John Sites, jr., Wm. Miller, William Henry, Gabriel Turner, Hugh Henry,Washington Young, Dabney A. Bowles, Levi B. Allen,Jacob Matthews, Elias Thrasher, Abraham Bird.

Jackson County, Missouri, Delinquent Tax List, 1829.

Benjamin Baron, Tapley Bingham, John Bostick, Jonathan G. Fugate, James Johnston, James P. Kipper, Joseph M. Kinion, Zachariah Zinnville, Joseph Matlock, Ashford Nolad, Rebecca Ware, Louis Uneau.

Chartion County, Missouri First Loan Office, Persons Listed On The Proceedings Of The County Clerk (Certificates, Interest, Warrants, etc.) From January 7, 1824 to July 7, 1825, Capitol Fire Documents, CFD 69, Folder 6549.

Pleasant Browder, Wm. Pearson, Solomon Kimsey, Joel King, John M. Bell, James Earickson, Abram Lock, Edward B. Cabell, Isaac Campbell, Jas. Richardson, Little B. Witt, John Moore, Ephraim Moore, Saml. Marrs, Nat. Todd, Lewis Newton, Eliza. Williams, John Holman, Wm. W. Monroe.

St. Charles County, Missouri, Third Loan Office, October 12, 1821 to January 11, 1822,Report On Certificates and Installments, Capitol Fire Documents, CFD 69, Folder 6559.

CERTIFICATES

Debtor	Loan Date	Due Date	Security
Anthony E. Reaile	10-12-1821	10-12-1822	Uriah S. Devore
William Postal	10-13-1821	10-13-1822	Real Estate
Hiram H. Baber	10-15-1821	10-15-1822	Uriah S. Devore
Uriah S. Devore	10-15-1821	10-15-1822	Hiram H. Baber
James Devore	10-15-1821	10-15-1822	S. M. Forman and J. Millington
Thomas French	10-15-1821	10-15-1822	Jerem. Millington
--- Leduc	10-15-1821	10-15-1822	Real Estate
Ebenezer Ayres	10-15-1821	10-15-1822	E. D. Ayres
Joseph W. Ganaty	10-16-1821	10-16-1822	Solomon Whitley
John Jacoby	10-17-1821	10-17-1822	Real Estate
Frances Allen	10-17-1821	10-17-1822	E. Collard
John F. McKnight	10-17-1821	10-17-1822	Wallace Kirkpatrick
Mashal Mann	10-18-1821	10-18-1822	Real Estate
Samuel Caldwell	10-18-1821	10-18-1822	Real Estate
Ruduff Peck	10-19-1821	10-19-1822	Chauncey Shepherd
Chauncey Shephard	10-19-1821	10-19-1822	Ruduff Peck
David Lamaster	10-19-1821	10-19-1822	John Green
David Bailey	10-19-1821	10-19-1822	Samuel Bailey
Samuel Bailey	10-19-1821	10-19-1822	David Bailey
Taylor P. Lilley	10-20-1821	10-20-1822	Real Estate
Griffith Brown	10-20-1821	10-20-1822	Real Estate
Peter Blount	10-20-1821	10-20-1822	Real Estate
William Lamme	10-22-1821	10-22-1822	Daniel Colgan,sr.
John McKay	10-23-1821	10-23-1822	David Lamaster
Zadoc Woods	10-25-1821	10-23-1822	James Woods
James Murdock	10-29-1821	10-29-1822	Antoine Reynold
Rufus Pettibone	10-29-1821	10-29-1822	Levi Pettibone
James Jones	10-29-1821	10-29-1822	Real Estate
Joasdose (sic) Robideux	10-29-1821	10-29-1822	Andre St. August
Jesse Morrison	10-30-1821	10-30-1822	Real Estate
Rufus Easton	10-30-1821	10-30-1822	Oliver Cottle
James Morrison	10-31-1821	10-30-1822	Real Estate
John Venables	10-31-1821	10-30-1822	James Johnson
Benjamin Emmons	11-01-1821	11-01-1822	Benona R. Gillett
Saml. K. Caldwell	11-01-1821	11-01-1822	John White and Jno. Venables
John Harriman	11-02-1821	11-02-1822	Osborn Thruett
George R. Spencer	11-02-1821	11-02-1822	Real Estate
John Estes	11-05-1821	02-05-1822	Beischell Allen
Alexander Garvin	11-05-1821	11-05-1822	John Garvin
Joel F. Praer(sic)	11-07-1822	11-07-1822	Charles Denny

(St. Charles Loan Office Continued)

Debtor	Loan Date	Due Date	Security
William Wooten	11-08-1821	11-08-1822	Real Estate
Levi Pettibone	11-09-1821	11-09-1822	Rufus Pettibon
Bernard F. Thornton	11-10-1821	11-10-1822	Andrew Wilson
David Gainsay	11-10-1821	11-10-1822	Real Estate
John Lanton (sic)	11-13-1821	11-13-1822	Real Estate
F. Craig Durouchier	11-13-1821	11-13-1822	Daniel Colgan,sr.
William A. Lynch	11-13-1821	11-13-1822	Nathaniel Lynch
De De Thier	11-14-1821	11-14-1822	Real Estate
Alexander Ford	11-15-1821	11-15-1822	Real Estate
William Eckert	11-14-1821	11-14-1822	John Rochester
Anthony E. Reile	11-14-1821	11-14-1822	Antoine Reynold

INSTALLMENTS

Receiver	Received Date	Amount
Peter Didier	10-11-1821	$4,300
Peter Didier	10-18-1821	4,000
Peter Didier	10-20-1821	4,000
Peter Didier	11-08-1821	5,000
Peter Didier	11-29-1821	600
Peter Didier	12-08-1821	600
Peter Didier	12-22-1821	1,300

St. Charles County, Missouri, Third Loan Office, Monies Received For Warrants and Certificates, Capitol Fire Documents, CFD 69, Folder 6565.

Name	Received Date
Joshua Beauchamp	January 14, 1826
Alexander Garvin	November 28, 1825
Foster I. McKnight	March 18, 1826
Michael I. Noyes	January 21, 1826
Ruduff Peck	March 31, 1826
John Richard	March 29, 1826
Prospect K. Robbins	March 29, 1826
William Watson	March 29, 1826
James Woods	February 9, 1826
James Reynolds	October 8, 1825

Marion County, Missouri, Members of the Grand Jury, February Term, 1829.

William Muldrow, James Leary, Reuben Long,Andrew Muldrow, Jeptha Thurman, William W. Lewis, Willian Whaley, Parmenium B. Pritchard, Albert Whaley, Jeremiah Turpin,Rich. W. Jones, John Lowry, Moses D. Bates, John Godman, Abraham Bird, John Rhodes, James B. Ryland, Brian Cockrum, Joseph Holdman, Jos. D. Gash, Benjamin Forman, Squire Bozarth.

Jasper County, Missouri, Cave Spring Cemetery.

Name	Born	Died
Bushrod W. Richardson	Jan. 11, 1823	Mar. 17, 1897
Angeline Nichols	Sep. 13, 1814	Jan. 30, 1880
Frederick B. Nichols	Aug. 20, 1811	May 26, 1869
Rebecca E. Mize	Jun. 27, 1837	Mar. 11, 1889
Harvey K. Hoshaw	Dec. 27, 1837	Dec. 25, 1876
Elizabeth Smith	1836	1891
S. T. Vittow	1817	1891
Sarah J. Vittow	1827	1892
Findley M. Hoshaw	Aug. 4, 1831	Jan. 3, 1874
*Jane Cox Hoshaw	Mar. 25, 1792	
*(Died Sangannon (sic) County, Illinois)		
Jacob Hoshaw	1770	1855
Betty A. Hoshaw	1835	1858
Nancy C. Abston	1822	1882
Celia Grigg	1837	1898
Beaty Forsythe	1802	1877
John W. Duncan	1834	1860
Eliza Duncan	1812	1884
William Duncan	1806	1892
Moses Duncan (age: 81 y)		1845
Sarah Duncan (age: 81 Y)		1848
Jackson Crockett	Feb. 7, 1823	Nov. 5, 1860
Delilah Arnold	Mar. 3, 1838	Jun. 8, 1898
Jane Blake	Dec. 14, 1821	Nov. 28, 1892
Joseph Blake	Sep. 6, 1825	Sep. 19, 1846
Joseph Blake (sic)	Feb. 17, 1817	Jul. 22, 1855
*Samuel P. Binney	Dec. 27, 1806	Oct. 19, 1878
*(Born Indiana)		
Martha A. Binney	Dec. 9, 1819	Mar. 1, 1878
Joshua Abston	1814	1862

Marion County, Missouri,Case of Abraham Huntsberry vs. Lewis Vanlandingham, February, 1829, Jury Members.

Jury: William S. Dickerson, Kemp Anderson,Joseph Maxwell, Robert G. Dusty, Edward White, Benjamin Means,Mathias Brant, William Garner, John Lear, James Kindrick, Abraham K. Frye, John Anderson.

Ralls County, Missouri,A List Of Persons From Whom The Clerk Collected Monies From January 1, 1826 to October 12, 1826, Capitol Fire Documents, CFD 26, Folder 742.

Name	Date Collected
M. D. Bates	February 1, 1826
L. Bohannon	February 15, 1826
A. Gamble	February 15, 1826
R. Easton	February 15, 1826
A. K. Fry	February 15, 1826

(Ralls County, Missouri Continued)

Name	Date Collected
C. Markle, jr.	February 18, 1826
M. D. Bates	February 18, 1826
E. White	March 15, 1826
J. Morris	March 15, 1826
Ralls' heirs	March 28, 1826
L. Rorter (sic)	April 20, 1826
W. Dunkin	April 22, 1826
R. R. Carson	April 22, 1826
E. White	May 4, 1826
J. D. Caldwell	May 10, 1826
John M'Gee	June 5, 1826
Stephen Glascock	June 5, 1826
J. Rolett	June 9, 1826
R. R. Carson	June 18, 1826
W. Wiley	June 18, 1826
A. Bird	June 18, 1826
P. Glascock	June 18, 1826
M. Gentry	June 19, 1826
A. Clark	August 7, 1826

Marion County, Missouri,State vs. Washington Young, February Term, 1830.

Jury: Preston Parent, Inskeep Forman, Staunton Buckner, Edward Whaley, Clement White, Site Hampton, Harrison Sparks, Benjamin Duncan, Benjamin Flemming, Stephen McRae, James Kendrick, Jesse Gentry.

Lincoln County, Missouri, Public Securities From February 5, 1827 to June 4, 1827, Capitol Fire Documents, CFD 26, Folder 753.

Name	Date Collected
John Geiger	February 8, 1827
Christopher Clark	February 8, 1827
August Chouteau	February 8, 1827
Richard Ripley	February 8, 1827
Murvin Ross	February 15, 1827
William Herbet	March 10, 1827
James Gibson	March 15, 1827
George Riply	March 19, 1827
David Porter	March 26, 1827
V. J. Peers	April 9, 1827
H. H. Hoodbridge	April 9, 1827
V. J. Peers	April 10, 1827
John Geiger	February 15, 1827
Z. G. Draper	June 2, 1827

Coroner's Inquest, State vs Samuel Means,Territoral Court, July 11, 1813.

Jury of inquest convicted Samuel Means on July 4, 1813 as causing the death of a negro boy.

Jury: Joseph James, Wm. Patterson, Elisha Patterson, Jehu Brown, Samuel Hodges,John Patterson,James James,Danl. Biggs, James Standley, John C. James, Robert Jefferies.

A List Of Persons Against Whom Warrants Were Executed,United States vs. Joseph Leblanc, May Term, 1814, Territorial Court

Mather Kerr, Baptist Belovit, William Jones, John Ball, George W. Ferguson, Adam Woolfort, Peter Primm, Francois M. Benoit, Henry Campbell, John Cromwell, Joshua Farland, John McKnight, Cornelius Barns, Charles Bossorion,Christian Witt, David Deloney, Joseph Phillipson, Jose D. Russell, Alexander Lucas, James Irvin, George Choutly, Antoine Bonoit, John H. Reed, Archd. McDonald, Alexander McCloud, Adam J. Whitside, Moses Martin, Abraham Musick, Jacob Eastwood, Josiah Fugitt, Charles Foublet, Vincent Coince, Elisha Patterson, Barnabas Harris, Paul Whittley, Joseph Pamms, John Houdershell,Martin Douglass, Thomas Washington, Levi Martin, sr., Bartholomew Berthold, Alexander Belluame, Joseph Cunningham, George C. Sibley.

Lafayette County, Missouri, Delinquent Tax List, 1837, Capitol Fire Docuemtns, CFD, 30, Folder 1239.

Ezekial Cox, Elihue Cox, Joshua Cox, Samuel Cox,Catharine Crisman, James Craig, Mary Callaway, George Coatney, William Dunnaway, Washington Coatney, Ellis Doctor, Jesse Lea, James Fulton, Charles Higgins, Jesse Lightner, Hezekiah Pollard, William Robineto, jr., Polly Robinetto, Robert I. Smith, Wm. Tisdale, Perry Stacy, Campbell Vineyard, Eli B. Wilson, John Gosham, Thomas Ferrel, Flannery Manoill, Hannah Rumard, Wm. A. Watson, Nathaniel Davis, Hisakiah Pollard, Adison Rice, Benjamin Porter,Arthur Scott,Benjamin Elliott,Robert Farley.

Boone County, Missouri, Grandview Cemetery, Rt. HH, North Of Columbia, Missouri.

Name	Born	Died
Alfred S. Kile	Sep. 24, 1825	Feb. 17, 1897
William Harrison Brown	Feb. 28, 1832	Jan. 22, 1898
D. A. Rouse	May 21, 1823	Nov. 2, 1890
Leonard Bugg	Sep. 14, 1822	Oct. 19, 1885
*Abner E. Armstrong	Apr. 17, 1809	Apr. 3, 1887
*(Born Fleming County, Kentucky)		
Nancy Berry (age: 61 y, 22 d)		Sep. 18, 1866
Evaline Drennon	Sep. 3, 1811	Feb. 28, 1887
Henry Berry (age: 73 y, 8 m, 24 d)		Jun. 20, 1867
Malina Rouse (age: 66 y, 7 m, 18 d)		Feb. 18, 1892

(Boone County, Missouri Continued)

Name	Born	Died
Susan H. Armstrong	Aug. 31, 1810	Feb. 9, 1899

Marion County, Missouri, Grand Jury Members, June, 1829.

James McWilliams, Robert G. Dudley, Anselm C. Parith,John
Gath, Josiah Culbertson, James Able, Thomas J. Davis,Preston
Parent, Thomas Threlkeld, David Jacobs, Joseph Haydon, Jacob
Matthews, James B. Ryland, Burgess Lake,Jeremiah Turpin,Hugh
M. Anderson, Ballard Lake, Elijah Rice, Benjamin Bowles,Geo.
A. Nesbitt, Henry Taylor.

Howard County, Missouri, Pre-emptions Granted,Franklin Land District, June 3, 1819, Registrar and Receiver's Office at Franklin, Missouri.

Name	Acres	Location
James Alcorn	240	S28-T48-R16
Middleton Anderson	236.74	S24-T49-R18
Isaac Drake	160	S7-T49-R16
William Wardin	160	S36-T49-R17
Peter Creason	260.50	S21-T49-R16
John Hancock	121.60	S14-T49-R18
William Thorp	187.47	S24-T49-R18
Otho Ashcraft	82.05	S31-T49-R17
John Cooley	160	S5-T49-R16
Andrew Smith	160	S24-T49-R17
Joseph Moody	240	S9-T49-R16
James Alexander	274.93	S5-R48-R17
Daniel Crump	160	S29-T49-R16
David McGee	160	S20-T49-R18
William Pipes	160	S20-T49-R16
Joseph Fields	103.04	S31-T49-R16
John Busby's heirs	187.26	S3 & 4-T49-R18
Fanny Cooper's heirs	162.12	S5-T49-R18
Gray Bynum	160	S18-T49-R18
James McMahan	160	S17-T49-R18
Hannah Cole	240	S25-T49-R18
David McClain	195.75	S30-T49-R16
Abner Johnson	240	S9-T49-R18
Joseph and David Boggs	480	S10-T49-R16
Samuel Brown, sr. and Robert Brown	444.40	S19-T49-R16
John Cooper	160	S11-T49-R18
Joseph Wolfscale	189.63	S23 & 13-T49-R18
Amos Barnes	192.64	S5-T48-R16
David Kinkaid	283.60	S31 & 38-T49-R16
John Ferril	160	S14-T49-R18
William Cooper	312.06	S12-T50-R19
Thomas Chandler	176.94	S31-T49-R16

(Howard County, Missouri Continued)

Name	Acres	Location
William Brown	171.36	S18-T49-R17
Joseph Cooley	220.25	S8-T49-R16
Perrin Cooley	259.75	S8-T49-R16
Sarshal Cooper's heirs	291.33	S14-T49-R16
Benjamin Cooper, jr.	160	S11-T49-R18
Benjamin Cooper, sr.	166.37	S11-T49-R18
Thomas McMahan	160	S17-T49-R18
William Reed and Frederick Hiatt	388	S7-T49-R18
Phoebe Cole	193.84	S31-T49-R16
Samuel McMahan's heirs	160	S20-T49-R18
David Jones and Stephen Turley	470.18	S28-T49-R18
Jesse Cox	160	S7-T50-R18
Jeremiah and Margarett Gregg heirs of Wm. Gregg	160	S12-T50-R19
Ruben Fugitt's heirs	160	S20-T49-R16
Abbot Hancock	160	S11-T49-R18
Robert Hancock	271.96	S35-T50-R18
Stephen Jackson	108	S24-T49-R18
Robert Irvin's heirs	80	S3-T49-R18
Mathew Kinkaid	203.70	S31-T49-R16
William McMahan	299.75	S25-T49-R18
Adam McCord	160	S35-T49-R17
James Richardson's heirs	240	S16-T49-R16
William Ridgway	167.64	S5-T48-R16
John Stevenson	240	S30-T49-R16
Levi Todd	240	S16-T49-R16
James Jones' heirs	189.63	S30-T49-R17
Adam Woods	221.22	S10-T49-R18

St. Charles County, Missouri, Third Loan Office,February 17, 1823 to April 1, 1825, Capiotl Fire Documents, CFD 69,Folder 6562.

Debtor	Due Date	Secured	1st Installment
Anthony E. Reile	Oct. 12, 1822	Personal	Apr. 12, 1823
Hiram Baber	Oct. 15, 1822	Personal	Apr. 15, 1823
Thomas French	Oct. 15, 1822	Personal	Apr. 15, 1823
Uriah I. Devore	Oct. 15, 1822	Personal	Apr. 15, 1823
James Devore	Oct. 15, 1822	Personal	Apr. 15, 1823
Antoine Leclair	Oct. 15, 1822	Mortgage	Apr. 15, 1823
Joseph W. Garraty	Oct. 16, 1822	Personal	Apr. 16, 1823
Solomon Whitley	Oct. 16, 1822	Personal	Apr. 16, 1823
John Jacoby	Oct. 17, 1822	Mortgage	Apr. 17, 1823
Francis Allen	Oct. 17, 1822	Personal	Apr. 17, 1823
Samuel K. Caldwell	Oct. 18, 1822	Mortgage	Apr. 18, 1823
David Lamasters	Oct. 19, 1822	personal	Apr. 19, 1823

(St. Charles County, Missouri Continued)

Debtor	Due Date	Secured	1st Installment
Peter Bland	Oct. 20, 1822	Mortgage	Apr. 20, 1823
Griffith Brown	Oct. 20, 1822	Mortgage	Apr. 20, 1823
Peter Brusterra	Oct. 22, 1822	Mortgage	Apr. 22, 1823
Zadock Woods	Oct. 25, 1822	Personal	Apr. 25, 1823
Rufus Pettibone	Oct. 29, 1822	Personal	Apr. 29, 1823
Rufus Easton	Oct. 30, 1822	Personal	Apr. 30, 1823
James Morrison	Oct. 31, 1822	Mortgage	Apr. 31, 1823
Benjamin Emmons	Nov. 1, 1822	Personal	May 1, 1823
Alexander Garvin	Nov. 5, 1822	Personal	May 5, 1823
F. Preur (sic)	Nov. 7, 1822	Personal	May 7, 1823
Levi Pettibone	Nov. 9, 1822	Personal	May 9, 1823
Howard F. Thornton	Nov. 10, 1822	Personal	May 10, 1823
John Stanton	Nov. 13, 1822	Mortgage	May 13, 1823
St. Croix Durocher	Nov. 13, 1822	Personal	May 13, 1823
William Eckert	Nov. 14, 1822	Personal	May 14, 1823
Prospeck K. Robbins	Nov. 20, 1822	Personal	May 20, 1823
A. E. Reile	Nov. 20, 1822	Personal	May 20, 1823
U. I. Devore	Nov. 24, 1822	Mortgage	May 24, 1823
James Green	Nov. 27, 1822	Personal	May 27, 1823
Thomas Jones	Nov. 27, 1822	Personal	May 27, 1823
James Woods	Nov. 22, 1822	Personal	May 22, 1823
Samuel K. Caldwell	Dec. 1, 1822	Personal	Jun. 1, 1823
Samuel H. Lewis	Dec. 1, 1822	Personal	Jun. 1, 1823
Antoine Janis, sr.	Dec, 3, 1822	Personal	June. 3, 1823
E. Lmasters	Dec. 6, 1822	Personal	Jun. 6, 1823
William G. Pettus	Dec. 8, 1822	Personal	Jun. 8, 1823
William Smith	Dec. 8, 1822	Personal	Jun. 8, 1823
John Richard	Dec. 8, 1822	Personal	Jun. 8, 1823
William Watson	Dec. 8, 1822	Personal	Jun. 8, 1823
Seth Allen	Dec. 11, 1822	Personal	Jun. 11, 1823
David Sharmon	Dec. 13, 1822	Mortgage	Jun 13, 1823
John McDonald	Dec. 13, 1822	Personal	Jun. 13, 1823
James Johns	Dec. 15, 1822	Mortgage	Jun. 15, 1823
James Watson	Dec. 17, 1822	Personal	Jun. 17, 1823
William Bray	Dec. 19, 1822	Personal	Jun. 19, 1823
Benjamin Garvin	Dec. 22, 1822	Personal	Jun. 22, 1823
Jacques Dubois	Dec. 22, 1822	Personal	Jun. 22, 1823
Andrew Wilson	Dec. 22, 1822	Mortgage	Jun. 22, 1823
John J. Wheeler	Dec. 22, 1822	Mortgage	Jun. 22, 1823
John Bivins	Jan. 5, 1823	Personal	Jul. 5, 1823
Charles S. Drury	Jan. 5, 1823	Personal	Jul. 5, 1823
L. F. Collins	Jan. 21, 1823	Personal	Jul. 21, 1823
Samuel Kean	Jan. 29, 1823	Mortgage	Jul. 29, 1823
Joseph B. Yater	Feb. 13, 1823	Personal	Aug. 16, 1823
John Martin	Feb. 16, 1823	Personal	Aug. 16, 1823
Kenedy Frier	Feb. 16, 1823	Personal	Aug. 16, 1823
Alphsono Boon	Feb. 16, 1823	Personal	Aug. 16, 1823

Debtor	Due Date	Secured	1st Installment
William Baxley	Mar. 1, 1823	Personal	Sep. 1, 1823
Charles Williams	Mar. 1, 1823	Personal	Sep. 1, 1823
Thomas Gibson	Mar. 2, 1823	Personal	Sep. 2, 1823
John Sullins	Mar. 2, 1823	Personal	Sep. 2, 1823
Richard Kerr	Mar. 2, 1823	Personal	Sep. 2, 1823
James Johnson	Mar. 4, 1823	Personal	Sep. 4, 1823
Nathaniel Simonds	Mar. 4, 1823	Mortgage	Sep. 4, 1823
C. C. Easton	Mar. 5, 1823	Personal	Sep. 5, 1823
Otis Peck	Mar. 9, 1823	Personal	Sep. 9, 1823
Sylvester Pattie	Mar.18, 1823	Personal	Sep. 18, 1823
Joseph Inks	Mar.19, 1823	Personal	Sep. 19, 1823
James Reynolds	Mar.22, 1823	Personal	Sep. 22, 1823
John Reynolds	Mar.22, 1823	Personal	Sep. 22, 1823
Elias Jackson	Mar.23, 1823	Personal	Sep. 23, 1823
Moses Kerrey	Mar.23, 1823	Personal	Sep. 23, 1823
Charles B. Rouse	Mar.23, 1823	Personal	Sep. 23, 1823
John E. Allen	Mar.23, 1823	Mortgage	Sep. 23, 1823
Michael J. Noyes	Mar.23, 1823	Personal	Sep. 23, 1823
Noah Caton	Mar.30, 1823	Personal	Sep. 30, 1823
John Griffey	Apr. 6, 1823	Mortgage	Oct. 6, 1823
Robert Muin	May 21, 1823	Personal	Nov. 21, 1823
Jacob Myers	Jul.13, 1823	Personal	Jan. 7, 1824
John Walls	Jul.30, 1823	Personal	Jan. 30, 1824
Benjamin F. Todd	Sep.30, 1823	Personal	Mar. 30, 1824
William V. Rector	Nov. 2, 1823	Personal	May 2, 1824
Isreal B. Read	Nov. 2, 1823	Personal	May 2, 1824
Arch. Watson, sr.	Nov.11, 1823	Personal	May 11, 1824
Seth Millington	Dec. 4, 1823	Personal	Jun. 4, 1824
James Jones	Dec. 3, 1823	Mortgage	Jun. 3, 1824
John Shwimmer	Nov. 1, 1823	Personal	May 1, 1824
James Johnson	Nov. 4, 1823	Mortgage	May 4, 1824
John Venables	Nov. 4, 1823	Personal	May 4, 1824
John F. McKnight	Nov. 6, 1823	Personal	May 6, 1824
Marshal Man	Nov. 6, 1823	Mortgage	May 6, 1824
Isadore Rubidoux	Nov. 7, 1823	Personal	May 7, 1824
David Gainsay	Nov. 9, 1823	Mortgage	May 9, 1824
William Postal	Oct.31, 1822	Mortgage	Apr. 13, 1823
Ebenezer Ayres	Oct.15, 1822	Personal	Apr. 15, 1823
Ruduff Peck	Oct.19, 1822	Personal	Apr. 19, 1823
Samuel Bailey	Oct.19, 1822	Personal	Apr. 19, 1823
David Bailey	Oct.19, 1822	Personal	Apr. 19, 1823
Chancy Shepherd	Oct.19, 1822	Personal	Apr. 19, 1823
James Murdoch	Oct.29, 1822	Personal	Apr. 29, 1823
Jesse Morrison	Oct.30, 1822	Mortgage	Apr. 30, 1823
William Wooson	Nov. 8, 1822	Mortgage	May 8, 1823
Alexander Ford	Nov.15, 1822	Personal	May 15, 1823
Joshua Beauchamp	Nov.22, 1822	Mortgage	May 22, 1823

(St. Charles County, Missouri Continued)

Debtor	Due Date	Secured	1st Installment
John Miller	Nov.24, 1822	Personal	May 24, 1823
E. D. Ayres	Nov.26, 1822	Personal	May 26, 1823
W. Warren	Nov.29, 1822	Personal	May 29, 1823
John B. Brugiere	Dec.16, 1822	Personal	Jun. 16, 1823
Ahab Bean	Dec.17, 1822	Personal	Jun. 17, 1823
David Bailey	Dec.25, 1822	Personal	Jun. 25, 1823
John Young	Jan.19, 1823	Personal	Jul. 19, 1823
William Elgin	Jan. 5, 1823	Personal	Jul. 5, 1823
E. Beasley	Jan. 5, 1823	Personal	Jul. 5, 1823

Audrain County, Missouri,Fee Bill Of Sunday Suits Of Indict-Ments, December 16, 1839.

Joel Haynes, clerk; John Willingham, sheriff;Josiah Gant, witness; Thos. Gant, witness; Joseph Cook, witness; William C. West, witness; John Fawcett,witness;J.B. Hatten, witness; Thos. Hundle, witness; Jas. E. Fenton, witness; H.J.M. Doan, witness; Joseph Pearson, witness; Eli Smith, witness; T. M. Barnett, witness; B. B. Wilkerson, witness; Caleb Williams, witness; Harrison Howell, witness; Thos. Stricklin, witness; Joseph McDonald, witness.

Jackson County, Missouri, February, 1830, Licenses.

Saml. D. Lucas, merchant and liquor; James Aull,merchant; William Everet, ferry; Joseph Roy, liquor; L. Chouteau, merchant; Eli Roberts, liquor.

Pettis County, Missouri, Members Of The Grand Jury,November, 1837.

Clinton Young, Josiah Hall, William B. Smiley, William E. Anderson, William B. Smiley, Leonard Bouldin, Elijah Layton, Greenbury Greer, Benjamin Willoughby, Zadock Powell, Thomas Beaman, James Martin, Samuel Read, Arthur Patrick, Mason G. Pemberton, Benjamin O. Harrison, William Moseby, Thomas B. Marton, Abner Clopton, jr.

St. Francois County, Missouri, Public Securities, March 10, 1826 to November 8, 1826.

Name	Date
Isaac Cunningham	October 20, 1826
James Clark	November 2, 1826
Thomas Dunlap	August 8, 1826
William Evans	August 8, 1826
Henry Hunt	October 9, 1826
Jackson Rucker	October 20, 1826
Thomas Johnston	October 20, 1826
John Manchester	April 11, 1826
John Hunter	May 7, 1826

(St. Francois County, Missouri Continued)

Name	Date
James McFarland	October 20, 1826
Jno. Perry	March 15, 1826
Jno. Perry	April 4, 1826
Jno. Perry	May 8, 1826
Jno. Perry	July 7, 1826
Henry Polin	August 18, 1826
James Perry	October 11, 1826

St. Charles County, Missouri, Third Loan Office, Monies Received from November 5, 1826 to May 12, 1827, Capitol Fire Documents, CFD 69, Folder 6564.

Name	Date
David Sherman	October 8, 1826
Noah Caton	November 7, 1826
James Jones	January 3, 1827
Marshall Mann	February 1, 1827
M. J. Noyes	February 2, 1827
Griffith Brown	November 22, 1826
David Bailey	February 24, 1827
Samuel Bailey	February 24, 1827
John F. McKnight	March 6, 1827
C. C. Easton	February 8, 1827
Alexander Ford	February 8, 1827
Richard Kerr	February 8, 1827
Charles R. Rowe	February 24, 1827
Alphonse Boone	March 27, 1827
David Garnsley	March 30, 1827
Samuel Kean	March 30, 1827
James Johnson	January 2, 1827
James Woods	April 18, 1827
Warren Elgin	May 12, 1827

Pettis County, Missouri, Members Of The Grand Jury, July, 1838
   Jonathan Lussey, Ninian Steele, Henry Small, jr., Reubin Curnett, Alexander M. Christian, Montville Huff, Lalton Warden, Oswald Kidd, Mortimer F. Collier, William Anderson, William Obannon, Jesse Swope, James Dickinson, William Wright, Alfred Brock, Isaac Carver, Thomas W. Brooks, James T. Roberts.

Lafayette County, Missouri, Higginsville Brand German Cemetery

Name	Born	Died
Wilhelmina Hefmuller	Feb. 2, 1833	Dec. 27, 1872
Wilhelmine Gunthe	Jun. 29, 1814	Oct. 2, 1886
F. W. Welpmann	Dec. 18, 1838	Oct. 15, 1886
Peter H. Brand	Mar. 15, 1809	Jul. 11, 1880
- Frederick Hader	Dec. 24, 1838	Jul. 4, 1896
M. Clara Greifi	Jan. 2, 1826	Jan. 5, 1887

(Lafayette County, Missouri Continued)

Name	Born	Died
Maria F. Brand	Jun. 20, 1813	Jul. 17, 1887
Wilhelmiene Hader	Nov. 17, 1816	Dec. 18, 1884
John G. Hader	Mar. 7, 1815	Dec. 6, 1884

St. Charles County, Missouri, Third Loan Office, Monies Collected From May 12, 1827 to November 1, 1827, Capitol Fire Documents, CFD 69, Folder 6564.

Name	Payment Date
E. Beasley	May 19, 1827
David Garnsley	May 25, 1827
James Johnston	June 19, 1827
Venables & Johnston	June 19, 1827
White & Venables	June 19, 1827
Todd & Elgin	June 19, 1827
Bean & Behurst	June 19, 1827
Elgin, Beasley & Johnson	June 19, 1827
Lamaster & Morgan	June 19, 1827
Rouse & Cook	June 19, 1827
James Murdock	July 16, 1827
James Woods	July 28, 1827
Ebenezer Ayres	July 27, 1827
Archd. Watson	June 18, 1827
Alexr. Garvin	August 25, 1827
William Smith	September 30, 1827
Wynkoop Warner	September 27, 1827
Joshua Beauchamp	October 6, 1827
Seth Millington	September 4, 1827
E. D. Ayres	October 16, 1827

Ripley County, Missouri, Delinquent Tax List, 1836, Capitol Fire Documents, CFD 30, Folder 1242.

Moore Township: Sally Capps, William Galaher, Wm. Luncy, Daniel Rose.

Union Township: William Dalton, William Drake, Benjamin Drake, John Hobs, Mary Hobs.

Washington Township: James Brown, Griffin Emons, Daniel Emons, James Harris, James Hogh, John Lee, Silas M. Lerner, Silas Lemons, Young Lemons, Dempsey Odom, Henry Polrin, John Rite, Moses Smith, Harrel Street, James Threat.

Current River: Jonathan Burleson, George Coppage, Daniel Null, Jesse Dorman, Hiram Hobaugh, John Hobaugh, jr., Wm. N. Finkler, Thomas Montgomery.

Washington Griffin Emons, Daniel Emons, Peggy Humby, John Matney, Dempsey Odom, Moses Smith, Herold Street, Abraham Thompson.

Kelly Township: Michael Bunget, Henly Black, Wm. Moore, John Moore, William Matney, Sally Ward.

St. Charles County, Third Loan Office,Monies Collected From November 1, 1827 to April 1, 1828, Capitol Fire Documents, CFD 69, Folder 6564.

Name	Payment Date
Seth Allen	November 7, 1827
E. D. Ayres	November 27, 1827
Samuel Kean	October 28, 1827
U. S. Devore	October 28, 1827
Wynkeep Warner	October 28, 1827
James Johnson	October 28, 1827
William Wooson	December 25, 1827
James Green	February 1, 1828
John F. McKnight	February 16, 1828
Joseph Inks	March 11, 1828
Samuel Kean	January 15, 1828
M. S. Noyes	February 8, 1828
David Garnsley	February 8, 1828
E. Beasley	February 8, 1828
E. Lamasters	February 8, 1828
Alexr. Ford	February 8, 1828
Chs. R. Rouse	March 30, 1828

Osage County, Missouri, Salem Presbyterian Cemetery, Salem, Missouri.

Name	Born	Died
Ernest H. Rosenbaum	1811	1893
Fritz Ehlert	1830	1872
Frank Schollmeyer	1800	1888
J. Friederich Pauck	1810	1873
Peter Casper Uetterling	1802	1885
August Hummert	1836	1896
Wilheime Hummert	1807	1875
H. C. Carl Hummert	1801	1860
Carolina Schollmeyer	1839	1885
Wilhelmina Hoffman	1837	1878
Matthias Helmer	1800	1870

Benton County, Missouri, Licenses, May, 1837, Capitol Fire Documents, CFD 30, Folder 1215.

N. M. Sterret, A. Cornwall, Ringo Hopplin, L. Bledsoe,Wm. Birdwater, John Spence, Frances Redman.

Boone County, Missouri, Tax On Convictions, June, 1825, Capitol Fire Documents, CFD 26, Folder 693.

Richard Bibb, Thomas Barnes, Thomas D. Chavis, William I. Rice, Samuel Lemon, John B. Clark, Richard Gentry, Roger A. Todd, James Harrison, George Harrison, James D. Kirtley, P. H. D. McBride, Thomas Harrison, James P. Laughlin, Richard Samuel, Amos Mamay, William Martin, William Martin (sic), S.

(Boone County, Missouri Continued)
P. Nolan, Samuel Potts, James Turley, Gilpin Tuttle, Jesse T.
Wood, Willis West, John Williams.

St. Charles County, Missouri, Third Loan Office, Names Of
Persons Indebted To The State On February 18, 1824 For Cer-
ticates, Capitol Fire Documents, CFD 69, Folder 6561.
     Anthony E. Reilhe, Hiram H. Baker, Thomas French, Uriah I.
Devore, James Devore, Antoine Leclair, Joseph W. Garray, John
Jacoby, Solomon Whitley, Samuel H. Coldwell, David Lamasters,
Peter Bland, Griffith Brown, Zadock Woods, Rufus Easton, St.
Croix Durocher, Benjamin Emmons, Alexander Garvin, Howard F.
Thornton, Antoine Reilhe, Prospect K. Robbins, Uriah I. Devore,
James Green, Thomas Jones, James Woods, Samuel H. Coldwell,
Samuel H. Lewis, Antoine Janis, sr., E. Lamasters, William
Smith, John Richards, William Watson, Seth Allen, Sylvester
Pattie, David Shearman, Jacques Dubois, John Bevens, Charles
Drury, L. F. Collins, Samuel Kean, Kennady Frier, Alphonso
Boone, William Bailey, Charles Williams, Thomas Gibson, John
Sullens, Richard Kerr, James Johnson, C. C. Easton, Joseph
Inks, James Reynolds, John Reynolds, James Watson, Wm. Elgin,
James Watson, James Johns, John McDonald, E. Beasley, David
Bailey, John Young, Ahab Bean, John B. Bruzier, Ebenezer B.
Ayres, W. Warner, Joshua Beauchamp, Alexander Fourd, William
Wooton, James Murdoch, David Bailey, Samuel Bailey, Ebenezer
Ayres, Ruluff Peck, William Postal, David Garnsay, Isadore
Robedeaux, Marshal Man, John F. McKnight, James Jones, John
Veneables, James Johnson, Seth Millington, Isreal B. Read,
Archibald Watson, jr., William V. Rector, Benjamin L. Todd,
John Watts, Jacob Myers, Robert Muin, John Griffey, Michael
S. Noyes, Noah Caton, John E. Allen.

Cooper County, Missouri, Second Loan Office, January 1, 1830,
Capitol Fire Documents, CFD 69, Folder 6557.

Debtors	Security
Isaac Clark	Peter Stephens & James Bruffee
Charles R. Berry	James Berry
James Long	Churchill B. Ross
George Edgar	Reuben B. Harris
Ira A. Emmons	Ezekiel Williams
Amos Horn	James Crockett & William Horn
William Horn	James Crockett & Amos Horn
Henry Marmon	George Cathey
John T. Son	Robt. Pogur
John Minrs	Churchill B. Ross
James D. Campbell	William D. Wilson
Marcus Williams	Robt. P. Clark
Samuel Lapslry	William H. Adams
Marcus Williams	Benjamin T. Hickox

203

Debtor	Security
Justainian Williams	Robt. Boyd
Robt. Boyd	Benjamin T. Hickox
Henry Ruby	Thos. Ruby and Wm. Reed
William Carlisle	Wm. D. Wilson and Richard D. Shackleford
Benjamin Chambers	David Todd
Wm. M. Adams	Saml. Lasslry
William Savage	Mortgage
James Edgar	Libourn Wright and Geo. Edgar
Ezekiel Williams	Wm. Curtis and Absalom Riam
Cornelius Davis	George Bennett
James W. Maney	Austin K. Songan
James S. Collins	Lilbourn Wright
Wm. Ross	Church B. Ross
Thos. Densman	Saml. Lasslry
Robt. P. Clark	Marcus Williams
James Brown	Reuben B. Harris
Bazabell W. Levins	Gilbert Shorrs
Jabez Hubbard	Thos. Hubbard
Reubin B. Harris	James Edgar
John Fitzhugh	Thos. Fitzhugh
Charles Fourd	Frederick Conner
James Alexander	Saml. Lasslry
John C. Rochester	Wm. D. Wilson
Thos. Lynville	William Samms
Levi Odiniel	Saml. Johnson
Solomon Brown	Reubin B.Harris
John Fitzhugh	James Fitzhugh
William D. Wilson	Mortgage
William C. Porter	Churchill B. Ross
William Young	Phillip W. Thompson
Jabez Hubbard	William Ross
Churchill B. Ross	John Potter
William Reed	---
Thos. Rogers	Churchill B. Ross
Nathan Huff	Job McClanahan
Thos Burgin	Edward Bradley
John Potter	Churchill B. Ross
George C. Hartt	Robt. P. Clark
James Bruffee	Marcus Williams
John Williams	Williamson Curtis
Nicholas Senetchfield	Wm. Murphy, Darin Murphy and Robt. Johnston
Davis Murphy	Robt. Johnston
Alfred K. Stephens	Saml. Westmann
Saml. Westman	Alfred K. Stephens
Thos. Barlow	James Colirs

(Cooper County, Missouri)

Debtor	Security
Isaac Davis	Thos. and Cornelius Davis
John C. Rochester	Churchill B. Ross
James Edgar	William Savage
Stephen Cole	William Ross
Absalom Rain	Williamson Curtis

Lincoln County, Missouri, Licenses,1823 to 1824,Capitol Fire Documents, CFD 26, Folder 640.

Name	Type	Date
Francis Parker	Liquor	Mar. 17, 1824
Richard Fenton	Merchant	Apr. 19, 1824
Cary K. Duncan	Merchant	Apr. 28, 1824
Minerva Woods	Liquor	Nov. 5, 1823
Francis Parker	Liquor	Nov. 26, 1823
Emanuel Block	Merchant	Oct. 16, 1823
Joshua N. Robbins	Merchant	Mar. 13, 1823

Chariton County, Missouri, Fine Tax, 1823, Capitol Fire Documents, CFD 26, Folder 630.

D. H. Campbell, Levi Ellis, Geo. I. Foster, Josiah Foster, Jas. I. Foster, Perry B. Ray, Right Hill, Thos. D. Loney.

Osage County, Missouri, Useful Cemetery, Useful, Missouri.

Name	Born	Died
Joseph N. Rice	1822	1898
E. W. Anderson	1823	1894

Macon County, Missouri, Ballinger Cemetery, Near Calleo, MO On Hwy 612.

Name	Born	Died
Gid. Skinner	Aug. 12, 1827	Feb. 19, 1890
Mary C. Smoot	Feb. 2, 1836	Jul. 9, 1894

Audrain County, Missouri, Purchasers Of Town Lots In Mexico, May, 1839.

John Willingham, William B. Evans, Washington Kilgore, Wm. Sims, Caleb Williams, Thomas Kigore, sr.

Perry County, Missouri, Naturalizations, July, 1838.

Anthony Butz, Joseph Volz, sr., Anthony Flect, Ignatuis Bonnert, Joseph Berhrle, Mortez Berhrle, Frederick Sutter, Godfred Bleche, Martin Schneider of Baden.

INDEX

This index references all surnames found in the text,
including "dit" names, or aliases, used by the French.

--AKEY, 143
ABBEY, 143
ABBOT, 1 2
ABBOTT, 32 160 161 166 167 169
ABERNATHY, 87 88 147 149 153 154
   181
ABLE, 195
ABNATHER, 129
ABRAHAM, 2
ABSTON, 192
ACKERMAN, 98
ACLES, 13
ACTHERTON, 93
ACTTESSEL, 2
ADAIR, 3 20 117 120 124 181
ADAMS, 2 3 23 30-32 87 92 112 113
   120 124 127 129 143 179 203 204
ADDAR, 27
ADKINS, 32-34
ADKINSON, 119
ADTENTINE, 2
AGEE, 3 17 20 83
AGEY, 22
AGNES, 162
AGNEW, 146 157 160 164 168 169
AGUS, 161
AIRES, 154
AKENS, 13
AKER, 33
AKIN, 119
ALARY, 135
ALBRIGHT, 31
ALCORN, 195
ALDERSON, 6
ALEXANDER, 2-4 8 11 14 18 21 30 75
   92 108 137 180 195 204

ALFORD, 1 2 74
ALFRED, 128
ALIN, 2
ALKIRE, 3
ALLAIR, 78
ALLAIRE, 134
ALLAN, 1
ALLARD, 117
ALLCOCK, 31
ALLE, 124
ALLEE, 117 118 121
ALLEN, 3 4 7 13 15 20 23-26 29 30-33
   74 83 92 96 97 122 127 129 135 142
   143 147 152 162 170-172 179 184
   188-190 196-198 202 203
ALLEY, 32 115 116
ALLISON, 30 88 170
ALLNUT, 32
ALSMAN, 154
ALSONON, 153
ALSOP, 169
AMBROIN, 30
AMET, 159
AMINEAUX, 129
AMMAUINS, 129
AMMEAUX, 129
AMOREUX, 182
AMOS, 2 171
AMOUREUX, 136
ANDERSON, 1 2 3 13 24 32 33 75 86-
   88 107 109 125 134 145 147 148
   150-155 157 158 160 162 164 165
   167-169 171 172 192 195 199 200
   205
ANDRAE, 106 107
ANDRES, 17

ANDREW, 128
ANDREWS, 107 140 185
ANTHONY, 30 108 114 118 119 121
APPERSOM, 126
APPERSON, 127
ARBUCKLE, 32 117
ARCHAMBEAU, 79 82 134
ARCHAMBIA, 109
ARGENBRIGHT, 114 115
ARMISTEAD, 189
ARMOUR, 181
ARMOUREAUX, 186 188
ARMSTEAD, 30 83 92
ARMSTRONG, 3 25 127 182 194 195
ARNOLD, 8 31-33 128 129 192
ARSHANBERRY, 129
ARTERBERRY, 87
ARTHUR, 33 111 165
ARTLETT, 141
ARUNDEL, 133
ASBOURNE, 118
ASHBRANNER, 112
ASHBRIDGE, 170
ASHBY, 32 33 86
ASHCRAFT, 195
ASHLEY, 74 116 139
ASHLOCK, 3
ASHLY, 87
ASKEW, 83
ASKIN, 1
ASLY, 1
ASSAW, 164
ATCHESON, 112
ATCHINSON, 112
ATCHISON, 32 33 133
ATCHLEY, 127
ATER, 31 126
ATKINSON, 32
ATKISSON, 132 133
ATWATER, 8
AUBASHON, 129
AUBASON, 129
AUBIN, 134
AUBUCHON, 135
AUGE, 90
AUGINUL, 170
AUGUST, 112
AULL, 31 199

AUREN, 2
AUSTIN, 3 14 25 108 111 139 166 182
AUTHERTON, 94
AVERETT, 117
AVERY, 163 164 166 168
AVIRAT, 161
AVOY, 160
AVRETT, 31
AYERS, 85
AYRES, 137 153 154 185 190 198 199
    201-203
BABER, 34 190 196
BACLAND, 86
BACON, 95 127
BADGLEY, 112
BAFORTA, 30
BAGBY, 4
BAGSBY, 112
BAILEY, 4 6 26 34 97 111 129 173 174
    178 190 198-200 203
BAILS, 87
BAILY, 30 88 178
BAINES, 23
BAINS, 81
BAIRD, 82 162
BAKER 3, 4 6 8-10 12 14 17 22 27 30
    83 86 87 93 110 112 115 129 138
    139 157 176 185 187 203
BALDRIDGE, 85 91 97
BALDWIN, 35 93 95
BALL, 33 81 194
BALLARD, 112
BALLENGER, 108
BALLEW, 133
BALLINGER, 87
BALY, 4
BAMFORD, 84
BANCROFT, 34 107 156 162 166 167
    175
BANKMAN, 30
BANKS, 179 180
BARBEE, 147 173 180
BARBER, 34 36 88
BARCLAY, 153 154
BARDO, 129
BARGER, 4 117-119 121 122
BARKER, 1
BARKMAN, 30

BARKWELL, 132
BARLETT, 120
BARLOW, 129 204
BARLTEY, 24
BARNES, 2 4 8 13 17 22 23 25 28 36 92
    112 116 137 155 168 173 174 178
    195 202
BARNETT, 75 92 108 120-122 153 199
BARNS, 85 145 179 194
BARNY, 17
BARON, 189
BARQFOW, 149
BARR, 157 163
BARRETT, 132
BARRI, 106
BARRINGER, 87
BARRY, 6 15 16 22
BARTELL, 153 160 170 171
BARTELSON, 36
BARTLETT, 111 120 141-143 145 147
    151-155 157 158 162 163 165-169
BARTLETTSON, 117
BARTLEY, 4 8 9 18 20 21
BARTON, 165
BARUTEL, 134 135
BASKETT, 10
BASKIN, 4
BASQUE, 135
BASS, 121
BASSETT, 36 86
BASSIER, 85
BASSITE, 30
BAST, 131
BATES, 2 111 141 144 150 152 156 159
    164 165 171 191-193
BATHUCK, 2
BATLOT, 112
BATTERSON, 132
BATTHROP, 146
BATTIE, 4
BATTU, 135
BAUGHMAN, 119
BAUVAIS, 135
BAVAN, 4
BAXLEY, 198
BAXTER, 35 135 181
BAYLEY, 83
BAYNHAM, 4 21

BEACH, 142
BEALL, 96 108 179
BEAMAN, 199
BEAN, 129 146-148 199 203
BEARD, 143
BEARN, 4
BEASLEY, 88 199 201-203
BEATTY, 92 131 137
BEATY, 97 155 188
BEAUCHAMP, 35 191 198 201 203
BEAULIEU, 133 134
BEAUMAN, 80
BEAUVAIS, 78 109 184
BEAUVUIS, 93
BEAVANS, 4
BEAVEN, 7
BEAVUIS, 93
BEAZLEY, 34
BEBE, 105
BECKELSIMER, 2
BECKETT, 160 161
BECKSLER, 126
BECKTITE, 161
BEDEN, 25
BEDFORD, 89
BEDWELL, 90
BEEBE, 167
BEGERON, 134
BEGUIN, 112
BEHURST, 201
BELAMA, 4
BELCHER, 35 88 173 178
BELDSOE, 88
BELL, 3 4 8 11 35 89 121 129 178 189
BELLAMA, 4
BELLOWS, 4
BELLUAME, 194
BELOTT, 129
BELOVIT, 194
BELSHA, 87
BELSHY, 129
BENEDICT, 98
BENEFIELD, 75
BENJAMIN, 100
BENNET, 159 160 181
BENNETT, 4 34 114 176 204
BENNING, 149
BENOIST, 149 184

BENOIT, 194
BENSON, 4 35
BENT, 182
BENTLEY, 14
BEQUET, 95 129
BEQUETT, 129
BEQUIT, 129
BERGER, 134
BERHRLE, 205
BERHUE, 110
BERK, 129
BERKETT, 6
BERNEY, 139
BERR, 107
BERRI, 106
BERRY, 5 30 34 36 118 124 129 137
    152 159 160 194 203
BERRYMAN, 6 20 33 34 169
BERTHOLD, 140 157 194
BERTHOLETT, 80
BESS, 87
BEST, 114
BEUAT, 93
BEVENS, 203
BEVIN, 75
BEVINS, 33 34
BHAUER, 108
BIBB, 187 202
BIBEAUX, 134
BIDDLE, 93 94
BIENENU, 135
BIENVENU, 135
BIENVENUE, 108 110
BIGELOW, 113
BIGGS, 126 133 163 193
BILDERBACK, 78 110
BILL, 112
BILLINGS, 127
BILLINGSLEY, 30
BILLOW, 151 155
BILLS, 30 120
BINGHAM, 75 174 179 189
BINNEY, 192
BINNOT, 163
BIRCH, 170
BIRD, 129 145 151 158 159 163 169 170
    175 176 189 191 193
BIRDEAU, 102

BIRDSONG, 121 124
BIRDWATER, 202
BIRON, 133 134
BISSON, 134
BISSONET, 134
BIVINS, 197
BLACK, 16 23 87 88 92 97 117 128 168
    201
BLACKBURN, 1 15
BLACKWELL, 5 139
BLAIN, 35
BLAIR, 186
BLAKE, 96 192
BLAKELY, 30 118 146 162 164 167
BLAKEY, 35 143 144-146 149 152 153
    157 158 162 169
BLAKLEY, 90
BLANCHARD, 104
BLAND, 122 147 197 203
BLANTON, 35
BLASSENGAME, 122
BLATTENBURGH, 14
BLAYLOCK, 30
BLAZE, 87
BLECHE, 205
BLEDSOE, 75 88 89 99 107 112 167
    202
BLESSING, 144 145
BLEVEN, 5
BLEVINS, 19
BLEW, 167
BLISS, 99
BLIZENBY, 151
BLOCK, 90 129 146 147 205
BLOOM, 112
BLOUNT, 8 190
BLOW, 169
BLUE, 92 159
BLUNCKALL, 5
BLUNT, 5
BLY, 14
BLYTHE, 21 30 98
BOAGIEN, 153
BOARTH, 36
BOAZ, 5
BODAUX, 129
BOENG, 181
BOGAER, 117

BOGGES, 5
BOGGESS, 33 34
BOGGS, 5 82 107 125 195
BOGIE, 36
BOGY, 30 78 79 129
BOHANNAN, 154
BOHANNON, 192
BOHN, 160 161
BOICE, 126
BOILVIN, 75 102 105
BOLAN, 122
BOLAND, 134
BOLDUC, 177
BOLDUKE, 129
BOLES, 89 120
BOLLINGER, 112 120 123 124 138 186
BOLLINS, 148
BOLTON, 107
BOMANE, 120
BOMER, 92
BOMPART, 104
BOND, 5 112
BONDS, 36
BONER, 124
BONHAM, 160 162
BONIS, 109
BONNEAU, 90
BONNERT, 205
BONNETT, 123
BONOIT, 194
BOOGS, 103
BOOKER, 5
BOON, 5 18 97 197
BOONARD, 119
BOONE, 3 5 6 8 13 14 17 26 85 96 128
   129 137 153 185 203
BOOTEN, 127
BOQUET, 134
BORAN, 118
BOSBY, 157
BOSIA, 129
BOSLEY, 153 162 165
BOSSIER, 93
BOSSIEUR, 136 183
BOSSORION, 194
BOSTICK, 181 189
BOSWELL, 150
BOTTS, 89 92

BOTTSFORD, 104
BOUCHARD, 82
BOUCHER, 97
BOUGY, 139
BOULDIN, 199
BOULIARD, 134
BOULIN, 112
BOULWARE, 2-19 21-29 141 161
BOUNDS, 90
BOURASSA, 133
BOURD, 5
BOURNE, 144
BOUSFIELD, 98
BOUVAIS, 85
BOVIA, 129
BOWAN, 153
BOWDRY, 36
BOWEN, 115 119 133 148 151-153 155
   156 158 161-163 165 169-171
BOWER, 159
BOWERS, 167
BOWLES, 165 189 195
BOWLIN, 111 154
BOWLING, 163
BOWLINGER, 121
BOWMAN, 81
BOX, 112
BOYCE, 5 141 144
BOYD, 2 5 7 15 18 116 117 120 138 181
   204
BOYDSTON, 36
BOYES, 6
BOYET, 98
BOYLES, 97
BOYS, 117
BOZARTH, 36 89 191
BOZORTH, 142 143 152 160
BRACKEN, 35
BRACKER, 2
BRADFORD, 24 87 172 173 178 179
BRADLEY, 33 96 132 133 145 153 204
BRADLY, 30 152-154
BRADSHAW, 105 126 147
BRADY, 82 93 134 138 169
BRAHAM, 6
BRALEY, 35
BRALY, 174 177
BRAM, 181

BRANABLE, 2
BRANAM, 34
BRAND, 99 200 201
BRANDON, 6 14
BRANE, 97
BRANHAM, 6
BRANSON, 9
BRANT, 148 192
BRANUM, 14
BRASHEAR, 156
BRASHEON, 153
BRATCHER, 112
BRATHER, 141
BRAWNER, 35 83
BRAY, 197
BRAZIER, 153
BRECKENRIDGE, 33
BRECKRIDGE, 24
BREECH, 126
BREIN, 121
BRENNEESEN, 107
BRENT, 183
BRERETON, 95
BRETTON, 21
BREVARD, 124
BREWER, 1 83 87 97 100 151
BRIANT, 6
BRICE, 128
BRIDE, 4
BRIDGER, 140
BRIGGS, 144 145 148 162
BRILEY, 86
BRIMBAL, 30
BRINGH, 30
BRINGLEY, 156 161
BRINKER, 106
BRISCOE, 118
BRISSON, 134 161
BRITE, 6 21 87
BRITTARIE, 99
BRITTINGHAM, 163
BROADDUS, 86
BROADHURST, 34 36
BROCK, 35 136 200
BROCKMAN, 6 83 124
BRODHEAD, 145
BROGUHTON, 150
BROOK, 136

BROOKINS, 154
BROOKS, 6 33-35 86 92 109 123 124
  129 136 176 200
BROTHER, 176
BROTHERS, 169 171
BROUGHTON, 24 150
BROWDER, 172 173 178 189
BROWER, 151
BROWN, 1 2 4-6 22 28 29 30 34-36 83
  86 87 92 95 96 99 115 116 119 128
  129 131 132 139 144 148 149 152
  154 156 161 163 165 167 168 170
  171 175 177 181 190 194-197 200
  201 203 204
BROWNSNET, 2
BROYLES, 36
BRUBAKER, 111
BRUCE, 1 92
BRUER, 117
BRUFFEE, 180 203 203
BRUGIERE, 199
BRUN, 141
BRUNE, 159
BRUNUM, 180
BRUSTERRA, 197
BRUZIER, 203
BRYAN, 17 20 24 26 29 88 92 131-133
BRYANT, 6 22 35
BRYNS, 92
BRYSON, 133
BUALE, 108
BUATE, 109
BUATT, 129
BUCHANAN, 142
BUCHANNAN, 6
BUCHANNON, 152
BUCHE, 90
BUCKANAN, 170
BUCKER, 1
BUCKLEY, 6 167
BUCKNER, 123 147-152 154 170 193
BUEGINS, 129
BUFORD, 128 163
BUGES, 89
BUGG, 194
BULE, 87
BULL, 88 175 180
BULLARD, 6 98 104 105

212

BULLIN, 158
BULLINGER, 87
BULLOCK, 141 143-147 162
BUMAN, 128
BUNCH, 6 22 30 97
BUNGET, 201
BURBEAU, 109
BURCH, 172 174 178 180
BURCKHARTT, 86
BURD, 120
BURDETT, 153
BURDINE, 98
BURDITT, 161
BURESS, 129
BURGAN, 97
BURGEE, 87
BURGEN, 112
BURGESS, 96
BURGET, 128
BURGETT, 88
BURGIN, 204
BURGUETT, 129
BURK, 87
BURKER, 121
BURKES, 143
BURKET, 29
BURKS, 6 127
BURLESON, 201
BURLSON, 128
BURMUM, 174
BURNASS, 85
BURNET, 6
BURNETT, 2 16 36 90 96 165
BURNHAM, 112 115 136
BURNS, 6 24 34 36 82 87 88 95 106 112
      114 121 129
BURNUM, 173 179
BURROWS, 80
BURRS, 87
BURT, 7 14 16 18-20 22 26 28
BURTON, 35 149 164
BUSBY, 195
BUSH, 36 161
BUSHARD, 129
BUSTER, 36
BUTCHER, 82 129 172
BUTEAU, 134
BUTLER, 34 75 109 124 169

BUTOTT, 129
BUTZ, 205
BUYAT, 135
BUZZ, 6
BUZZARD, 116
BYBEE, 121
BYEE, 121
BYNUM, 178 195
BYRD, 137 138 175 178 184 188
BYRNE, 123 124 138
BYRUM, 112
BYWATER, 165
CABASSIER, 134
CABEEN, 87
CABEL, 118
CABELL, 86 87 173 178-180 189
CADRON, 133
CAIMAN, 170
CAIN, 37 41 79 132
CAIRNS, 112
CALAHAN, 128
CALAWAY, 129
CALBERT, 143
CALDWELL, 1 6 8 133 153 155 161
      163 184 190 193 196 197
CALE, 147
CALFEE, 119
CALIOTT, 129
CALLAHAN, 135
CALLAWAY, 6 7 10 12 19 93 136 152
      163 168 185 188 194
CALLE, 156
CALLIS, 141 152-154
CALLISON, 5 7 13 118
CALVERT, 129
CALVIN, 10
CAMDEN, 161
CAMEGY, 160
CAMERN, 87
CAMERON, 37 39
CAMMEL, 92
CAMMENS, 39
CAMPBELL, 7 11 21 39 40 77 80 84 87
      93 96 101 102 105 119 122 129 156
      160 162 165 166 167 169 172 174
      176-178 189 194 203 205
CAMPEAU, 133
CAMPSTER, 129

CAMRON, 39
CAMUR, 160
CANADIEN, 134
CANAHAN, 30
CANES, 167
CANNON, 93-95 143 167
CANNOY, 160
CANON, 77
CANS, 40
CANTERBURY, 92
CANTLEY, 136
CAOMPARET, 134
CAPER, 162
CAPPS, 128 201
CARDIN, 74
CARDINAL, 112 181
CARDWELL, 92
CAREY, 40 112
CARICO, 184
CARISLE, 145
CARL, 108
CARLISLE, 204
CARLOCK, 112
CARLOW, 146
CARMAN, 170 171
CARMEGY, 162 166
CARNAP, 151
CARNEGY, 146 148 150 152 154 156
    157
CARNES, 143
CARNS, 112
CAROU, 105
CAROW, 129
CARPENTER, 39 75 78 79 109 124 131
CARR, 1 85 112
CARRINGTON, 7
CARROLL, 37 39 120
CARROW, 129
CARRUTH, 7
CARRUTHERS, 96
CARRY, 37 41
CARSON, 149 153-155 157 164 193
CARSTARSHEN, 158
CARTEE, 116
CARTER, 1 7 21 39 96 158
CARTHALL, 152
CARTHEA, 40
CARTHURS, 178

CARUTH, 175
CARVER, 88 200
CARY, 40
CASETY, 1
CASEY, 37 38
CASHION, 87
CASON, 7
CASS, 95
CASSIDY, 30
CASSIO, 137
CASSOU, 135
CASTAPHERN, 165
CASTERLINE, 133
CASTOR, 105
CASWELL, 168
CATE, 37
CATES, 139 140
CATHEY, 180 203
CATON, 75 198 200 203
CATRON, 91 148-150
CATTLEMAN, 150
CATTS, 37 41
CAUK, 188
CAULK, 140 184
CAVE, 7 110 155
CAVIELL, 40
CEARS, 129
CEBRAN, 129
CELY, 150
CERRE, 78 85
CESSELL, 136
CHAK, 2
CHALFIN, 133
CHALISS, 169
CHAMBERLAIN, 95
CHAMBERLIN, 95
CHAMBERS, 85 87 129 204
CHAMPLAIN, 134
CHANCE, 36 37 41
CHANDER, 168
CHANDLER, 37 40 41 80 88 143 148
    149 195
CHANEY, 40 99
CHAOUTEAU, 81
CHAPEL, 23
CHAPMAN, 7 119 121 141 142 160
CHAPRON, 154
CHARBONEAU, 77 79 80

COGER, 143
COINCE, 194
COLDWEL, 129
COLDWELL, 129 203
COLE, 83 88 115 117 195 196 205
COLEBURN, 2
COLGAN, 190
COLINE, 109
COLIRS, 204
COLLAMS, 2
COLLAND, 2
COLLARD, 137 190
COLLEY, 40 41
COLLIER, 30 40 146 147 168 200
COLLIN, 30
COLLINS, 2 40 120 136 166 169 181
    197 203 204
COLWELL, 161
COMBS, 120 126 143
COMEGY, 170
COMEGYS, 2
COMMER, 8
COMSTOCK, 186 187
CONGER, 8 16 20 22
CONGO, 18
CONN, 118
CONNER, 170 204
CONNROY, 159
CONRAD, 87 155
CONVISA, 40
CONWAY, 96 140 147 164 166 169 178
CONYERS, 75
COOK, 1 8 118 119 124 126 128 134
    136 163 167 170 171 185 199 201
COOLEY, 38 195 196
COONEE, 169
COONS, 5 7 8 12 19 20 24 26 28 187
COOPER, 30 38 91 96 112 114 118 137
    138 144 161 162 165 166 168 169
    181 195 196
COOTS, 37 38
COPE, 164 165 169 171
COPELAND, 99 108 162
COPPAGE, 128 201
CORLEW, 170
CORLEY, 8
CORMIER, 153
CORNELIUS, 37 41

CORNELUIS, 41 99
CORNET, 181
CORNIELSON, 132 133
CORNWALL, 1 202
CORPIN, 159
CORREN, 82
CORSER, 126 127
CORTEEN, 129
CORUM, 36 37 41
COSBY, 83
COSSITT, 144 146
COSTE, 134
COTEAUX, 83
COTHRAN, 129
COTTE, 81
COTTLE, 97 185 190
COTTRELL, 145 146
COUCE, 2
COULNY, 161
COULTIER, 23
COUNINS, 129
COUNSEL, 129
COUPLAND, 169
COURED, 104
COURIE, 134
COURSOLLE, 137
COURTNEY, 40 145 149-151 160
COURTOIS, 134
COURTOIX, 135
COVINGTON, 8
COWAN, 99 181
COWIN, 129
COWLE, 132
COWLING, 160 162 164 168 169
COX, 1 2 18 40 88 98 116 119 147 194
    196
COXE, 147
CRACRAFT, 175
CRACROFT, 175-177
CRADDOCK, 175
CRADER, 124
CRAFT, 30
CRAGBARN, 143
CRAGG, 18
CRAGHEAD, 6 8 16 18
CRAIG, 2 7 8 13 25 37 85 86 141 154
    157 172-174 178-180 194
CRAIGHEAD, 11 136

216

CRAIN, 7 28 117
CRAMER, 81
CRANE, 77 102
CRANNY, 40
CRASENTO, 8
CRAWFORD, 9 15 38 114 177
CREACY, 92
CREASON, 112 195
CREATH, 123 175
CREED, 8 89
CREEK, 38
CRENSHAW, 126 142 158
CRESON, 39
CRESSON, 169
CREWS, 129 142 143 150
CRICKMAN, 1
CRISMAN, 194
CRIST, 111
CRISWELL, 164
CRITES, 112
CRITTENDEN, 96
CROCKER, 145 148 149
CROCKET, 172
CROCKETT, 13 14 39 40 92 178 192 203
CROMWELL, 194
CROOK, 115 159
CROPPER, 161
CROSSET, 38
CROSSETT, 38
CROSSWAITE, 8
CROSSWHITE, 92
CROUCH, 92
CROUGHTON, 152
CROW, 96 97 129 169
CROWELL, 95
CROWLEY, 36-40
CROWSON, 8 28
CRUD, 92
CRUISE, 142
CRUMP, 8-10 21 114 117 131 195
CRUNK, 127
CRUTCHER, 150 151
CRYER, 30
CULBERTSON, 141 195
CULLEN, 113
CULLUM, 1
CULLY, 87

CULP, 37 39
CULSIN, 107
CULVAR, 154
CULVIR, 154
CUMMING, 1
CUMMINS, 30 99
CUNNINGHAM, 2 117 159 164 194 199
CURD, 9 164 168 170 171
CURNETT, 200
CURO, 153
CUROPIN, 90
CURRIN, 30 139
CURRY, 20 27 104
CURTIS, 104 179 181 204 205
CURTS, 152
CUSHING, 166
CUYLER, 87
D'LASHMUITT, 123
D'LASHMUT, 94
D'LASHMUTT, 123 124
D'LASHOMITT, 176
DA---, 163
DAGGETT, 149
DAGLEY, 42 83
DAILEY, 2
DAILY, 129 155 157 158
DALE, 41 42 87
DALEY, 87
DALLINS, 92
DALRYMPLE, 158
DALTON, 147 201
DANAH, 155
DANGEN, 82
DANHORN, 90
DANIEL, 2 24 30 111 118 123 143
DANIS, 134 135
DAQUIET, 85
DARBY, 129 168
DARDENNE, 84
DARNEILLE, 112
DARNELL, 154
DARR, 166
DARRAH, 156 159-167 169-171
DARRELL, 118
DARST, 85 131
DART, 129
DARTING, 27
DAUBUCHON, 134

DAUGHERTY, 123 124
DAVENPORT, 42 43 132 133
DAVID, 189
DAVIDSON, 5 85 110 118 121 128 131 150
DAVIS, 2 3 5 9 12 14 18 19 22 23 26 27 30 41-43 74 83 86-88 91-93 95 99 100 109 113 117 119 131 147 149 154-157 160-162 164 166 167 169 170 173 176 180 186 194 195 204 205
DAVISON, 106
DAWSON, 30 42 84 110 128
DAY, 2 4 8 9 23 25 29 78 92
DEAKINS, 118
DEAN, 16 30 41
DEANING, 128
DEARING, 26 162 165
DEBO, 9
DECKENS, 117
DECKER, 9
DEEN, 87
DEFOUR, 129
DEGEAS, 129
DEGUIRE, 114
DEHART, 30
DEHERTE, 137
DEHETRE, 135
DELANEY, 85 92 173 178
DELAP, 2
DELAUNAY, 186
DELBA, 89
DELCHEMENDY, 110
DELLINGER, 107
DELNEY, 115
DELOGE, 134
DELONEY, 194
DELORME, 133
DELOUISSES, 129
DEMENT, 112
DEMETER, 133
DEMPEWOLF, 113
DENBORN, 43
DENING, 113
DENISON, 113
DENNIS, 104 121 132 133 137
DENNY, 41 42 111 190
DENSMAN, 204

DENT, 82 128
DEPESTON, 129
DEQUER, 129
DERINGER, 96
DERIOE, 155
DEROUSSE, 78 134
DERUISSEAUX, 30
DESHAZO, 9
DESSHA, 93
DESUSSEAUX, 30
DETCHEMENDZ, 129
DETWEILER, 127
DEVEAL, 129
DEVORE, 3 190 196 197 202 203
DIAMON, 168
DIANNE, 30
DIBBLE, 43
DICKERSON, 22 141 145-149 152 156 162 163 167 192
DICKESON, 172
DICKEY, 42
DICKIE, 42
DICKINSON, 129 200
DICKSON, 30 87 88 128 147 148 167
DIDIER, 191
DIEL, 85
DIGGS, 9
DILBOURN, 90
DILE, 9
DILIARD, 74
DILL, 9 164
DILLARD, 11 114
DILLINGHAM, 170
DILLON, 93 136 168
DILLOSS, 163
DINESNE, 133
DINNING, 145
DINSMAN, 180
DISARD, 92
DISMUKES, 146
DIVINE, 87
DIXON, 2 9 129 151 161 167 176
DOAN, 23 27 92 199
DOBBINS, 98 119 121
DOBYN, 159 162 166 169
DOBYON, 161
DOBZ, 1
DOCKERRY, 112

FAGGITT, 46
FAGOT, 189
FAIRBRIDGE, 113
FAIRHERTT, 88
FALLIS, 184
FANELL, 162
FANNERY, 92
FANNIN, 160
FANNING, 96
FAREBEAU, 105
FARIS, 10 188
FARLAND, 194
FARLEY, 194
FARMER, 10 46 128 182
FARNAN, 168
FARRAR, 87 103 182
FARREL, 87
FARRENS, 45
FARRIS, 90 99
FAUBION, 46
FAUCETT, 92
FAUK, 87
FAUSSEE, 90
FAVIER, 10
FAWCETT, 199
FEAGAN, 162
FEARIS, 86
FEAZEL, 189
FEAZLE, 157
FECLET, 81
FELAND, 99
FELLOW, 159
FELLOWS, 124
FELPS, 158 160
FELT, 156
FELTS, 157
FENCH, 120
FENTESCHE, 10
FENTON, 92 93 132 133 199 205
FENWICK, 83 85 88 130
FERANDIS, 97
FERGSIN, 163
FERGUENAN, 166
FERGUSON, 4 10-13 19-21 25 29 103
    143 145-147 153 162 163 165 167
    169 170 194
FERNANDE, 135

FERQUERAN, 149
FERQUERMAN, 142
FERREL, 45 108 194
FERRIER, 11 22
FERRIL, 195
FEY, 100 110
FICKLIN, 2 8
FIDLER, 99
FIELDER, 157
FIELDLER, 108
FIELDS, 11 45 96 97 98 195
FILCHER, 74
FILFERT, 167
FINCH, 87
FINDLEY, 11 120 122 125 179
FINKLER, 201
FINKS, 89
FINLEY, 11 45 46 96
FINNEL, 172 174 180
FINNELL, 86
FISHER, 1 11 18 25-27 89 95 117 118
    120 121 125 126 144 166
FITZGERALD, 83 146
FITZHUGH, 117 122 204
FLAHARTY, 87
FLANAGAN, 30
FLANEGAN, 30
FLANEY, 128
FLAUGHERTY, 137 183
FLECHER, 11
FLECT, 205
FLEETWOOD, 86 179
FLEMMING, 193
FLETCHER, 11 29 45 46 95 114 143
    149
FLEURANT, 134
FLING, 87
FLINN, 1
FLINT, 130
FLOURNOY, 146
FLUBARDEAU, 93
FLYNN, 82 88 164 166
FOETUS, 2
FOLEY, 119
FOLSOM, 93 94
FOOY, 30 188 189
FORBES, 145

FORCE, 46
FORD, 1 131 156 163 166 170 173 179 191 198 200 202
FOREMAN, 150
FORMAN, 141 143 147-149 159 160 163 164 166-171 190 191 193
FORQUERAN, 146
FORQUEREAN, 148
FORSITH, 1
FORSTH, 1
FORSYTH, 1 75 96 101
FORSYTHE, 192
FORT, 7 92
FORTA, 130
FOSTER, 2 11 100 110 172-174 178 179 182 205
FOUBLET, 194
FOURD, 203 204
FOURNIER, 77
FOURNIQUET, 157
FOWLER, 1 11 46 75 83 132 145 148 150 173 174 177 179 180
FOX, 27
FOXWORTHY, 29
FOY, 11
FRAIZER, 163 166
FRAMMELL, 91
FRANCES, 168
FRANCHER, 116
FRANCIS, 153 155
FRANCOIS, 160
FRANIER, 77
FRANKLIN, 45 46
FRASER, 1
FRAUK, 130
FRAY, 148
FRAZEL, 114
FRAZER, 1
FRAZIER, 30 107 110 141 145 152
FRAZIERUR, 130
FRAZURE, 30
FREE, 170
FREEMAN, 6 11 16 141 148 173
FREIYER, 166
FREMONT, 160
FRENCH, 11 87 115 119 190 196 203
FRENCHMAN, 111
FRENTH, 92

FREY, 11
FRIAR, 87
FRICKE, 175
FRIEND, 75 83 93 94
FRIER, 197 203
FRISTOE, 2 97 174 178
FROMBERGER, 169
FROST, 46 157
FRUIT, 5 6 9-11 13 15-17 19-21 26 27
FRUNIAN, 178
FRY, 45 46 103 128 141-145 148 149 151 152 156 158 192
FRYE, 141 143 178 192
FRYEND, 138
FUDGE, 46
FUGATE, 92 158 189
FUGETT, 46
FUGITT, 46 194 196
FULKERSON, 87 90 93
FULKS, 13 119 120
FULL, 157
FULLBRIGHT, 11
FULSOM, 30 94
FULSON, 94
FULTERTON, 2
FULTON, 194
FUNK, 107
FURIT, 13
FURMAN, 165
FUTRAL, 30
GABEER, 180
GABRETH, 92
GACHARD, 90
GADSDEN, 95
GAGE, 179 180
GAHAN, 89
GAILY, 169
GAINES, 47 48 184
GAINETO, 162
GAINSAY, 191 198
GAIRRON, 130
GAITHER, 178 180
GALAHER, 165 201
GALBREATH, 5 11 86 91
GALBRETH, 92
GALE, 130
GALEHAR, 128
GALLAHER, 159

GALLAWAY, 48
GALLOHER, 135
GALLS, 2
GAMBLE, 192
GAMES, 24
GAMETON, 164
GANATY, 190
GANT, 199
GAPPER, 89
GARDENER, 16
GARMAN, 106
GARNER, 8 123 124 145 153 158 192
GARNETT, 146 162
GARNSAY, 203
GARNSLEY, 200-202
GARRARD, 33
GARRATY, 196
GARRAY, 203
GARRETT, 11 87
GARROTSON, 133
GARTELL, 150
GARTRELL, 160 165
GARVIN, 148 190 191 197 201 203
GARY, 178 179
GASG, 163
GASH, 48 141 144 145 151 157 168 189
191
GASKILL, 164
GATES, 46 128 129
GATEWOOD, 150
GATH, 195
GATHER, 87 154
GAUD, 134
GAUDIN, Dedication
GAUN, 2
GAY, 142 151 152 154 158 163 166 171
GAYLORD, 2
GEE, 11
GEHON, 118 120 122
GEIGER, 193
GEIZER, 135
GELLIER, 170
GELSTON, 96
GENDRON, 135
GENTRY, 46 48 142 145 149 152 156
157 162 165 193 202
GEORGE, 2 47 112 120 160 179
GEOSHANG, 91

GERMAIN, 134
GERMAN, 117 120 125
GERVALIS, 133
GEST, 118 125 159 165 170 171
GHSKLETT, 157
GIBBONS, 147 149 153
GIBBS, 108 147
GIBSON, 3 10 95 112 130 139 187 193
198 203
GIEBER, 91
GIEL, 130
GIGNARES, 85
GILBERT, 18 26 169
GILCHRIST, 150
GILES, 124
GILL, 48 87 129 170
GILLASBY, 93
GILLASPIE, 151 176 177
GILLESPIE, 47 94 127 171
GILLESPY, 112
GILLET, 174 179
GILLETT, 190
GILLHAM, 112
GILLIAM, 47 178
GILLIS, 110
GILLMORE, 12
GILLS, 2
GILLUM, 173
GILMAN, 6 7 12
GILMON, 12
GILMOOR, 81
GILMORE, 12 47 120 122 179 180
GINSON, 137
GIROUX, 134
GIRRAD, 134
GIRTY, 1
GISH, 47
GIST, 119
GLADDEN, 47
GLADWELL, 12
GLASCOCK, 87 142 146 149 151 152
155 157-162 167 169 171 176 193
GLASCOE, 163
GLASGOW, 97
GLASS, 30 143
GLASSCOCK, 146
GLASSEN, 139
GLASSGLOW, 167

GLAVES, 30
GLEASON, 154 155
GLENDAY, 141
GLENDI, 12
GLENN, 108 153 170
GLENSAY, 145
GLIVENZ, 155
GLOVER, 4 12
GOALLY, 92
GOBBONS, 155
GOCHER, 47
GODAK, 114
GODDARD, 105
GODIN, (Dedication) 134
GODMAN, 141 149 191
GOEGER, 140
GOFORTH, 139
GOIN, 130
GOINGES, 112
GOINGS, 112
GOIROIUEX, 130
GONDRON, 134
GONEVILLE, 134
GONVILLE, 134
GOOCH, 90 150 151 163
GOOCHE, 139
GOOD, 113
GOODE, 48
GOODIN, 91
GOODMAN, 147
GOODNIGHT, 86
GOODRICH, 12 89 120 187
GOODSPEED, 130
GOODWIN, 107 153 166
GORDAN, 12
GORDON, 1 2 8 12 14 48
GORHAM, 86
GORNOE, 130
GOSESHOW, 130
GOSHAM, 194
GOSLIN, 110 132 133
GOSSETT, 30
GOSSIAUX, 134
GOTCHER, 47
GOTTERMAN, 100
GOUIE, 1
GOVIROX, 130
GOZA, 30 82 85 95 130

GRADAVENE, 4
GRADY, 176
GRAGG, 47 48
GRAHAM, 75 88 95 100 106 110 159
GRANDBOIS, 134
GRANDER, 30
GRANES, 4
GRANNON, 2
GRANT, 1 4 12 17 92 108 141
GRASON, 130
GRATIOT, 183
GRATIOTT, 158
GRATZ, 141
GRAVEROD, 1
GRAVES, 29 97 117 173 175 178 181
GRAVIER, 30
GRAY, 7 12 26 30 83 90 95 106 115 135
    137 139 155 171
GREAR, 12
GREASON, 92
GREEN, 4 12 25 30 46 47 83 86 95 97
    98 103 110 119 121 126 143 146 149
    150 152 170 172 173 175 179 180
    182 185 190 197 202 203
GREENE, 130
GREENLEE, 164
GREENWALT, 30 130
GREENWELL, 83
GREENWOOD, 156 158 159
GREER, 116 181 199
GREGG, 28 46 48 49 92 97 196
GREGOIS, 130
GREGORY, 163 182
GREIFI, 200
GRENIER, 134
GRENN, 88
GRENNEY, 1
GRENON, 90
GREY, 114
GRICE, 2
GRIFFEY, 198 203
GRIFFIN, 87 97 110 117 153
GRIFFITH, 12 47 83 137 159 170
GRIGG, 92 192
GRIGGS, 12 112
GRIGGSBY, 48
GRIGSBY, 149
GRIMES, 48

GRIMM, 46
GRISBY, 152
GROESBECK, 1
GROMER, 46 47
GRONDINE, 134
GROOM, 47 48
GROOMER, 46 83
GROOMS, 48
GROSHONG, 137
GROSLE, 134
GROSS, 47
GROTZ, 133
GROUND, 114 138
GROUNDS, 87
GROVE, 111
GROVENOR, 112
GROVES, 123 124
GROWER, 81
GUERRANT, 12
GUGER, 103
GUILD, 123 124
GUINN, 46
GUITARSH, 130
GUITTARD, 134
GUMME, 109
GUNDELFINGER, 106
GUNN, 100 115
GUNTER, 47
GUNTHE, 200
GURNEAU, 82
GURTHEE, 117
GUTHERIE, 12
GUYER, 119
GUYMAN, 160
GUYNN, 167
GUYOL, 140
GUYON, 135
GYLMARE, 12
HACKET, 30
HACKNEY, 6
HADEN, 30 130 139 142
HADER, 200 201
HADLEY, 50
HAE, 167
HAESLIP, 168
HAFF, 148
HAGAN, 50 83 87 130
HAGANS, 49

HAGEN, 1 30
HAILE, 175
HAINES, 3 155 156 159-165 167-171
HALBITT, 86
HALCOME, 2
HALE, 2 120
HALES, 167
HALL, 11 12 49-51 83 87 92 123 136
    142 144 154 168 169 199
HALLOWELL, 166 170
HAM, 3 5 6 9 10 12 13 15-20 22-24 26-
    29 87 89
HAMBLIN, 5 13 26
HAMILTON, 2 3 5 13 24 50 144-146
    185
HAMINGTON, 30
HAMISTIAN, 130
HAMMON, 180
HAMMOND, 89 104 180 187
HAMMONS, 180
HAMPTON, 30 115 143 147 193
HANCOCK, 87 96 132 173 178 180 195
    196
HAND, 1
HANKINS, 158
HANKS, 30 50 140
HANNA, 158
HANNAH, 13
HANNEY, 115
HANSBERRY, 13
HANSON, 49 50 162
HARBESON, 128
HARBOUR, 166 171
HARCALL, 150
HARD, 112
HARDIN, 12 52
HARDING, 144 170 171
HARDOVICH, 1
HARDWICK, 50 173 177-180
HARDY, 86 149 150 157 159 163
HARFFY, 1
HARFLY, 1
HARGIS, 171
HARGROVE, 2
HARINS, 50
HARMAND, 133
HARMON, 118 120
HARNESS, 133

HARPER, 23 27 28
HARREL, 1
HARRELSON, 52
HARRIMAN, 190
HARRINGTON, 50-52 85
HARRIS, 6 11 13 50 52 83 86 87 93 108
    117 119 120 122 123 125 130 148
    151 154 179 181 194 201 203 204
HARRISON, 13 16 19 28 30 87 113 114
    129 142 148 169 181 199 202
HARROW, 1
HARRY, 92
HARRYFORD, 24
HARRYMAN, 13 172 180
HARSEL, 51
HARSEN, 1
HARST, 75
HART, 2 13 20 53 91 160 181 185 187
    188
HARTT, 137 138 180 204
HARVER, 13
HARVEY, 50
HARWOOD, 170
HASE, 26 87
HASKINS, 13
HASSINGER, 165
HASTINGS, 155
HATFIELD, 117 120 122 125 173 179
HATHERLY, 136
HATTEN, 92 199
HATTON, 10 21
HAUK, 128
HAUN, 131
HAUPT, 92
HAVILAND, 113
HAVINS, 50
HAWES, 167
HAWK, 125
HAWKEN, 116
HAWKINS, 2 13 49 50 83 118 130 142-
    145 148 152 161-164 166 168 169
    171 182
HAY, 112
HAYDEN, 87 88 114 142 148 150 157
    162
HAYDON, 13 87 141-143 146 156-158
    160 162 163 165 170 171 182 195
HAYES, 92 153

HAYNE, 96
HAYNES, 9 13 16 23 24 92 106 199
HAYS, 4-7 9 13 19 75 96 97 104 112
    117 185
HAYTON, 13
HAYWOOD, 2
HEAD, 133 137 173 174 178
HEART, 13 22
HEARTT, 50
HEASICK, 13
HEATHER, 118 122
HEAVANS, 178
HEAVINGTON, 1
HEBERT, 134
HECTOR, 176 177
HEDDLESTON, 27
HEDDY, 94
HEE, 1
HEFFLINGER, 126
HEFMULLER, 200
HEINTZ, 108
HEISER, 78
HEISKILL, 168
HEIZER, 79
HELLAR, 88
HELMER, 202
HELMS, 75
HEMBY, 128
HEMPHILL, 30
HEMPSTEAD, 91 123 130 137 167
HENDERICKS, 142
HENDERSON, 1 4 5 7 10-14 16 19 24
    28 30 49 50 83 90 133 140 143 183
HENDETETER, 87
HENDRICKS, 123 133 144 150
HENDRICKSON, 89
HENNY, 30
HENRY, 2 30 96 107 112 130 139 157
    183 189
HENSEL, 106 107
HENSLEY, 51 52
HENTON, 112
HENWICK, 128
HERBET, 193
HEREFORD, 14 24
HERNDON, 127 153
HERRICK, 175
HERRIFORD, 14

HERRIN, 110
HERRISON, 97
HERTICK, 136
HESKENE, 126
HETH, 188
HEWETT, 158
HIATT, 196
HICKADAY, 24
HICKCOX, 180
HICKERSON, 14
HICKEY, 163 166
HICKLIN, 142
HICKMAN, 49 50 87 153 176
HICKOCK, 90
HICKOX, 181 203 204
HICKS, 2 112 168 170
HICKSON, 49
HIETT, 49 51
HIGGINS, 87 153 194
HIGGINTOTTERS, 167
HIGHHART, 14
HIGHNOGHT, 87
HIGHT, 137 183
HIGHTOWER, 50
HIGNIGHT, 30
HILDEBRUM, 155
HILES, 175
HILL, 6 11 19 88 96 113 118 123 125
    205
HINCH, 130
HINER, 50
HINES, 138
HINKSTON, 49 50
HITCHCOCK, 2 114
HITE, 167
HIX, 120-122
HIXON, 49 50
HOBAUGH, 128 201
HOBS, 128 201
HOCKADAY, 17 21 106
HOCKINS, 14
HODGE, 14
HODGES, 159 194
HOFF, 118 168
HOFFMAN, 149 202
HOFUIS, 106 107
HOGAN, 112 139 184
HOGARD, 87 88

HOGGARD, 2
HOGGINS, 109
HOGH, 201
HOKE, 162
HOKIT, 52
HOLCOMBE, 2
HOLDER, 114 115
HOLDERMAN, 145
HOLDIN, 131
HOLDMAN, 145 191
HOLEMAN, 49 112
HOLEUES, 167
HOLIDAY, 165
HOLLAND, 81 146
HOLLIDAY, 171
HOLLINGSWORTH, 90
HOLLINGWORTH, 167
HOLLIWAY, 8 16
HOLLOWAY, 10 14 110 132 173 174
    178 179
HOLLYMAN, 100 143 155
HOLMAN, 6 49 50 174 175 179 180 189
HOLMES, 49 155 157
HOLSTEAD, 112
HOLSTER, 83 130
HOLT, 12 14 21 25 49 50 106 154
HOLTSCLAW, 43
HOLTZCLAW, 51
HOMER, 163
HOMES, 159
HOMN, 159
HONEY, 189
HONORE, 76 79 80 102 104
HOOD, 160 169
HOODBRIDGE, 193
HOOK, 27 92 117
HOOKER, 127
HOOLOW, 168
HOOPER, 114
HOOPMAN, 85
HOOTEN, 153
HOOTON, 145 162 163 171 180
HOPE, 11 12 30
HOPKINS, 5 6 9 11 14 16 19 23 25 27
    84 94 95 148 150 156 161
HOPPER, 3 75
HOPPLIN, 202
HOR, 2

HORD, 171
HORINE, 136
HORN, 90 203
HORNBACK, 112 148 149
HORNBUCKLE, 6 14 23 27
HORNE, 139
HORNICAN, 153
HORNS, 87
HORNSBY, 88
HORRELL, 87
HORTON, 117
HOSHAW, 192
HOSKINS, 180
HOSTETTER, 137
HOTCHKISS, 112
HOTSTOTTER, 97
HOUDERSHELL, 194
HOUGH, 26 167
HOUGHTON, 160-162
HOUNICAN, 164
HOUSE, 14
HOUSER, 17
HOUSHAW, 88
HOUSTON, 14 96 121
HOUTS, 94 95 177
HOW, 130
HOWARD, 14 22 27 30 92 110 118 119
    121 125
HOWE, 14 161
HOWELL, 30 85 96 141 156 168 171
    199
HOWSER, 100 110 117 125
HOXEY, 12 17
HOXSEN, 5
HUARESBOROUGH, 135
HUBARDOO, 130
HUBBARD, 14 92 131 204
HUBBERT, 159
HUBBLE, 1 181
HUCHAU, 130
HUDDLESTON, 25 136
HUDGENS, 49 50
HUDSELL, 30
HUDSON, 52
HUDSPETH, 111
HUFF, 15 118 119 133 200 204
HUFFAKER, 49 50
HUFFMAN, 50 51 87 94 96 97 181

HUFFTAKER, 49
HUGGART, 110
HUGH, 128 174
HUGHART, 13
HUGHES, 5 8 14 29 49-52 88 118 140
HUGHS, 1 30 118
HULCE, 51
HULEN, 86
HULETT, 115
HULL, 14
HULTS, 15 128 129
HULTZ, 15 29
HUMBY, 201
HUME, 50
HUMMERT, 202
HUMPHREY, 108
HUMPHREYS, 184
HUMPHRIES, 5 15 23 95
HUNDLE, 92 199
HUNGATE, 92
HUNGERFORD, 162 163
HUNKER, 87
HUNQUEL, 92
HUNSAKER, 143
HUNT, 3 20 24 28 52 82 143 157 199
HUNTER, 15 18 22 74 83 85 86 93 95
    98 106 126 138 159 187 199
HUNTINGTON, 166
HUNTSBERRY, 141 142 144 146 148
    149 156 160 162 171
HUSKILL, 170
HUSTEN, 108
HUTCHERSON, 15
HUTCHINGS, 179 180
HUTCHINS, 172
HUTCHISON, 116 156
HUTSON, 94
HUTTCHINGS, 178
HUTTON, 94
HYATT, 166
HYDE, 147 156 159 162-164 169
HYMON, 133
IMBAU, 30
IMBODEN, 98
INCLABB, 81
INGRAHAM, 30 166
INGRAM, 90 125 138 156 158
INK, 136

INKS, 198 202 203
INYART, 52
IOLA, 130
IRBY, 2
IRVIN, 4 52 194 196
IRVINE, 14 15 142 145 182
IRWIN, 52 96
ISH, 91
ISHAM, 25
IVEY, 127
IZNER, 138
JACABO, 89
JACK, 133 172 179
JACKMAN, 15 92
JACKSON, 5 11 87 92 114 116 118 120
   122 128 130 143 153 181 196 198
JACOBS, 30 87 115 121 188 195
JACOBY, 190 196 203
JAHS, 24
JAMERSON, 130
JAMES, Dedication 2 15 52 53 84 86 88
   130 139 140 162 182 194
JAMESON, 4 15 29 138 144
JAMILL, 130
JAMISON, 17 25 128
JANE, 150
JANELS, 30
JANES, 15 113
JANICE, 130
JANIS, 81 110 134 185 197 203
JANNEY, 162 167
JARDEUS, 30
JARETT, 130
JARROT, 97 112
JARVIS, 168
JASSEPH, 52
JAWAN, 15
JEFFERIES, 53 163 167 170 194
JEFFERS, 52 99
JEFFERY, 138
JEFFERYS, 146
JEFFRIES, 52
JENIFER, 141
JENKINS, 157 162-165 168 170
JENNINGS, 112 169
JESSE, 2 15 52 53 92
JEWELL, 154
JEWETT, 96

JOACHIME, 115
JOACHIMI, 114
JOBE, 53
JOHNS, 197 203
JOHNSAN, 163
JOHNSON, 2 5 15 28 30 53 82 92 95 96
   97 110 112 114 117 120 123 127 138
   146-148 152 158 161 162 166-168
   170 171 175 181 184 190 195 198
   200-204
JOHNSTON, 3 24 52 53 96 125 130 136
   147 163 189 199 201 204
JOINER, 181
JONES, 1 2 7 10 12 15 16 18-21 30 52
   53 87-89 106 118 120-122 131-134
   146 151 153-155 158 162 168-170
   190 191 194 196-198 200 203
JONICAN, 122
JOPLIN, 92
JORDAN, 128
JORDON, 22
JOURNEY, 88 96 137
JUDAH, 99 100
JUDIN, 123
JUDY, 52 135
JUILEIUS, 166
JULIEN, 105
JURDY, 135
JUSTICE, 52
JUTTON, 123
KAIN, 85
KANADY, 130
KANCKIN, 180
KARGES, 106
KARPPI, 13
KATES, 53
KAVANUAGH, 114
KEACH, 154
KEALE, 168
KEAN, 167 197 200 202 203
KEANES, 130
KEANS, 1
KEATON, 16
KECTON, 92
KEEL, 128
KEEN, 127 128
KEENAN, 148 149 151
KEENY, 116

KEESLER, 94
KEITHLY, 90
KELISON, 16
KELLER, 80
KELLEY, 114
KELLISON, 122
KELLY, 120 129 149 152 155 158 162
    165 167 168 170 171 185
KELSAY, 117 121
KELSO, 26 28
KEMP, 7 16 121
KEMPER, 110 162
KENADEY, 88
KENDAL, 184
KENDALL, 135 187
KENDRICK, 30 139 149 150 152 153
    166 170 193
KENEARSIN, 130
KENES, 130
KENLEY, 143
KENNEDY, 115
KENNERLY, 78 79 103
KENNETT, 5
KENNON, 110
KENNY, 2 16
KERNS, 53
KERR, 156 168 194 198 200 203
KERREY, 198
KESEE, 146
KESS, 151
KESSLER, 30
KESTER, 16
KEY, 9
KEYS, 7
KEYTE, 151
KIBBEY, 16 183
KIDD, 112 200
KIDWELL, 21
KIEL, 82
KIESER, 141-144
KIGORE, 205
KILE, 130 194
KILGORE, 16 92 168 205
KILLEKREW, 91
KILLIAM, 30
KILLION, 87
KILY, 130
KIMMEL, 88

KIMSEY, 189
KINCAID, 53
KINDRICK, 169 192
KINEDEY, 173
KINERSON, 130
KING, 9-11 16 22-24 27 30 53 96 128
    154 160 165 168 172-174 178 189
KINGSBERRY, 94
KINION, 2 114 189
KINISON, 83
KINKAID, 195 196
KINKEAD, 16 135
KINNESON, 88
KINNEY, 178
KINNISON, 175
KINNSEY, 177
KINNY, 179
KINSEY, 174 177
KINSLOW, 128
KINZEI, 1
KINZEY, 53
KIPPER, 189
KIRBY, 170
KIRKMAN, 100
KIRKPATRICK, 3 5 7 8 9 11-14 18 20
    25-27 122 190
KIRPATRICK, 5 8 19
KIRTLEY, 202
KISER, 151
KISSEE, 166
KITCHUM, 53
KIZER, 152
KNIGHT, 53 96
KNIP, 149
KNON, 123 131
KNOT, 2
KNOTT, 137
KNOX, 88
KRYTZ, 138
KUTZ, 53
KUYKENDALL, 30 53
KYES, 100
LABBADIE, 99
LABBE, 134
LABRIERE, 135
LABUMAN, 130
LABURNDIER, 130
LABUXIERE, 133 134

LACEY, 175
LACHANCE, 114 134 136
LACHAPELLE, 134
LACLAVE, 130
LACROISE, 88
LACROIX, 134
LADEROUTE, 135
LAELARE, 130
LAFARME, 135
LAFFORD, 152 154
LAFLAMME, 133 134
LAFLETT, 154
LAFLEUR, 78
LAFON, 146
LAFONT, 83 90
LAFOON, 53
LAFORGE, 74 138
LAFRESNIERE, 188
LAGANERN, 31
LAGANOIS, 130
LAGAUTERIE, 135
LAGE, 153
LAGMAN, 162
LAIDLAW, 54
LAIL, 152
LAIN, 107
LAINHART, 54
LAIR, 143 150 182
LAJOR, 89
LAKE, 110 195
LAKEMAN, 79 105
LALAFFORD, 151
LALANDE, 134
LALOR, 156
LALUMADIER, 130
LALUMADIERE, 90
LALUMARDIET, 130
LAMASTER, 190 201
LAMASTERS, 196 202 203
LAMB, 121 153
LAMBERT, 16 80 94 102
LAMINE, 55
LAMKIN, 147
LAMME, 85 96 142 158 190
LAMOT, 169
LAMPKIN, 170
LAMPKINS, 12 21
LAMPTON, 23 114

LAMUEL, 155
LANCE, 164
LANCEY, 128
LAND, 177
LANDER, 151
LANE, 2 54 130 149 151 154 156 157
    159 163 169 171 189
LANEY, 53
LANGLEY, 1 6 16 28 128 171
LANGLOIS, 130
LANGLY, 28
LANIER, 119 142
LANKFORD, 116
LANSABANCA, 130
LANSDALE, 148
LANSING, 53 161
LANTER, 145
LANTON, 191
LAPENCE, 133
LAPERCHE, 133
LAPLAINT, 130
LAPLANT, 130
LAPLANTE, 84
LAPORT, 130
LAPSLRY, 203
LARD, 135
LARMARCHE, 134
LARUE, 16 30
LASAFFORD, 151
LASEFIELD, 126
LASERMUET, 95
LASHPELLE, 110
LASOURCE, 135
LASSEUR, 99
LASSLRY, 204
LATHLIN, 17
LATROURNEAU, 134
LAUGHERTY, 95
LAUGHLIN, 128 202
LAUGHTON, 1
LAUMANDIER, 130
LAUTER, 55 145
LAVERTU, 134
LAVIN, 30
LAW, 90
LAWLESS, 91
LAWRENCE, 17 81 87 112
LAYSON, 17

LAYTON, 1 2 83 87 130 199
LEA, 194
LEACH, 92 128
LEAK, 154
LEAKY, 54
LEAQUE, 158
LEAR, 54 158 161 192
LEARS, 172
LEARY, 191
LEATT, 131
LEAVEN, 176
LEBEAUME, 183
LEBEUASSE, 134
LEBLANC, 134
LEBO, 120
LECLAIR, 196 203
LECOMPTE, 105 108
LECUYER, 134
LEDGEWOOD, 54 179
LEDUC, 183 184 190
LEE, 2 95 128 131 143 146 162 169 201
LEEK, 93
LEEPER, 3 17 27 97 179
LEETS, 31
LEFEVERE, 134
LEFEVRE, 139
LEFORD, 160
LEGGET, 94
LEGGETT, 94 117
LEIPER, 17
LEISSTER, 128
·LEMA, 88
LEMAY, 134
LEMEILLEUS, 85
LEMIEUX, 134 135
LEMON, 54 133 202
LEMONS, 128 201
LENARD, 17
LENOX, 121
LEONARD, 82 87 166
LEONE, 31
LEPAGE, 133 134
LEPLANTE, 134
LERENARD, 134
LERNER, 201
LESIEUR, 84 185 186
LESLEY, 112
LETANG, 134

LETCHWORTH, 54 55 118
LEVEL, 17
LEVELL, 128
LEVERING, 169
LEVIER, 171
LEVINS, 204
LEWIS, 1 2 4 10 17 21 54 78 79 89 90
    96 97 106 113 123 124 128 137 145
    152-154 159 169 171 172 174 178
    179 182 189 191 197 203
LIDICK, 152
LIETH, 1
LIFERN, 30
LIGGETT, 55
LIGHT, 103
LIGHTNER, 194
LIGON, 54 55
LILFORD, 161
LILLEY, 190
LIME, 118
LIMMONS, 162
LINCH, 104
LINCOLN, 54
LIND, 167
LINDELL, 91
LINDSEY, 2 88 99 126 174
LING, 162
LINGENFELTER, 53-55
LINK, 112 140
LINKHORN, 130
LINN, 175
LINNEL, 172
LINSEY, 2
LINVILLE, 29 54
LINZ, 162
LIPSCOMB, 162
LISA, 140
LITERAL, 92
LITLING, 168
LITTIZ, 171
LITTLE, 17 87 123 128
LITTON, 122
LIVINGSTON, 20 54 55
LIZE, 134
LIZENBY, 151
LMASTERS, 197
LOCHRIDGE, 16 92
LOCK, 175 180 189

M'MILLIN, 97
M'MULLIN, 93
M'PERION, 125
M'PHERION, 125
M'PHERON, 125
M'PIKE, 93
MABERRY, 128 170
MACAFFERY, 112
MACDANIEL, 20
MACKAY, 184 186
MACKENTIRE, 25
MACKEY, 85 96
MACKINTOSH, 1 96
MACLEOD, 115
MACOMB, 1
MACON, 133
MADDIN, 85
MADDOCK, 87 166
MADDOX, 100 142 161
MADEN, 31
MADIN, 130
MAGAN, 167
MAGEE, 164
MAGILL, 49 58 59
MAGIOT, 134
MAGNEDES, 170
MAGOFFIN, 169
MAHAIN, 158
MAHAN, 20 92 128 154 162
MAHANEY, 92
MAHANY, 58
MAHN, 155
MAHONEY, 17
MAIDS, 58
MAINWARING, 59
MAJOR, 10 57
MAJORS, 56
MALBONE, 96
MALES, 58
MALETT, 112
MALETTE, 79
MALICE, 122
MALLACK, 164
MALLIO, 143
MALLORY, 92
MALONE, 14 75 98 158 172 178
MALONEY, 79
MALOT, 56

MALOTT, 58 59
MAMAY, 202
MAN, 198 203
MANCHESTER, 58 172 179 199
MANEGRE, 112 133
MANER, 122
MANEY, 204
MANIFEE, 168
MANN, 145-148 169 190 200
MANNING, 2 83 87 130
MANOILL, 194
MANSFIELD, 92 126 127
MANTERDEAU, 59
MARDERS, 147 149
MARDIS, 154
MARIE, 84 133
MARKEN, 97
MARKLE, 156 157 193
MARKS, 112 147
MARKSBURY, 57
MARLEAUX, 134
MARLEY, 1
MARLIN, 171
MARLOW, 134 143 144
MARLY, 80
MARMADUKE, 152 170 171
MARMEDUKE, 145
MARMON, 203
MARROW, 17
MARRS, 172 173 178 189
MARS, 133 179
MARSH, 57 59
MARSHAL, 88 93
MARSHALL, 164 165
MARTENS, 112
MARTIN, 1 4 7 15 17 19 20 23 24 27 29
    30 55 57 59 87 92 97 108 115 116
    124 134 140 145 155 158 161 168
    172 194 197 199 202
MARTINE, 112
MARTON, 17 199
MARYE, 111
MASEAU, 161
MASK, 17
MASON, 17 19 58
MASQUERIER, 141
MASSEE, 59
MASSEY, 87

MASSIE, 144 150 151 154

MASTEN, 31

MASTERS, 118

MASTHENA, 92

MASTIN, 92

MATEER, 22

MATHENY, 10

MATHER, 177

MATHEW, 94

MATHEWS, 57 58 84 142 154 186

MATHUS, 2

MATIER, 20

MATIN, 161

MATINGLY, 130

MATKIN, 112

MATLOCK, 160 189

MATNEY, 128 201

MATRICK, 159

MATSON, 143 166 168

MATTER, 18

MATTERSON, 147

MATTHERS, 186

MATTHEWS, 18 138 153 156 157 189 195

MATTINGLY, 87

MATTOCK, 18

MATUE, 161

MAUCH, 112

MAULSBY, 94 97

MAUPIN, 136

MAXEY, 6 173 179

MAXWELL, 141 192

MAY, 1 9 18 21 25 26 29 89 95 100 118 130 163

MAYBERRY, 128

MAYO, 56

MAYS, 18 21 92 145 155 160

MAYSE, 92

MCAFEE, 3 4 6 9-11 13 15 18-22 27-29 57 166 169

MCAFFEE, 152

MCALISTER, 158

MCALLISTER, 89

MCALPIN, 1 127

MCARTHUR, 85 130 136 175

MCAULEY, 87

MCAUSTIN, 87

MCBRIDE, 87 202

MCBROWN, 119

MCCABE, 128 175 177

MCCALL, 18 95 130 136 152

MCCAMPBELL, 8 18

MCCANN, 112

MCCARMICK, 170

MCCARTHY, 114

MCCARTY, 92 100 181

MCCLAIN, 18 56 195

MCCLANAHAN, 122 204

MCCLEAMS, 164

MCCLELLAND, 18 20 23

MCCLENDON, 116

MCCLOUD, 194

MCCLURE, 10 13 18

MCCOIN, 127

MCCOLLUM, 177

MCCOMBS, 120

MCCONNELL, 18 26 58 137 185

MCCORD, 122 152 196

MCCORDI, 118

MCCORKLE, 56-58

MCCORMACK, 18 92 163 166

MCCORMICK, 1 26 28 112

MCCOUGHAE, 130

MCCOY, 55 56 59 117

MCCRARY, 56 148

MCCRAY, 4 127

MCCREA, 1

MCCREDIE, 18

MCCREERY, 147

MCCROREY, 56

MCCULAH, 121

MCCULLOCH, 186

MCCULLOCK, 135

MCCULLOM, 174

MCCULLOUCH, 30

MCCULLOUGH, 56

MCCULY, 57

MCCUNE, 98

MCCUTCHEN, 118

MCDANIEL, 18 31 57-59 92 140 143 144 145 147 163 164 168

MCDANIELS, 153

MCDNL, 163

MCDONALD, 18 92 135 145 152 169 194 197 199 203

MCDONEL, 144

MCDOWALL, 171
MCDOWNS, 135
MCDURMITT, 124
MCELDON, 107
MCELROY, 147 149-151 154 155 159-
   161 165 169
MCELWEE, 55 56 58 59
MCFADDEN, 113
MCFALL, 145
MCFARLAND, 112 116 117 120-122
   125 136 176 200
MCFERRON, 187
MCGANNEGLE, 164
MCGARY, 8 19
MCGAUHER, 100
MCGAUHEY, 100
MCGEE, 58 59 89 92 118 195
MCGILL, 58 59 163 165 166 168
MCGINNESS, 57 59
MCGINNIGLE, 164
MCGINNIS, 2 56 57 87
MCGREGGOR, 1
MCGRUDER, 153
MCGUIRE, 9 20 56 58
MCGUIVE, 175
MCGUNNIAGLE, 164
MCHENRY, 88 112
MCILVAIN, 56 57
MCILVAINE, 144 145
MCINTIRE, 19 23
MCINTOSH, 1
MCINTYRE, 92 113 114
MCK---, 161
MCKAMEY, 4
MCKAMMEY, 19
MCKAY, 55 56 188 190
MCKEE, 1 56 117 153 159 160 162-164
   166-168 170 171
MCKEEN, 56
MCKENSIE, 1
MCKENZIE, 132 133
MCKINNEY, 6 18 19 131 173 178
MCKIRTLE, 111
MCKISSACK, 59
MCKISSICK, 58 59
MCKITCHEN, 147
MCKNIGHT, 130 140 190 191 194 198
   200 202 203

MCKOWN, 59 165
MCLAIN, 130
MCLANAHAN, 17 122
MCLANE, 1 160
MCLAUGHLIN, 6 7 19 87 133 139
MCLEAD, 114
MCLEAN, 87 95 124 167
MCLEHAN, 130
MCMAHAN, 19 91 113 137 195 196
MCMAHON, 112
MCMANAMA, 143 159 161
MCMANES, 85
MCMANS, 93
MCMEIS, 178
MCMILLEN, 96
MCMILLIN, 19
MCMINN, 95
MCMURRY, 165
MCMURTY, 5 14 19
MCNABB, 112 134 135
MCNAIR, 135 184 186
MCNALLY, 89
MCNANAMA, 143
MCNEILL, 1
MCNENSE, 108
MCNULTY, 143
MCPETERS, 96
MCPHEETERS, 17
MCPHERSON, 1 118 119
MCPHILLIP, 1
MCQUADDY, 57 58
MCQUEAMEY, 56
MCQUEEN, 148
MCQUITTY, 137
MCRAE, 189 193
MCROBERTS, 133
MCSPARHEN, 100
MCSWAIN, 92
MCTAGGART, 56
MCWILLIAMS, 58 59 140 141 143 189
   195
MEACHAM, 19
MEAD, 19
MEADER, 118
MEADOWS, 7
MEANS, 55 57 58 143 149 152-155 174
   179 181 192 194
MEARD, 75

236

MEDCALF, 120
MEDE, 19
MEDLEY, 81 127 172 174 178
MEEK, 58
MEELOR, 14
MEESIA, 130
MEHON, 117
MEIN, 128
MELDRUM, 1
MELIN, 171
MEMISTON, 128
MENARD, 31 76 77 84 101 102 106 108
   109 135
MENDLER, 127
MENDOZA, 133
MENG, 21
MENIFEE, 19
MEPHANS, 114
MERCIER, 134
MEREDITH, 20 27 106 130
MERREL, 150
MERRELL, 145
MERRIE, 158
MERRILL, 147 153 167
MERRITT, 118
MERRY, 120 149
MERTON, 163
METCALF, 92
METEER, 15
METIVIER, 134
MEUDETT, 130
MEUR, 12
MEYERS, 27 79
MICHAEL, 87
MICHEL, 94
MICKEL, 88
MIDDLETON, 92
MIDGET, 111
MIGNESON, 103
MIGREN, 89
MILCE, 120
MILES, 87 130 161 168
MILIGAN, 95
MILL, 128
MILLAN, 161 166 167
MILLARD, 140 177
MILLER, 4 5 8 15 19 20 22 27 30 56 57
   82 87 92 96 106 107 112 117 118

MILLER (continued)
   123 125 126 128 130 135 136 138
   141 142 146 152 156-158 161 162
   175 176 178 179 189 199
MILLES, 160
MILLIN, 166 170
MILLINGTON, 190 198 201 203
MILLON, 162
MILLS, 78 79 115 128 146
MILMURRY, 31
MILTON, 155 157 158 160 162 165
   167-169 171
MIMANS, 166
MINGERON, 80
MINNES, 166
MINRS, 203
MINTER, 57
MIOTT, 130
MIRES, 20
MISSAHAS, 31
MISSPLAY, 89
MITCHEL, 31 112 122
MITCHELL, 1 31 83 114 147 151 153
   164 166 169
MIZE, 192
MOBERLY, 145 156
MOBLEY, 118 121
MOCK, 122
MOCKBEE, 144
MOEHLE, 108
MOEN, 130
MOFFETT, 145
MOFFOT, 113
MONNAUGHAN, 106
MONNIJU, 159
MONOEY, 177
MONROE, 13 20 58 87 119 173 178 180
   189
MONTAGNE, 104
MONTEER, 20
MONTGOMERY, 31 98 145 171 177
   201
MONTIER, 82
MONTRAY, 100
MONTRE, 102
MONTREAL, 78
MONTRENY, 77
MONTREUIL, 78 109 110

OWEN, 31 54 128 151 152
OWENS, 60 163 164
OWNBEY, 116 125
OWNBY, 86
OWSLET, 166
OWSLEY, 154 168-171
OWSLY, 155
OXFORD, 128
P---, 169
PAC, 123
PACE, 6 7 16 21 23 25 28 29
PACK, 126
PADGET, 21
PADGETT, 21
PAGE, 2
PAINE, 105
PALMER, 61 91 112 122 132 156
PAMMS, 194
PANCRASS, 134
PAORE, 151
PAQUIN, 90
PARENT, 129 193 195
PARISEN, 134
PARISH, 96 141
PARITH, 195
PARK, 1 62
PARKER, 11 21 28 29 31 87 115 120
    154 171 205
PARKES, 120-122
PARKS, 2 60 88 120
PARMER, 112 172 173 177-180
PARRIS, 96
PARRISH, 150
PARROTT, 61
PARRY, 31
PARSONS, 61 111 112
PARUE, 8
PASCHALL, 130
PASKU, 160
PATE, 21 91 93
PATEN, 20
PATERSON, 31 130
PATRICK, 89 199
PATRIDGE, 157
PATTERSON, 88 89 91 95 135 136 140
    142 153 169 174 194
PATTIE, 137 198 203
PATTON, 10 21 42 100

PATTY, 22 26
PAUCK, 202
PAUL, 81 82
PAULGEL, 21
PAYATTE, 139
PAYNE, 22 61 62 96 108 143 152 153
    176 177
PAYTON, 90 118
PEABODY, 154
PEAKE, 157 158 162 165 166 169 170
PEARCE, 178 180
PEARL, 131
PEARSON, 6 22 93 172 178 189 199
PEASE, 168
PEBLEY, 37 60 61
PECK, 190 191 198 203
PECKETT, 163 164
PEEBLES, 98
PEERS, 193
PELHAM, 95 112
PELKY, 112
PELOW, 61
PELTIER, 85
PEMBERTON, 22 149 199
PEMINO, 160
PENCE, 60 61
PENICK, 110
PENNIMAN, 185
PENNINGTON, 150
PENNYMAN, 182
PEPPER, 161 172
PERAULT, 105
PERCIVAL, 96
PEREY, 112
PERIOR, 77
PERKINS, 24 93 108 121 187
PERRIN, 88
PERRY, 61 96 161 187 200
PERTLE, 88
PETERS, 61 62
PETERSON, 31
PETTERS, 145
PETTIBONE, 190 191 197
PETTIT, 97 139
PETTITT, 31 114
PETTLE, 77 101 102
PETTUS, 145 146 197
PETTY, 11 15 22 26 93

240

PEYTON, 14 22 126 127
PFISTERER, 61
PHEGAN, 1
PHELPS, 139 140
PHELPST, 74
PHILBROOK, 96
PHILIPS, 13 15 17 22 31 88 130 142
PHILIPSON, 130
PHILLIPS, 10 74 94 95 107 110 118 120
    141 146 166
PHILLIPSON, 194
PHIPPS, 128
PHULL, 157
PHYE, 22
PICARD, 134
PICKENS, 121
PICKETT, 152 158 162 166 168
PIERCE, 113 128
PIERRE, 134
PIERSON, 119
PIGG, 132
PIGGOT, 133
PIGGOTT, 133
PILET, 134
PINCOMEAU, 134
PINDLE, 62
PINKLETON, 88
PINKLEY, 82 130
PINKSTON, 11
PIPER, 85
PIPES, 195
PISIER, 82
PISS, 133
PITZER, 79
PLACEE, 130
PLACES, 31
PLACET, 89 110
PLACETT, 130
PLEDGE, 22
PLEYER, 100
PLOWMAN, 126
PLUMB, 106
PLUMMER, 2
POAGE, 61
POAGUE, 62
POER, 117 119 121
POERS, 128
POGUE, 180

POGUR, 203
POIRIE, 134
POIRIER, 134
POKE, 128
POLHERMUS, 167
POLIN, 200
POLLARD, 30 62 152 153 156-161
    165-168 170-172 194
POLLOCK, 98
POLRIN, 201
POOL, 149 150 159
POOR, 120 122 125 147 157-159 167
    171
POPE, 144 156
POPLIN, 128
POQUE, 158
PORTER, 75 89 112 133 146 148 159
    163 193 194 204
PORTUGAIS, 134
POSEY, 60 93
POSTAL, 190 198 203
POSTEN, 116
POSTON, 136
POTEAT, 61
POTEET, 61
POTTAN, 150
POTTER, 15 22 28 60 61 118 165 204
POTTERS, 167
POTTS, 29 82 203
POTTZ, 93
POWEL, 157
POWELL, 11 93 94 169 199
POWER, 22
POWERS, 88 116 133
PRA---, 176
PRAER, 190
PRAG, 95
PRAT, 157
PRATHER, 62 118
PRATT, 22 29 31 88 130 154 155-158
    160-162 168 170
PRATTE, 88 183 187
PRESLEY, 2
PRESSON, 87
PRESTON, 88 91 130
PREUR, 197
PRICE, 11 15 16 22 60 79 88 89 97 126
    127 147 153 155 168 170 171 187

PRIEST, 176
PRIME, 91
PRIMM, 194
PRINCE, 96
PRINE, 181
PRINGLE, 131
PRITCHARD, 143 191
PRITCHETT, 144 147 148 152-154
PROCTOR, 31 156 170
PROFFER, 112
PROVANCHIER, 104
PROVEAUX, 109
PROVOST, 133 134
PROVOT, 78
PRYOR, 61
PUGH, 22
PUKILL, 171
PULHAM, 13 171
PULIS, 93
PULLEY, 125
PULLIAM, 22 30 61 168
PULLIM, 88
PULLMAN, 22
PUNNELS, 19
PURDOM, 60
PURDY, 113
PURTLE, 75 94
PUSEY, 93
PYE, 165-167 171
QUARLES, 98
QUICK, 126 131
QUINCY, 156
QUINN, 12
RABE, 148 151-154 158 169
RABIN, 146
RACINE, 31
RADFORD, 128
RADICAN, 22
RAELY, 160
RAFFERTY, 106
RAIN, 205
RAINS, 107 115
RAJEN, 159
RALAFORIA, 157
RALATHEIN, 90
RALLS, 189 193
RALPH, 87
RAMEY, 62

RAMSEY, 10 12 14 15 19 20 22 25 27
    28 30 81 83 93-95 109 174 178
RANDALL, 138 170
RANDLES, 123
RANDOL, 124 176 189
RANDOLF, 23
RANDOLPH, 7 21 23 169
RANGEA, 130
RANKIN, 139 140 186 187
RANNEY, 123
RANOUSSE, 134
RANSOM, 27
RANSONS, 113
RAPELAIS, 134
RAPER, 82 133
RAPIER, 153
RAPP, 100
RARIDDON, 88
RATCLIFF, 112
RATEKIN, 7-9 23
RATIA, 130
RATICAN, 5
RATNOR, 133
RAULINGS, 45
RAVENSCRAFT, 87 94 138
RAVENSCROFT, 176
RAWLS, 188
RAY, 180 205
REA, 121
READ, 93 160 198 199 203
READY, 63
REAGAN, 23 94
REAILE, 190
REANOLDS, 23
REAUM, 91
REAVES, 111
RECTOR, 23 87 98 178 198 203
REDD, 178 179
REDDICK, 143
REDDING, 87 151
REDFORD, 88
REDMAN, 5 8 10 12 15 26 202
REED, 12 20 23 62-64 113 139 140 143
    144 145 148 149 174 187 194 196
    204
REEDE, 23
REEDER, 89
REEL, 147

REESE, 170
REEVES, 165
REFELD, 189
REFELO, 31
REGUALDIS, 113
REHLE, 134
REID, 23 86
REIHLE, 134
REILE, 191 196 197
REILHE, 203
REINHART, 149 153
RENFRO, 23 25
RENICK, 63 64 90
RENICT, 64
RENNIE, 23
RENNOIS, 23
RENOE, 21 23
RESSEN, 2
RESSLEVIN, 95
REUBEN, 112
REVISHELD, 2
REYNALDS, 1
REYNOLD, 190
REYNOLDS, 2 23 29 31 62 64 75 85 93
    97 107 116 141-146 155 191 198 203
RHEA, 89 118 119
RHOADES, 23
RHOADS, 23
RHODES, 16 89 191
RHOUR, 6
RIAM, 204
RICE, 7 17 23 25 63 64 88 96 174 179
    194 195 202 205
RICHARD, 115 159 191 197
RICHARDS, 63 64 91 104 108 153
    156-158 203
RICHARDSON, 23 119 121 122 144
    145 147 149 151-155 169 173 177
    178 179 189 192 196
RICHIE, 64
RICKETTS, 63
RICKMAN, 62
RIDDICK, 135 182 184
RIDDLE, 110
RIDER, 127
RIDGELY, 151
RIDGEWAY, 14 23
RIDGLEY, 155

RIDGON, 95
RIDGWAY, 7 10 18 27 196
RIGDON, 136
RIGG, 64
RIGGINS, 23
RIGGS, 23 62-64 97 140 154 173
RIGHTER, 146 152 156 167
RILEY, 1 62-64 83 86 99 130 147 168
RINEY, 1 84 88 136 165
RINGER, 155 156 158-161 165-167 171
RINGGO, 159
RINGGOLD, 157
RINGO, 63 64
RINGOLD, 161 166
RIPLEY, 113 193
RIPLY, 193
RIPPETE, 100
RITCHEY, 116
RITCHIE, 134
RITE, 201
RIVARD, 137
ROBB, 161
ROBBINS, 23 133 191 197 203 205
ROBEDEAUX, 203
ROBERSON, 28
ROBERT, 110 130 164
ROBERTS, 4 62-64 81 85 88 100 126
    151 162 171 199 200
ROBERTSON, 17 23 30 62-64 110 117
    125 138 157
ROBESON, 104
ROBEY, 146
ROBIDEUX, 190
ROBIN, 134
ROBINET, 18 24
ROBINETO, 194
ROBINETTO, 194
ROBINSON, 2 24 31 62 90 96 110 115
    118 132 166
ROBNETT, 142
ROCHE, 188
ROCHER, 134
ROCHESTER, 204 205
ROCK, 15
ROCKHELL, 155
ROCKHILL, 157 159 169
ROCKHOLD, 64
RODES, 88 148 166

SHERMAN, 25 162 170 200
SHIEFFLIEN, 1
SHIELDS, 12 138
SHIVERS, 24
SHOBE, 131
SHOCK, 93 132
SHOOK, 112 114
SHOPSHIRE, 152
SHORRS, 204
SHORT, 179
SHORTRIDGE, 26
SHOUSE, 68
SHOUTTS, 1
SHRADER, 94 183
SHROPSHIRE, 150-154 156 162 164-
    171
SHUBAEL, 163
SHUGART, 148 153
SHULL, 8
SHULTS, 88
SHUMAN, 121
SHUMLEY, 128
SHURLEY, 122
SHWIMMER, 198
SIBERT, 89
SIBLEY, 76 102 194
SIDES, 114
SIDLER, 127
SIDNEY, 2
SIKE, 123
SILES, 170
SILVERO, 75
SIMCO, 11
SIMIONE, 130
SIMMOE, 130
SIMMONS, 145 150 156 158-160 171
    172 174 178 179
SIMMS, 65-67 89
SIMONDS, 137 198
SIMONEAU, 80
SIMONS, 96 176 177
SIMPSON, 2 11 16 88 94 96 117 135
    149 159 165 166 173 177
SIMS, 25 88 130 136 205
SINGLETON, 67 147 155 160 166
SIPPLE, 87
SISSON, 66
SITER, 168

SITES, 142 144 181 189
SITTON, 3 11 16 25
SKAGGS, 1
SKIDMORE, 88
SKINNER, 131 142 169 205
SLACKER, 168
SLATE, 94
SLATER, 119
SLATEY, 147
SLAUGHTER, 67 90 143 144 145
SLAVE Rhoda, 150 Tina 152
SLAVEN, 170
SLEBY, 24
SLINKARD, 112
SLOAN, 25 67 68 146 158
SLOANE, 154
SLOM, 1
SLUSHER, 128
SMALL, 90 200
SMALLEY, 100
SMART, 3 15 25 28
SMILEY, 199
SMITH, 1 2 7 8 11-13 15 16 20 21 25 26
    31 64-68 75 86 87 89 91-93 96 99
    100 103 107 108 111 112 114 116
    119 121 125-128 130 133 135 138
    141-143 145 146-148 150 153 157
    162 164 167 168 171 182 185 188
    192 194 195 197 199 201 203
SMOOT, 90 130 160 205
SMS, 88
SNEED, 97
SNELL, 9 25 66 157 158 160 166 168
    171
SNIDER, 2 112
SNOWDEN, 97 115 117
SNYDER, 115 161
SODOWSKY, 162 164 168 171
SOLE, 111
SOLLERS, 66
SOLOMON, 186
SOMMERS, 108
SON, 203
SONE, 107
SONGAN, 204
SOUCIER, 137
SOULARD, 98
SOWDOSKY, 155

SPALDING, 164 169
SPARKMAN, 1
SPARKS, 150 193
SPARLIN, 116
SPEAR, 155 158 164 165
SPENCE, 116 155 161 202
SPENCER, 99 120 125 137 159 190
SPERA, 93
SPIVER, 128
SPRADLING, 112
SPRIGG, 175 176
SPRING, 175
SPRINGER, 65 168
SPURGEON, 116
SQUIRE, 112
STACY, 128 151 194
STALLCUP, 94 95 176
STANDLEY, 30 194
STANFIELD, 165
STANLEY, 25
STANTON, 67 197
STAPP, 178 179
STARK, 67 110
STARKES, 122
STEEL, 91 117 121 122 143
STEELE, 9 125 200
STEPHEN, 25
STEPHENS, 2 3 4 7 9 13-15 17 18 21
    23-25 27-29 65 86 90 111 125 126
    145 147 148 157 166 203 204
STEPHENSON, 65 67 88 111 152 173
    179 180
STEPNEY, 150
STERLING, 158
STERRET, 202
STEVENS, 1 66 86 121 147 148 155-157
    163 166
STEVENSON, 196
STEWARD, 26 88 89 119 121 158 187
STEWART, 5 8 17-20 22 25 26 67 82 88
    97 122 130 146 163 167 170
STICKNEY, 96
STILL, 93
STILLWELL, 31 189
STINSON, 117 119
STITES, 26
STOKER, 26
STOKES, 26 29 75

STOLLINGS, 66
STONE, 26 66 67 91 93 112 140 155 157
    159 162
STOREY, 67
STORRS, 178
STORY, 1 67 89
STOTHART, 66-68
STOULL, 160
STOUR, 2
STOUT, 154 155 157 159 163 166 167
    169 170
STOUTT, 157 161
STOVER, 115
STRAHERN, 84
STRATTON, 89
STREET, 96 128 201
STRIBLING, 66
STRICKLAND, 89 111 130
STRICKLIN, 2 93 128 199
STRINGER, 1 138 166
STRINHAM, 111
STRODE, 26 64 65 159
STROLLINGS, 66
STRONG, 31
STROOPS, 31
STROTHER, 2 64 140
STROTHERS, 177
STUART, 88 107
STUBBLEFIELD, 2
STURDUINE, 83
STURDUVANT, 1
STURGES, 82 105
STUSSEL, 114
STWINSON, 2
SUBLET, 8
SUBLETT, 156 169 175
SUBLETTE, 132
SUCET, 7
SUELL, 161
SUGGETT, 3-5 7 8 13-17 21-26 28
SULCHER, 117
SULLEN, 93
SULLENS, 115 203
SULLINS, 133 198
SULLIVAN, 97 121 133 146 182
SUMERS, 122
SUMMER, 75 121
SUMMERS, 84 117 119 122 150

TINDALL, 94
TINGLEY, 158
TINIVER, 130 131
TINQUE, 130 131
TINSLY, 93
TIPPETS, 69
TIPTON, 68 96 110
TISDALE, 194
TMAN, 153
TOALSON, 132
TOBIN, 102 103 146
TOD, 27
TODD, 29 68 69 112 133 148 171 174
    179 189 196 198 202-204
TOFFEIMIER, 69
TOLAND, 154
TOLSON, 96
TOMIER, 130 131
TOMILSON, 81
TOMISH, 131
TOMPKINS, 135 145 156
TOMPSON, 88 169
TOMSAN, 169
TOMWIER, 131
TON, 180
TONEY, 98
TOOLER, 178
TOOLEY, 173 174 178
TOUCHET, 134
TOULOSE, 134
TOULOUSE, 134 135
TOWEN, 80
TOWLSON, 83
TOWLY, 153
TOWNSEND, 3 28
TOWNSON, 13
TRABUE, 147 168
TRACY, 103
TRASK, 91
TREADO, 131
TRENT, 120
TRICKEY, 88
TRIGG, 98
TRIMBLE, 17
TRINCE, 31
TROTIER, 134
TROTTER, 88 94 100 142 188
TROULOUSE, 135

TROUTMAN, 162
TRUDEAU, 85
TRUDEAUS, 31
TRUMAN, 2
TUCKER, 1 6 14 27 88 89 130 131 163
    186
TUGGLE, 149
TULL, 167
TULLOCK, 117 164
TULLOT, 161
TULLOTT, 161
TULLY, 10
TUNLEY, 75
TURCOTT, 92
TURGEON, 134
TURICK, 131
TURLEY, 24 27 196 203
TURMAN, 128
TURMOT, 74
TURNAN, 168
TURNEDGE, 70
TURNER, 6 12 16 27 69 70 75 93 94
    100 110 117 122 132 157 163 189
TURNHAM, 69 70
TURPIN, 169 191 195
TURRIES, 114
TUSLEY, 93
TUTT, 114
TUTTLE, 20 168 203
TWYMAN, 88
TYLER, 157
UANNOY, 153
UEHER, 128
UETTERLING, 202
ULIMOEN, 126 127
UMSTATTD, 89
UNCAPNER, 106
UNDERWOOD, 99
UNEAU, 91 189
UNO, 27
UPDIKE, 28
UPPTERGROVE, 122
UPTERGROVE, 2
UPTON, 117 120 169
URNAN, 168
URQUHART, 1
UTTERBACK, 70
VABIA, 131

VADBONONCOEUR, 134
VAIRIN, 147
VAIRU, 147
VALENTIN, 134
VALIA, 131
VALLANDINGHAM, 108
VALLE, 77 79 85 110 123
VANARSDALL, 27
VANBBER, 137
VANBBIER, 128
VANBIBBER, 15 99 128
VANCARNAP, 141
VANCE, 70 71 82 87 115 154 177
VANCLEANE, 23
VANDERBURGH, 97
VANDERGRAPH, 120
VANDERSLIC, 150
VANDETT, 134
VANHORN, 123 131
VANIER, 102
VANLANDINGHAM, 141 144 158 163
    171
VANNER, 144
VANNOY, 152 166
VANPHUL, 166
VANQUICKENBORNE, 29
VANSANT, 136
VARBLE, 70
VARNER, 111 112 131
VARNEY, 160
VASSUER, 31
VAUDRY, 134
VAUGHAN, 87
VAUGHN, 27 70 71
VAUGHT, 120
VAUGIN, 31
VAUGINE, 189
VAUNOY, 144
VELAR, 131
VENABLES, 190 198 201
VENDEMANS, 70
VENEABLES, 203
VENIBB, 93
VENNIBB, 93
VERREJOT, 11
VESSELS, 88
VEST, 27
VESTAL, 99

VIDMORE, 131
VILEMONT, 31
VILLARET, 133
VINCENT, 14 27 31 71 89
VINEYARD, 194
VINSON, 14
VINSTON, 125
VIRGIN, 83
VITAL, 131
VITTOW, 192
VIZINA, 134
VOLZ, 205
VON PHUL, 163 165 168
VON PHULL, 158
VON PULL, 159
VOORHEES, 80
WADDEL, 112
WADDELL, 112
WADDLE, 133
WADE, 72 73
WADKINS, 124
WADLEY, 7 9 27
WAGGENER, 25
WAGGONER, 27 30
WAHRENDORF, 103
WAINSCOTT, 28
WAIT, 95
WALDEN, 87 126
WALDRING, 27
WALKER, 8 9 20 28 31 71-73 78 88 89
    97 103 127 138 139 141 156 162 166
    171
WALKISON, 176
WALLACE, 1 90 99 128 149 166 190
WALLE, 1
WALLINDORF, 106
WALLS, 28 198
WALSH, 165
WALTER, 144 150
WALTERS, 94
WALTHALL, 152
WALTON, 2 95 96 121 125
WALTOP, 125
WALTTAS, 154
WAMBLEY, 73
WAMMOCK, 2
WANTON, 153 158
WARBURTON, 144

WARD, 28 72 90 93 95 96 141 150 156
201
WARDEN, 200
WARDIN, 195
WARE, 133 136 189
WARFIELD, 148
WARNER, 161 201-203
WARNOCK, 132
WARREN, 6 10 12 22 72 73 91 114 199
WARTHON, 82
WASH, 87 151
WASHINGTON, 3 136 150 194
WASSON, 180
WATERS, 1 82 84 88 93 95 98 131 139
170
WATHAN, 74
WATHEN, 93-95
WATKIN, 128
WATKINS, 2 28 71-73 88 148 176 181
WATSON, 86 87 94 128 131 154 155
158 163 173 174 177 179 180 191
194 197 198 201 203
WATTERS, 126
WATTS, 93 203
WAYHART, 111
WAYNE, 3 21 28 93
WEAR, 114
WEARE, 31
WEATHERFORD, 28 116
WEAVER, 89 117 121 143
WEBEERT, 28
WEEDEN, 72
WEEDS, 185
WEHLING, 108
WEIGHT, 158
WEITZ, 116
WELCH, 31 73 79 80 88 93 145
WELD, 116
WELDON, 71 72
WELLBORN, 185
WELLBORNE, 31
WELLS, 28 31 86 112
WELLZ, 156
WELPMANN, 200
WELSH, 1 114
WELT, 81
WELTON, 71

WERNECK, 142
WERNICK, 144 147
WEST, 1 2 7 9 11 18 30 82 93 127 128
133 158-160 168 199 203
WESTBROOK, 26 138
WESTFALL, 96
WESTMAN, 204
WESTMANN, 204
WESTOVER, 88 139 187
WESTZ, 2
WHALEY, 141 146 148-152 154 160
182 191 193
WHALL, 165
WHARBURTON, 147
WHEAT, 74 146
WHEATLEY, 133
WHEATON, 1
WHEELER, 124 149 197
WHELENBURGER, 88
WHERELY, 128
WHERLEY, 128
WHERRY, 188
WHETSTONE, 31
WHILE, 31
WHITE, 1 22 71 86 88 92 93 96 114 129
133 141-146 149 152-155 157 161
163 168 190 192 193
WHITESIDE, 112 134
WHITESIDES, 92
WHITFIELD, 151
WHITLEDGE, 88
WHITLEY, 190 196 203
WHITLOCK, 72 74
WHITLOW, 131
WHITNER, 114
WHITS, 147
WHITSETT, 90
WHITSIDE, 86 194
WHITSITT, 71
WHITTENBURG, 177
WHITTEY, 18
WHITTLESEY, 182
WHITTLEY, 194
WHITTON, 146
WHORTON, 72
WIDEN, 108
WIETT, 72

WIGGINS, 81 104 105 109
WIGGINSON, 23
WIGGINTON, 106 179
WILBORN, 115 164
WILBRUNE, 165
WILBURN, 1 5 27 28
WILCOCKSON, 25 28
WILCOX, 73 114 122 146 151 153 159
    171
WILCOXAN, 153 167 169
WILE, 150
WILEY, 10 75 100 151 158 193
WILFLEY, 4 9 28
WILHITE, 72 132
WILHOIT, 72 73 83
WILKERSON, 22 26 28 73 74 88 99 131
    133 199
WILKES, 28 126
WILKINSON, 88 93 139 176 177
WILLARD, 139
WILLCOXIN, 161
WILLES, 156
WILLETT, 156
WILLIAM, 125
WILLIAMS, 1 2 12 15-17 26 28 29 71-
    74 87 88 92 93 96 98 99 106 117 120
    126 127 136 155 159 162-164 166
    169 173 174 178-181 189 198 199
    203-205
WILLIAMSON, 166
WILLING, 28
WILLINGHAM, 16 28 93 199 205
WILLIS, 2 100 155 160 164
WILLOCK, 155
WILLON, 2
WILLOUGHBY, 199
WILLS, 5 8-10 19 22 29 72 73 117 154
WILSON, 11 24 29 55 71-73 88 89 93 96
    108 109 111 112 119 120 122 124-
    127 141 142 155 167 171 194 197
    203 204
WINCHESTER, 93 94
WINDLE, 126
WINDSOR, 127
WINFIELD, 83 88
WINGATE, 164
WINGO, 132
WINLOCK, 147 150-152 164 169

WINN, 29 73 87 134 170
WINNINGHAM, 72
WINNSOT, 83
WINSCOTT, 28
WINSFIELD, 131
WINSLOW, 153
WINSOR, 138
WINTERTOWER, 29
WINTHROP, 30
WIRT, 72 162
WISDOM, 96
WISE, 142 143 157-159 162 163 165
WISEMAN, 168
WISLEY, 82
WISLIZENNS, 114
WIST, 154
WITHERS, 71 154 155 158 162 167
WITHURINGTON, 29
WITT, 71 82 99 173 174 177 179 189
    194
WOLFE, 133
WOLFSCALE, 195
WONDERLY, 170 171
WOOD, 7 23 75 100 119 120 139 142
    145 161 168 203
WOODFIN, 120
WOODFORD, 119
WOODLAND, 11
WOODRUFF, 113
WOODS, 3 20 21 24 29 72 73 82 91 93
    96 190 191 196 197 200 201 203 205
WOODSON, 2 186
WOOLFOLK, 141 166
WOOLFORT, 194
WOOLRICK, 166
WOOLSEY, 31
WOOLWITCH, 113
WOOLWORTH, 142
WOOSLEY, 83
WOOSON, 198 202
WOOTEN, 117 191
WOOTON, 203
WOOTTEN, 117
WORBURTON, 160
WORLEY, 92 133
WORSHAM, 29
WORTHINGTON, 95 151
WRAY, 29